KU-030-446

501 MUST-TAKE JOURNEYS

501 MUST-TAKE JOURNEYS

Bounty
Books

An Hachette UK Company
www.hachette.co.uk

First published in Great Britain in 2008 by Bounty Books,
a division of Octopus Publishing Group Ltd
Carmelite House
50 Victoria Embankment
London EC4Y 0DZ
www.octopusbooks.co.uk

This revised edition published in 2017

Copyright © Octopus Publishing Group Limited 2008, 2013, 2017

All rights reserved. No part of this publication may be reproduced, stored in a retrieval system,
or transmitted, in any form or by any means, electronic, mechanical, photocopying, recording
or otherwise without the prior written permission of the publisher.

ISBN: 978-0-7537-3254-0

A CIP catalogue record is available from the British Library

Printed and bound in China

10 9 8 7 6 5 4 3 2 1

Publisher: Lucy Pessell
Designer: Lisa Layton
Editor: Sarah Vaughan
Production Controller: Marina Maher

Notes
For your own safety please note this book is only intended as a guide. Octopus Publishing
Group is not responsible for the actions or precautionary measures taken by readers. Please
check with your government's own foreign travel advice before travelling.

CONTENTS

INTRODUCTION 6

AMERICAS & THE CARIBBEAN... 8

Arthur Findlay, Kieran Fogarty, Joe Toussaint,
Sarah Oliver and David Brown

AFRICA 92

Sarah Oliver, Jackum Brown, Bob Mitchell and Janet Zoro

EUROPE 124

Kieran Fogarty, Janet Zoro, Jackum Brown,
Bob Mitchell, Joe Toussaint, Sarah Oliver
and Arthur Findlay

AUSTRALASIA & PACIFIC..262

Roland Matthews and Arthur Findlay

ASIA.. 296

Joe Toussaint, Kieran Fogarty, Sarah Oliver,

Jackum Brown, Arthur Findlay and David Brown

EASTERN MED & MIDDLE EAST 362

Sarah Oliver, Bob Mitchell and Janet Zoro

INDEX 380

INTRODUCTION

Journeys – journeys to work, to school or university, to the theatre or cinema, to do the shopping or laundry or pick up the kids – most of us are taking journeys every day. We see the same old sights each time and mostly we let our brains work on automatic, failing to derive any pleasure from the actual trip, because we just don't expect to. Our most ardent wish, if ever expressed, would be for the journey to be over with just a click of the fingers. The destination is all.

Many sun-seeking holiday makers would also much rather reach their seaside holiday destination without the trials of the trip there – the queues at the airport, the flight, the walking, the traffic. Yet in recent years increasing numbers of people, though still not immune to the occasional lazy pleasures of beach life, have become fascinated by the variety of interests and challenges presented by all manner of different journeys. They have realized that to take a journey can enable them to have more unusual experiences, to encounter and interact with local people, to observe and explore new places, different cultures, historic landmarks and superb scenery.

There's an eclectic variety of fascinating journeys described in this book – some of them take only an hour or two to complete while others could last up to six months. Most modes of transport are covered: on foot, by bicycle, car, boat, train, plane, horse, mule and even dog sled. There are trips to be taken at different times of year, through mountains and valleys, jungles and pine forests, rivers and seas, from the snowy wastes of the Arctic Circle to the mind-numbing heat of the Sahara Desert. They encompass journeys taken for the extraordinary beauty of the landscape, to reach ancient monuments, to meet people living in remote regions and to see wildlife of all descriptions.

Whether it's canoeing down the Yukon, mountain trekking in Bulgaria, a boat trip up the Norwegian coast, a rail trip in the Himalayas, touring the Chilean vineyards or cycling in Northern Australia – there are journeys here to satisfy even the most jaded of travelling palates.

Some of the journeys – the walk along the Great Wall of China, or driving the famous US Route 66, or a camel trek from Timbuktu on part of the old Salt Road – are well known classics; others are little known and rarely travelled. Some require feats of endurance and that you are at the very peak of fitness. On others you can relax in the lap of luxury with very little physical exertion: South Africa's famous Blue Train, for example, provides you with 5-star accommodation and haute cuisine as you travel from Cape Town to Pretoria and marvel through the window from the comfort of your carriage at the landscape, the elephants striding across the plains and the herds of giraffes and antelopes grazing peacefully before you. Quite a few of the journeys can be taken more or less on the spur of the moment; other very different types of journey in some distant land could involve months of planning.

There are all sorts of reasons for making a journey. You might want to see mysterious Mayan pyramids, or make a pilgrimage to an important religious site. You might want to feel at one with nature in part of the Canadian wilderness or simply walk an ancient trail beside a lake. Perhaps you are an active person, one whose idea of bliss is to trek through rainforest, or cycle in southern Italy – or you might want to keep the kids happy with a trip inland from a seaside resort. You may have a special interest: bird watching, whale watching, art, the Roman empire, food or wine – whatever your preferences, there is certain to be a journey to take that will fulfil your dream.

Having made your choice of journey, you should take the time to read and research it as thoroughly as possible. You need to be prepared, to take appropriate clothing and footwear, maps, medication, food and water, camping gear – anything you may need en route. While some journeys are easy, and you will never be far from help, others are seriously remote, and what you carry with you is desperately important.

Happily much of the time it's not a question of either the destination or the journey – you can have both! In many cases you have the opportunity to visit your chosen destination and have an exciting and interesting trip as well. The beautiful city of Luang Prabang in Laos is truly a joy to behold, but if you are able to reach there by gently travelling down the Mekong River from Huay Xai, then your whole experience of the visit will be much enhanced.

So have a good look through this book, find a journey that speaks to your soul – and get going.

AMERICAS & THE CARIBBEAN

TRANS-CANADA TRAIN JOURNEY
North America/Canada

The sights you see and the people you meet on this epic trip will stay in the memory for the rest of your life. Nearly all those who make the journey from Halifax to Vancouver do so for fun (flying is cheaper and quicker) and this gives the whole experience a real party feel. The first stage from Halifax to Montreal takes you from the extremely picturesque Nova Scotia coast, through New Brunswick. Skirting the Appalachian Mountains, you are then transported to Montreal, the beating heart of French Canada. The second leg allows you to sample the most modern railway Canada has to offer. The Montreal to Toronto link feels strangely normal compared with the rest of the trip. Business people barely look up from their laptops as the train passes along the St Lawrence River, past the Thousand Islands and along the shore of Lake Ontario.

From Toronto, Canada's most modern of cities, you embark on the truly monumental part of the train ride. The seemingly endless forests of Northern Ontario eventually give way to wide prairies as you cross the Continent's interior – the vastness of it all is quite breathtaking. After two nights on board, the train approaches the Rockies. Waterfalls and sheer rock faces heave in to view one after another and this is the time to grab a seat in the panoramic dome car. After this, Kamloops is the last major stop before arriving in Vancouver and your chance to experience the city often voted the 'World's Best Place to Live'.

WHEN SHOULD I VISIT?:
Year round, but schedules can be disrupted in winter (November–April).

HIGHLIGHTS:
The Thousand Islands – the islands that gave you the dressing.
Old Montreal – fabulous, French and funky.
Mount Robson and Pyramid Falls – in the Rockies.
Vancouver – it really is as good as they say: the sea, mountains, excellent affordable eating and really friendly people.

FRASER DISCOVERY ROUTE ON THE ROCKY MOUNTAINEER
North America/Canada

HIGHLIGHTS:
Mount Robson is the biggest vertical rock face you will find anywhere on Earth.
The Fraser River – which in spring is one of the fastest flowing rivers in the world.

Starting in the ski resort of Whistler, you travel eastbound through the rich farmland of the Pemberton Valley before the train wends its way along the shores of Anderson and Seton Lakes. Breathtaking views of the Fraser Canyon feed the eye as you near the improbably high Deep Creek Bridge. The train runs alongside the mighty Fraser River until it reaches the sleepy town of Quesnel where it stops for the night, allowing you to explore one of the Canadian interior's oldest towns, home to the world's largest gold pan.

The next morning you enter the Rocky Mountain Trench and the upper reaches of the Fraser River. The route then leaves the Fraser River at Tête Jaune Cache, and climbs past majestic Mount Robson, the highest peak in the Canadian Rockies at 3,954 m (12,972 ft) and the highlight of the journey. The train crosses the top of the Yellowhead Pass and enters the province of Alberta. ending as the Rocky Mountaineer descends through Jasper National Park to the perfect little town of Jasper.

THE SKEENA TRAIN
North America/Canada

HIGHLIGHTS: The Rockies – the wow factor never goes away.
The chance to glimpse wildlife feeding and grazing on the riverbanks.

Billed as Canada's best-kept secret, the 1160 km (721 mi) long Skeena Railway takes passengers between Jasper National Park and Prince Rupert on the Pacific coast. The railway links many otherwise isolated communities and gives travellers a chance to view hidden Canada at first hand. This region is one of North America's last great wildernesses and it's sprinkled with tantalizing reminders of its rich First Nations history. Soon after leaving Jasper, the train passes Mount Robson and the Pyramid Falls, two of the most stunning sights the Rockies have to offer. The track then heads in a north-westerly direction, skirting the spectacular Columbia Mountains alongside the Fraser River and down to Prince George for an overnight hotel stop.

This sumptuous land of waterfalls, huge rivers, lakes and wilderness is home to bear, elk, wolves and moose and such is the gentle pace of the train that the driver often slows down for people to take photographs.

The last leg of the journey, between the 'two Princes' takes you to ever more remote communities. Following the Skeena River, the train then reaches its final destination – Prince Rupert, gateway to Haida Gwai, northern Vancouver Island and Alaska.

THE BRUCE TRAIL

North America/Canada

HIGHLIGHTS:
Blue Mountains Section
(Lavender to Craigleith).
Beaver Valley Section
(Craigleith to Blantyre) –
offering fine views of rocky
crevasses.
Sydenham Section (Blantyre
to Wiarton) – teeming with
nature.

WHEN SHOULD I VISIT?:
During the fall colours
(September–October) is
best, but really any time from
May–October is good.

The 800 km (500 mi) Bruce trail in Ontario is the oldest and longest marked trail in Canada, taking the hiker along the Niagara Escarpment from Niagara to the tip of the Bruce Peninsula. There are also about 300 km (187 mi) of additional side trails that link well with the Bruce. The iconic waterfalls at Niagara are a great place to start and having left with the sound of crashing water in your ears and ozone in your lungs, it is a short hike to the main trail proper.

This well-maintained trail, with its clear markings and efficiently run campgrounds is the most ambitious of projects. The nine chapters of the Bruce Trail Association work hard at protecting this UNESCO World Biosphere Reserve, acquiring new land and opening up this most beautiful, fragile environment for all to see. Hence, it is important to take nothing and leave nothing, except memories and photographs. The fact that the campsites provide all necessary camping gear, to avoid outside contamination, means that you can travel light and cover more ground than you would otherwise.

This ancient escarpment shelters a rare bio-diversity and is home to an array of woodland dwellers, from chipmunks to bear and chickadees to Canada geese. The further north you venture the more isolated the trail becomes and the more likely you are to witness the resident fauna in its natural environment. A good pair of binoculars and a soft step is all you need – enjoy.

An experienced hiker could expect to complete the trail inside 20 days, but, since 200 km (125 mi) of the Bruce is paved road, it is probably best tackled in sections.

THE EAST COAST TRAIL
North America/Canada

HIGHLIGHTS: The Spout (a wave driven geyser)
The suspension bridge at the historic abandoned community of La Manche.

The 540 km (337 mi) East Coast Trail hugs the scenic shores of the Avalon Peninsula of Newfoundland and Labrador. This grand trail is very much a work in progress, with 220 km (138 mi) of the trail well marked. The remainder of it is accessible but un-signposted and provides a greater challenge. The marked section of the Trail stretches from Fort Amherst, in historic St. John's, to Cappahayden, on the beautiful southern shore. It is equipped with trail signage, maps and supporting trail information to enhance your hiking experience along the coast and through the wilderness. It consists of a series of 18 paths each with a northern and a southern trailhead. Each of these paths can be hiked individually, some are easy strolls, whille others are longer and more demanding.

As is fitting for a trail of this magnitude there is much to see and explore. This system of what were backcountry routes and hunting trails takes the hiker through provincial parks, national historic sites and ecological reserves. Sustenance and rest can be taken at any one of the charming fishing villages which line the route.

THE MANTARIO TRAIL

North America/Canada

Running along part of the Canadian Shield, this most inviting of trails offers dramatic views at every turn. A large portion of the 63 km (39 mi) trail is a dedicated Wilderness Zone, where hunting and motorized vehicles are forbidden. This gives the whole hiking experience a pedestrian feel in the best sense of the word, with only the sound of the wildlife, the wind through the trees and the sound of your step breaking the silence Each stage of the hike takes you up and along granite ridges, which offer wonderful panoramic views of lakes and gullies. Variety is the watchword for this well maintained trail. Spruce, balsam, jack pine and white birch all thrive here, giving the forest a wonderfully diverse feel. Campgrounds are plentiful and in good order and the huge variety of outdoor activities should keep all happy. The fact that vehicular access is confined to the north and south trailheads adds to the sense of being alone with nature.

WHEN SHOULD I VISIT?:
Try to see the spectacular fall (September/October) colours of this diverse woodland.

ACROSS VANCOUVER ISLAND

North America/Canada

A seaplane ride from Vancouver takes you over the Lions Gate Bridge and across the Georgia Strait giving you a first full glimpse of this most verdant of lands. When reaching the island, the lush ancient forest, specked with the odd lake, feeds the eye. About halfway across, the Alberni Inlet guides the plane along to the Pacific Rim National Park with its long sandy beaches framed by rich temperate rainforest. Then finally you land in the heart of Tofino.

Alternatively, the views along the road linking the main ferry terminal at Nanaimo to both Ucluelet and Tofino are spectacular. Leaving Highway 1 from Nanaimo you turn onto Highway 4 and enter Cathedral Grove, an area of 800-year-old majestic Douglas firs, some measuring 9 m (29.5 ft) in circumference. After Port Alberni you come to Sproat Lake. In spring brown bears, waking from hibernation, come to eat the dandelion heads that grow near the road – don't leave your vehicle but have your camera ready. Finally the road winds its way past Kennedy Lake and then onto the Pacific Rim Highway that runs parallel to the golden sands of Long Beach.

HIGHLIGHTS:
Long Beach – a 16 km (10 mi) long stretch of pristine Pacific sandy beach. Tofino Botanical Gardens – an unconventional garden with boardwalks and paths through sculptures and forest.

HIGHLIGHTS: The wildflower meadows in spring (April/May). The fragrant smell of the pine forests from late May–September. The bucolic charm of the settlements along the way.

THE P'TIT TRAIN DU NORD

North America/Canada

Running north from St-Jérôme to Mont Laurier, the P'tit Train du Nord utilizes an old railway line, decommissioned in 1989, and is popular with hikers and cyclists in summer, while the winters are given over to Nordic skiing and other snow-based activities. The dozen or so villages linked by the trail in the Laurentian hills north of Montreal, offer fine-dining and bountiful delicatessens as befits French Canada.

Good use has been made of the defunct stations and many are given over to service areas. As one would expect of a former railway, the gradients are not steep, making it a perfect trail for groups of all ages and abilities. However, it is sometimes surprising how high you can get – and the views of this rolling countryside are quite lovely from the several 'peaks' along the way. The trail is very much a work in progress, with some of the gravel tracks being upgraded to paved roadways making it even more accessible for summer visitors. In winter the area changes markedly and becomes the domain of cross-country skiers, the toughest sportsmen and women to be found anywhere in the world. Gentle inclines become muscle-testing mountains, as the sub-zero temperatures attempt to freeze every inward breath and the need to carry emergency supplies adds to the challenge.

THE DEMPSTER HIGHWAY

North America/Canada

An engineering miracle, first opened in 1979 to link the mineral wealth of the north with southern Canada, this gravel road has now become a magnet for thrill seekers from around the globe. Those who like their roads even and services regularly spaced should keep away. This is the most challenging journey of them all, through the most magnificent of Arctic landscapes. From the Klondike gold fields to the Mackenzie Delta you cross mountain ranges, traverse valleys and have the chance to view nature red in tooth and claw.

The area is home to all the wildlife you would expect in northern Canada – and more. Both black and grizzly bear can be found as well as a host of caribou, sheep and mountain goats. With such a bountiful supply of food, predators are plentiful, so keep your eyes open for lynx, foxes and above all any patrolling wolves, the most magical of sights.

Each season brings new wonder, from the midnight sun in the summertime to the icy calm of winter, when ferries on the route are replaced by ice bridges, thus obliging you to place your trust in nature even as you marvel at it. The 741 km (463 mi) highway is a true test of man (or woman) and machine. Along the way there are abundant opportunities for adventure, so load up your kayak and pack your hiking boots.

HIGHLIGHTS:
The sheer magnitude of it all, as you cross rivers and negotiate mountain passes. The explosion of colour which heralds the short Arctic summer (July–August).

THE COQUIHALLA HIGHWAY
North America/Canada

HIGHLIGHTS: The Okanagan Valley – Canada's premier fruit and wine producing region.
The town of Merritt – a ranching and recreation centre.

The Coquihalla Highway (pronounced 'coke-a-hal-a') is a major toll highway that connects the Greater Vancouver region with the interior of British Columbia. It is a four-seasons-in-one-day, pedal-to-the-metal, ear-popping, super highway through the magnificent Cascade Mountains. The dramatic changes of environment are always exhilarating, as you go from misty coastal cedars and tall firs to bright sunlight on the high rock faces in the space of half an hour. The Coq, as it is affectionately known, travels northwards from Hope to Kamloops via Merritt on Highway 5, passing through Monck and Lac Le Jeune Provincial Parks. The road then climbs through the Great Bear Snow Shed to the summit of the Coquihalla Pass, at 1,240 m (4,068 ft), then crosses the top of the Thompson Plateau, with side roads leading off into rolling countryside speckled with fishing lakes.

Pine, spruce and Douglas fir can be found at the lower elevations around Merritt and the grasslands support moose, mule deer, bear and elk. The strain that the many inclines put on vehicles means that there is less commercial traffic than on many of the region's roads, so you are always guaranteed a smooth passage – weather permitting.

DON'T MISS
Cheticamp – an Acadian village famous for fish and fiddle playing.

THE CABOT TRAIL
North America/Canada

Located in the Cape Breton National Park in Nova Scotia, the Cabot Trail winds spectacularly along the flanks of the mountains. The 282 km (175 mi) loop is popular with experienced cyclists. One breathtaking view after another unfolds, and the plunging descent from Mount MacKenzie to Pleasant Bay will be one you will never forget.

The park has 27 hiking tracks branching off the Cabot Trail. Many excursions are quite short and have the feel of an amble rather than a hearty tramp, but those who welcome a challenge will find something to suit. The Glasgow Lake Lookoff is a relatively gentle round-trip hike that takes you through barren and scrub forest to a rocky bald headland overlooking a series of pristine highland lakes, with distant views of the ocean. The trail is alternately swampy and rocky, so strong footwear is advised.

Further along the Cabot Trail, the Bog Trail offers a glimpse of the tableland's unique bogs from a dry boardwalk. Lone Shieling is an easy loop through a verdant hardwood forest in a lush valley that includes 300-year-old sugar maples (most stunning in fall).

ICEFIELDS PARKWAY
North America/Canada

HIGHLIGHTS: The Columbia Icefield – a chance to witness a pristine wilderness.
Lake Louise – with its turquoise lake and overhanging glacier.
The Crossings – a chance to reflect and anticipate.

Fur traders and First Nations peoples dubbed this 230 km (144 mi) route the Wonder Trail. It climbs steadily north through forest, until you reach the alpine meadow at Bow Summit, the journey's highest point. The next section, which drops down to the Saskatchewan River, offers the best chance to see black bears and moose. The Crossings section is famous the world over for its breathtaking scenery as Mount Athabasca and the Columbia Glacier heave into view.

The outstanding features of the final leg of the journey, from Tangle Ridge to Jasper, are the Sunwapta and Athabasca Falls and the opportunity to spot grizzly bears and mountain caribou. Although over a million people make the trip each year to experience this 'window on the wilderness', the sheer vastness of the landscape still means it can rarely seem crowded.

CANOE DOWN THE YUKON RIVER
North America/Canada

HIGHLIGHTS: The abandoned settlement at Hottalinqua.
Fort Selkirk – a renovated pioneer and First Nations settlement.
The vibrant colours of the glacial melt waters.

Starting at Whitehorse near the border with northern British Columbia, this 580 km (362 mi) canoe trip down the Yukon should only be undertaken by the most experienced of adventurers. Even the name of the river conjures up images of the frontier, and this journey takes you through early Canadian history as the river propels you on your way. So harsh is this environment that forward planning is a must. Sudden storms can cause long delays and the area is home to around 5,000 grizzly bears, so great care needs to be taken when setting up camp.

The spectacular Lake Lebarge offers a good target for your first stop. At 48 km (30 mi) long and on average 5 km (3.1 mi) wide, the lake offers the most challenging of paddles. Almost benign on a calm day, it can without much warning turn in to a bubbling cauldron and pose great danger.

Once through the lake, the river gathers pace and takes you past abandoned wood yards and gold mining settlements – a reminder of the folly of yesteryear, when the lure of potential wealth brought many to the region. Carmacks, some 350 km (219 mi) into the trip, offers the first opportunity to stock up and this cute little town of 500 even has a couple of hotels and restaurants.

The snow-covered mountains, shining in the midnight sun, frame the river as it runs fast towards the Arctic Circle and your final destination, Dawson City.

THE INSIDE PASSAGE FERRY
North America/Canada

WHEN SHOULD I VISIT?:
Best in the summer months
(May–September) when the
voyage takes place entirely in
daylight.

TIME IT TAKES:
15 hours.

HIGHLIGHTS:
The sight of schools of
migrating whales and
dolphins.
Campania Island – a
perfectly formed rocky
island.
The never-ending wonders of
the amazing scenery.
Prince Rupert – a
cosmopolitan town full of
surprises.

The Inside Passage can be travelled as part of a longer cruise between California and Alaska. However it is difficult to beat the intimacy and affordability of the regular ferry service between Port Hardy on Vancouver Island and Prince Rupert in northern British Columbia. This 500 km (312 mi) voyage is one of North America's truly great journeys.

The first two hours of the trip involve crossing the open sea between Vancouver Island and Rivers Inlet and offers a chance to grab a coffee, soak up the atmosphere on board and get to know your fellow passengers. Soon it will be time to climb to the sometimes optimistically named sundeck, as the spectacular Central Coast Archipelago heaves into view. The route north then meanders through a narrow maze of channels, passes and reaches. The mountains soar up majestically from the ocean floor, their peaks covered in snow and ice. So rugged is most of the coast here that if you were exploring by kayak, you would struggle to find a welcoming landing site. Passengers should keep their eyes peeled for whales or dolphins in Queen Charlotte Sound. With a little luck, you might even see a white-coated Kermode bear on Princess Royal Island's lengthy shoreline. Snow-capped peaks delight the eye as the vessel travels through the improbably narrow channel between Pitt and Banks Islands. The open waters of Chatham Sound then await you before Prince Rupert comes in to view.

This BC Ferries operation is more than just a tourist route, it forms part of a vital network connecting outlying communities – your co-travellers may therefore be your best interpreters.

YOU SHOULD KNOW
Unless you are travelling on to Haida Gwai or Alaska, the most affordable way back is by ferry, so be prepared for a round-trip. Also you should book your hotel in Prince Rupert well in advance, as rooms are scarce when the ferry pulls in to town.

SAIL UP THE ST LAWRENCE

North America/Canada

The main pleasure of riverboat cruising is in its constant proximity to the land, meaning that almost every moment brings something new. Your boat up the St Lawrence heads eastwards from Kingston, with Lake Ontario behind you, and after it has rounded Wolfe Island you are greeted by one of North America's most fabulous sights, the iconic Thousand Islands. As most of the islands are the exclusive preserve of the rich or reserved for nature, this really is the best way to see them. From your ringside seat you can marvel at such sights as the abandoned Boldt Castle, while other islands are little more than rocks. The St Lawrence Seaway, a triumph of co-operation between the US and Canada, opens up the heart of the Great Lakes to the Eastern Seaboard. Its strategic importance is evidenced by the prevalence of settlements visible on both banks. For the next 100 km (62.5 mi), rolling pastures frame the river on both sides until it widens at Lac St-François and Lac St-Louis. The names of the towns tell you that you are entering French Canada and that grande dame of Canadian cities, Montreal comes in to view. Most notable among all Montreal's wonderful French colonial architecture is the magnificent dome of St Joseph's Oratory. In the final leg of the voyage, settlements become more spaced out and the hills to your left contrast with the bucolic flatland to the right. The river then widens and the St Lawrence wends its way to Quebec City.

WHEN SHOULD I VISIT?:
Best between the months
May–October.

TIME IT TAKES:
Around one week.

HIGHLIGHTS:
The Thousand Islands in the
fall (September–October) –
featuring a spectacular array
of colours.
The riverfront of Old
Montreal.
Historic, majestic Old
Quebec City.
The ever-changing scenery,
the sunsets and the vibrancy
of the river.

NAHANNI RIVER ON A RAFT
North America/Canada

HIGHLIGHTS: Virginia Falls – difficult to tear oneself away. The thrilling run through Painted Canyon.

A Nahanni rafting expedition is truly a trip of a lifetime. Over the course of this 94 km (150 mi) journey from Virginia Falls to Blackstone Landing, this fast flowing river drops a heart pumping 396 m (1,300 ft). You tumble through Hell's Gate, pass Headless Creek and camp out in Deadmen Valley. So remote is this region of north-western Canada that the only practical way to arrive is by air. This start to the voyage could not be more spectacular, as you land alongside the towering Virginia Falls.

The Nahanni River provides the rafter with the most thrilling of rides. From the figure-of-eight rapids of

Hell's Gate to the giant waves of George's Riffle, this is a true test of oars, people and raft. The welcome respite of overnight camping could not be in more imposing surroundings, and the 1,200 m (3,900 ft) walls of Third Canyon are the most magnificent of sights to wake up to in the morning.

Towards the end of this epic voyage you pass, as if by design, Kraus' Hotsprings where you can soothe your aching limbs. It is then just a short paddle along the braided channels of The Splits where the river finally loses some of its rage.

WHEN TO GO: April–October, but most spectacular in the fall (September–October) when the first dustings of snow cover the mountains.

THE INTERNATIONAL SELKIRK LOOP
North America/Canada

This is a 450 km (281 mi) scenic drive, through an area of forested hillsides, dazzling waterfalls, snow-capped rocky peaks, and charismatic small towns. Much of the land within the Loop is protected National Forest and hundreds of miles of trails are available for hiking, biking, riding, skiing and snowmobiling.

There is no better place to start than the sleepy town of Nelson. Tucked away in the interior of British Columbia, this idyllic place has over 350 heritage homes, though its laid-back townsfolk make it feel like somewhere out of the 1960s. Having stocked up, it is a short ride to Balfour to take the longest free ferry ride in the world, across the Kootenay Lake.

Verdant forests and the lake's deep blue water continue to enrich the senses as you head across the American border into Idaho. With the majestic Cabinet Mountains behind you, the Loop takes you into Washington State and the most beautiful corner of America.

The excellent provision of campgrounds and RV parks is married with the need to preserve the region's endangered wildlife, such as the woodland caribou, grizzly bear and the white sturgeon deer.

THE GREAT DIVIDE TRAIL

North America/Canada-USA

WHEN SHOULD I VISIT?:
The degree of difficulty is less from April–September, although you always have to tread a fine line between extreme cold and extreme heat.

HIGHLIGHTS:
The Canadian Rockies – the ride south from Banff is spectacular.
The mountains of Southern Colorado.
The Flatlands of New Mexico – a chance to build up some strength in your legs.
Getting to the end!

Created by the Adventure Cycling Association of North America with the goal of staying within 80 km (50 mi) of the Continental Divide, this is the mother and father of all bike rides. Originally confined to the USA, it was recently extended to include southern Canada, making the journey an epic 4,238 km (2,711 mi). It has become customary to ride The Divide from north to south but you are not obliged to do so.

The route begins in the glacial valleys of Banff National Park in the Southern Canadian Rockies. It then passes through the densely forested mountains of Montana and Idaho, wends its way down into the barren high desert lands of Wyoming's Great Basin, rises again up and over several 3,000 m (10,000 ft) passes in Colorado, before switching back through rugged mountainous sections of New Mexico and it finally drops down into the Chihuahuan Desert.

The route's highest point, Indiana Pass in Colorado, is around 3,600 m (11,910 ft) above sea level. The first half of the Albertan section and the segments in Montana and New Mexico are the most rugged and challenging, but such is the magnitude of this journey that difficulties can crop up at any point. Violent thunderstorms are common and can be the biggest obstacle to your progress as they often make the riding surface impassable. Be prepared to stop and take stock at a moment's notice. Carrying good lightweight camping gear is essential.

The sense of achievement is almost overpowering as you near the Mexican border. It is at this point that even a few miles can feel like a marathon. The incentive provided by doing the journey as a sponsored ride can add power to your legs as you near the finishing line. Only then can you take in what you have seen and done.

YOU SHOULD KNOW

You have to be fit – very fit – to complete this ride within any reasonable timescale. It is best tackled in a group of people of similar ability. Take advice from the people who designed the route, namely the Adventure Cycling Association.

HISTORIC ROUTE 66

North America/USA

With vast distances and a well-developed railway system, the USA had roads that were little more than local tracks until well into the 20th century. In 1919 the War Department's first Transcontinental Motor Convoy – an expedition that included future World War II Supreme Commander Dwight Eisenhower – took months to cross from east to west. When a Federal highway system was developed, Route 66 – established in 1926, signed in 1927 and fully paved by 1938 – was one of the first.

This iconic road – from Chicago to Los Angeles through eight states and the heart of America, covering some 3,940 km (2,450 mi) – was nicknamed 'The Main Street of America', bringing prosperity to towns along the way and serving as the major route for westward migration during the Great Depression of the 1930s and industrial boom of World War II. Subsequently, Route 66 facilitated tourist development and acquired legendary status, featuring widely in literature (John Steinbeck christened it 'The Mother Road'), films and popular music. But its death warrant was signed in 1956 by the aforementioned Dwight Eisenhower – by then President – when he put his name to the Interstate Highway Act, which led to today's freeway network and made US-66 redundant, though it didn't vanish from maps until 1985. Many sections were incorporated into freeways, and it is now impossible to follow the original route, which anyway varied over the years. But happily nostalgia soon set in and much of the old road has been designated – and marked – as Historic Route 66, with new sections constantly being added. These may be found especially in Illinois, New Mexico and Arizona, and with the help of patience and specialist maps, those who warm to the romance of this famous road can still retrace much of its length – or simply drive individual sections for a reminder of the way America once travelled, not so long ago.

YOU SHOULD KNOW

American fast food culture was born on Route 66, when Red's Giant Hamburgs in Springfield, Missouri became the world's first drive-through restaurant in the late 1940s.

WHEN SHOULD I VISIT?:
April–October for easy driving conditions.

TIME IT TAKES:
Allow several weeks for a realistic attempt to travel the entire length of Historic Route 66.

HIGHLIGHTS:
The Historic Odell Standard Oil Gasoline Station in Illinois, opened beside Route 66 in 1932 and now restored to its original condition.
The National Museum of Transportation in St Louis, Missouri, with a huge collection of historic vehicles and memorabilia, including a unit from the old Coral Court Motel that once fronted Route 66.
The National Route 66 Museum in Elk City, Oklahoma, that allows visitors to recreate a journey along the entire length of Route 66.

Right: Historic Route 66

CALIFORNIA STATE ROUTE 1

North America/USA

Often called Highway 1, this classic West Coast road runs for 1,055 km (655 mi) along much of California's beautiful Pacific shoreline. It starts in Orange County to the south and ends in Mendocino County to the north. Different sections have different names, including Pacific Coast Highway, Cabrillo Highway and Shoreline Highway.

Along the way, this rewarding route can be multi-lane highway or two-lane blacktop, and driving its entire length produces extraordinary contrasts between urban sprawl and some of the finest coastal scenery in the USA,

plus the opportunity to visit many important heritage sites. Highway 1 has mile markers that help locate any listed feature or attraction, numbered from south to north, each bearing the abbreviated name of the relevant county. Highway 1 is best driven from south to north as the reverse direction ends anti-climactically with Los Angeles smog. Starting in San Juan Capistra, the road travels through Los Angeles and the Beach cities, Santa Monica, Malibu, Santa Barbara, Lompoc, Santa Maria, San Luis Obispo, Morro Bay, Carmel (former Mayor – Clint Eastwood), Pacific Grove, Monterey, Watsonville, Santa Cruz, Half Moon Day, Pacifica, San Francisco, Mill Valley and Fort Bragg. It terminates at Leggett, where it meets US Highway 101 (with which it actually shares several sections of the coastal route) for the last time. Many of the place names serve as a reminder of California's historical ties with Spain, and there are a number of old Spanish settlements along Highway 1.

Despite some stretches that are inescapably modern freeways, the leisurely traveller best remembers the characteristic feel of a narrow, winding coast road amidst stunning scenery – not for nothing is it said that to drive Highway 1 is to understand the heart and soul of California.

HIGHLIGHTS:
Unspoiled Big Sur with its rugged cliffs,
Halfway between Los Angeles and San Francisco – Hearst Castle in San Simeon, the extravagant edifice built by newspaper tycoon William Randolph Hearst.

WHEN TO GO:
May–September.

PACIFIC CREST TRAIL

North America/USA

This long-distance hiking route is only for the super-fit. The Trail stretches from the Mexican border up into Canada, a distance of 4,240 km (2,650 mi), following the high country of the Sierra Nevada and Cascade Range, inland from and parallel to the USA's West Coast. The PCT mostly crosses forests and protected wilderness, avoiding civilization and even roads wherever possible. Those who just wish to experience a section of this rugged Trail often opt for the northern section in Washington. Start at the Bridge of the Gods across the Columbia River; from there on it's uphill most of the way, as the Trail goes through National Forests, skirts Mount Adams and crosses a vast wilderness. It enters Mount Rainier National Park, and then continues into the Lake Chelan National Recreational Area and North Cascades National Park.

GLACIER BAY NATIONAL PARK AND PRESERVE

North America/USA

Situated on the Gulf of Alaska in the southeastern part of the country, Glacier Bay National Park and Preserve is an icy wonderland of snowy mountains and dazzling glaciers. It was designated a national monument in 1925, and added to the UNESCO World Heritage Site as part of a vast trans-border park system that includes Canada's Tatshenshini–Alsek and Kluane National Parks. The park covers 13,053 sq km (8,160 sq miles) and includes much of Mount Fairweather and the American section of the Alsek river as well as Glacier Bay itself. In 1794, Captain George Vancouver discovered Icy Strait, situated at the southern end of the bay. All he could find was an enormous glacier, but by 1879 John Muir, the naturalist, found that the glacier had retreated 80 km (50 mi), leaving Glacier Bay in its wake. Today the park is formed from the largest group of high peaks on the continent, the largest ice fields outside the polar caps and 16 huge tidewater glaciers. These last are still retreating every year, and vast icebergs sheer off and plunge into the water.

HIGHLIGHTS:
The Ansell Adams Wilderness in California's Sierra Nevada, named after the famous 20th-century landscape photographer who was inspired by these mountains. A civilized stop-off at Timberline Lodge, built within Oregon's Mount Hood National Forest as a work-generation project in the Great Depression, now a National Historic Landmark and popular tourist destination. Crater Lake National Park in Oregon, the most notable feature of which is the eponymous Crater Lake, a volcanic caldera lake famous for its deep-blue colour.

COAST STARLIGHT TRAIN
North America/USA

WORTH A DETOUR: A break in Paso Robles, with dozens of wineries to tour… before relaxing in the rejuvenating waters of natural hot springs.

Who says the romance of rail travel is dead? It isn't if you save up your pennies and travel on Amtrak's Coast Starlight service, connecting Seattle's King Street Station with Union Station in Los Angeles via Portland, Eugene-Springfield, Klamath Falls, Sacramento, Oakland, the San Francisco Bay area, Salinas and Santa Barbara. Along the 2,216 km (1,377 mi) route, the train passes through some truly spectacular West Coast scenery encompassing virgin forests, snow-capped mountains, lush valleys… and long stretches of fabulous and unspoiled Pacific coastline. No wonder it's rated as one of the world's most beautiful rail journeys. Amtrak gives every passenger a Route Guide that details what to look out for along the way and includes photo symbols indicating the most photogenic spots.

To take full advantage of all that natural beauty, the train uses double-decker Superliner rolling stock, including a Sightseer Lounge car with floor-to-ceiling windows. If you did indeed accumulate those pennies, you can travel in pampered luxury in the first-class Pacific Parlour Lounge car, with sleeping berths, a library, wine tasting, movie theatre and complimentary drinks. The train is hauled by Amtrak's mighty Genesis series locomotives.

A gentle word of warning – the Coast Starlight has sometimes arrived up to 11 hours late, though timekeeping has recently improved dramatically.

HIGHLIGHTS: John Pennekamp Coral Reef State Park. Ernest Hemingway Home and Museum in Whitehead Street, Key West. The southernmost house in the continental USA – a wonderful turreted Victorian confection in pink, at 1400 Duval Street in Key West.

FLORIDA KEYS SCENIC DRIVE
North America/USA

From the tip of Florida, the Overseas Highway (US-1) runs for 203 km (126 mi) along a chain of subtropical isles where the Atlantic meets the Gulf of Mexico, connected by over 40 bridges. It features the southern tip of the Everglades, bustling Key Largo, and Islamorada (Purple Isle), where a memorial at Mile 82 commemorates victims of a 1935 hurricane that was one of the most powerful ever recorded in the USA.

Seven Mile Bridge is one of the world's longest. Now, the keys seem to become more isolated, and wildlife becomes more obvious – like the endangered miniature deer on Big Pine Key (visit their sanctuary) and a profusion of birds such as eagles, red-tailed hawks and falcons.

For the final section, the road crosses a succession of small keys that almost seem to merge, before arriving at the end of the line – Key West, a quirky place that seems to owe more to Caribbean culture than American. It is truly eccentric and unlike anywhere else in the USA, and this is one drive where both journey and destination more than come up to expectations.

Right: Florida Keys Scenic Drive

LEWIS & CLARK'S NATIONAL SCENIC TRAIL
North America/USA

TIME IT TAKES: By car, the entire Trail can be followed inside two weeks without hurrying. Best avoid this route during the harsh northern winters.

If there's one thing the USA isn't short of, it's long distances. Lewis & Clark's route across North America underlines the point, covering 5,960 km (3,700 mi) from Illinois to the Pacific. Meriwether Lewis and William

Clark undertook their two-year saga from 1804 to 1806 at the instigation of President Thomas Jefferson, who dreamed of exploiting unexplored lands to the west. Nowadays, the trail they blazed is the second longest of the USA's 23 National Scenic and Historic Trails. Starting at Hartford, Illinois, it goes through ten more states – Missouri, Kansas, Iowa, Nebraska, South Dakota, North Dakota, Montana, Idaho, Oregon and Washington.

It is not literally possible to follow the pioneers' footsteps, but retracement opportunities are available, under the auspices of the National Park Service. Water segments follow parts of the expedition's waterborne route by boat or canoe. Overland hiking and horse-riding sections are being established and there are marked motor routes where roads nearly or precisely follow the original trail. Perhaps the most complete option is to follow the Lewis & Clark Trail Highway established in the 1960s, which uses modern roads.

YOU SHOULD KNOW
Movie star Ginger Rogers owned a ranch on the Rogue River for more than 50 years, living there full time and greatly enjoying the fishing.

HIGHLIGHTS:
Whiskey Creek Cabin – a 19th-century mining cabin
Gold panning – there is still gold to be found in Rogue River gravel.

ROGUE RIVER TRAIL
North America/USA

Wild and rugged are adjectives that spring readily to mind when describing the Rogue River's wilderness surroundings and seething white water. The 65 km (40 mi) Rogue River National Recreation Trail along the river's north bank offers a splendid way of seeing the impressive Rogue River Canyon. Both the eastern and western trailheads (and the middle of the trail) can be reached by road. Most people hike in an easterly direction so the sun is on their backs in the afternoon.

The Trail is not too demanding terrain-wise, with a well-constructed trailbed and moderate grades, though it should not be attempted by the inexperienced or unfit. It is necessary to backpack, carrying adequate water and supplies along with camping gear, though it is possible to restock along the way. For those who prefer not to camp, lodge accommodation is available (pre-booking essential) at regular intervals. Potential hazards along the Trail include black bears, rattlesnakes, ticks and poison oak.

APPALACHIAN TRAIL

North America/USA

WHEN SHOULD I VISIT?:
Best between April–October
(after which hiking in Maine is
seriously discouraged).

TIME IT TAKES:
A complete 'thru hike' takes
four–seven months.

HIGHLIGHTS:
Flora – the Appalachian Trail
passes through spectacular
forests that vary enormously,
depending on climate and
elevation, and there are
a number of sub-alpine
and alpine sections with
interesting plant life.
Fauna – there are numerous
animals, birds and reptiles
to be seen along the trail,
including black bear, deer,
elk, moose, smaller mammals,
rattlesnakes... and (on the
down side) a variety of
biting insects.

Officially known as the Appalachian National Scenic Trail – unofficially the AT – this marked trail in the eastern USA is a magnet for thousands of hikers each year. Some 3,200 km (2,000 mi) long, it runs from Springer Mountain in Georgia to Mount Katahdin in Maine, passing through North Carolina, Tennessee, Virginia, West Virginia, Maryland, Pennsylvania, New Jersey, New York, Connecticut, Massachusetts, Vermont and New Hampshire as it goes. After that, you know you've had a serious stroll – mostly enjoying the solitary splendour of wilderness, though a few stretches traverse towns.

Many attempt the full length in one hit and about a third of these 'thru hikers' make it. Many more are so-called 'sectional hikers' who either complete the AT bit by bit over a number of years, or just choose one or more choice sections to hike and never essay the whole. Thru hikers generally start in Georgia in early spring to take advantage of warm weather moving north. There are numerous simple shelters along the AT, but these get crowded in summer and most hikers carry basic camping gear. Indeed, living rough on the Trail is very much part of the attraction and this is definitely not an adventure for the faint-hearted.

The Appalachian Trail is largely owned by the National Park Service and has been fully mapped and marked to assist hikers. The main markers are white blazes on trees, with blue blazes indicating side trails to shelters, viewpoints, parking areas and even (whisper it if you dare!) shortcuts.

A word of warning – the Maine section is particularly tough and demanding. And speaking of Maine, don't start along the wrong trail by mistake! The International Appalachian Trail goes north from Maine into New Brunswick and Quebec, with an extension to Newfoundland planned.

OREGON COAST TRAIL

North America/USA

The Oregon Coast Trail (OCT) follows the state's Pacific coastline, from Astoria on the Columbia River in the north to the California border near Brookings – a distance of 600 km (360 mi). It clings to the shoreline, with only an occasional inland detour where the beach is impassable, usually at rocky headlands like Cape Kiwanda. Where the Trail goes through a coastal town, it usually follows the streets closest to the water. This is one of the most beautiful and dramatic coastlines to be found anywhere in the USA (maybe the world!) where the hiker truly feels at one with awesome Nature. Many travel the Trail and camp as they go. Camping is allowed on many beaches and where it is forbidden (within state parks) there are alternative campgrounds. Others prefer the many yurts along the way – conical shelters modelled on the Mongolian original that can be used for a small fee. There are also plenty of bed-and-breakfast establishments that offer walkers a warm welcome and hot showers. Be aware that some sections of the Trail can only be walked at low tide, necessitating a hold-up or sometimes-demanding detour if you arrive at the wrong time. Oregon's Pacific beaches certainly justify a visit, even if you have no intention of travelling the whole Trail. An excellent way of experiencing this wild and unspoiled coastline is to choose a section of the trail that can be walked in a day – there will almost always be a local bus to return you to your starting point at the end of the leisurely hike. For those who don't 'do' walking, US-101 more or less follows the OCT.

HIGHLIGHTS:

The secluded section of the OCT between Port Orford and Brandon – offering four days of pristine wilderness hiking for those willing to camp… and swim a river along the way.
A night in the yurt at Beachside State Park, just south of Waldport.

DON'T MISS
Edinburg – a village on
the picturesque banks
of Stoney Creek.

SHENANDOAH VALLEY
North America/USA

The Shenandoah Valley was a scene of ferocious conflict in the American Civil War when it was known as 'The Breadbasket of the Confederacy'. It lies between the Blue Ridge Mountains to the east and the Allegheny Mountains to the west, stretching for 320 km (200 mi). A journey through the Shenandoah Valley must involve leisurely progress along US-11 – a former turnpike known as 'The Great Valley Road' – from Roanoke in the south to Harpers Ferry in the north. This trip will allow you to experience traditional 'Mom and Apple pie America' at its very best and provide real insight into the pioneer spirit that made the country great. The people are friendly and there's usually some sort of festival, celebration or re-enactment to be found. The picture-postcard landscape combines natural beauty with traditional farmsteads and historic towns with buildings dating back to the 18th and 19th centuries.

BLUE RIDGE PARKWAY
North America/USA

This 755 km (469 mi) National Parkway and All-American Road runs through the famously scenic Blue Ridge mountain chain, part of the Appalachians. The road was a 1930s job-creation project, and the effort was worthwhile – the scenery is stunning (those mountains really are a study in misty blues!), whilst the road passes through unspoiled lands maintained by the National Park Service and the US Forest Service. There are 26 tunnels along the way, together with six viaducts and 168 bridges that carry the parkway across ravines, rivers and across roads to ensure an uninterrupted journey.

A drive along the Blue Ridge Parkway is a memorable experience, but to make the most of this unique landscape it really is necessary to stop frequently and explore some of the numerous side roads and trails which often lead to stunning vistas that change according to the seasons, with a variety of trees, colourful foliage and flowers to be enjoyed, especially in spring and autumn.

HIGHLIGHTS:
The Mabry Mill by its tranquil pool at Milepost 176.1, where a trail leads to this vintage gristmill, sawmill and blacksmith shop where old-time skills are demonstrated throughout the summer. Mount Mitchell – the highest point in eastern North America, reached via a road off the Parkway at Milepost 355.4… what a view!

CHESAPEAKE BAY BRIDGE-TUNNEL

North America/USA

WORTH A DETOUR: Fisherman Island at the entrance to the Bay – a barrier island traversed by US-13 that is part of a National Wildlife Refuge, the habitat of varied waterfowl, shorebirds and waterbirds.

US Highway 13 across the Chesapeake Bay Bridge-Tunnel (CBBT) from Virginia's Eastern Shore at Cape Charles to the mainland at Virginia Beach near Norfolk is known as 'The East Coast's Scenic Shortcut'. The CBBT was opened in 1964, and is a dramatic 37 km (23 mi) crossing of Chesapeake Bay utilizing bridges and tunnels, the latter requiring artificial islands as portals. The actual water crossing over this ocean strait is some 28 km (17 mi) long and has been called 'one of the seven engineering wonders of the modern world'. The CBBT consists of low-level trestle bridges connected by two tunnels beneath shipping lanes, then two high-level bridges over two other navigation channels. The motorist and passengers mainly have a view of the Atlantic seascape during the crossing, but the bridges do curve to give views of other sections of the CBBT and there are usually plenty of ships to be seen, often including US Navy warships. One novel option is making the crossing by night (perhaps a return journey after a daylight trip?), which offers a fascinating light show. And as a bonus, if you do decide to return within 24 hours, the toll is more than halved.

DON'T MISS
The Fulton Market Building for interesting shops and cafés.

LOWER MANHATTAN

North America/USA

New Amsterdam, the Dutch colony that grew into New York City, has long disappeared under Lower Manhattan – yet it remains a fascinating part of the great city to explore. But first look from the water – ride the subway to South Ferry and take a free round trip on the Staten Island Ferry. Those harbour views are to die for.

Back in Manhattan, walk into Battery Park, with its Castle Clinton National Monument and superb waterfront views of the Statue of Liberty and Ellis Island. Head up State Street to the Bowling Green at the foot of Broadway. The city's oldest park offers a fine view of the impressive Alexander Hamilton Customs House. Go down Whitehall Street to the junction with Water Street. Turn left, walk a block east and go left again up Broad Street, then right into Pearl Street. Go up Pearl (pausing for refreshment at the atmospheric Georgian Fraunces Tavern) and turn left into Wall Street, lined with spectacular skyscrapers and noble buildings, including the Stock Exchange, Morgan Guaranty Trust Company and Citibank. Rest awhile in the tranquil graveyard of Trinity Church at the junction with Broadway. Turn north past historic St Paul's Chapel and go on to City Hall Park, overlooked by the fabulous Woolworth Building and home to New York's venerable City Hall.

WORTH A DETOUR: The extraordinary lighthouse on the north tip of Roosevelt Island, built in 1872 – a great viewpoint overlooking the river, Manhattan's Upper East Side and Triborough Bridge.

ROOSEVELT ISLAND TRAMWAY
North America/USA

Completed in 1976, this aerial tramway (cableway to Europeans) spans the East River, connecting Manhattan to Roosevelt Island. Each car has a capacity of 125 people and there are 115 trips per day across the 940 m (3,100 ft) distance. It was grounded after malfunctioning twice, in 2005 and 2006, stranding passengers in mid-air. After refurbishment, the service was reinstated though (just in case) each car now carries blankets, food, water... and a toilet with privacy curtain.

Roosevelt Island had various names over the centuries – Minnahononck, Varckens Island, Manning's Island, Blackwell's Island and Welfare Island – before its final renaming in anticipation of a Presidential monument to Franklin Delano Roosevelt that never got built. In the 19th-century hospitals, asylums and prisons were located on the island, it is now subject to intensive residential redevelopment.

HUDSON RIVER TRIP
North America/USA

The mighty Hudson River rises in the Adirondack Mountains and is 507 km (315 mi) from source to sea. Looking out at the hustle and bustle of New York Harbour, it's easy to forget that the river has great historical significance, reflected in the Hudson Valley's status as a National Heritage Area. It attracted many of the earliest European settlers and a canal connection to the Great Lakes in the 19th century helped to open up the vast interior of this great continent.

A splendid way to appreciate the contrast is to take a Hudson River Cruise, thus enjoying this striking American landscape much as the pioneers first saw it. Key ports of call are Tarrytown, Nyack, West Haverstraw, Peekskill, Garrison, Cold Spring, West Point, Newburgh, Poughkeepsie, Kingston, Catskill, Hudson, Albany (the state capital) and Troy.

The dramatic journey that will not only include wonderful natural beauty but also historic sights – from splendid old plantation houses through the massive mansions of robber barons to battlefields and George Washington's Revolutionary War headquarters.

WORTH A DETOUR: Vanderbilt Mansion National Historic Site and Franklin D Roosevelt Presidential Library & Museum, both in Hyde Park township, Dutchess County.

CAPE COD SCENIC ROUTE 6A

North America/USA

The arm-shaped peninsula that forms the easternmost part of Massachusetts is technically an island, following the completion of the Cape Cod Canal in 1914, but few refer to it as such. Bridges connect 'the Cape' to the mainland, and in summer they're busy with holiday traffic rushing to enjoy the wonderful beachfronts and small-town character of this unique part of New England.

Massachusetts Route 6A is the official title of parts of former US Highway 6 on Cape Cod, generally known as the Old King's Highway, which runs along the north coast that fronts the enclosed Cape Cod Bay. This is considered to be the Cape's most historic and scenic road, and a journey along it (and back) provides a rewarding opportunity to explore an historic maritime landscape and its quaint New England towns.

These delightful places are all well worth exploring – full of character, antique shops, galleries, craft outlets and seafood restaurants... but also thousands of vacationers in high season. In order to experience the beauty of Cape Cod without fighting through hordes of like minded visitors, a journey in late spring or early autumn can pay dividends, though the weather may be cool and some attractions will be closed.

> **WORTH A DETOUR:** Whale watching out of Provincetown, a former whaling harbour that has gained a new lease of life as a result of tourist interest in its former quarry.

> **WORTH A DETOUR:** Before or after the road journey, take a trip on the Durango & Silverton Narrow Gauge Railway, riding rolling stock dating back to the 1880s and hauled by classic steam locomotives.

THE CATSKILL MOUNTAINS

North America/USA

The San Juan Skyway Scenic Byway takes travellers from Durango, through the San Juan National Forest, down the San Juan River down to Placerville, and on to Ridgway. Here, it turns south on US-550, before crossing Bear Creek Falls and entering the valley of Ironton Park, Eventually it returns to San Juan National Forest and descends through the Chattanooga Valley (no, not the Chattanooga of 'Choo Choo' fame, which is in Tennessee) to the historic mining town of Silverton. The fabulous mountain views, sheer cliffs, rushing rivers, plunging waterfalls, rocky terrain, old mines, ghost towns, historic railways and Victorian towns make driving the Skyway a unique experience, as it snakes around mountains, twists through valleys and wriggles through canyons. It's no wonder the San Juan Skyway was designated by the US Government as an All-American Road in 1996. This is the highest possible classification, an accolade that's well deserved.

GRAND CIRCLE ROAD TRIP

North America/USA

HIGHLIGHTS:

Kolob Arch in Zion National Park, thought to be the world's largest free-standing arch at 95 m (310 ft) – see it whilst exploring the amazing Zion National Park Byway.

Hell's Backbone Byway, a dramatic stretch of road near Boulder that travels a ridge with a sheer drop on each side.

Looking straight down into the Grand Canyon from one of the new glass-floored observation platforms.

Viva Las Vegas! But having said that, move on for one of the best sight-seeing road journeys in the USA. This drive of some 1,915 km (1,190 mi) will eventually return you to the world's gambling capital, but not before you've seen some extraordinary natural marvels. First stop is St George, and the attraction here is Zion National Park. Take to the road again, and you're travelling Utah Highway Scenic Byway 12, one of the top scenic drives in America. It winds through National Parks, State Parks and endless scenic vistas encompassing sandstone spikes, petrified forest, desert and snow-capped mountains.

First stop is Bryce Canyon National Park, with colourful rock formations known as 'hoodoos'. Then take the long and winding road to Capitol Reef National Park. Another long stint through stunning desert landscape will bring you to Arches National Park with its wealth of extraordinary rock arches. Go on to Monument Valley Tribal Park, with some of the most famous scenery in America – huge sandstone towers amidst unspoiled wilderness. Last but not least, it's time for the South Rim of the Grand Canyon, 1,830 m (6,000 ft) deep and up to 20 km (15 mi) wide.

GRAND TETON NATIONAL PARK
North America/USA

DON'T MISS
American bison grazing the lowlands, survivors of slaughter in the 19th century.

Part of the Rocky Mountains, the snow-dusted Teton Range soars without foothills from the level floor of Jackson Hole, a long, narrow valley in Wyoming. This special place is preserved as Grand Teton National Park, named after the highest peak that rises to an impressive 4,200 m (13,775 ft). With over 320 km (200 mi) of roads and trails, the Park offers wonderful hiking and biking opportunities.

Mountain bikers can ride the Park from end to end, starting at Jackson, 8 km (5 mi) outside the south entrance. Stay on the road until it forks, giving a choice – Teton Park Road goes over the Snake River and up beside Cottonwood Creek to Jenny Lake, then on past Jackson Lake to rejoin the eastern route. The latter is more straightforward, following the Snake River all the way to Jackson Lake Lodge at the junction with the western route. Thereafter, the road continues alongside the water through Colter Bay Village, to Lizard Creek at the head of Jackson Lake and then up (and up!) to Flagg Ranch Village. Shortly thereafter, the scenic journey is complete.

WORTH A DETOUR: The terrific Arkansas Museum of Natural Resources at Smackover – a 1920s scene of one of the wildest mineral booms in North American history as crude oil came bubbling from the ground.

ARKANSAS HIGHWAY 7
North America/USA

Arkansas bills itself as 'The Natural State' – and when you drive Highway 7, the first state-designated Scenic Byway, it's easy to see why. This 465 km (290 mi) journey shows you many different faces of Arkansas, starting north of the Louisiana state line on the West Gulf Coastal Plain, where an oil boom began near El Dorado in 1921. From there, the road continues to Camden and Arkadelphia through rolling country of river valleys and dense forest.

Highway 7 then enters the Ouachita Mountains, famed for producing amazing quartz crystals en route to Hot Springs National Park. The road enters the level terrain of the Arkansas River Valley at Russellville. But not for long – it soon climbs into the Ozark Mountains, swinging through the Ozark National Forest and finally on to Harrison. It's almost impossible not to linger in Hot Springs, which features the USA's oldest National Park, pre-dating the much-touted Yellowstone by 40 years (plunging into therapeutic hot springs mandatory!) Further north, the Buffalo River is one of the few remaining unpolluted and free-flowing rivers in the USA, as it cuts its way through the Ozarks between massive bluffs.

WORTH A DETOUR: Stopping off at the summit of Washington Pass, the journey's literal highlight at 1,699 m (5,477 ft) – admire jutting Liberty Bell and Early Winter Spires (among others).

NORTH CASCADES SCENIC HIGHWAY

North America/USA

The North Cascades Highway, also known as SR-20, runs across Washington State from Puget Sound in the west to Idaho in the east. Most travellers focus on the Scenic Highway, a 225 km (130 mi) section that has some of the most dramatic scenery in the northwestern USA.

The North Cascades Scenic Highway begins at Sedro-Woolley on SR-20 and enters the rugged North Cascade Range through the Skagit Wild and Scenic River Corridor, following the Skagit through Hamilton, Concrete (true!), Rockport and Marblemount. The road then enters North Cascades National Park, bisecting a vast wilderness before passing dams that create Diablo and Ross Lakes, providers of hydroelectric power for energy-hungry Seattle. The most demanding stretch of the Highway now climbs towards two incredible high points – Rainy Pass and Washington Pass, From there, it's all downhill as the Highway winds down through Mazama to Winthrop, a 19th-century staging post for gold miners.

RIM OF THE WORLD DRIVE

North America/USA

This 172 km (107 mi) National Scenic Byway runs along the crest of the San Bernadino Mountains, passing through magnificent scenery as it connects some of the most popular destinations in the Greater Los Angeles area – Crestline, Lake Arrowhead, Running Springs and Big Bear Lake.

Yet it still manages to twist and turn through some of the last unspoiled country left in Southern California, offering great panoramas at almost every turn. It begins at the Mormon Rock Fire Station; at Cajon Pass, several historic routes intersect (the Old Spanish Trail, Santa Fe Trail, Santa Fe Railway and John Brown's Toll Road). From there, the road goes through Horsethief Canyon, which tells its own tale.

SR-18 carries the Byway along the rim, with great vistas across San Bernadino and the Los Angeles Basin. There are numerous stopping points and tempting side routes to explore. At its end, the Byway travels through delightful mountain communities to the Mill Creek Ranger Station.

HIGHLIGHTS:
Before starting off, take the short hike from Mormon Rock Fire Station to view the eponymous Mormon Rocks – a striking pink sandstone formation that stands on the old Mormon trail to Utah. Silverwood Lake State Recreation Area – take one of the side roads down to the lake itself.

WORTH A DETOUR: Balboa Park, largest urban cultural park in North America, with Spanish revival buildings dating from the Expositions of 1915 and 1935 – find Old Globe Theatre complex and lush gardens.

SAN DIEGO SCENIC DRIVE
North America/USA

The 95 km (59 mi) San Diego Scenic Drive guides visitors all around this laid-back city. It is clearly marked with blue-and-yellow signs, illustrated with a bold white seagull. Among too many to list individually, high points along the way include Harbor Island (wonderful views of San Diego Bay), Spanish Landing, Point Loma (historic lighthouse), Cabrillo National Monument (commemorates the first European visitor, Portuguese explorer Juan Rodriguez Cabrillo, in 1542), Sunset Cliffs, Ocean Beach, Mission Bay Aquatic Park (endless beaches), Soledad Mountain Park (best view in town), the University of California and Salk Institute, La Jolla Cove and Cave, Pacific Beach, Mission Beach, Sports Arena, Old Town State Historic Park (former Hispanic town centre), Hillcrest, Balboa Park (museum and cultural focus), the financial district, and Seaport Village (a trendy shopping complex). The route continues on to the historic heart of San Diego, the Gaslamp Quarter – once the home of opium dens, gambling halls and saloons, now a vibrant entertainment district. If you're not sidetracked there, continue to the end of the San Diego Scenic Drive in the ultra-modern Horton Plaza, for shopping and dining.

BEARTOOTH HIGHWAY
North America/USA

Few would disagree that the Beartooth Highway in Montana and Wyoming is one of the most beautiful drives in America. It is a section of US Highway 212 between Red Lodge, Montana and Cooke City, Montana – a journey of just 111 km (69 mi), but what a journey. It ascends to the Beartooth Plateau, zigzagging and switchbacking as it crosses the Montana-Wyoming state line, just north of Yellowstone National Park, climbing above the tree line to offer expansive views. To the south – canyons eroded by the Clarks Fork River over millennia. To the north – the Absaroka-Beartooth Wilderness, complete with the sharply etched spike known as Bear's Tooth that gave these massive mountains their name. Then the Highway climbs to the summit of mighty 3,345 m (10,974 ft) Beartooth Pass.

From there, it's a downhill run into lake country. There are over a thousand in the wilderness with Long, Little Bear, Island and Beartooth Lakes alongside the Highway. The Beartooth Highway then runs down into the old gold mining town of Cooke City. This is the northeastern gateway to Yellowstone, and there will be time a-plenty to take a peek… if you're not already suffering from an overdose of memorable scenery.

WHEN SHOULD I VISIT?:
June–August.

Left: San Diego Scenic Drive

PETER NORBECK SCENIC BYWAY

North America/USA

'Take me back to the Black Hills, the Black Hills of Dakota', croons the seductive song. It's certainly a trip worth making and one way of getting the most from a visit is to follow the Peter Norbeck Scenic Byway, named after the early-1900s South Dakota Governor and conservation minded Senator. This 110 km (68 mi) route loops through the Black Hills National Forest and Custer State Park in southwestern Dakota.

Start at the town of Custer, named after the late, not-so-great General who camped here in 1874 on his first, not-so-fatal expedition to the Black Hills. Head north on Highway 89, to a section called the Needles Highway where the road winds around hillsides and through tunnels, all the while passing the spectacular granite spires that give the road its name. Turning north on Highway 87 takes you past Peter Norbeck Wildlife reserve, onto the aptly named Iron Mountain Road, famous for one-lane tunnels aligned with Mount Rushmore. From there, take US-16A along to Mount Rushmore, where the faces of four great Presidents were carved into the mountain's solid granite by sculptor Gutzon Borglum and his crew between 1927 and 1941. After admiring Washington, Jefferson, Roosevelt and Lincoln, head on past towering Harney Peak on Highway 244 to the edge of the Black Hills National Forest, where Highway 87 and then Highway 89 will return you to the starting point. Along the way you will have seen the American West at its best – soaring mountains, rugged rock formations, caves, forests, grasslands, canyons, gulches, rushing rivers and lakes, all made accessible to the motor car by amazing roads built with ingenuity and engineering skills of the highest order.

HIGHLIGHTS:
Pigtail bridges on Iron Mountain Road
Crazy Horse Monument – an ongoing project to create a massive granite likeness of the mounted chief, which will be the world's largest sculpture – alongside the Indian Museum of North America and Native American Cultural Center.
Wind Cave National Park, near Custer.

OLD SPANISH TRAIL
North America/USA

WORTH A DETOUR: Las Vegas – original travellers of the Trail valued the place for its artesian springs, a welcome life-saver in the arid desert, but you may find other reasons for visiting.

This 2,000 km (1,200 mi) long trade route from Santa Fe to Los Angeles was explored by European pioneers in the 1770s. In its heyday the Trail was renowned for all the less endearing characteristics of the Wild West – rip-roaring frontier towns, naked commercial opportunism, banditry, horse stealing and raids – as mainly Mexican pack trains went from Sante Fe to Los Angeles to trade slaves and woollen goods for horses and mules raised on Californian ranches. The demanding journey encompassed six modern states – New Mexico, Colorado, Utah, Arizona, Nevada and California, running through high mountains, deserts and canyon country. Today, few traces of the original Trail remain, though it is remembered by many historical markers, road and street names. The only way to retrace its course is by car.

The Old Spanish National Historic Trail offers dramatic landscapes and a rich legacy of pioneering spirit, western adventure and American history, and you can plot your own journey or get a special map that does it for you.

SANTE FE TRAIL
North America/USA

DON'T MISS
The Fort Union National Monument north of Watrous, New Mexico.

Santa Fe was pivotal in the development of the American Southwest. This charming adobe city featured on the El Camino Real Trail up from Mexico and was both the starting point of the Old Spanish Trail to California and end-point of the Santa Fe Trail from Missouri through the modern states of Kansas, Oklahoma and New Mexico. The latter was a vital trade route from its inauguration in 1821 to 1880, when the railway's arrival at Santa Fe made it obsolete. Depending on the route, the Trail was around 1,255 km (780 mi) long. The original Trail took a northern path up to Las Vegas (no gambling then at this one-horse town!), San José and Pecos. The southern route – the Cimarron Cutoff – was shorter but more dangerous, with little water. There were many variations, especially of the Mountain Route, but those who wish to follow the Santa Fe National Historic Trail from beginning to end can do so on modern highways that duplicate the general course of both routes, though some sections are inaccessible. The Historic Trail is administered and promoted by the US National Park Service, who offer specialist maps and a wealth of useful information. Those who follow the Trail today (in vehicular comfort!) can only marvel at the courage and determination of those who travelled only on foot, horseback or by wagon.

MISSISSIPPI RIVERBOAT CRUISE

North America/USA

WHEN SHOULD I VISIT?:
Cruises are available all year round.

TIME IT TAKES:
Most cruises are seven nights, but there are shorter and longer options to be found.

HIGHLIGHTS:
Hearing (or even playing!) a calliope – these steam-powered organs were, and still are, very much a part of the riverboat scene.
Small-town America at its best (plus 29 locks) on an Upper Mississippi cruise from St Paul down to St Louis (seven nights).
All the charm and elegance of the old Deep South on a Lower Mississippi cruise from New Orleans to Memphis (seven nights).

YOU SHOULD KNOW
Louis Armstrong knew what he was talking about when he sang the classic song 'Ol' Man River – he travelled up the river from New Orleans by paddle steamer, stopping at towns along the way to play.

An enduring image of 19th-century America is the riverboat – a sternwheeler belching wood smoke from tall twin stacks as she dashed up and down the Mississippi, Ohio or Missouri Rivers. There was probably a high-stakes poker game going on within the fancy white superstructure, ending in gunplay when five aces came down in the same hand, whilst Mark Twain watched from the bank, pen in hand. Well, maybe it wasn't quite like that, but these stylish craft certainly played a vital role in developing the central-southern and midwestern USA.

Americans are good at marrying tradition with commerce, so it's still possible to experience the delights of this traditional river transport by taking a paddlesteamer trip. The modestly named Majestic America Line runs a variety of cruises using a couple of late 20th-century steamboats – American Queen (the largest river steamboat ever built) and the Mississippi Queen. Each is the ultimate in old-fashioned comfort and style, though American Queen is something of an impostor – she looks the part and has a sternwheel driven by steam, but her main source of propulsion is diesel-powered propellers. The company's Delta Queen, built in 1927, is a National Historic Landmark, but sadly her cruising future is on hold as a result of modern safety regulations.

These steamboats offer both a selection of 'see the river' cruises and theme cruises including the popular Jazz and Civil War itineraries. A cruise won't be cheap, but really is an opportunity to experience the elegant atmosphere and travelling style of a bygone era. Oh, the romance of paddle steamers is infectious. If you don't fancy the Mississippi, sternwheelers are now working Alaska's Inside Passage and the great rivers of the northwestern USA (Columbia, Willamette and Snake) for the first time in a century.

Right: Mississippi Roverboat

DEATH VALLEY

North America/USA

WHEN I SHOULD VISIT?: The heat in Death Valley can be lethal. Best visit between November–March.

HIGHLIGHTS:
Towne Pass, a 1,510 m (4,955 ft) summit that greets you just inside the Park. Mosaic Canyon near Stovepipe Wells – extraordinary walls of polished multicoloured rock. Zabriskie Point – no, not the iconic Antonioni movie, but the real thing – it's an amazing rock formation.

Here's one for the tough and super fit – a cycle trip through the notorious Death Valley in California and Nevada. It's the lowest place in America at 86 m (282 ft) below sea level, and also one of the hottest on earth with temperatures regularly reaching 54°C (130°F) in the day (but sometimes freezing at night). Death Valley National Park is a unique environment, offering an atmospheric landscape of sand dunes, salt flats, multicoloured rocks, canyons, snow-capped mountains and seemingly endless wilderness. The Park has a number of roads, mostly narrow and twisting, and not even the most dedicated mountain biker can explore them all.

A good journey follows California Route 190, which crosses the middle of Death Valley (albeit not in a straight line!) from Panamint Springs in the southwestern corner of the Park. From there it's a 29 km (18 mi) run to Emigrant, then another 13 km (8 mi) to Stovepipe Wells Village, which has all the facilities required for a little R&R. You'll need it – the next leg is the 44 km (28 mi) slog along CA-190, which turns sharply south before reaching the Furnace Creek Visitor Center. Continue on CA-190 and make the straight run to the Park exit and on to Death Valley Junction, a 45 km (28 mi) ride. If that's not enough to test your cycling prowess, you can take the State Line Road to Pahrump, Nevada – or even (if you're feeling lucky) cycle on from there to Las Vegas. Wimps can do Death Valley by air-conditioned car – which does give them the opportunity to explore the Park's many wonders more thoroughly.

DON'T MISS
Savannah's captivating
downtown area – one
of the largest National
Historic Districts in the USA.

SEA ISLANDS
North America/USA

This chain of barrier islands runs down the USA's Atlantic Coast off South Carolina, Georgia and Florida. The Sea Islands are captivating and with over 100 to choose from it's possible to plan a journey with ample opportunity to explore this delightful coast. One excellent route is from Jacksonville in Florida to Charleston in South Carolina, allowing you to find and visit Sea Islands in all three states. The Coast Road, this mainly follows the line of Interstate-95, but is a route that allows you to take interesting side-trips all the way to Charleston.

From the town of Brunswick, a number of roads lead down to the water if you want the sea for yourself, as there are no major resorts in this area. The Georgian town of Savannah merits a long stop, with a wonderful waterfront and access to more islands. The route finishes in the elegant southern city of Charleston.

THE ARIZONA TRAIL
North America/USA

WORTH A DETOUR: The Coronada National Memorial celebrates the first European expedition to southwestern America, in 1540, so the Trail follows in the hoof prints of conquistadors.

Ambitious mountain biker?
Cycle the newly signed Arizona Trail, designed to provide a physical challenge even as it showcases the widest possible variety of terrain and ecosystems (including lung-busting mountains!), together with Arizona's cultural and historic diversity. The idea is to keep things simple (primitive, even, though there are campgrounds) so this is a rough, tough adventure that will take you through some of the most rugged and spectacular scenery in western America. Ready, steady, pedal…

The Trail begins at the Coronado National Memorial near the Mexican border and goes north through the Huachuca, Santa Rita and Rincon Mountains. Before you can draw breath, you'll be in the Santa Catalina Mountains north of Tucson, then the Mazatzals. But there's more climbing in store, into the San Francisco

Peaks. At last, there's easier going – the Coconino Plateau all the way to the Grand Canyon, across the Colorado River and the final Kaibab Plateau stretch to the Arizona-Utah border.

You won't see much human habitation. Apart from the tiny town of Patagonia shortly after starting, the only other place on the Trail is Flagstaff, and even there you can take a detour. The Trail incorporates many established paths, so it is possible to pick and choose rewarding sections without doing the whole thing.

THE JOHN MUIR TRAIL

North America/USA

HIGHLIGHTS:

The impressive granite Half Dome at the eastern end of Yosemite Valley.
The Devils Postpile – a basalt cliff made of old lava columns, topped by trees and standing above a slope of fallen columns.

This is a terrific hike for those with strong legs and stronger lungs, running for 340 km (211 mi) along California's Sierra Nevada mountain range from the Happy Isles trailhead in Yosemite Valley to Mount Whitney in the south. And that's the direction to go on the John Muir Trail (JMT), allowing the hiker to become acclimatized to the thin atmosphere before tackling the more remote, demanding southern half. The JMT attracts plenty of day hikers, but the true challenge is backpacking the entire Trail. A permit is required to hike, to be obtained from the National Park or Forest where the journey begins.

The JMT is mostly over 2,440 m (8,000 ft) in elevation, above and beyond the height most people ever experience for extended periods. And that's not all – the journey crosses six passes (Donohue, Muir, Mather, Pinchot, Glen and Forester). The last – Forester – is the highest at a mighty 4,010 m (13,155 ft). After running through Tuolomne Meadows the JMT parallels the main range of the Sierra Nevada thorough Yosemite National Park, Inyo and Sierra National Forests, Devils Postpile National Monument, Kings Canyon National Park and Sequoia National Park. Even after gallantly reaching the end of the JMT by climbing to the summit of Mount Whitney, there's a sting in the tail – a further hike to civilization at the nearest trailhead at Whitney Portal, 18 km (11 mi) farther on. One of the true wonders of the USA is that – for all the country's sprawling and apparently insatiable urban development – it takes such care of (and pride in) preserving its pristine wildernesses.

HIGHLIGHTS: The view from the top of Mount Magazine Brightly coloured butterflies, from April onwards. Guided ATV tours of the Huckleberry Mountain Trail.

HUCKLEBERRY MOUNTAIN HORSE TRAIL
North America/USA

This glorious scenic journey is in the Ozark National Forest of northwest Arkansas, and for a short distance within adjacent Mount Magazine State Park. Anyone who wishes to tackle the Huckleberry Mountain Horse Trail has a choice of steeds – the good old-fashioned horses for which it was designed, the two well-shod feet of Shanks' Pony, the thoroughly modern lightweight alloy wheels of a mountain bike or an All-Terrain Vehicle (ATV).

The Trail shows the Ozarks at their best, offering a rugged landscape of shady forests and stunning mountain vistas. It consists of two loops, together offering some 55 km (34 mi) of well-marked scenic horseback riding, if that's the delightfully relaxed way you choose to travel. The terrain is varied – deep, winding valleys and creeks are overlooked by mountain bluffs. There are clear mountain streams and numerous trailside ponds for watering the horses.

After rain, some of the creeks and streams can become dangerous and should be crossed with extreme care – especially Shoal Creek. It's not difficult to stray off-route, so a Trail map is a wise investment.

TAHOE RIM TRAIL
North America/USA

WORTH A DETOUR:
A stunning display of wild flowers (at their best in the first two weeks of July) or fall foliage (September and October).

Lake Tahoe is a deep-blue, natural mountain lake, some 35 km (22 mi) long by 19 km (12 mi) wide. It is surrounded by snow-capped mountains, volcanic peaks, granite cliffs, lush forests, jewel-like small lakes, alpine meadows and a rich diversity of flora and fauna. The Tahoe Rim Trail (TRT) that girdles this natural marvel is 266 km (165 mi) long, going through two states, six counties, one State Park, three National Forests and three Wilderness Areas. It's an all demanding terrain that presents a real challenge to the dedicated hiker, who will need to carry all the essentials for survival in a single backpack.

The TRT is open to skiers in winter, but is not marked then. A permit is required to enter Desolation Wilderness (the Echo Lake to Barker Pass section of the Trail). There are blue triangular TRT markers at regular intervals, but anyone attempting the entire journey should get a detailed map. Those who don't have the time (or strength) to undertake the entire journey but wish to see something of this magical landscape can access the Trail at many points for a day hike.

MASON-DIXON TRAIL

North America/USA

WORTH A DETOUR: Codorus Creek – once owned by James Smith, a signatory of the Declaration of Independence, this furnace built in 1765 supplied ammunition to colonists during the American Revolution.

Connecting the Appalachian and Brandywine Trails, the Mason-Dixon Trail (M-DT) is 310 km (193 mi) long and starts in Pennsylvania at Whiskey Springs on the Appalachian Trail. It then goes east to the Susquehanna River, passing through Pinchot State Park along the way. The M-DT continues along the west bank of the Susquehanna south to Havre de Grace in Maryland, crosses the river and continues east through the Elk Neck State Forest into Delaware's Iron Hill Park. From there, the M-DT heads north along the Christina River and White Clay Creek to the White Clay Creek Reserve. It then turns northeast for the last leg to the eastern trailhead at Chadds Ford on the Brandywine River, back in Pennsylvania. The Trail is well marked by blue blazes, but is no wilderness excursion designed to avoid human habitation.

True, it does go through much pleasing open countryside, but in so doing often follows narrow back roads where traffic can be dangerous. It also passes through plenty of small towns and developed areas. That said, it does offer some fine vistas, along with long and scenic stretches of hilly, rolling terrain that is well wooded, plus rocky climbs out of side gorges along the Susquehanna River.

WORTH A DETOUR: Longmire Buildings in the Nisqually River Valley – a brief dose of civilization with an inn, museum and Wilderness Information Center.

WONDERLAND TRAIL

North America/USA

This rough-country route shuns roads and human habitation as it journeys around mighty Mount Rainier in the National Park of the same name, arriving back at the starting point after 150 km (93 mi). The cumulative elevation gain during the circumnavigation is around 6,000 m (20,000 ft), which adds up to a serious physical effort as the Trail crosses ridge after soaring ridge. But Wonderland it is – the Mount Rainier National Park offers a variety of eco-systems, from lowland forest to sub-alpine meadows, and Mount Rainier itself reveals a series of spectacular glaciers as the journey unfolds. The Trail crosses many rivers, often by simple log bridges, occasionally by more dramatic suspension bridges. Though there are a number of trailheads that will be busy in summer, many stretches of the Trail provide complete solitude amidst natural grandeur. But hikers should be aware that weather conditions can be treacherous, with dangerous storms always a possibility (especially in September). A backcountry permit is required to hike the entire Trail, and the challenge is so alluring that early application is advisable (in March), as a ballot is held in April to allocate a limited number of permits, thus ensuring the Wonderland Trail will never be spoiled by over-exploitation.

WORTH A DETOUR: Ruby Canyon on the Colorado River, with its towering red sandstone formations – unless you raft in, the only way to see the place is from the Zephyr.

CALIFORNIA ZEPHYR

North America/USA

No argument – this is one of the world's great train journeys, sheer heaven for the scenically minded. In 51 hours, it covers 3,925 km (2,440 mi) from Chicago to the Pacific coast, traversing Illinois, Iowa, Nebraska, Colorado, Utah, Nevada and California. In so doing, it crosses the American Midwest before heading over the Rocky Mountains and Sierra Nevadas to California. This luxury service was inaugurated in 1949 and has gone through various changes since those early days, though things have stabilized since Amtrak initiated the modern Superliner service (choice of roomy coach seats or private sleepers) in 1983. Look out for the amazing series of switchback turns the track takes as it descends from Soldier Summit in Utah's Wasatch Mountains, and Cape Horn, the steepest slope on the entire route (carved out by Chinese labourers lowered in baskets).

For those who are hooked on the romance of railways, it's possible to revisit the Zephyr's 'golden age' – an evocative collection of classic CZ silver rolling stock plus locomotive at the Western Pacific Railway Museum in Portola, northeastern California.

SAN FRANCISCO STREETCAR

North America/USA

WORTH A DETOUR: The Cable Car Museum beneath the car barn at Washington and Jackson Streets, where you can also descend to a large basement where the haulage cables are routed to the street.

The first streetcars (technically cable cars) capable of handling San Francisco's steep hillsides were introduced in 1873 and were an instant success – to such a degree that several new lines were opened. The boom was short-lived – cheaper electric streetcars arrived and the great earthquake of 1906 damaged many lines. By the 1940s the old streetcars were in terminal decline, as buses were by then capable of handling the acute gradients. Happily, a citizens' revolt saw the retention of three streetcar lines, which remain to this day as a much-loved part of the city's character.

The survivors are the Powell-Mason, Powell-Hide and California Street Lines, now used mostly by tourists. A journey on one or more of these splendid old streetcars (preferably hanging onto the outside!) is a mandatory part of the San Francisco experience. Two of the lines use single-ended, partially open cars that have to be rotated on turntables at the end of each run. Line 61 uses double-ended cars with open sides and an enclosed middle section. To maintain the romance, all lines use cars that are either restored originals or faithful replicas, and the changing views from the moving streetcars are among the best in SF.

MOUNT WASHINGTON COG RAILWAY

North America/USA

DON'T MISS
Old Faithful Geyser;
Grand Prismatic Springs.

In 1858, after climbing Mount Washington ('home of the world's worst weather'), Sylvester Marsh, nicknamed 'Crazy' Marsh, rashly proposed building a railway to the summit, at the dizzy height of 1,917 m (6,288 ft). After the laughing stopped, the New Hampshire State Assembly granted permission for the summit. So guess who had the last laugh? The first loco ran in 1867 and the line was completed in 1869, since which time Sylvester Marsh's quirky creation has carried over five million passengers.

Laid on trestle all the way, this extraordinary engineering feat has a maximum gradient of 37.41 per cent, and custom-built steam engines push carriages up a 4.9 km (3.1 mi) track, belching smoke as they use a tonne of coal and a 3,785 litres (1,000 gallons) of water on every journey. Many of the locomotives, each of which has a name, date back to the 19th century (though much rebuilt over the years) and today's passengers enjoy much the same experience as those who were first captivated by the Mount Washington Cog Railway 150 years ago.

The locos look weird on the flat, with forward-tilting boilers that are designed to be level when climbing and descending the mountain. Both engine and coach are pulled up the mountain (and eased back down) by a 19-tooth cog that meshes into the track's central rail. At the same time, reassuring ratchets that prevent backward slippage are engaged on ascents. After a scenic ride that offers majestic mountain vistas, be prepared to avert your eyes as the summit approaches – a trail crosses the tracks, and there's something of a tradition whereby hikers await the train and 'moon'.

In winter there is a limited service (mainly weekends and school holidays) up through the snow to Kroflite Camp at 1,250 m (4,100 ft).

HIGHLIGHTS:
Peppersass, named for its likeness to a pepper sauce bottle – the first engine used in the construction of the line from 1867, now on display at the Marshfield Base Station. Jacob's Ladder, the steepest section of the track – a raised trestle that angles round the mountainside.
Summit buildings, including Tip Top House (built in 1853) – some days you can see four states, Canada and the Atlantic Ocean, and on other days nothing but swirling cloud!

YOU SHOULD KNOW

Camp on the US bank and carry identity documents to show Border Patrol you're not 'illegal'.

RIO GRANDE
North America/USA

Big Bend National Park in Texas is like the state itself – larger than life and many countries. This vast area is bound by the Rio Grande to the south, which forms the border with Mexico, and the Park is a land of extremes – from desert to mountain, majestic rivers to inaccessible wilderness. The variety of plants and wildlife – especially birds – is extraordinary, and the Park's facilities are often stretched during high season (cooler winter months). But there's one way of getting round that problem – taking to the water, to kayak through the Chihuahuan Desert with open views and a dramatic river-scape that includes canyons up to 460 m (1,500 ft) deep.

The Rio Grande runs for 190 km (118 mi) within the Park, and a further 205 km (127 mi) downstream is designated a Wild and Scenic River. There is plenty of calm water, but this is not a journey for beginners as there are periodic encounters with rapids of varying severity, especially when the water is high. Unfortunately, extraction means it often isn't. The preferred option for experienced paddlers is a one- or two-person inflatable kayak, and even then this magnificent river is so remote that most people travel with a guide or organized party. It is possible to use your own equipment or hire locally (though not in the Park). Permits are required for self-organized trips, allowing you to stop off and explore interesting side canyons.

To run the Rio Grande through the Park, start at Lajitas on Texas Highway 170. Be aware that there are few facilities and a limited number of take-outs along the route and plan accordingly. Unless you intend to run the full length of the Wild and Scenic section, you end this unique journey at the Highway 2627 bridge in La Linda. This is a 200 km (125 mi) trip.

HIGHLIGHTS:
The beautiful journey through Santa Elena Canyon – great scenery, serenity, and the excitement of the Rockslide Rapids.
Sunset over Mexico's remote Sierra del Carmen (Carmen Mountains), south of the river.
Marsical Canyon, the most remote in Big Bend National Park – just 16 km (10 mi) long but with varied scenery, towering limestone cliffs, some rapids and ample stop-off points along the canyon bottom.

GOING-TO-THE-SUN ROAD

North America/USA

Named after the mountain of the same name, Going-to-the-Sun Road runs through Glacier National Park in Montana. It was completed in the 1930s after a dozen years of construction, and this ambitious engineering project was one of the first National Park Service projects to be specifically undertaken with automobile-borne tourists in mind. The massive construction effort was justified – the parkway runs for 85 km (53 mi) through the craggiest of mountain scenery. Strong nerves are required, as the roadway is both narrow and winding, often clinging to the mountainside without

WORTH A DETOUR:
St Mary Lake – so scenic that it has featured in at least two major movies – Forrest Gump and The Shining.

guardrails (they have been attempted, but always get swept away by late-winter avalanches). For those who prefer to watch the scenery rather than the road, there is a fleet of shuttle buses that allow visitors to explore the route at their leisure, hopping on and off at any one of numerous stops and catching the first bus along when they've finished sightseeing or exploring.

SEWARD HIGHWAY

North America/USA

YOU SHOULD KNOW
Beware quicksands! The mudflats and beaches on the coast from Anchorage to Portage should be approached with extreme caution.

The sometimes-moody Seward Highway was completed in 1951 and is 204 km (127 mi) long, though it follows a route used by Russian fur traders in the 1700s and native peoples for thousands of years before that. This incredible road runs along the Turnagain Arm and across the Kenai Peninsula, whose collective scenic glories have earned a coveted triple classification: All-American-Road, US Forest Service Scenic Byway and Alaska Scenic Byway. The natural beauty of the Seward Highway is unlike any other to be found in the USA – stunning fjords and crystal-clear lakes, glaciers and waterfalls, ridges and valleys, alpine meadows and a profusion of wild flowers in season. The area has become a magnet for adventurous tourists who, drawn by a plethora of outdoor recreational options, arrive all year round. Salmon season is May to mid-October and (ironically) the Seward Highway stays open all winter where many Scenic Byways in states farther south do not. That said, occasional avalanches do briefly close the road in winter, but the sweepers soon open it up again.

YOU SHOULD KNOW
The Trail finally fell into disuse
when the railway reached
New Mexico in 1880.

EL CAMINO REAL HISTORIC TRAIL

North America/USA

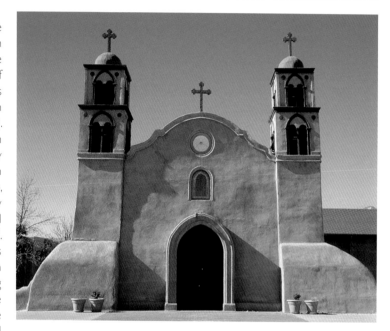

For decades before the Mayflower arrived in North America, El Camino Real de Tierra Adentro (Royal Road of the Interior) brought Europeans up from Mexico to Santa Fe in 'New Spain' (now New Mexico). The significance of this migration route has been recognized by classification of the 650 km (404 mi) US section (from El Paso, Texas to San Juan Pueblo, New Mexico) as a National Historic Trail.

The Trail runs along today's Interstate-25 corridor, with the modern highway following much of the old route. Before they arrived at what is now the Mexico-US border, settlers had endured a three-month voyage from Spain, a trek across the rugged Sierra Madre Mountains to Mexico City then a gruelling 1,770 km (1,100 mi) wagon journey to the Rio Grande. The last leg through dangerously inhospitable country was still to come, a reality that discourages modern attempts to hike the Trail.

However, it is possible to plan a self-guided car journey that follows the Trail and sees some remaining sites. First visit the new El Camino Real International Heritage Center, midway between Socorro and Truth or Consequences on I-25 (Exit 115). It overlooks the Trail where it crosses the fearsome Jornado del Muerto (Journey of the Dead Man) desert basin, a reminder of the hazards facing early travellers. One recommended journey involves travelling between the historic plazas of the main towns along the Trail – Santa Fe, Albuquerque, Socorro, Las Cruces and El Paso, stopping off to look at impressive Trail heritage along the way.

HIGHLIGHTS:
San Miguel Mission, also in Santa Fe – the oldest church in the USA, built at the last major stopover on the Trail in the early 17th century.
Fort Selden near Las Cruces, a mid-19th-century army post designed to protect travellers.
The historic district in the heart of Socorro, around a plaza that still holds the essence of the Trail.

THE PAN-AMERICAN HIGHWAY

North America/USA

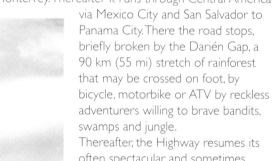

DON'T MISS
Sunrise; the Ohanapecosh river; Longmire.

HIGHLIGHTS:
The Alamo where a gallant band including Davy Crockett defied the Mexican army in 1836, before perishing to a man.
Quito – the capital city of Ecuador is a charming city that shows urban South America at its very best.

The world's longest drivable road is the Pan-American Highway, a system with a total length of some 48,000 km (30,000 mi). The intrepid traveller must drive from Prudhoe Bay in Alaska down to the Panama Canal. Although the Pan-American Highway has no official status in the USA and Canada, the accepted route follows the Alaska Highway. After reaching Canada, the road splits at Edmonton, one route going via the Great Lakes, Minneapolis and Dallas, the other taking in Calgary, Denver and Albuquerque. The two meet at San Antonio in Texas, before reaching the 'official' Pan-American Highway at the Mexican border south of Monterrey. Thereafter it runs through Central America via Mexico City and San Salvador to Panama City. There the road stops, briefly broken by the Darién Gap, a 90 km (55 mi) stretch of rainforest that may be crossed on foot, by bicycle, motorbike or ATV by reckless adventurers willing to brave bandits, swamps and jungle.

Thereafter, the Highway resumes its often spectacular and sometimes dangerous journey, as the road follows the Pacific coast down through Cali, Quito, Antofagasta and Valparaiso, before cutting across to the Atlantic at Buenos Aires. That marks the official end of the Highway, but there are two unofficial branches – one continuing down the west coast from Valparaiso to Quellon, the other from Buenos Aires to Ushuaia at the tip of South America. This latter route is, of course, mandatory for anyone who wishes to be one of the few individuals on the planet to have travelled America from top to toe.

HIGHLIGHTS: The view from Divisadero: enjoy the sensational vista of three canyons (Tararecua, Urique and del Cobre).
Chihuahua itself – a splendid historic city full of colonial treasures.

THE COPPER CANYON
North America/Mexico

The awesome Copper Canyon complex in the Sierra Tarahumara consists of six linked canyons, collectively four times larger (and deeper) than the Grand Canyon.
Happily, you don't have to hike this rugged country to experience Copper Canyon's incredible scenery, just catch a train. El Chepe, as the Chihuahua al Pacifico train is known, runs from the city of Chihuahua to Los Mochis near the Sea of Cortez, a distance of some 650 km (400 mi), traversing the principal canyon of Urique (North America's deepest). The line, completed in 1961, is a magnificent engineering feat, with 37 bridges and 86 tunnels. The quality of the scenery along the route is pretty good too – recognized by El Chepe's classification as 'one of the top ten most spectacular train trips in the world' in 2005. This accolade is justified – the extraordinary diversity of this unique landscape ranges from snow-capped mountains to tropical forests in canyon bottoms.

RIO SONORA
North America/Mexico

DON'T MISS
The magnificent 17th-century Nuestra Señora de la Asunción Church in Arizpe.

To follow the Rio Sonora is to journey through Mexican history, experiencing both the harsh natural beauty surrounding this life-giving river and the traditional towns that have grown along its banks since the Jesuits first arrived in the 17th century. Rough terrain and an uncertain water supply have combined to ensure that the river communities retain their rural roots, so this really is a step back in time. The river – and journey – starts just across from Arizona at Cananea. Highway 118 loosely follows the river all the way down to Mazocahui, where a right turn onto Highway 14 completes the route to Hermosillo. It's worth exploring along the way, as this is a journey that can offer fascinating insight into Old Mexico, framed by the sweeping vistas of typically arid Sierra Madre scenery.
Sonora is a mining town just a century old – and the massive copper mine west of the city is the largest in Mexico. The road next passes through a couple of ranching centres founded around 1650 – Bacoachi and Arizpe – before reaching Banamichi, settled by Jesuits in 1639. The town's Hidalgo Plaza contains the Piedra Historica, an ancient petroglyph thought to be an irrigation map. At Huépac, look inside San Lorenzo, a 17th-century church with a fine interior. Ures was once the state capital of Sonora, and the town's historic roots are very evident in the Plaza Zaragoza and San Miguel Cathedral. Mazocahui is the last sleepy pueblo before you reach the provincial capital of Hermosillo, one of the largest towns in northern Mexico.

YUCATÁN

North America/Mexico

HIGHLIGHTS:
Ciudad del Carmen, the 'Pearl of the Gulf' – try the seafood.
Progresso – Mérida's busy port, 30 km (18 mi) to the north, for amazing salt flats and extraordinary flocks of flamingoes.
Mérida's central Plaza, with America's oldest Cathedral (1556–1599), Palacio Municipal (1735) and Casa de Montejo (1542), former home of the founding conquistador.
An outing to the evocative Mayan ruins at Chichen-Itza and the nearby Caves of Balankanche.

The Yucatán Peninsula in southeastern Mexico separates two great bodies of water – the Caribbean Sea and the Gulf of Mexico. It has been rapidly developed for tourism in recent years, with the once-tiny fishing port of Cancun now a thriving boom town and the Mayan Riviera on the east coast a major resort destination for those seeking sun-sea-and-sand holidays.

For those more interested in the ancestral heartland of the ancient Mayan civilization, the 300 km (185 mi) journey from Villahermosa in the adjacent state of Tabasco to Mérida, Yucatán's 'White City', will be fascinating. Until recently, Yucatán was isolated, looking more to its Mayan roots and out to the Caribbean than inwards to Mexico,

so it has a unique atmosphere and culture. You will appreciate this as you drive, perhaps diverting to explore this special land of jungle, thorny scrub, hills, Mayan ruins, haciendas, colonial cities, wildlife preserves and pristine beaches.

From Villahermosa, head north on Highway 180 through Frontera, where you reach the Gulf. Keep going, enjoying stunning coastal scenery all the way (especially the amazing bridge crossing of the Laguna De Términos through Zacatal, Ciudad del Carmen and Puerto Real) before continuing to Chapoton and Campeche. From there, stay with 180 as the road cuts inland and heads for Mérida, via Chencoyi, Tenabo and Calkini. Mérida is worth waiting for. Founded by conquistadors on the site of a Mayan city, it is the oldest continually occupied city in the Americas, and displays much of the traditional splendour and charm of colonial Mexico.

WORTH A DETOUR: Roadside banana sellers – be amazed by how many varieties you'll be offered, plus you get to see what a freshly gathered cashew nut looks like.

OAXACA CITY TO PUERTO ANGEL

North America/Mexico

The experience begins in cosmopolitan Oaxaca City, then you find Highway 175 and head south. This two-lane road twists and turns violently as it winds through the mountains, to the point where motion sickness is a real possibility. What's more, the road surface is rarely the best – rainy season always sees damage to 175, which in true Mexican style barely gets repaired before the next rainy season.

But there's no point in hurrying. The Sierra Madre del Sur are noted for their biodiversity, and this road reveals stunning new vistas at every turn. You will have pictures of cloud forests with pines in the mist and lush tropical forest when the road descends. The villages along 175 often have wonderful indigenous crafts on sale. Eventually the road runs down out of the mountains towards the Pacific Ocean. Puerto Angel is an old-fashioned harbour town crouched around an enclosed bay with a fleet of small fishing craft.

ESPIRITU SANCTU AND ISLA PARTIDA

North America/Mexico

HIGHLIGHTS:
Interesting sea caves within walking distance of Isla Partida's south coast.
A mangrove bay on Espiritu Sanctu, providing a welcome mass of greenery that may be explored by kayak.
The Malecon waterfront promenade around the bay in La Paz, a quintessentially Mexican town that pays only lip service to tourism.

Describe the difference between the Gulf of California, Sea of Cortez and Mar de Cortéz? Of course they're all the same place – that long, narrow body of water separating the Baja California Peninsula from the Mexican mainland. The enchanting island of Espiritu Sanctu is connected by a narrow isthmus to Isla Partida, and together they are a protected UNESCO biosphere.

The way to explore the rocky wilderness islands in the Sea of Cortez north of La Paz on the rugged Baja California Peninsula is journeying by kayak, camping as you go. Take along a snorkel and flippers, as the diving is memorable. You can hire kayaks and canoes for a circumnavigation locally, or choose from a number of guided tours. It is possible to paddle out to the islands, though some prefer to be delivered by motorboat to allow the maximum possible time around the islands. Either way, it's a classic sea-kayaking trip. Being on the water gives you every opportunity to see many species – look especially for humpback whales, California grey whales, whale sharks, leatherback turtles, sea lions, dolphins and giant manta rays.

RIO USUMACINTA

North America/Mexico

WHEN SHOULD I VISIT?:
Avoid the rainy season
(May–November).

Ready for a real wilderness adventure? Something ever-so-slightly dangerous? This is border country, where smuggling between Guatemala and southeastern Mexico is rife. Bandits stalk the roads. Zapatista rebels have been active, so the Mexican army is in evidence. But the security situation has improved and – as the only way to make this incredible journey is as part of an organized group with experienced guides – the danger is not acute.

The river is formed in a great natural basin by the merging of two others – the Salinas and Pasión Rivers –

and serves as the border between the Mexican state of Chiapas and Guatemala, after which it wanders through the state of Tabasco to the Gulf of Mexico: the only physical boundary between the Yucatan Peninsula and the rest of Mexico. The trip involves overnight camping on river beaches and numerous stops to swim or explore interesting features and historic sites along the banks. The scenery varies from jungle-covered bluffs, cascading waterfalls, through tumbling rapids and canyons to the slower sections towards the take-out point at Tenosique.

HIGHLIGHTS:
The magnificent Temple
of the Jaguar.
The glorious jungle flora and
fauna of the region.

LA RUTA MAYA

Central America/Guatemala

La Ruta Maya, far from being a route trodden by the ancients, is a construct of 20th-century American travel writing. This often-travelled route links sites which were mysteriously abandoned by the Mayan civilization over a thousand years ago. La Ruta starts in Southern Mexico and takes you down the spine of Central America to Belize. The least visited and perhaps the most mystical part of the route lies within the modern day boundaries of Guatemala. Hidden by thick jungle until the 19th century, Tikal is one of the most stunning archaeological sites to be found anywhere in the world. Once one of the largest and most influential cities of the Mayan era, the city disappeared over the centuries, swallowed up by the lush jungle. The scale of the development can be seen by climbing up Temple IV to view distant structures still half hidden in the forest canopy.

This is but one of many important Mayan cities, hidden over many centuries and now re-discovered. Some were home to grand palaces; others were of more modest proportions. All however have something to reveal about the fascinating ancient Mayan empire.

YOU SHOULD KNOW
Whilst falling in number, guns are quite common. You are relatively safe in the park, where rangers are employed for security, but it is a good idea to travel in a group.

VOLCANO PACAYA
Central America/Guatemala

Located in the southwest coastal region of Guatemala, Pacaya began its most recent active phase in 1965. More often than not, it spews little more than gaseous emissions and relatively small steam eruptions, but its constant activity has made it a magnet for vulcanologists from around the globe and predictions of major eruptions such as the one in 2006 have increased in accuracy.

The ascent is definitely not easy, especially towards the top. Loose ash and volcanic rock make walking difficult, while clouds of sulphur can hinder breathing. Hazards aside, when you reach the top the views are astounding, like standing in a lunar landscape.

MOUNTAIN PINE RIDGE FOREST RESERVE
Central America/Belize

HIGHLIGHTS: Barton Creek Cave – full of Mayan artefacts. The Hidden Valley Falls – a viewing platform gives a great vantage point to the 460 m (1,500 ft) high waterfalls.

Pine forests are not the first things that spring to mind when you think of Central America, but the unique Mountain Pine Ridge in Belize has surprises around every corner. This 1020 m (3,400 ft) tall ridge is a natural wonderland of spectacular waterfalls, wild orchids, vibrantly coloured parrots, keel-billed toucans among a myriad of exotic flora and fauna.

Located in the Mountain Pine Ridge Forest Reserve, the trail leads you through thick jungle, past ancient rock formations and most notably to Caracol, the largest Mayan ruins in Belize. Excavation of these relics is still in its infancy – it's fascinating to see the forest slowly giving up its secrets.

All around you the forest invades the senses with ambient noise, colour and smell. Mossy ferns and abundant vegetation form a soft canvas, while exotic birds perch among the treetops and other wildlife plays between the branches. The area is dotted with cool mountain pools to swim in and caves to walk through – if only all life were like this! The tempo of this magnificent walk is perfect. The altitude of the climb takes the edge off the tropical heat and the often misty summit of the ridge provides a magical backdrop.

It is probable that the forest is the remnant of a volcanic island that collided with the mainland several millennia ago. This would explain the feeling of isolation you get from climbing the trail. This is truly a paradise gained.

MONTEVERDE CLOUD FOREST

Central America/Costa Rica

YOU SHOULD KNOW

If travelling with a guide ask for testimonials or get a recommendation from the local tourist authority, as some operators can be shady. Make sure that the horses look healthy and that the guide keeps to well-trodden paths.

Bathed in a curtain of life-giving mist, the Monteverde Cloud Forest in the mountains of Costa Rica is a profusion of saturated greenery that stands as an icon of modern day conservation. Originally founded by Quakers fleeing the draft in 1960s America, this privately owned reserve has now been expanded to cover over 10,500 hectares (26,000 acres).

With altitudes ranging between 600 m and 1,800 m (1,970 and 5,900 ft), the Forest Preserve is one of the most flourishing biological sanctuaries in the world. Over 100 species of mammals, 400 species of birds, 120 species of amphibians and reptiles, and 2,500 species of plants, as well as tens of thousands of insect species reside within its borders. In addition, larger animal species including the jaguar, ocelot, resplendent quetzal and baird's tapir inhabit the Preserve's boundaries.

HIGHLIGHTS:
The forest scenery and the views from the top.
The surrounding National Park – as close to a pristine jungle as you could wish to experience.

CERRO CHIRRIPO

Central America/Costa Rica

There can be few more intense fusions of pleasure and pain than the hike up Cerro Chirripo, with its 18 km (11 mi) climb to a 3,000 m (10,000 ft) high summit. If the gradient doesn't slow you down, then the diminishing oxygen at altitude will add extra pressure to the lungs. The rewards, however, for making it to the top are bountiful. On a clear day it's possible to see both the Pacific and the Caribbean by just turning your head!

A permit is needed to make this climb and the monies raised go towards trail maintenance and the employment of park rangers. So with ticket in hand and a rucksack stocked for all eventualities, it is time to breathe in the tropical air and start the climb. Everything from sun block to a sleeping bag is essential, as the hot tropical sun can easily burn you and it has been known to snow near the summit. Thankfully there are a couple of dormitory-style huts along the way.

As befits a jungle environment, the slippery trail can make progress hard work. Short of out-and-out mountaineering this is probably the most difficult 18 km (11.25 mi) you will ever travel. Its inaccessibility is what keeps this area special and free from the development and exploitation that blights much of Central America. Besides the challenge of climbing Costa Rica's highest peak, there are numerous trails that wind through more ecological zones than you will find in most entire countries.

YOU SHOULD KNOW

The delicate ecosystem that surrounds the canal is threatened by deforestation, as a result of illegal logging.

PANAMA CANAL AND LAKE GUTAN

Central America/Panama

For sheer drama it is difficult to top the 77 km (48 mi) passage through the Panama Canal. Built to cut sailing times between the east and west coasts of America, one-twentieth of the world's shipping now passes through its locks. It is the perfect marriage of engineering efficiency and Italianate architecture that makes it a true wonder of the modern world.

The locks themselves utilize the waters of the surrounding rainforest to send vessels on their way through improbably narrow passages. The region's rivers and lakes are dammed, and, along with the locks, these dams control the release of 236 million litres (52 million gallons) of freshwater per passing vessel. Where else in the world can you lean over the side of large cruise ship and touch land? When the ship is ready to change locks, it is mesmerising to look down from the stern. With only 10 m (33 ft) between propellers and lock gates the commotion caused by the water is quite incredible.

The canal marks the lowest point at which you can cross the American Continental Divide as you sail through the 13 km (8 mi) of the dramatic Gaillard Cut, where the mountain was literally sliced open to allow passage. Such is the dramatic nature of the scenery that it appears to the eye that you are heading straight towards a cliff as you head through the final lock that takes you into Lake Gutan. Here there is a chance to disembark or simply marvel at the sheer volume of shipping waiting to pass through the canal.

HIGHLIGHTS:

Marvelling at the mechanics of it all.

The evergreen tropical jungle, which adorns both sides of the canal.

The contrast between the bubbling excitement of the canal and the tranquillity of Lake Gatun.

Watching passing ships travel close by in the opposite direction on the section between Culebra Cut and Lake Gutan.

TRAIL TO VOLCAN BARU

Central America/Panama

WHEN SHOULD I VISIT?:
Year round – it's almost
deserted between
November–March.

TIME IT TAKES:
Allow a full day – six hours
up, four hours down.

HIGHLIGHTS:
The sounds of the jungle.
The misty forest.
El Respingo – a bird-
watcher's paradise, nearby.
The surrounding National
Park.

Volcan Baru forms the focal point of a sumptuous National Park that shares its name. The highest point in Panama, it has become a Mecca for outdoor adventurers, bird-watchers and nature lovers of all kinds.

It is quite probable that your first view of this 3,474 m (11,398 ft) high iconic symbol of the Central American rainforest will be fleeting, as the summit is usually shrouded in cloud. This is an important consideration when planning a climb and an early morning start is vital in order to maximize your chances of enjoying good views from the top. When the clouds clear, a carpet of green lies before you, framed by the azure waters of both the Pacific Ocean and the Caribbean Sea.

Because of the volcano's height and isolation, this area is considered a bioclimatic island. Its forest is home to distinctive species of orchids and rare flora such as magnolia and giant oak trees, some of which are over 800 years old. You'll also see wild bamboo gardens and gigantic, knotted trees dripping with vines and sprouting prehistoric-looking bromeliads from their stems.

The rainforest also provides a home to over 200 species of bird, the most notable of which is the resplendent quetzal, whose extraordinary beauty puts it in the number-one spot on many bird-watchers' lists. Other rare birds here include the silky flycatcher, the three-wattled bellbird, and the hairy woodpecker. In higher reaches, an intermittent cloud forest creates an eerie ambience.

DON'T MISS
The quaint,
garage-size
old railway stations.

RAILWAY TRAIL
Bermuda

The Railway Trail traces a traffic-free path through the archipelago – a thoroughfare for walkers, pedal-cyclists and riders. It runs for some 34 km (21 mi) along the roadbed of the narrow-gauge railway torn up in 1948, its continuity broken into seven sections where original trestle bridges no longer exist. From Sandys Parish in the west to St George's in the east, the trail bypasses every town and village, but provides tranquil access to all of them. It is a treasure trove of fascinating sights, unavailable any other way. It winds through sun-dappled countryside, revealing a succession of glorious seascapes. You see beautiful houses with characteristic Bermudan stepped roofs of whitewashed limestone, and skirt magnificent Georgian mansions. You pass pink sandy beaches, marshlands and mangroves. You share the scent of roses with the migrating birds in the upland forest sanctuary of Heydon Trust; and you enjoy the commanding view of the Sound from 19th-century Fort Scaur, the smallest drawbridge in the world, and a dozen other wonderful ways to remove yourself from urban Bermuda.

BLUE MOUNTAIN DOWNHILL
Caribbean/Jamaica

WORTH A DETOUR: The demonstration (including much drinking) of Blue Mountain coffee, the most expensive and among the best in the world, at one of the plantations.

It is effortlessly simple. If you want to see the Blue Mountains, have yourself driven to the highest point accessible by vehicle, Hardware Gap (1,707 m/5,600 ft), deep in Holywell National Park and in the immediate shadow of the Blue Mountain peak itself, at 2,257 m (7,402 ft) the highest point in the Caribbean. The forest, Kingston and the sea are spread below you. All you have to do is put on the required helmet and knee pads, mount your bike, and roll gently downhill for 29 km (18 mi).

The actual riding time is about 2 ½ hours, but the journey can take all day depending on your starting point. Enthusiasts come from as far as Ocho Rios, adding five hours driving to the ride. In any case, the downhill is punctuated by extremely well chosen photo opportunities and refreshment pauses, culminating in mid-afternoon with a short walk to a forest pool, with creepers and vines dangling from a rock face over which cascades a 30 m (100 ft) waterfall. You'll be ready for the swim. It's a chance to reflect on everything you've seen and everything you've been told about descending through several different ecosystems. Because the mountain roads are small, and bikes don't make a lot of noise, you really do get close to some of the blazing colours of Jamaican bird species, and of the clouds of flowers that turn densely packed rainforest trees into floral totems. You can stop and listen any time, or take a better look at plants that catch your eye. But probably you'll be content to drift on down while all your other senses enjoy the feast.

TREK TO THE BOILING LAKE

Caribbean/Dominica

YOU SHOULD KNOW

1. Go with a guide, because the trail becomes indistinct. 2. Wear proper footwear and scruffy clothes – you will get dirty. 3. Try to go in a group of six to ten, so that there is likely to be someone of similar ability to walk with.

The Boiling Lake trek is Dominica's ultimate trial of strength. The volcanic island is the most rugged and mountainous in the Caribbean. The combination of tropical location and active volcanism make it a rainforest paradise of streams and cascades – much of it protected in the wilderness National Park that surrounds its highest peaks, the Morne Trois Pitons. The Boiling Lake lies at its heart, a fittingly dramatic finale to what feels like a mythic adventure into a new world.

The Valley of Desolation lies, wreathed in the bubbling sulphur steam of 50 fumaroles and hot springs that colour rocks like stained-glass. The water may flow black, milky, bright yellow or iron-red. But not even the bizarre formations or the mosses and rare orchids that survive here are preparation for the exhilaration of emerging suddenly, after another hard climb through clouds and steam, at the cliff edge of the Boiling Lake itself.

WORTH A DETOUR: Above 'Dupuy Pit', just past 'la Dècouverte', the view of the leeward coast of Basse-Terre across the Caribbean to Les Saintes is breathtaking.

LA SOUFRIÈRE SUMMIT HIKE

Caribbean/Guadeloupe

Clambering to the summit of La Soufrière, you enter another world, completely invisible from below. Instead of a single immense crater, since the massive eruption of 1976 La Soufrière is capped by a cluster of eruptive vents arranged along the fracture zones. The pits and pools form a lunar landscape of damage where the hail of stones and sludge projectiles utterly destroyed previously lush vegetation. Green posts mark the trail through the mist of sulphurous fumes leaking from this wasteland, once so rich in plants it was called 'le jardin Herminier' (in honour of an early 19th-century Guadeloupean doctor and botanist), and now known as 'la Porte d'Enfer'.

Here you cross the 'Great Fault' by a natural rock bridge and loop right to the multiple fumaroles of 'Piton Napoleon', until you reach the bubbling cauldron of the south crater. Often invisible in fog or hidden by its own thick vapour, you can smell it and feel its radiating heat at some distance. In fact the hellish landscape is a fascinating demonstration of recovery. La Soufrière's summit plateau of bizarre rock formations is covered with the flora of recolonization – a wonderful surprise and a rewarding hike.

HIGHLIGHTS:
The hairpin ascent up a near vertical slope from the airport to Hell's Gate.
Vanishing into cloud on Mt Scenery – at 877 m (2,850 ft).
The descent from Windwardside, the village where most visitors stay, via The Bottom to Fort Bay.
The 15 minute taxi drive combines the thrills of the Road with a temperature rise of 30 degrees at sea level.

THE ROAD

Caribbean/Saba

Close to St Maarten, the peak of an extinct volcano called Mount Scenery rears out of the Caribbean, the centrepiece of Saba's 13 sq km (5 sq mi) of vertiginous cliffs and lush, forested mountains. So steep are its hills that for centuries the only way to get around was by hiking up long stone stairways, using donkeys to carry produce and household goods: the world's engineers agreed that it was impossible to build a road on Saba's rugged terrain. With the determination of a Joseph Conrad hero, a local man decided otherwise. Guided only by a correspondence course in engineering, between 1938 and 1961 he browbeat the rock into submission using just dedicated local labour and a wheelbarrow. The Road is his testament. It is literally the only road on the island. The Road defies gravity, common sense, and all the rules of engineering. It's a stomach-churning 14 km (8.75 mi) switchback made of concrete, with no blacktop, edging or markings. It connects the airport on the northeast side and the harbour at Fort Bay on the southwest, twisting and turning through all four of Saba's villages en route. Mango, guava, avocado, lemon and banana trees line it where its narrow ribbon isn't already crowded by the uniform white, red-roofed houses walling its sides. It makes no concessions to fear or vertigo as it careers past sheer drops into the ocean, and plunges up, down and round within the villages. Sabans take it at speed – and wily locals choose laborious hiking trails rather than walk the Road.

Even by taxi, the Road is an adrenaline rush. Given Saba's incomparable flora, the natural beauty of its rainforest, and its reputation as a world-class dive site, it's appropriate that just travelling between its charms should be a unique journey in itself.

Be sure to arrive by plane – Saba's runway is just 400 m (1,200 ft) long with a sheer drop into the ocean at either end.

PICO DUARTE

Caribbean/Dominican Republic

DON'T MISS
Snorkelling in
Stingray City.

HIGHLIGHTS:
Climbing the highest
mountain in North America,
east of the Mississippi.
The variety and numbers of
birds – including trogons,
hispaniolan parrots, palm
chats, woodpeckers, red-
tailed hawks, and zumbador
hummingbirds.
Riding mules (you can hire as
many as you want: the rule of
thumb is one guide and one
mule for every five hikers).

Pico Duarte (3,087 m/10,128 ft) is the highest mountain in the
Caribbean. More significantly, it is the centrepiece of the huge
Cordillera Central Reserve of Bermúdez National Park, and almost
untouched by the kind of tourism that threatens to make a Disney
World of other parts of the Dominican Republic. The Park is
uninhabited, a pristine wilderness of clear mountain rivers, jungle
forests alive with the darting colours of hummingbirds and parrots, and
the most magnificent landscapes in the Caribbean. Pico Duarte itself is
only one of several similar peaks, and incorporates distinct sub-tropical
eco-zones ranging from coconut palms and swaying bamboo groves to
mountain rainforest and cool alpine scrub and pine.
Of the five routes to Pico Duarte, all are strenuous hikes of between
3 to 6 days and 46–108 km (28–67 mi). The most popular starts
25 km (13 mi) south west of Jarabacoa, from the village of La Cienaga
where you have to register for the 46 km (28 mi) round trip, and hire
a guide and mule (the mule is all but mandatory – if only as insurance
for porterage and safety). Early in the morning, you follow the bubbling

rivers up into the wild woodlands,
serenaded by Mourning Doves.
The dense forest thins, and gaps
in the canopy reveal more and
more of Hispaniola's fabled,
translucent beauty. By nightfall you
reach a ramshackle cabin called
La Compartición, where the trails
meet and hiking parties prepare
for the pre-dawn scramble up the
last 5 km (3 mi), through scented
pines and open meadows, to
greet the sunrise from the bare,
rocky summit.
On a clear day with the clouds
flushed pink below you, with the
emerald forest and blue sea sharp
contrasts in the distance.

TREN FRANCES

Caribbean/Cuba

YOU SHOULD KNOW

1. Foreign visitors pay more than Cubans for rail travel; and they pay neither in pesos nor dollars, but in Cuban Convertible dollars (CUC$).
2. It's best to reserve your seat at least 24 hours in advance, and at both Havana and Santiago stations you do so at a special booth (NOT the normal Booking Office). You may be asked to show your passport, and/or to confirm your ticket one hour before scheduled departure, at the same place.

Cuba is so big, with so much to see, that sooner or later visitors need to get from one end of the country to the other. The most rewarding method of travel is the train – and the Tren Frances is FC's (Ferrocarriles de Cuba) flagship service. On odd days (1st, 3rd, 5th of the month, etc) it leaves Havana for Santa Clara, Camaguey and Santiago; and on even days (2nd, 4th, 6th, etc) it makes the return journey. It's a stately schedule befitting the air-conditioned, stainless steel rolling stock acquired from France in 2001 after its retirement as a workhorse of the Trans-Europe Express between Paris, Brussels and Amsterdam. With reclining seats, carpets and cafeteria service, the Tren Frances still offers two classes: basic leatherette especial (2 + 2 seats across) and primera especial, with fabric seats spaciously arranged 2 + 1 across the aisle. It's comfortable, fast and (despite frequent moans from downright unlucky passengers) relatively reliable. It has to be: if it's more than an hour late, you get the fare refunded in full.

But watching the backyard of Cuba's glorious countryside unfurl, punctuated by visions of its colonialist past and the grinding demands of its agro-industrial economic present, you realize quite how extraordinary this train really is in its Cuban context. It's a statement about the country's determined ambition to make do, mend and better itself on its own terms. The Tren Frances really is the best way to see the 'real' Cuba – and the daily evidence is the other passengers. Most are Cuban, keen to talk and share, and (in marked contrast to the grumpy clientele on the 'tourist-only' bus network) thoroughly cheerful about life and its vicissitudes. Primera especial may be grubby and worn, but only the Tren Frances provides a first-class insight to match the country you see from its windows.

HIGHLIGHTS:
The powerful air-conditioning.
Breaking the ice with fellow passengers.
In Santiago, the station is opposite the Caney rum factory.
Sub-tropical dusk and dawn.
The sense of intimacy with Cuba you retain, even long after stepping off the train in either Havana or Santiago.

WHEN SHOULD I VISIT?:
Year-round.

TIME IT TAKES:
Over 12 hours for the one-way journey of 861 km (533 mi).

REVOLUTIONARY TRAIL IN THE SIERRA MAESTRA

Caribbean/Cuba

YOU SHOULD KNOW

You need to carry all the food and water you require with you.

HIGHLIGHTS:

Listening to revolutionary songs sung by Quinteto Rebelde in Santo Domingo.

Getting politically hyped-up by the enthusiasm of fellow hikers along the trails or in the campsites.

With history at every turn, the naturalist's paradise of the Sierra Maestra makes this some of the world's most stimulating trekking.

The friendly and informative researchers at the bio-stations.

Virtually unchanged since the momentous days of Cuba's revolution, the entire Sierra Maestra region is full of important revolutionary sights – but the Sierra's status as a National Park derives equally from the necessity to preserve some of Cuba's most beautiful landscapes and very best wildlife. Trekking the revolutionary trail is therefore a double whammy for political and ecological heritage.

Head for the small town of Santo Domingo (itself the site of a key battle) at the north entrance to the Park. From here, you can join tours (the only way to get the necessary permits). Two are essential. La Comandancia de la Plata was Castro's field headquarters, in a forest clearing on a western spur of Pico Turquino. The wooden huts where Castro lived, and Che (a qualified doctor) ran a tiny hospital, retain their full dramatic potency in their remote, desperate setting up a single tortuous track of mud and rocks. The other is the tough, two-day hike to Pico Turquino's summit, a ritual political pilgrimage for many young Cubans. A famous picture shows Castro on the peak, gun in hand, looking imperiously over the country he was to rule for 49 years.

WORTH A DETOUR: The single-storey, wooden houses with characteristic porch-balconies that make the town of Vinales feel like a timewarp.

MARIEL TO VALLE DE VINALES
Caribbean/Cuba

Cuba's far west has always been isolated from development or tourism by dense forests and rugged mountains. Its remote beauty has been made accessible by the extension of the Circuito Norte – the autopista that links Havana east and west along its north coast – to Pinar del Rio, and the paving of access roads close to some of the region's most breathtaking charms.

With the sea sparkling on one side, you drive out of the port of Mariel into the green hills of the Sierra del Rosario, a protected UNESCO Biosphere Reserve of tropical mountain forests. Cut by numerous rivers and waterfalls, the Reserve is both stunningly beautiful and home to 100 bird species and more than half of Cuba's endemic species of flora and fauna. From the Circuito Norte, visit Las Terrazas, a woodland eco-community where you can swim in the forest waterfalls and pools of the San Claudio Cascade.

HIGHWAY 901
Caribbean/Puerto Rico

WORTH A DETOUR: The Punta Tuna west beach, protected from development so that light pollution does not distract hatching leatherback and hawksbill turtles.

Highway 901 is a sideshow, a scenic corniche road that has so far escaped the horrifying urbanization and development of Puerto Rico's fabulous coastline. From Yabucoa it leads straight to the sea at Playa Lucia, a bedraggled but lovely palm-lined beach kept free of crowds by frankly dangerous currents. Highway 901 climbs quickly past the beach, rising to the very cliff edge some 100 m (328 ft) high above the Caribbean, curling round the tail of the Cuchilla de Panduras Mountains as they drop into the sea. From here, you get a glorious view along the top of the cliffs: with a classic white lighthouse drawing your eye to the distance. Driving is hair-raising enough without going fast, because at several points the edge of the road is the edge of the drop.

The lighthouse is not open to the public, but you can stop outside it to admire the vistas either side of Punta Tuna, on which it stands. Below the rocky promontory, on both sides sandy coves are hemmed in with thick vegetation bursting with colourful flowers, their scent on the air. In crowded Puerto Rico, the breezy solitude is pure balm for the soul: it's usually impossible to resist a scramble down to the beach itself before driving on. Above you, 901 swings back inland to join the roar of traffic at Maunabo, forming the northwestern boundary to the Punta Tuna wetland area of freshwater swamp and three kinds of mangrove. Like Highway 901, the reserve is a wonderful reminder that Puerto Rico's coast isn't all freeways.

RUTA DE LAS NIEVES
South America/Venezuela

WORTH A DETOUR: The backcountry of the paramo eco-zone – high grassland full of wildflowers and the endemic, soft-green velvet frailejón.

From the coastal jungle around Maracaibo, Venezuela's cordillera rises rapidly to the thriving town of Valera. Now called the Trans-Andean Highway, the road twines upwards into the glories of the Sierra Nevada National Park, passing the Venezuelan Andes' highest peaks and most dramatic landscapes before dropping down to the lovely old colonial city of Mérida. Woven into the snow-capped mountains, the Ruta de las Nieves is an astonishing introduction to the extreme contrasts of Andean ecosystems, culture and way of life. Valley bottoms are a mesh of stone walls and streams enclosing trout fisheries or pasture for horses and cattle – a system as ancient as the carefully-tended terraces (andenes) that climb slopes 1,000 m (3,200 ft) high. The Ruta ascends through cloud forest to the high mountain paramo of windswept grassland, through 17th-century stone villages like Mucuchies or its neighbour San Rafael, Venezuela's highest (3,140 m/ 10,330 ft) community. It follows the high ridge between Timotes and Apartaderos – said to be the most scenic drive or bike-ride in the country – with vast panoramas of the Sierra Nevada on either side. The greys and whites of the jagged upper peaks shift with pink and pale-gold reflections from banks of scree and snow; and 200 glacial lake surfaces race with the movement of the sky.

Marvellous as it is just to drive, the Ruta de las Nieves also provides access to some of Venezuela's best hiking, mountain-biking, riding, climbing and eco-tourism.

WHEN SHOULD I VISIT?: December–February offers the clearest weather, but many visitors prefer July–September when there is more snow on the mountains.

TELEFÉRICO DE MÉRIDA
South America/Venezuela

This is the closest you will ever come to flying on a magic carpet: the longest and highest cable car journey in the world. The ascent is pure drama. Mérida is a lovely 16th-century colonial city set like a bowl of flowers wedged into the green slopes of Venezuela's Sierra Nevada National Park. The Teleférico terminal just east of Plaza Bolivar makes a surreal contribution to the antiquity of Mérida's historic heart, and as the city dwindles into pint-sized perfection, most visitors are fixated by the contrast. The focal point changes at the first station, La Montana (2,542 m/8,338 ft). It's a good idea to walk about and breathe deeply, to get accustomed to the sudden increase in altitude – for now the true majesty of the mountains becomes apparent. During the next two sections (La Aguada 3,452 m/11,323 ft, and Loma Redonda 4,050 m/12,263 ft), huge vistas open up of the saw-toothed high peaks stacked behind one another. Reaching into the distance, you can see how Venezuela's cordillera shares the triple spine that characterizes the Andes through Peru, Bolivia and Chile; and nearer, how apparently insignificant trickles and water cascades have carved mighty canyons and broad river valleys. Finally, the Teleférico climbs into a world of ice, rock, glaciers and still lakes.

YOU SHOULD KNOW

1. Whatever you take up the tepui, you must take back down, including all forms of paper and other refuse.
2. Taking souvenirs – even a single stone or crystal – from the tepui is a serious offence; and your baggage is likely to be searched back in Paraitepui.

RORAIMA TEPUI

South America/Venezuela

The Gran Sabana of southeast Venezuela's Canaima National Park is a remote wilderness of jungle, tropical savannah, rain- and cloud forests, rivers and waterfalls. Over 1,500 million years, erosion studded the region with huge table-mountains, once connected but now isolated into individual colossi whose sheer cliffs rise 1,000 m (3,280 ft) and much more. Roraima is the highest of these tepuis, and its 2,810 m (9,217 ft) summit is a geologist's and botanist's paradise. With a microclimate, topography and endemic flora and fauna evolved in virtual isolation, it is a fantastic world of surreal rock formations, fissures, gorges, pools, waterfalls and sandy 'beaches', valleys of sparkling multicoloured crystals, insectivorous flowers in gaudy red and yellow, and flashing hummingbirds. Minerals in the rock turn streams into liquid rainbows of blue, red and green; and mist, fog, hot sunshine and driving rain make a lottery of the weather

Getting there starts with a flight (by scheduled Cessna!) to Santa Elena, where you must buy all the food you will need, and then a 4x4 to the Pemon Indian village of Paraitepui, where you (or a tour agency) sort out the Park entrance fee, guides and porters. A full day's trek across rolling grassland, fording the Tek and Kukenan Rivers, brings you to the 1,800 m (5,900 ft) base of Roraima. It takes a further four–five hour (minimum) diagonal climb up 'the ramp', through cloud forest, waterfalls, and ancient rock formations to the top, where you camp in one of the sandy areas overhung by rock called hoteles. Trails lead in all directions to the summit's best sites, like the Valley of Crystals. From the rim, you understand how Roraima's strange reality beggars imagination, and how it inspired Conan Doyle to believe in a 'Lost World'.

HIGHLIGHTS:

The 'Kukenan Window' – a two-hour dawn hike to catch the view of Roraima's eastern wall, with Matawitepui in the distance and the jungle of Guyana below, before the clouds form.

The guacharos (oil birds) in the massive vertical fissures on one section of Roraima's sheer rim: these are thought to be evidence of the break-up of Pangaea.

ANGEL FALLS
South America/Venezuela

DON'T MISS
The Churun river rapids pass through Devil's Canyon.

Sixteen times higher than Niagara, Angel Falls (Salto Angel) has an uninterrupted drop of 979 m (3,212 ft), and are the highest in the world.

You might take two, or six or even ten days to reach Angel Falls by boat. Starting southeast of Auyantepui, you can explore the orchid and bird-filled jungle paradise skirting the mesa, spending an adventurous week aboard a motorized curiara (dugout canoe) and sleeping in a hammock. You pause to swim through canyons (kavac) and frolic underneath waterfalls tumbling out of tangled flowers and foliage high in the riverbanks (toma de agua). Eventually, you thread your passage through mild rapids on the Akanan River to the Carrao River, where you will meet other canoe parties heading for Angel Falls. Some will have flown direct to Canaima, intending to visit the Falls in two days: they will miss the pink and orange-coloured river beaches, the cascades glowing gold in the sunset, the insights into their river and rainforest world you glean from talking to your Pemon guides and the villagers at campsites – the richness of 'other world' experience that makes the breathtaking first sight of Angel Falls a culmination instead of a tick on a list.

WORTH A DETOUR: The Logrono Caves – a side trip deep into caves of huge stalactites and falling water. With Wagnerian noise and drama, the torrent crashes in from outside.

RAFTING THE UPANO RIVER
South America/Ecuador

On its swift-flowing path from the Andes to the Ecuadorian Amazon, the Upano River becomes a broad jungle waterway spun with thrilling rapids. Occasional clearings in the dense forest on its banks are home to the indigenous Shuar people, whose frail balsa rafts are the only river traffic. The descending river powers through canyons trailed with vines and foliage, then twists into a narrow gorge choked by massive boulders. A dozen waterfalls crash hundreds of metres from the high canyon walls, adding their sparkle to the drenching spume of contorted water.

You join the river at the frontier town of Macas, where it runs broad, a flight path for egrets, parrots, raptors, and the darting brightness of songbirds galore. Shuar guides share their knowledge of the forest and of culture in the headwaters of the Amazon. After the Patuca Bridge, the Upano enters a series of rocky gorges, culminating in the Canyon of the Sacred Waterfalls. By the time you leave the river at Santiago, 104 km (65 mi) downstream, you feel exhilarated not just by the speed thrills of distance rafting, but by the feeling of having learned a bit about the Shuar and the Amazon rainforest.

YOU SHOULD KNOW

Visit from December–August;
later in the year it's much
colder and often misty.

LA RUTA DEL SOL

South America/Ecuador

La Ruta del Sol is Ecuador's Pacific Coast Highway. Officially, the name applies to the southern stretch from Salinas north to Puerto Cayo, but in practice it extends all the way to Esmeraldas. It makes good sense, because La Ruta del Sol is a catch-all for Ecuador's best beaches, reef dive sites, loveliest and wildest coastal landscapes, party-town resorts, and National Parks along the way. But resort development scarcely exists except near the Ruta del Sol's southern end. Great surfing attracts an international crowd to la Punta and the closest town, Montanita; and it's the nearest good beach for Guayaquileños at weekends. The party only stops when you head north. Suddenly, beach follows deserted beach. Apart from small and ancient fishing communities, there are scarcely any buildings. La Ruta leads to a wilderness coastline that gets increasingly pristine the further north you get. The few small towns lining the highway are each of them gateways to delights like the reef at Isla de la Plata or the ecological marvel of the Machalilla National Park, which has both humid and dry tropical forests side by side. Also near Puerto Lopez is the tropical magnificence of Los Frailes beach.

Unfortunately, visiting cruise ships and a local USAF base have recently damaged the charm of Manta, once the source of Panama hat straw; but the best begins at Bahia de Caraquez. Close by are four distinct eco-systems, home to over 350 different bird species. You can go from mangroves to one of the last tropical dry forests in the world, where golden orioles nest in giant ceibo trees, and you can look down on estuarine marsh filled with roseate spoonbills. You can walk, cycle, ride or drive it: the Ruta del Sol seems to include almost everything people want to do for sport, pleasure, or curiosity.

HIGHLIGHTS:

The Pacific Ocean sailing community, who congregate in the Bahia de Caraquez. The Awa and Cayapas Indian culture still extant in Cotocachi-Cayapas, and around the estuary of the Cayapas-Mataje Mangrove Reserve near Esmeraldas. Spending all day in a hammock beneath swaying palms near Santa Elena, then partying all night with the surfers in Montanita.

DEVIL'S NOSE RAILWAY

South America/Ecuador

DON'T MISS
'Riding the Roof' on trains that run as far as Alausi.

The Devil's Nose Railway used to connect Quito with Guayaquil. Recently weather-damaged by El Niño, it now operates only between Riobamba and Alausi. It's a spectacular four-hour ride along twisting gorges and high bridges over ravines, and through fertile valley bottoms lined with colourful villages and small towns. But at Alausi, nobody leaves the train, because ahead lies the Devil's Nose itself. One of the world's greatest railway engineering feats, the track switchbacks down an almost perpendicular 1,000 m (3,250 ft) wall of rock to Sibambe.

The descent from Alausi takes an hour of constant advancing and backing up, zigzagging across the sheer mountain side; and another to re-ascend. Meanwhile you have a matchless view, forever renewed as the train shifts position and height, of the patchwork panorama of fields: yellow, green and grey rectangles moulded to every contour on the hillsides.

The Devil's Nose Railway is enormous fun, and an ideal prelude for travellers intending to trek the Inca Trail to Ingapirca. From Alausi it's only a short drive to the mountain hamlet of Achupallas (3,300 m/10,824 ft) where the Trail begins. Alausi is also en route to the 16th- and 17th-century colonial splendour blended into the Inca city of Cuenca, the World Heritage Site to the southeast.

HIGHLIGHTS: Condors wheeling above the pass at Tres Cruces. The mighty stones that make up the 500 year-old Inca roadway – part of a continuous system that extended further than the Roman Empire's.

INGAPIRCA INCA TRAIL

South America/Ecuador

The Ingapirca Trail is a 35 km (22 mi) remnant of the 5,000 km (3,125 mi) of well-maintained roads that united the Inca Empire from Chile to Ecuador. At first the Inca road follows the Rio Cadrul across the hills and wild paramos (high grasslands) to the lake at Tres Cruces. It's clear that in 500 years, nothing very much can have changed in the spectacular landscape. But above Tres Cruces, at 4,300 m (14,104 ft) on the saddle of the pass and the trek's highest point, the panorama is breathtaking. You can gaze across the high peaks in every direction, and look down on blue gems of lakes in the valley pockets. Near Ingapirca, the close-set stones show the original Inca roadway to be 7 m (23 ft) wide, a colossal highway through the roof of the world. It's a powerful reminder that the temple to the sun and other buildings at Ingapirca whose walls have been tumbled by wind and grasses, was a mere motel to the culture that built Machu-Picchu.

AMAZON JOURNEY

South America/Brazil

WORTH A DETOUR:
The jungle tower at Ariau, providing access to aerial walkways in the forest canopy.

The Amazon is the dramatic highway for people and freight to cross the continent to Colombia, Ecuador and Peru; and boats of all sizes and degrees of comfort make the trip. From Manaus you can explore the pristine wilderness surrounding the confluence of the Amazon and its biggest tributary the Rio Negro. West and north of the confluence the rainforest is almost untouched, and barely inhabited. Over a few days, you can reach deep into all three types – the igapo, seasonally flooded with dark water and an orchid-filled, bromeliad-trailing cathedral of fishing-birds; or terre firme, where giant trees with buttresses like rocket fins create the high canopy for howlers and other monkeys; and the varzea, flooded with rich silts and with a totally distinct flora that attracts large concentrations of birds, mammals and black caiman. You may be able to visit a deep-forest settlement, and learn something of the medicines as well as nourishment provided by the jungle, or stalk birds on aerial walkways.

SERRA VERDE EXPRESS

South America/Brazil

HIGHLIGHTS: Marumbi – you can access very rare Atlantic rainforest easily.
The Sao Joao Bridge, 55 m (180 ft) above the riverbed.

The Serra Verde Express takes you from Curitiba in southeastern Brazil to Paranaguá on the coast. It's the most spectacular train ride in Brazil. Forty minutes after you leave the high-rise modernity of Curitiba and the conventional drab of its suburbs, you emerge from the first tunnel into the completely unexpected, revelatory world of the Serra do Mar. Buckled like a concertina into a series of soaring peaks and precipitous valleys, the Serra do Mar drops 900 m (2,950 ft) from Curitiba to the delicate old colonial town of Morretes at sea-level. These mountains form the largest and best-preserved slice of Brazil's pristine Atlantic rainforest, protected as the UNESCO World Heritage Site and Biosphere Reserve of Marumbi. The dense forest of banana trees, palmetto, hard woods, orchids and creeper vines is shot with rivers and waterfalls, and alive to the colour and movement of toucans and monkeys.

There are two kinds of Serra Verde Express. The smart, expensive version is the weekend-only air-conditioned 'Litorina', which halts in the mountains for photo opportunities, but does continue to Paranaguá. It's always crowded. On weekdays, the third-class 'Convencional' chugs as far as Morretes, but stops at Marumbi (Km 59) for visitors to the Reserve. It's a working train – a passenger equivalent of the great freight trains that still haul produce out of the mountains to the sea. There is no on-board service, but at the frequent unscheduled halts, people offer you coffee, fruit, pastries and bottles of local banana liqueur through the window.

PANTANAL FAZENDAS

South America/Brazil

The Pantanal of southwestern Brazil covers 140,000 sq km (87,500 sq mi). Fourteen times bigger than Florida's Everglades, it's the world's largest freshwater marsh. Between October and March every year it floods, and plant life explodes across its vast network of rivers and black waterways, knee-deep floodplains, lush savannahs, ponds, thick forests and lily-covered lagoons. From April the waters recede, returning newly-refreshed pasture and habitat both to the staggering numbers and variety of birds and mammals who make it their home, and to the fazendas – the enormous cattle ranches of the region, whose prosperity depends on their ability to adapt to the dramatic annual transformation.

Fazendas exist throughout the Pantanal wherever the land remains higher than the surrounding floodwaters. They make it possible for travellers to find good (often deluxe) food and lodgings while exploring the region. They provide horses, canoes or boats, and above all, local knowledge and expertise in finding the best sites and species habitats, which vary from year to year. Some fazendas even offer visitors the opportunity to live like Panatanal cowboys, roping, herding and branding specially bred cattle. Horses make the best transport, providing the extra height you need to see down into the shallows, and a commanding view above the vegetation line and through the forest. Their stamina ensures you see much more than you could on foot; and by portaging canoes, or pre-arranging them, you can cross huge areas. Many fazendas co-operate so you can travel from one to another enjoying some of the 650 bird species, giant otter families taking breakfast, alligators, anacondas, howler monkeys, piranhas and even jaguars that contribute to giving the Pantanal one of the highest concentrations of wildlife on earth. Fazendas are part of the region's ecology and culture.

HIGHLIGHTS:

The best birdwatching on the planet. Rarities in abundance, of aquatic, shore, field, forest and savannah, and of every size and colour. Mammals and reptiles in and out of the water, mangroves, forest canopy or on open ground: if you've ever seen them, it was never this closely. The blissful luxury available overnight at some fazendas. Viewing the rainforest and flooded plains from horseback.

ROTA ROMANTICA

South America/Brazil

Rota Romantica is Portuguese for 'Romantic Route'. In the mountains of Rio Grande do Sul, Brazil's southernmost state; it's the name for the 184 km (114 mi) scenic road that winds from São Leopoldo to São Francisco de Paula through the Serra Gaucha. It is a fairytale landscape of wooded hills, vineyards, broad rivers, canyons, waterfalls, bluffs and green pastures. It looks almost European, a look enhanced by the predominant German and Italian cultures of its original colonists. Many of the local Brazilians have blond hair and look northern European; and even speak the local Riograndenser Hunsruckish German dialect. The towns are full of black-and-white half-timbered, or Swiss chalet-style, buildings. The shops are full of German and Italian specialities; and Oktoberfest is sacred. Add to this an arcadia worthy of Poussin, in all the moods and colours of four full seasons, and the Rota Romantica is unlike any other Brazilian experience. For visitors, Gramado and Canela are the hub of the Rota Romantica's attractions, and of the serra alemana, the towns with the Rota's typical German flavour. From Gramado it is easy to join the Rota's sister routes, the Italian-influenced Caminhos da Colonia, which runs through the Italian wine-making towns in the parallel serra italiana, and the specifically wine-inspired Rota de Uva e o Vinho. Gramado, Canela and the shoemaking and dairy town of Novo Petropolis also form part of the stunning Região de Hortênsias – a shorter road tour through miles of dazzling blue hydrangeas. One of the region's greatest delights is the constant incongruity of its Euro-Brazilian character and the Rota Romantica's popularity thrives on it. It is also the Rota's only drawback: for many northern Brazilians, the emphasis on old-world cultures practised in the Serra Gaucha's communities is a political issue about 'being Brazilian'.

HIGHLIGHTS:
The late 19th-century medieval-style half-timbered buildings of Picada Café, along with Novo Petropolis, among the most obviously Germanic towns on the Rota.
The 131 m (430 ft) waterfall plunging off the cliff into the dense growth of Canela's Parque de Caracol.

CORCOVADO RACK RAILWAY
South America/Brazil

HIGHLIGHTS: The vast skies arcing across Rio's bays, beaches, and beautiful grography.
The VIP train's 'office' suite – for one of the world's great views.

The 38 m (125 ft) statue of Christ the Redeemer, standing arms outstretched on a mountain, is the symbol of Rio de Janeiro. Corcovado Rack Railway takes you up to it.

Opened in 1884 by the Emperor Dom Pedro II, it runs on the Riggenbach ladder rack system for 3.8 km (2.4 mi) from Cosme Velho Station, climbing the steep, forested hillside to emerge just behind and below the statue. From here, you can choose to climb 222 steps to the statue itself, or take a panoramic elevator all the way.

The rail trip only takes 20 minutes, but there are just four electrically driven trains with two cars each, so capacity is limited to 360 people an hour.

The rack cranks you up Corcovado's granite crags by way of the Tijuca Forest National Park. Originally cleared by early coffee growers, the mountain was replanted with native species between 1855–70 to safeguard the springs that supplied Rio with water. Now the Park is the biggest urban forest in the world, and for visitors to the viewing platform above it, a green frame to the 360 degree panorama of downtown Rio, the Sugarloaf (from its best 'sleeping giant' angle), the Lagoa, Copacabana, Ipanema, Niteroi and several favelas.

YOU SHOULD KNOW
At the railway's highest point, there is 40 per cent less oxygen in the air than at Lima. People describe feeling drunk, shell-shocked or nauseous. But help is at hand, and it will pass as you descend.

LIMA TO HUANCAYO
South America/Peru

The Lima-Huancayo line soars 4,829 m (15,839 ft) up into the Andes, a masterpiece of engineering and a thrilling ride. It was, and still is a working train; so it works well as a visitors' introduction to Peru. It's a comfortable train, and it needs to be. For six hours you climb steadily from sea level at Lima to the frozen wilderness of the high Andes, feeding your growing altitude headache with coca tea from the trolley. When you stretch your legs at what is still thought to be the world's highest station, Ticlio (4,758 m/15,606 ft), you may gasp for air and need the help of the Oxygen Matron who patrols the train. Most people do. The cold is bitter but the scenery is breathtaking. It gets even better as you revive, watching flowing robes and llamas raising dust in the settlements of the altiplano. By the time you reach Huancayo, you feel you've travelled through the heart of Peru's economic future as well as its highlands.

CUZCO TO MACHU PICCHU

South America/Peru

WORTH A DETOUR:
The Qente waterfall, and the pristine subtropical flora around it.

Three kinds of train run between Cuzco, the Inca capital, and Machu Picchu, the 'Lost City' hidden in the high peaks of the Andes. The 'Expedition' (formerly the 'Backpacker') is the most economical. The 'Vistadome' offers the premium service of greater comfort. Both leave Cuzco at 6 am for the roughly 4 hour, 112 km (70 mi) long journey, but spend the first half hour climbing steeply up a series of switchbacks called the Zigzag to Poroy, the first stop. The luxury train, the 'Hiram Bingham' starts its journey from Poroy. The railway runs through typical Andean valley farms and passes whole hillsides of broken terracing, dotted with ruined Inca forts. It climbs past the ruins of Qente into a valley where the microclimate is fed by a waterfall, and giant hummingbirds are common among the bright flowers of the morning. At Chachabamba, rocky outcrops are overhung with bromeliads and orchids, and tall ceibos crowd the train. Then the view opens as it pulls up at Machu Picchu Town, 2 km (1.25 mi) below the Citadel.

CORDILLERA BLANCA

South America/Peru

The Cordillera Blanca of central Peru is the world's highest tropical mountain range. With 29 summits over 6,000 m (19,680 ft), its landscape of snow-capped peaks, glaciers, lakes, rivers and treeless tundra is among the most dramatic in the Andes. For mountain bikers, there's a classic 7-day circuit of the Cordillera that runs past Laguna Querococha, up over the watershed to the extraordinary archaeological ruins of Chavin de Huantar, and along the Conchucos Valley altiplano. With

WORTH A DETOUR:
The 'folded mountains' above the lovely Laguna Purhuay – a geological wonder of a mountain of rock apparently melted, like chocolate, and petrified in mid-flow.

the Andes ranked behind them into the misty distance, you stand in what feels like touching distance of Nevado Huascaran, Chopicalqui, Chacraraju and Huandoy peaks. Then you launch into an incredible flying descent past the Llanganuco lakes to the route's end, at 2,500 m (8,200 ft), Yungay town. The Cordillera Blanca makes you feel you reinvented mountain biking.

THE INCA TRAIL

South America/Peru

YOU SHOULD KNOW

Restrictions on the number of Trail permits mean that they sell out months in advance.

The trek to Machu Picchu, the Lost City of the Incas, is one of the world's most famous. Even though the route to it is crowded, it's only because of the imaginative appeal of its destination. Crowds don't matter when you first arrive at the Trail's end – the stone portal of Intipunku, the Gateway of the Sun, through which you first see the ruins of Machu Picchu.

The traditional route begins at Cuzco, once the imperial capital of the Incas' Andean Empire. Most visitors choose to acclimatize to the altitude while browsing Cuzco's Inca and Spanish colonial history, architecture and artefacts. The trek leads up the Urubamba River valley from Chilca to the Inca ruins at Llactapata; past the gentle farmland slopes and woods of Wayllabamba to a steep climb through cloud forest to the second campsite at Llulluchapampa. The plants, flowers and birds are completely different in the open terrain before Abra de Huarmihuanasca, the 'Dead Woman's Pass', at 4,200 m (13,776 ft) the highest point of the trek; but the hard work of climbing at altitude is worth it for the panorama of the Vilcanota and Vilcabamba mountain ranges. The Trail drops to cross the Pacaymayo River but at the next pass, Runku Raccay, you come to a series of ancient stone steps descending to the Inca town of Sayac Marca, from which a still superbly-paved Inca highway disappears through amazing cloud forest to Phuyupatamarca ('Cloud-Level Town'). This campsite is close to the extensive Inca site of Huinay Huayna, from which the Trail drops through forest until it levels out and climbs to Intipunku itself. No photograph prepares you for the reality of Machu Picchu. The legendary magnificence of the panorama is magnified by the physical investment you make in Inca history and culture on the ascent.

HIGHLIGHTS:

Acclimatizing at the Inca fortress of Ollantaytambo, and the market and ruins of Pisac – among various Inca sites on the Urubamba River known collectively as the Sacred Valley.

The pre-dawn cloud forest hike to reach Intipunku as the sun rises.

The Inca paving stones, stairways, tunnel and multiple other ruins.

The unexpected orchids among the mosses of the mature cloud forest before Huinay.

THE HUAYHUASH CIRCUIT

South America/Peru

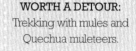

WORTH A DETOUR:
Trekking with mules and
Quechua muleteers.

The Cordillera Huayhuash (pronounced 'why-wash') is isolated, rugged, difficult and dangerous to trek in. The Circuit trek is the most challenging of all its routes. The reward for completing it – available only to experienced and determined travellers – is a mythic sense of communion with seriously high mountains. The panorama ahead improves each day as you follow the green valleys and high passes deeper into the mountains, until the terrain above the Atocshaico lakes becomes a wilderness of boulder-strewn ridges before you reach the end at Laguna Jahuacocha, nestled in a huge amphitheatre of the Cordillera's most impressive peaks. From here the Quebrada Huanactapay is the first of a series of valleys, passes, waterfalls, lakes and glaciers that ends after some twelve days at Laguna Jahuacocha, nestled in a huge amphitheatre of impressive peaks.

HIGHLIGHTS: The colossal Pacaya Samiria Reserve, a pristine jungle jewel.
Swimming below 35 m (115 ft) Aguashiyacu waterfall.

HEADWATERS OF THE AMAZON

South America/Peru

Chiclayo is the major regional centre for northern Peru, the crossroads between the coast, the highlands, and the jungle. Iquitos lies on the other side of the Andes, a major city that can only be reached by air or by boat along the Amazon and its headwaters.

It's a ten-hour drive up and across the watershed to Chachapoyas, through the wonders of the cloud forest and mountain jungle; but curiosity will divert you to Cajamarca, where the conquistadors imprisoned Inca Atahualpa, or the fortress sites of Sipán and Kuelap. The region's rich history is hand in hand with its astonishing natural beauty.

Tarapoto is as famous for the multiple waterfalls in its surrounding forests, and the variety of rare birds and butterflies, as for the Quechua music, art and dancing of local villages, and the 2,500 orchid species in its leafy environs.

The road ends at Yurimaguas, where cargo boats leave for the two-day journey to Iquitos. You get some idea of how the forest people live, and the extraordinary biodiversity of the upper Amazon. Most of all, you feel an urgent desire to stop and explore.

EL CHORO

South America/Bolivia

HIGHLIGHTS: Coroico – the charming and relaxed main town of Las Yungas, around which there are some lovely short hikes. Monkeys swinging through the trees.

El Choro is a 70 km (40 mi) long, ancient Inca road that connects the high mountains of the Altiplano with the sub-tropical jungle of Las Yungas. From La Cumbre, near La Paz, you scramble your way up the barren mountainside to the Chucuro Pass, high above the tree line at nearly 5,000 m (16,000 ft). You wind your way down, past gushing waterfalls and torrential rivers, across old wooden bridges, alongside ancient dry stone walls, pre-Columbian ruins and isolated thatched huts. You will encounter itinerant Aymará Indians in their traditional brightly coloured costumes.

Desolate mountain rock gives way to the mysterious twisted and stunted trees of the Challapampa cloud forest, and the rarified high-altitude air becomes ever more dense and humid, ripe with the smells of the rainforest, and the vegetation starts to grow luxuriantly thick and green. By the third day, you find yourself in a paradise of verdant jungle, with all your senses quickened by the exotic sights and scents and sounds of Las Yungas. You will reach the laid-back hill town of Coroico glowing with a real sense of achievement at having accomplished one of the best treks in South America.

THE LOST WORLD OF HUANCHACA AND THE CAPARÚ PLATEAU

South America/Bolivia

HIGHLIGHTS:
Aerial view of the plateau, rivers and waterfalls.
Swimming in the pool of El Encanto waterfall.
Sights of rare birds and animals including spider monkeys, jaguars and macaws.
Los Torres rocks.

The 600 m (1,968 ft) high Caparú Plateau, an 150 km (95 mi) long pre-Cambrian sandstone mesa (table mountain) emerges abruptly out of the midst of the primeval Huanchaca rainforest conservation area in northeast Bolivia.

Flor d'Oro, in the far north of Huanchaca National Park, is only accessible by light aircraft or a long boat journey up the River Iténez, the border with Brazil. On the flight from Santa Cruz, there are spectacular aerial views. The sky is reflected in the land below, an endless patchwork of rainforest, wetlands, and lakes threaded through with huge rivers. Out of this kaleidoscopic swirl of greens, greys and blues, a rust-red wall of cliff suddenly rises to the savannah plain of the Caparú – a complete contrast to the lowland tangle of jungle. From above, you witness the surreal spectacle of rivers tipping over the sheer edge of the plateau in huge cascades.

The region is one of the last virgin areas on the planet, with a diversity of habitats and species unmatched anywhere in the Americas. As you trek from Flor d'Oro to Lago Caiman and then scramble up Caparú, you will pass through four different eco-regions, seeing all sorts of exotic plants, birds and animals. Eventually you clamber up to Mirador de los Monos (Monkey Point) and gaze down at the wetlands below.

WHEN SHOULD I VISIT?: February–October. (6 August to experience Independence Day celebrations in Copacabana – one of the best fiestas in Bolivia.)

TO THE HOME OF THE SUN GOD
South America/Bolivia

From the picturesque town of Copacabana, on the southwestern shore of Lake Titicaca, it is only a boat ride to the heartland of the Incas. In Incan mythology, the rugged island mountain of Isla del Sol is venerated as the birthplace of civilization. Here the Sun God created the first Incan, Manco Capac, out of the sacred waters of Lake Titicaca. Today, the Aymará Indians still cultivate the same ancient terraces that their ancestors carved into the mountainsides more than a thousand years ago.

The lake stretches before you as you make the ferry crossing – 8,000 sq km (3,120 sq mi) of the bluest water you have ever seen, encircled by the tallest mountains in the western hemisphere. You are in a place untouched by time: campesinos patiently until the unyielding soil with wooden hoes, bowler-hatted Aymará women trudge uphill bearing loads larger than themselves, and raggedy urchins scamper along the terraces after their skinny sheep. As you sit in the ruins of an Incan palace watching the sun go down over the lake, the glistening peaks of the Cordillera Real take on an almost mystical hue. It is only too easy to believe that you have reached the origin of the world.

ACROSS THE PATAGONIAN CORDILLERA
South America/Chile

HIGHLIGHTS:
Crossing Rio Puelo in a wooden boat with your horse swimming alongside.
La Pasarela del Rio Puelo – spectacular rapids and waterfalls.

A packhorse is the only realistic means of travel in this uncharted Andean wilderness, a land that is just as it was 500 years ago when the first pioneers and missionaries made their way across it. There are no roads at all, only ancient Indian paths and drovers' tracks, known only to the arrieros (mule drivers) and vaquearos (cattle and sheep drovers). From Lago Puelo in Argentina, the Puelo River flows through Lago Inferior on the Chilean side of the border to the Reloncavi estuary on the Pacific Coast. This is the starting point for your ride into the wilds, some 100 km (60 mi) from the city of Puerto Montt.

The tranquil ride from the village of Puelo along the Reloncavi fjord is a scenic treat with the Yate Volcano towering ahead of you. After loading your horse onto the ferry to cross Lago Tagua-Tagua you then take to the narrow trails that lead through verdant rainforest scored with tumbling rivers, dramatic waterfalls and rapids, to high mountain plateaux of wild flower meadows, sparkling streams and azure lakes. Apart from isolated farmhouses, you really are in the back of beyond, entirely reliant on your guide to pick your way along the valleys and ridges, across the lakes and rivers to Lago Inferior on the border with Argentina. Here you must say farewell to your horse and take a boat across Lago Inferior to Argentina where you disembark in the steppes of Lago Puelo National Park under the snowy peaks of Tres Picos.

TORRES DEL PAINE 'W' TRAIL

South America/Chile

The 'W' Trail through the Torres del Paine Biosphere Reserve is one of the world's classic treks. The spectacular scenery, shaped by the combined forces of glaciation and fierce Patagonian winds, is a dream-like landscape of spiky mountains, water and ice – a phantasmagoria of colour and form. You camp beside turquoise, aquamarine and green lakes strewn with icebergs, cross tumultuous rivers and waterfalls, walk through wild grasslands and primeval forests, gaze hypnotically at blue-tinted glaciers, and marvel

at wondrous rock spires soaring to 3,000 m (9,800 ft). An initial boat journey northwards across Lake Grey takes you to the trailhead. From the boat, you will see great chunks of ice dropping off the face of Glacier Grey and icebergs drifting along the lake. The Trail leads along the eastern shore where you can view Glacier Grey from above. This huge fractured river of ice, over 3 km (2 mi) wide, reflects the constantly changing skies, with a mesmerising effect of dancing shapes of light and shade.

The strenuous climb through French Valley – a cirque of spectacular sheer cliffs – leads you to a heart-stopping view over the lakes and another glacier. Walking the 13 km (8 mi) Sendero Paso los Cuernos (Horns Pass Way) along the northern shore of Lake Nordenskjold, you will see guanacos and humueles roaming the grasslands, and condors wheeling gracefully around the horned peaks of the bizarre bi-coloured slate and granite Cuernos mountains, possessing the sky. The last leg of the trek is a scramble over a steep moraine of boulders to the most dramatic view of all – the Torres. These three stark granite monoliths, from which the Reserve gets its name, loom over the land like sentinels, dwarfing you beneath the power of nature.

HIGHLIGHTS:
The lake crossing with views
of Grey Glacier.
Mirador Francés.
Cuernos del Paine.
Torres del Pain.
Wildlife sightings.

WHEN SHOULD I VISIT?:
High season is from
December–March when
there is up to 18 hours of
daylight.

TIME IT TAKES:
Four–six days.

THROUGH THE PATAGONIAN CHANNELS

South America/Chile

DON'T MISS

Messier Channel – the changing colours of the water from the rivers pouring down from the icefield.

The ferry that travels the wind-lashed west coast of Southern Patagonia takes you through the intricate glacial labyrinth of channels, islands and fjords at the tail end of the Andes Cordillera.

From the port of Puerto Montt, the ferry weaves through the Gulfs of Ancud and Corcovado, passing by picturesque wooden villages on stilts huddled on the shore of the Isla de Chiloé and the beautiful thickly forested islets of the Chonos Archipelago, before heading round the Taitao Peninsula, the westernmost promontory of the Chilean coast, and across the wild, windswept waters of the Golfo de Penas (Gulf of Sorrows). It almost defies belief that the Kawesqar Indians, the pre-Hispanic nomadic inhabitants of the Patagonian Channels, habitually crossed this tempestuous sea in their dugout canoes.

At the end of the Messier Channel, one of the deepest fjords in the world, the lush scenery becomes bleaker, and the further south you go, the lower the snowline creeps down the wild, barren mountainsides. The passage continues through miles of narrows, often scarcely wide enough for the boat to negotiate. It finally enters Ultima Esperanza (Last Hope) Sound, with stunning views of the mountains of the Patagonian Icefield, and journey's end at Puerto Natales, gateway to the iconic granite spires of Torres del Paine National Park. You will look back on your voyage with fond memories, for the human camaraderie among the disparate bunch of passengers and motley ship's crew as much for the magnificent glacial scenery.

HIGHLIGHTS: Casa Silva – the oldest and most traditional winery in the Colchagua Valley. Huasos – Chilean 'cowboys' in traditional dress.

WINE ROUTE

South America/Chile

The wine region is a fertile basin of eight upland valleys between the Andes and the Pacific. The 120 km (75 mi) long Colchagua Valley produces the best world-class red wines of all and is Chile's first official Ruta del Vino. The route starts at San Fernando, heart of the country's Hispanic folk-culture, homeland of the rodeo and the huaso – the chic Chilean equivalent of a cowboy, kitted out in long leather silver-spurred boots, swirling poncho and broad-brimmed hat.

The Wine Train chugs through the scenic agricultural landscape of fruit orchards, wheat fields and wineries at a gentle 30–40 kph (20–25 mph), its 1920s German-built carriages pulled by a heritage Chiean steam engine. There are panoramic views of snow-capped Andean volcanoes, oak-forested hills, and huasos on horseback riding down country roads lined with slender poplar trees. At Santa Cruz, you find yourself in a charming traditional country town.

CARRETERA AUSTRAL

South America/Chile

HIGHLIGHTS:
Queulat National Park – Pedro
Aguirre Cerda Lagoon,
glaciers, cascades.
Caleta Tortel – picturesque
coastal village, built on stilts.

Otherwise known as 'Pinochet's Folly', the construction of the 1,200 km (750 mi) Carretera Austral trunk road was part of the Chilean dictator's scheme to open up the impoverished, sparsely populated region of Aisén. Thirty years and millions of dollars later, it is still a work in progress, a potholed dirt and gravel track barely wide enough for two vehicles, only paved around the larger towns, with ferry crossings wherever the complex coastal topography bars its path. From the port of Puerto Montt to the sleepy southern village of Villa O'Higgins on the edge of the Patagonian Icefield, the road carves a path through phenomenal scenery.

Within minutes of hitting the road you hop on and off a ferry into stunning volcanic scenery of sub-tropical rainforest. At the precipitous cliffs of Hornopirén you face more water – five hours crossing the bay to Caleta Gonzalo. This initial cyclist's frustration is worth enduring for what follows – hundreds of kilometres of fantastic cycling. After a bumpy ride through the glorious forest and fjord country of Pumalin National Park to the fishing town of Chaitén, you cycle 425 km (265 mi) along a switchback of mountain ridges and lush valleys, across tumbling rivers with glaciers and waterfalls to the beautiful turquoise lakes around Coihaique, the regional capital. A final 440 km (275 mi) stretch through the awe-inspiring, isolated mountain terrain around Cochrane and Tamango National Park takes you to road's end.

TREN A LAS NUBES

South America/Argentina

HIGHLIGHTS: The condors flying above.
Puerta Tastil – ruins and rock paintings.
Salta – a beautifully preserved colonial city.

Built in the 1940s, the Tren a las Nubes (Train to the Clouds) is the third highest railway in the world. It is worth travelling along for the sheer technical wizardry of the railway line itself, quite apart from the mind-blowing terrain it goes through on its skyward journey, a thrilling 220 km (136 mi) zigzag switchback ride crossing some of most complex topography on the planet by means of 13 viaducts, 29 bridges and 21 tunnels. There are two huge loops along the route where the track virtually doubles back on itself in order to gain height. You feel that you have been given a front row seat over the world as you gaze from vertiginous mountain heights.

From the sub-tropical colonial city of Salta, the train passes quaint mud-built villages and red-flowering ceibo trees as it heads into the Quebrada del Toro (Bull's Gorge) and across the rocky salt desert canyons of the Andes. Marvel at the awesome rock formations, blasted into grotesque shapes by aeons of erosion.

THE END OF THE WORLD TRAIN

South America/Argentina

HIGHLIGHTS: Cascada La Macarena waterfall
Ushuaia Museo del Presidio – Prison Museum.
Cañadón del Toro gorge.

On this journey, not only are you travelling on the world's southernmost railway line but you are pulled by one of several heritage steam engines along a narrow gauge track with a fascinating past.

The railway starts 8 km (5 mi) from Ushuaia and runs for some 14 km (9 mi) into Tierra del Fuego National Park, a protected area of 630 sq km (240 sq mi) once inhabited by Yamaha Indians. As the train meanders along the River Pipo valley at a sedate 15 kph (9 mph) you have breathtaking views of the wild glacial landscape of the South Andes Cordillera – steep snow-capped mountains, rivers, waterfalls, woods and lakes interspersed with tundra plateau carpeted in lichens and mosses. The journey ends at Estación del Parque from where you can explore this remote region on foot.

Although today the End of the World Train is a tourist attraction, it was originally built to fulfil an altogether murkier purpose – the transportation of forced labour to the hinterland forest and of felled trees back to the coast. By the end of the 19th century the Argentinian authorities had established a penal colony as far away from civilization as possible, at the tip of South America. From these inauspicious beginnings emerged today's city of Ushuaia, its earliest buildings constructed by convicts using timber from the surrounding sub-polar forests. The prison was transformed into a naval base in 1947 and the railway was decommissioned in 1952 after an earthquake badly damaged the track.

RUTA DE LAS SIETE LAGOS

South America/Argentina

YOU SHOULD KNOW

The Lake District is a very popular area for sports activities. Cerro Catedral, near Bariloche, is one of Argentina's main ski resorts. In the summer you can go sailing, rafting and fly-fishing as well as mountain hiking, horse riding, off-road driving and cycling.

HIGHLIGHTS:
Valle Encantada – strange rock formations.
Los Arrayanes National Park – forest of rare 300-year old and 20 m (66 ft) high arrayán trees, said to be Disney's source of inspiration for the film Bambi.

The 200 km (125 mi) drive from Bariloche on the southern shore of Lago Nahuel Huapi up to the mountain resort of San Martin takes you through two national parks along a winding road with panoramic views round every bend.

From the beautiful city of Bariloche, a scenic 70 km (40 mi) lakeside drive takes you to the charming resort town of Villa La Angostura, the starting point of the famous Ruta de las Siete Lagos (Road of the Seven Lakes). The road zigzags its tortuous way along the narrow river valleys and ridges of Nahuel Huapi, the oldest of Argentina's national parks. The lower slopes of the rugged Patagonian mountains are swathed in evergreen coigüe forest, lightened by paintbox colours of wild flowers and shrubs – eye-catching daubs of yellow, red, orange and pink. The savage dark rocks and snowy peaks tower above you and, at every turn, just when you think you have seen the view of a lifetime, you are greeted with yet another incredible sight to take your breath away.

The road takes you through Villa Traful, a picturesque Andean village of wood and stone houses overlooking a turquoise lake, past Lago Escondido (Hidden Lake) twinkling behind its forest canopy, the twin lakes, Villarino and Falkner, joined by an isthmus, and the most beautiful of all, Lago Hermoso. At the entrance to Lanín National Park the landscape becomes drier, the thick evergreen forest gives way to southern beech woods, and you soon catch sight of the immaculately still waters of Lago Machonico. The road ends at the tranquil tourist town of San Martin, nestling among the mountains on the shore of Lake Lácar.

HIGHLIGHTS: Sierra de las Quijadas National Park – otherworldly fossil landscape. Aconacagua – the highest peak in the western hemisphere.

THE NORTHERN LOOP

South America/Argentina

This 5,000 km (3,000 mi) road trip enables you to see sights and landscapes that you would not even glimpse from a plane, takes you to four great cities, across the pampas, into the wine lands, up into the Andes, through desert, ending in the sinister rainforest borderland of Brazil and Paraguay. From Buenos Aires, sultry tango capital, you start on the most gruelling stretch of road – 1,000 km (600 mi) cross-country through the stark monotony of the pampas to the beautiful green city of Mendoza. You head northeastwards through wild green mountains and picturesque hill villages to see the sublime colonial architecture of Córdoba, and continue north to Tucumán, 'the garden of the republic'. Travelling back eastwards through the cactus-dotted plains of the Chaco and the verdant wetlands of Corrientes you reach the historic northeastern province of Misiones, a rainforest region of deep red ferrous earth and lush green jungle, named after the brutal Jesuit missionaries who converted the Guarani Indians to Christianity by force. The road to the Brazilian border ends at the spectacular Iguazú Falls, one of the greatest natural wonders of the world.

THE BEAGLE CHANNEL & MAGELLAN STRAIT

South America/Argentina

HIGHLIGHTS: Cape Horn National Park – stark promontory with sheer 400 m (1,300 ft) cliffs. Wulaia Bay – beautiful Magellanic forest scenery.

Short of travelling to Antarctica, the southern hemisphere's most incredible scenery is to be found in the crazy maze of channels, islands and bays that make up the southwestern coastline of Tierra del Fuego. The sea passages connecting the Atlantic and Pacific are notoriously hard to navigate. You will see dolphins, penguins, seals and cormorants, hear the creaking sounds of the glaciers and the thunderous crashes as great chunks of ice break off into the sea, and experience a sub-polar wilderness of forest and mountain. The Beagle Channel is named after the eponymous surveying ship that the great naturalist Charles Darwin sailed on. His description of the landscape is just as valid today as it was in 1839: 'The lofty mountains on the north side... are covered by a wide mantle of perpetual snow... numerous cascades pour their waters through the woods into the narrow channel below... magnificent glaciers extend from the mountainside to the water's edge. It is scarcely possible to imagine anything more beautiful than the beryl-like blue of these glaciers and especially as contrasted with the dead white of the upper expanse of snow. The fragments which had fallen from the glacier into the water were floating away and the channel with the icebergs presented... a miniature likeness of the Polar Sea'.
You disembark at Punta Arenas, a charming colonial town of red-roofed houses and a lovely tree-lined central square with a statue of Ferdinand Magellan, the first explorer to sail from the Atlantic into the Pacific.

SOUTH PATAGONIA ICE CAP TREK
South America/Argentina

HIGHLIGHTS: Snoe-shoeing on the Viedma Glacier.
Rio Eléctrico – beechwoods, rare birds and exotic flowers.
View of Mt Fitz Roy at dawn when the granite spires glow pink.

Los Glaciares National Park in the Patagonian Icefield is a 4,450 sq km (1,720 sq mi) wonderland – a maze of rivers and glaciers, milky glacial lakes, and mountain spires soaring like cathedrals into the sky. This is a landscape from another planet – unimaginably strange and overwhelmingly beautiful.

The starting point for any trek is El Chaltén, an isolated mountain village at the confluence of two rivers north of Lake Viedma. From here, after you have hiked through the romantic lenga beechwoods along the

banks of the Rio Eléctrico, you hike up to Paso Marconi for incredible views of Mount Fitz Roy and don your snow shoes for the tough but scenic journey across the icefield, traversing the Viedma and Upsala glaciers through magical ice landscapes, bivouacking in rough shelters along the way.

At last, as you scramble across Upsala's rocky moraine ridge, Lake Argentino comes into view. The boat ride across the lake to the southern edge of the Park, passing the glacier faces, is a fitting grand finale to your trek – both spell-binding and scary. These relentless rivers of ice make awesome creaking and juddering sounds as the iceface continually fractures and falls. Huge chunks come crashing down into the weird milky-green coloured water and then sail calmly off.

CYCLE ACROSS THE ANDES TO THE ATACAMA
South America/Argentina

HIGHLIGHTS: Salinas Grandes.
Quebrada (Gorge) of Humahuaca.
Purmamarca's beautiful 16th–17th-century Chapel.

The road between San Salvador de Jujuy in northwest Argentina and the Atacama, the world's driest desert, is the highest route in the Americas.

The 400 km (250 mi) of tough mountain road starts gently enough, pedalling slowly along the ancient Camino Inca, constantly distracted by the incredible multicoloured rock of the Quebrada de Humahuaca. After about 60 km (40 mi) you turn off to the picturesque mud-built village of Purmamarca, admire the Cerro de Siete Colores (Seven Coloured Mountain) and prepare for some serious cycling. The Cuesta de Lipan is a hair-raising stretch of fiendish bends through desolate wilderness, spiralling up to 4,000 m (13,000 ft). From the top, you gaze down at a hallucinatory view of blank whiteness – the entrancing salt landscape of the Salinas Grandes. Eventually you are there – at the top of the world. The Atacama Desert spreads below you, and beyond, the dream of the Pacific Ocean. The descent to San Pedro is fantastic. You hurtle downhill in a spirit of wild exhilaration to a tourist town chock-full of backpackers. You will be only too grateful for the creature comforts it provides.

HIGHLIGHTS: The sea lion and seal colonies.
Boat ride out to sea from Puerto Piràmides to see dolphins.
The saltpans of Valdés Peninsula.

EXPLORE THE PENÍNSULA VALDÉS

South America/Argentina

You would be hard put to find anywhere more inspiring than the windswept shores and blue waters of the Patagonian coast. This magical region of multicoloured pebble beaches, steep cliffs, jagged rocks, and miles of sand flats is one of the most precious wildlife habitats in the world where, among a plethora of sea and land creatures, you can see dolphins playing, orcas out on a seal hunt, and the largest southern right whale breeding grounds in the world.

The drive from Puerto Madryn, on Golfo Nuevo, along the Ameghino Isthmus to the tip of the World Heritage wilderness of Península Valdés, plunges you straight into the savage beauty of the natural world. You can hear the southern right whales calling to each other as you watch them play in the water along the remote shores of El Doradillo beach. You drive along dirt tracks through desolate country of steppe and saltpans where guanacos, rheas, maras and grey foxes roam at will among the sheep. On the mudflats of Puento Norte, while you watch the elephant seals and sea lions, you will see opportunistic orcas lurking offshore ready to pounce on any unprotected pup and drag it into the water. At Valdés Caleta, a long gravel spit, you can observe a colony of Magellan penguins among the thousands of seabirds that congregate here. At the end of the road, at Punta Delgada lighthouse on the southeastern tip of the peninsula, you gaze down from the high cliffs at the huge colony of elephant seals on the beach below.

CHE GUEVARA'S REVOLUTIONARY ROAD

Chile

TIME IT TAKES: Che famously took nine months. Once, two actors took a year, making a film on the way. Three months is normally considered the minimum.

Heading south from Buenos Aires in 1952, 23-year-old Che Guevara circled South America on a motorbike, with a friend. Down Argentina, across the Andes, up Chile to Peru, then from Cuzco through the Amazon headwaters to Iquitos and (via Leticia) Colombia and Venezuela – Che's diaries provide much more than just the inspiration to keep your eyes properly open. His carefree exuberance is infectious, a reminder to take opportunities to share the back of a dusty truck with whoever, or to swim when the ferry needs pushing. His route goes deep into remote backcountry, to borders and regions which can still be dangerous. Seek help where you can from local people – but use the tourist infrastructure where it is useful. Balance some of your curiosity with caution (e.g. when hitch-hiking, as Che did), but enjoy unexpected adventures when they happen.

AFRICA

KROM RIVER TRAIL

Southern Africa/South Africa

YOU SHOULD KNOW

Be prepared to meet anglers along the Trail – the Krom is a popular trout-fishing river.

HIGHLIGHTS:
A plunge into one of the splendidly cooling swimming pools that greet you enticingly at either end of the Krom River Trail.
Views of Du Toits Peak – highest point of the Limietberg Nature Reserve at 1,996 m (6,557 ft).
The animals and birds – including klipspringer, baboon, caracal, an occasional leopard, Cape sugarbird, protea canary and black eagle.

Sadly this great river, along with its associated wetlands, is coming under increasing pressure from the development demands of modern South Africa, with consequent degradation. But it is still possible to experience the pristine beauty of the Krom River and environs as it has always been by hiking various marked trails in Limietberg Nature Reserve, which is located in the De Toitskloof Pass between Paar and Worcester in the Western Cape. To hike the Krom River Trail, approach through the Huguenot Tunnel from the Worcester side and park. A permit from Cape Nature is required.

The Trail is 7 km (4.4 mi) long, and can be comfortably walked in half a day. No guide is needed, though sensible pre-hike precautions (appropriate clothing plus a basic supply of food and water) should be taken. The Trail crosses the Molenaars River and ascends along the right-hand slope above the Krom River. It passes through an area of indigenous forest and reaches a waterfall with pool beneath. There is then a hair-raising climb up a chain ladder to a second fall and pool – this waterfall in its lush setting is one of the very best in the whole Western Cape. The Trail then returns by the same route.

There are other rewarding trails in the park – each different, each taking no more than a day. The Rock Hopper Trail from Eerste Tol to Tweede Tol is more adventurous, and involves finding your own way down (or up) an 8 km (5 mi) stretch of the Witte River's boulder-strewn riverbed, using a combination of walking, swimming and rock-scrambling. This Trail requires a drop-off at the beginning and pick-up at the end. The Elands Trail initially involves a steep climb, providing great valley and river views, before descending to Fisherman's Cave with its inviting pool.

DON'T MISS
The Robertson Wine
Festival, which takes
place every October.

CAPE WINE ROUTE
Southern Africa/South Africa

If you are interested in glorious scenery and delicious wines, a trip along Route 62, in South Africa's Western Cape region, is a must. Some 50 years ago, a highway was opened here, and Route 62 became a forgotten road, with little traffic and fewer visitors. Surprisingly, this was a godsend for the area: its fruitful farming communities were left in peace. The result is probably the longest wine route in the world, meandering through some of the most sublime scenery and prolific vineyards you can imagine. Leaving Cape Town, the road climbs through majestic mountains, over a series of dramatic passes, alongside crystal clear streams, through fertile valleys rich with magnificent vineyards and orchards. The approach to Montagu, the first town en route, is astonishing. Set in a narrow valley, by a mountain stream, with towering ochre cliffs to either side, and peach and apricot trees laden with blossom, this Victorian era town might be in the Garden of Eden. Continuing through the Breede River Valley, the Worcester winelands provide 27 per cent of the country's wine as well as being the main brandy producing area.

HIGHLIGHTS: The views from the top of Cape Town's Table Mountain.
A trip to the infamous apartheid era prison on Robben Island.

THE BLUE TRAIN
Southern Africa/South Africa

The Blue Train is one of the world's most prestigious train journeys, luxury on wheels, right up there with the Orient Express. Its origins go back to 1923, when trains were introduced to carry passengers from Johannesburg to Cape Town, where they embarked on the long voyage to England. In 1933, a dining saloon was introduced, and gradually further luxuries were added. After a break for World War II, the service returned, and this time it was named the Blue Train after its blue carriages. Three years after the end of apartheid, in 1997, the service was re-launched in all its present day glory.
Passengers are ushered into a splendid check-in lounge, where sparkling wine and delicious nibbles are offered before a butler takes you to your suite. This is 5-star accommodation: top quality bed linen, goose down duvets, marble bathroom, a desk set by the window, even a multiple choice entertainment centre. The train glides smoothly through superb scenery. From its windows you'll see tea and citrus estates, vineyards, thick, indigenous forests, cliffs and gorges, and deserts where giraffes, zebras and elephants roam in peace. Enjoy an off-train visit to the privately owned Aquila Game Reserve at Kleinstraat, where you can experience a close encounter with cheetahs. Back on board, wonder at the extravagant sunset as you sip your pre-dinner drink before enjoying a gourmet meal and a great night's sleep. After a leisurely breakfast, in your suite if you wish, the Blue Train reaches Pretoria, the end of its 1,600 km (1,000 mi) journey.

GARDEN ROUTE

Southern Africa/South Africa

YOU SHOULD KNOW

The Garden Route and the Wine Route
are sufficiently close together to move
easily between the two. If this is your
plan, give yourself a few extra days.

HIGHLIGHTS:
Go cage diving with great
white sharks at Gansbaii.
Cable slide across the
rainforest canopy in
Tsitsikamma.

South Africa's Garden Route is a spectacular road trip along the coast from Mossel Bay east to Storms River. The road is named not for its floral gardens but because of its lush and varied vegetation, so different from the country's harsh, dry interior.

The N2 links a series of charming towns, with areas of great natural beauty in between. This is part of the Cape Floral Region, famed for its fynbos, natural heathland vegetation that includes 9,000 species, 6,200 of which are endemic. Of these, many are flowering and others are fragrant. Rooibos and honeybush are both commercially harvested.

Pass through the Wilderness National Park – its lagoons and wetlands are home to 250 species of bird, including Knysna Lourie, a bright green bird with red wings, and many kingfishers. You can feast on oysters, and of course the local wines are excellent. From Plettenberg Bay, another seaside resort, the road descends sharply, winding through old growth forest until it reaches the finest stretch of untamed coastline in Tsitsikamma National Park, before reaching the journey's end at Storms River.

Along the way there is much to do, hiking, diving, kayaking or even playing golf. Keep an eye open for the very rare Knysna elephants. Perhaps you'd like to travel on the last continuously operating steam train on the continent, the steam train Choo Tjoe, currently running only between Mossel Bay and George, after mud slides in 2006 damaged the track.

RUNNING THE ORANGE RIVER
Southern Africa/South Africa

WORTH A DETOUR: Rapids like Dead Man's Rapid and Sjambok Rapid – not too dangerous, but definitely enough to get the blood pounding.

For those in search of adventure, running the Orange River in the Richtersveldt National Park on the border of South Africa and Namibia is just the ticket. In this isolated part of the Northern Cape, the Orange River's long journey from the Drakensberg range to the Atlantic Ocean finally ends. Here, this majestic river is a long, green-fringed oasis that offers scenic stretches of serene water as it twists and turns through a striking desert landscape, with occasional fun rapids to spice up the journey.

This is a river run to be undertaken with a guide, either solo or with a group. The Orange River is usually tackled using two-person inflatable rafts, kayaks or canoes, sometimes with the support of a larger raft carrying supplies. A typical trip will be around 80 km (50 mi) long and different guides and organizers use various starting and take-out points. There is usually a base camp at the start where personal belongings may be left, with transport back at the end of the trip. Most expeditions assemble at Vioolsdrift on the Namibian border, just upriver from the Park – and some 350 km (217 mi) from the mouth of the Orange River – from where paddlers are driven to base camp.

TABLE MOUNTAIN AERIAL CABLEWAY
Southern Africa/South Africa

WORTH A DETOUR: An extraordinary diversity of plant life on the summit – look especially for the sunshine conebushes in full flower (summer only).

Opened in 1929, and extensively refurbished in 1997 when new cars and double cabling were introduced, the Table Mountain Aerial Cableway has transported more than 16 million people to the top of Table Mountain, a dramatic ride which offers wonderful views of Cape Town and surrounds, both on the way up and from the summit.

This isn't a journey for the faint-hearted (or vertigo sufferers). Some 1,200 m (3,940 ft) of cable link the Lower Cable Station on Tafelberg Road near Kloof Nek with the Upper Cable Station on the westernmost end of the Table Mountain Plateau. In the course of their upward journey, the cars rise steeply from a height of 302 m (990 ft) to 1,067 m (3,500 ft). The latest Rotair cars can each carry 65 passengers, more than doubling the capacity of the old cars.

Once up, there are various pathways leading to stunning views over Cape Town, Table Bay, Robben Island,

Cape Flats and the Cape Peninsula. There are three signed walks. Klipspinger Walk follows the plateau edge above Platteklip Gorge. Agama Walk has been designed to give wonderful all-round views of Cape Town. Dassie Walk offers spectacular views to the north, south and west.

ROBBEN ISLAND FERRY

Southern Africa/South Africa

Cape Town's Victoria & Alfred Waterfront is the departure point for one of the city's essential activities – the ferry trip to Robben Island, for centuries a safe dumping ground for those deemed undesirable by the authorities, from Muslim leaders and Dutch colonial dissenters through lepers to anti-apartheid freedom fighters – among the latter Nelson Mandela, who went on to become a Nobel Peace Prize winner and South Africa's first black President. During the apartheid years the prison on Robben Island (established in 1959) became known for brutality. The harsh regime failed to achieve its objective and Robben Island became known in Africa and throughout the world as a symbol of resistance to tyranny.

Today, the prison has become a living museum, where many of the guides are former political prisoners who really do know what they're talking about. After a period of neglect, resources are being devoted to sprucing up the prison and the island. Sailings by five ancient ferries were once frequently cancelled as a result of mechanical problems, but the launch of a new 300-seater ferry, the Sikhululekile ('We are free'), has restored reliability. Even so, the ferry journey can be an exciting roller-coaster ride – or not take place at all – if one of the sudden storms for which the area is famed blows up. It's a risk worth taking, as there are stunning bay views during the approach to Robben Island, with Table Mountain as the brooding backdrop.

HIGHLIGHTS:
Cell number 46664, where Nelson Mandela was incarcerated for 18 years. Observation of the over-active and ever-entertaining penguin colony.

CHAPMAN'S PEAK DRIVE

Southern Africa/South Africa

HIGHLIGHTS:

Stopping at one or more of the many scenic overlooks above the sea to have a picnic – or simply drink in the staggering seascapes.
Sunset over Hout's Bay, seen from the Chapman's Point lookout.
Parking and hiking the trail to the top of Chapman's Peak for truly amazing views (four–five hours needed, take water).

The journey may not be long – just 9 km (5.6 mi) – but Chapman's Peak Drive on the Atlantic Coast at South Africa's southwestern tip is one of the world's most spectacular marine cliff roads. Starting from the picturesque horseshoe-shaped fishing harbour of Hout Bay, the Drive skirts Chapman's Peak, the southerly extension of Constantia Berg. It winds up towards Chapman's Point, offering views down to sandy coves below, from whence it descends to sea level at Noordhoek. That sounds simple enough, but doesn't begin to hint at the drama that will be enjoyed as this unique toll road unfolds.

It was constructed between 1915 and 1922, and has 114 bends and sections blasted out of sheer rock faces. The effort was worthwhile. The geology is fascinating – the road was cut where base granite meets sedimentary limestone above, creating brilliantly coloured layers of orange, red-yellow silt shot with lines of dark purple manganese. But that's not the main attraction, because Chapman's Peak Drive delivers almost unbelievable views of the Atlantic Ocean as it snakes towards journey's end.

Those who wish to see the sights without worrying that it's dangerous to drive while eye-balling the views can take a bus. These may travel only from the Hout's Bay end in the interests of safety, though short tours that include Chapman's Peak Drive are freely available from various start points. This is the best direction to drive, too, as it makes pulling off into scenic overlooks easier. The Drive may be hiked from either end but not right through – walkers are barred from the central section. It is occasionally closed to all traffic as a result of adverse weather conditions.

DRAKENSBERG TRAVERSE

Southern Africa/South Africa

Call it Quathlamba or call it Drakensberg, the end result is the same – the rugged mountain range that extends for 1,125 km (700 mi) from Mpumalanga (formerly Eastern Transvaal) to Eastern Cape Province. Traversing the Drakensberg (Dragon Mountains) involves a wilderness adventure, camping out (unless there's a handy cave as night approaches) and backpacking everything needed during the trip. This is a guided expedition, as only extremely experienced wilderness hikers could contemplate going solo. The main challenge is the altitude, with thin mountain air making physical effort more difficult, testing resolve and endurance to the limit. Daily distances of 8 km (5 mi) to 16 km (10 mi) are the norm. There are lots of routes to choose from, in Drakensberg, usually titled according to length – Mini-Traverse (five days), Classic-Traverse (seven days), Super-Traverse (14 days) or Grand-Traverse (21 days). One option is trekking in the Drakensberg Park, two hours from Durban, with all the magic of these mountains plus ancient cave dwellings with rock paintings. Traverses begin with an ascent to the escarpment, either by climbing a steep pass or using the local specialty shortcut – metal ladders bolted to the sloping rock – after which each party treks for the set distance and time before descending back to civilization. Although the parameters of each Traverse are loosely established, the sort of flexibility dictated by unknown factors like weather conditions and the party marching at the pace of the slowest will determine final itinerary.

One thing never changes – these mountains always offer an opportunity to experience an enchanting wilderness of peaks and high escarpment, astonishing natural architecture, incredible views… and the sense of achievement that comes from undertaking and making one of the world's greatest hikes.

HIGHLIGHTS:
Intense starry nights, way above light pollution.

YOU SHOULD KNOW
Drakensberg weather can be severe – storms blow up from nowhere and, while there are no snowfields, snowfall has been recorded on every day of the year.

YOU SHOULD KNOW

Visitors to Sossusvlei need a park entry permit. 4x4s can drive up to the Pan; other vehicles use a car park a long, hot walk away – take water.

NAMIB DESERT

Southern Africa/South Africa

The name 'Namib' means 'Vast Dry Plain', and the Namib Desert extends along the Atlantic coast, with vast seas of towering dunes rolling inland towards gravel plains and isolated mountain ranges. This is one of the oldest and driest deserts in the world.

Windhoek, Namibia's capital, is a graceful city set on low hills; the road southwest (C26) crosses lovely countryside and desert hills. South of Solitaire on the C14 a signed road leads south to Sesriem and the Namib Dunes.

These are 'dynamic' dunes – they shift and change shape, sculpted by the wind. They are made of quartz sand, and their colours also change, from cream to copper, red to violet. Some of these enormous sandhills are easily accessible, by foot or 4x4.

Sossusvlei, 60 km (37 m) deeper into the desert is the most photographed place in Namibia. It consists of a huge clay pan surrounded by massive red dunes, some as high as 300 m (975 ft). When the Tsauchab River fills and spills into it, this briefly becomes a turquoise lake, flocked by aquatic birds. The park opens at sunrise and closes at sunset; to experience the glorious technicolour effects it is necessary to stay around Sesriem.

The road northwest towards Swakopmund, the C14, runs along the eastern edge of the dunes then through the Gaub Pass and the Kuiseb Pass, turning west to cross the Namib-Naukluft Park, an area of gravel plains and occasional hills. It reaches the coast at Walvis Bay, a busy harbour town. Swakopmund, 30 km (19 mi) north, is an attractive German-colonial seaside resort, and Namibia's most popular holiday destination, with a wide range of adventure sports on offer on land and sea.

WHEN TO GO:
May–October.

HIGHLIGHTS:
Sossusvlei – climb one of the dunes and look down over the waves of the Sand Dune Sea.
Escape the crowds at Hidden Vlei, a low landscape surrounded by lonely dunes.
Bird watching at Walvis Bay. Huge numbers of bright pink flamingoes visit the surrounding wetlands.

OKAVANGA DELTA

Southern Africa/Botswana

DON'T MISS
The many spectacular
birds and butterflies.

HIGHLIGHTS:
Wildlife – you will spot
hippos and crocodiles in
the waterways, and you may
see elephants and antelopes
while trekking.
Local knowledge – as well
as identifying wildlife, polers
can explain Delta life.

YOU SHOULD KNOW
Wildlife can be dangerous:
camp sensibly and never
swim without checking with
your poler.

The Okavango River rises in Angola, flows south through Namibia and into Botswana; then the river's waters spread, sprawling over the sandy wastes of the Kalahari Desert to form an immense, extraordinary inland delta. The waters of this, the largest landlocked delta in the world, never reach the sea; trapped in the parched Kalahari this watery wilderness is a magnet for wildlife. In the lush forests and along the floodplains, hundreds of species of bird flourish and lions, elephants, hippos and crocodiles, as well as smaller animals, congregate. The beauty and serenity of the Delta is drifting along passageways of papyrus, gliding across the pale golden waters in a shallow-draft dugout canoe, a mokoro. Traditionally made from logs of ebony or sausage tree wood, these amazingly stable craft are now often constructed of fibreglass – international conservation groups encourage this to save the slow-growing trees. Generally a mokoro carries two passengers, supplies and a poler, who stands at the back with the ngashi, a long pole made from the mogonono tree.

Two- or three-day trips can be arranged, overnighting in campsites in the Delta. Trips combine poling and trekking – poling is hard work. Most polers speak some English, and are very knowledgeable about the flora and fauna, though they tend to be rather shy.

HIIGHLIGHTS: The vegetation – umbrella acacias, Mokolae palms (the sap makes palm wine and the fronds, baskets). Baines' Baobabs, immortalized by the artist/traveller in 1862.

NXAI PAN OLD CATTLE TREK

Southern Africa/Botswana

In the heat of August, the Nxai, Sowa and Ntwetwe Pans, form a land of dizzying mirages, but with the rains, temporary lakes form in the depressions and the earth greens. Herd animals, including elephant and zebra, arrive in their thousands and waterbirds, most spectacularly flamingoes, flock to feed on algae and crustaceans. Nxai Pan lies north of the highway which cuts through the Park area. To visit, a 4x4 is essential. The permanent residents of the grassy expanse include lion, giraffe, kudu, impala and ostrich, and during the migration period the huge herds are followed by predators. Running inside the western boundary of the Old Cattle Trek route is the Pandamatenga Trail. It runs to the Zambian border. In a 4x4 it is still possible to follow this trail out of the Park, northeastwards to Pandamatenga, some 200 km (125 mi) away.

JOBO MOUNTAIN ADVENTURE DRIVE

Southern Africa/Lesotho

YOU SHOULD KNOW

Each summer several people die from lightning strikes, so avoid high, open ground during storms.

Rural Lesotho is perfect trekking country. Dominated by mountain ranges, this is a land without fences where herd-boys drive their flocks and blanket-wrapped farmers ride. In the south, a relatively small area around the village of Malealea seems to offer all the best features of the highlands. Here are precipitous mountains and gorges, ancient rock paintings, waterfalls and a scattering of remote villages fluttering with bright flags. These flags are colour-coded advertisements for the available comestibles – red and green for meat and vegetables, white and yellow for sorghum or barley beer. Fittingly, this area is reached through the Gates of Paradise Pass.

The lodge here will advise on routes for walkers and drivers of 4x4s and arrange pony treks. Ponies and guides are provided by the villages, and longer treks spend nights in village huts. The Basuto are a nation of horsemen and their small, strong, surefooted ponies are the ideal form of transport. No wild gallops here, though: the ponies pick their way carefully up and down the steep tracks. Very gentle, they are ideal for non-riders.

A trek to Jobo Mountain and village is one of the most rewarding and exciting journeys. The route covers the Sani rock paintings and the Botso'ela Waterfall and the final climb is along a precarious pass between two beautiful, deep gorges. Most 4x4 drivers prefer to walk the last, vertiginous section.

SKELETON COAST
Southern Africa/Namibia

The Skeleton Coast stretches from Swakopmund to the Angolan border 500 km (300 m) north. This is an inhospitable place, where immense stretches of beach are beaten by breakers, engulfed by fog and cut off by trackless, shifting dunes. Early Portuguese sailors knew it as 'The Sands of Hell', for the crew of a foundering ship was doomed. The narrow strip of dunes was proclaimed a Nature Reserve in 1971. This ancient, untouched wilderness has a fascinating ecosystem – although almost rainless, the desert is moistened by the dense fogs that

are brought by the icy Benuela Current and blown inshore. Plants and lichens adapt to the extreme conditions by taking on strange forms. The coast road runs along the margin of the dunes, but there is no access. A sightseeing flight from Swakopmund is a good option – these low-level flights allow a view of the vast graveyard of the shore and the mesmerising changing shapes and colours of the dunes.

HIGHLIGHTS:
The Ugab Formations, whose black ridges contrast with the white desert.
Sarusa Springs Oasis – a perennial water source.

YOU SHOULD KNOW
The dense coastal fogs occur most mornings and evenings.

WORTH A DETOUR:
The Welwitschia mirabilis, a tree dwarfed by the extremes of the desert, lives for over 1,000 years.

DAMARALAND
Southern Africa/Namibia

Damaraland occupies the area between the Skeleton Coast and Namibia's central plateau. Here, desert hills are interspersed with mountains and gravel plains. The rugged landscape is networked by streams which streak the land with green, providing water for the Damara people and their livestock and for many desert-adapted, free-ranging animals including elephants, zebras and the rare black rhino.

This region is rich in geological features – mountains, craters, strange rock formations and the renowned petroglyphs. These paintings and engravings on rock are found nearby.

Here are many quiet roads and tracks, off the main tourist routes, and some companies offer mountain bike safaris. These typically start from Swakopmund, with visits to the Spitzkoppe (the 'Matterhorn of Africa') and Namibia's highest mountain, the Brandberg. A night is spent in the remote and beautiful landscape of the Ugab River in a camp run by the Save the Rhino Trust, after which the route climbs the Damara steppe and eventually reaches Twyfelfontein.

WORTH A DETOUR: 'Palm Springs' at the end of the demanding first section. This spot offers good camping and the bliss of a soak in the hot, bubbling water.

FISH RIVER CANYON TRAIL
Southern Africa/Namibia

The second largest canyon in the world, Fish River Canyon winds and twists (legend suggests it was formed by the frantic writhings of a giant serpent) for over 160 km (100 mi). Because of flash flooding in the rainy season and the extreme heat of summer, the canyon is open for a limited season to trekkers for the challenging walk down the 85 km (52 mi) trail from Hobas to Ai-Ais near the southern end. From Hobas a gravel road leads to Hikers' Viewpoint, the start of the route, and from here those not braving the walk can enjoy an awe-inspiring panorama. The first part of the walk is the most exhausting, with the steep descent of the canyon wall and several miles of rough sand and boulders. The route follows the course of the river past sulphur springs, viewpoints and strange rock formations. There are shortcuts bypassing the longer bends. At Ai-Ais (the name means 'scalding hot') the weary but triumphant walker will find the Hot Springs Resort with all its welcome facilities.

YOU SHOULD KNOW
This very tough walk can only be attempted by experienced hikers. A medical certificate is required.

TRANS-ORANJE
Southern Africa/Namibia

HIGHLIGHTS:
The biggest man-made hole in the world, on the left just after Kimberley station.
The Karoo Desert landscape as night falls – the train is timed to allow travellers to enjoy spectacular sunsets.

One of South Africa's great train services is the Trans-Oranje's twice-weekly run between Cape Town and Durban (or vice versa), the longest inter-city train journey in South Africa. From Cape Town, the multicoloured Trans-Oranje heads out across the arid Karoo Desert. It then passes the famous De Beers diamond mine in Kimberley, crosses the plains of the Orange Free State and continues on into Natal, passing through the mountainous landscapes of Cliffdale, Ntshongweni, Situndu Hills and Marianhill before arriving on the shores of the sparkling Indian Ocean at Durban, that humid city of bananas, sugar cane and fun. Along the way the train stops at names writ large in the annals of South African history, including Kimberley, Bloemfontein and Ladysmith. The ideal journey is a return trip, allowing full appreciation of the varied sights of this extraordinary land of contrasts afforded by a journey on the Trans-Oranje – from ever-changing scenery to shanty towns.

THE TEA ROAD

Southern Africa/Swaziland

DON'T MISS

Sheba's Breasts, twin peaks traditionally the site of King Solomon's Mines.

One of the smallest African countries, Swaziland, under its king Mswati III, has a strong sense of pride; the King represents and maintains the traditional way of life.
The superb scenery of this relaxed and friendly country ranges from rainforest and savannah scrub to jagged mountains and high veld. Originally set aside for the royal hunt, several of the excellent game and nature reserves owe their existence to the king and this is one of the best areas to see rhinos, despite poaching. The Tea Road is named after a failed project to establish tea plantations. The route runs north from the main road from Mbabane, climbing into the Mzdzimba Range, the burial place of the kings. The ridge provides a panoramic view of the beautiful Royal Valley, Ezulwini. At its centre, the town of Lobamba contains the palace, parliament and the royal kraal, where the King participates in the two magnificent annual ceremonies. A boulder marked gravel road crosses the mountains through Swazi villages and descends to the Malkerne Valley, a lovely area famous for skilled craftwork. North of the country road back towards Mbabne, the mountainous Miliwane Wildlife Sanctuary has a variety of wildlife and good walks.

YOU SHOULD KNOW

Winds, tides and sandbanks can be hazards for dhows; if you arrange your own trip, check the reliability of your dhow with the tourist office.

BAZARUTO ARCHIPELAGO

East Africa/Mozambique

Vilankulo is a charming town with a lively market and lovely beaches, and the gateway to the Bazaruto Archipelago. The whole area is protected as a conservation area. The sand dunes, tidal flats and saline lakes support a wide variety of seabirds; the coral reefs teem with fish and marine mammals.
With billowing sails and graceful silhouettes, dhows epitomise a romantic dream of travel. In reality traditional, sail-only dhows, fighting wind, wave and current, becalmed or grounded, with nothing but a rudimentary toilet, have their drawbacks. Dhows with auxiliary outboards and more comfortable facilities offer catering and on-board sleeping arrangements and camping options.
Typically a trip will call at Margaruque for snorkelling and the beach and continue to Benguerra. The journey

on to Bazaruto, with its high dunes, anchors at Two Mile Reef for diving. The deep waters around Santa Carolina offer good game fishing. All these low-lying islands have white, palm-fringed beaches – wild and wave-beaten on the windward side, calm turquoise waters and glorious sunsets on the leeward. The diving in these protected reefs is first class. Uncrowded dive-sites have excellent visibility; as well as a rainbow of small fish, dolphins, rays, humpback whales and turtles are widespread.

ZAMBEZI RIVER CRUISE TO VICTORIA FALLS

East Africa/Zambia

HIGHLIGHTS:
A sunset cruise with cocktails has a touch of colonial elegance.
Livingstone Island is in the middle of the river, right by the falls.
Wildlife – from the river you might be lucky enough to see a rhino as well as elephants and hippos.
The Monument Site Park opens during full moons for the lunar rainbow.

David Livingstone first saw Victoria Falls in 1855. In awe he wrote that 'angels in their flight must have gazed' on such sights. Though he named the falls for his queen, the Kolola name, 'the smoke that thunders', is more evocative. Here, the Zambezi races over a cliff nearly 2 km (1.2 mi) wide and plunges into the Batoka Gorge more than 100 m (325 ft) below. When the river is in flood, the spray can be seen from miles away.

The falls must be seen, felt and heard from close quarters. At the Victoria Falls World Heritage National Monument Site a walk over a narrow footbridge leads to a buttress, the Knife Edge, with a dizzying view of the falls and the sheer drop. A steep track leads down to the river and a whirlpool called the Boiling Pot. There are advantages to visiting in both the wet season – the falls are at awe-inspiring full flow – and the dry when, though the flow is reduced, the size and structure can be seen clearly.

The range of adventure activities on offer around the foot of the falls includes abseiling, bungee jumping and river boarding as well as white water rafting. However, a river cruise is a leisurely and luxurious way to see the falls from the top and, on the stately progress upstream, watch for wildlife in the parks on both sides of the river. Various cruises are on offer, but the double-or triple-decker craft have a certain style. They leave from the Royal Mile, named for George VI, who visited the Falls in 1947. There is a choice of sunrise and sunset, breakfast, lunch and dinner cruises.

YOU SHOULD KNOW

The situation on the northern border with Sudan and the southwestern border with Congo is volatile.

THE ALBERTINE ESCARPMENT

East Africa/Uganda

Uganda has superb landscapes – mountain ranges, rolling countryside, lakes, rivers and waterfalls. Lake Albert stretches about 160 km (100 mi) along the Congo border to the Albert Nile and spectacular Murchison Falls, where the Victoria Nile rushes and tumbles along its way. Masindi, five hours west of Kampala, is the gateway to the Falls area. Between Masindi and the Lake lies the Budongo Forest National Park. The road south along the escarpment is not good: little used and often very steep, it requires a 4x4, but it crosses some of the loveliest country in Uganda. Ringed by eucalyptus trees planted in colonial times, Hoima lies on a plain. In 1862 it became the capital of the King of Banjora, and the throne room of the current Kitari is open by arrangement. South of Hoima the road rises again, passing through mountainous, lushly forested countryside where occasional cultivated areas allow views for miles around. Finally, the road reaches the hilly greenness surrounding Fort Portal. One of the most attractive towns in Uganda, Fort Portal lies high in the well-watered foothills of the Rwenzie among tea-estates.

MOUNT ELGON & SASA RIVER TRAIL

East Africa/Uganda

WORTH A DETOUR: Sipi Falls is an impressive, three-tiered waterfall; the lowest section drops over a sheer cliff.

A single, massive extinct volcano towering over the plains, Mount Elgon straddles Uganda's border with Kenya. Wagagi, the highest peak of the caldera ring, is, at 4,321 m (14,043 ft). The ascent traverses fertile cultivated foothills (coffee and fruit), montane forest, bamboo and low canopy forest, heath and, above 3,800 m (12,350 ft), Afro-alpine moorland, supporting rare plants. The larger animal residents are rarely spotted, though the forest abounds in monkeys and birds.

Mount Elgon is uncrowded and unspoilt. It rises in a series of quite gentle slopes punctuated by steep cliffs and scrambles, and is a straightforward climb which can be made by non-mountaineers. The Sasa Trail is the most direct route to the summit, though the first day is strenuous, scaling the cliff by the 'ladders', a series of steep steps and muddy passages. The descent can be made by the Piswa/Sipi Trail, ending at the pretty, relaxing resort at Sipi Falls. After the 'ladders' the trail leads through forests and open moorlands, affording breathtaking views. Wagagi is reached by way of Jackson's Hole; then the path follows the caldera rim and joins the Piswa Trail. This passes through lovely terrain – streams, waterfalls and gorges. The last leg follows the Sipi Trail down to Kapkwai, upstream from Sipi Falls.

YOU SHOULD KNOW

Ranger-led tours are a must: much of the wildlife is dangerous.

MOUNT KILIMANJARO

East Africa/Tanzania

This is Africa's highest mountain and one of the world's highest volcanoes. Uhuru Peak, one of a jagged group to the east of Kibo, reaches 5896 m (19162 ft). Kibo itself appears as a snow-covered dome, but this is a dormant volcano with a huge crater.

Every year hundreds set out – in theory no specialized expertise or equipment is needed – but a large percentage do not reach the summit. Though the climb can officially be undertaken all year, the rains make the paths slippery and the unpredictability of the weather should never be underestimated. Altitude sickness is a problem which can be alleviated by acclimatization. All treks should be organized through a tour company, but one essential is to allow enough time. Whatever route is chosen, variables such as local conditions and illness must be allowed for in flexible timetabling. The Machame Route, though not the easiest, is one of the most scenic. It follows steep paths through magnificent forests and over moorland plains, followed by a long track running runs east below the precipitous glaciated cliffs, traversing scree and ridges. This leg importantly gives time to acclimatize at around 4,000 m (13,000 ft). After a night at Bafa Hut, the last day of the ascent involves and early start and a gruelling climb up a bleak and barren section (often snow-covered) to the caldera rim and onwards to Uhuru. The trek down is by the steeper but more direct Mweka Route.

YOU SHOULD KNOW

This climb is rated Grade 4, strenuous, and is best suited to fit climbers with experience of high altitude. Take your own maps and compass. Make sure everything is waterproofed.

LAKE MANYARA NATIONAL PARK
East Africa/Tanzania

HIGHLIGHTS: Elephants – they are relaxed around vehicles. Hippos – it is possible to observe them at quite close range. Tree-climbing lions are rarely seen; stop in the acacia.

Lake Manyara, a large, shallow, soda lake, is dramatically situated at the foot of the western escarpment of the Rift Valley. The National Park, a UNESCO World Biosphere Reserve, occupies its northwest corner; though one of the smaller parks it enjoys diverse vegetation, which provides a variety of habitats. The wildlife species are not as numerous as in better known parks (though this is home to the elusive tree-climbing lion), but the birdlife is a huge attraction, particularly flamingoes.

Early morning is the best time to arrive, to catch the game drive. It is very peaceful, with more chance of spotting animals. The safari trips visit in the afternoons, when the Park can be crowded. The road runs the length of the park through marsh, savannah and acacia woodlands and close to the steep escarpment wall, where a variety of trees grow. It passes two sulphur springs, and ends. Tracks and loops off the main road, lead to different habitats – the lake, plains where buffalo, zebra and impala graze, and a pool which is home to hippo and flamingoes.

WORTH A DETOUR:
Selous Game Reserve – in the daylight, elephants, zebras, giraffes, monkeys and birds of all sorts are easily spotted from the train.

TAZARA RAILWAY
East Africa/Tanzania

The Tanzania and Zambia Railway Authority runs trains from Dar es Salaam to Mbeya in Tanzania's Southern Highlands and on to Kapiri Mposhi in Zambia. It's a notoriously unreliable train service, particularly west to east, but without the railway, much of the Southern Highlands is hard to reach and the journey is enjoyable – staff and passengers are friendly and the line runs through some marvellous countryside.

Two fast trains a week leave Dar in late afternoon, and one slow train in the morning. If time is of no concern and landscape is, take the slow train and break the journey at Ifakara, a leafy old trading-station town eight hours southwest of Dar. This means a daylight journey through the lovely, verdant countryside west of Dar and the huge expanse of the Selous Game Reserve where the train crosses woodlands, grasslands and waterways teeming with wildlife.

The fast train reaches Ifakara after midnight and, after some hours of darkness, offers views of the Highlands – the lushly forested slopes of the Udzungu Mountains towering to the north, the ranges, one after another, southwards towards Lake Nyasa. This train arrives in Mbeya at lunchtime. Mbeya, a major trade and transit centre, is set in low hills clothed in tea plantations, coffee, bananas and cocoa. It is surrounded by mountains and the climate is pleasantly cool.

YOU SHOULD KNOW

Treks into the craters must
be made with an
armed ranger.

NGORONGORO CRATER HIGHLANDS TREK

East Africa/Tanzania

Ngorongoro Crater is one of Africa's best known reserves, with its huge, steep-sided crater and an unequalled concentration of wildlife. The beautiful and rugged Crater Highlands, formed from volcanoes and collapsed volcanoes, extend in a chain along the east of the area. Several of the peaks top 3,000 m (9,750 ft), and the collapsed volcanoes have produced the eponymous craters. This remote and little-visited area offers remarkable scenery, plenty of wildlife and very good trekking.

The area is also home to the Datoga pastoralists and Hadzabae foragers, and guides may be able to negotiate visits to villages.

There are no designated routes in the Highlands, so the places visited will vary. Deserted Empakaai Crater, with its deep, flamingo-crowded lake, offers dramatic views over the whole area from the caldera rim; wooded Olmoti Crater is the source of the Munge River. The soda lakes of Eyasi and Makat are home to many waterbirds (and their predators) and the river gorges provide breeding grounds for raptors and water for the Maasai cattle. Higher peaks include Oldeani with its forested crater, and the still-active Ol Doinyo Lengai (Mountain of God). The acacia forests are rich in wildlife.

MOMBASA TO ZANZIBAR CRUISE

WORTH A DETOUR: Mombasa's Fort Jesus and its museum are a must for anyone interested in the history of East Africa.

East Africa/Kenya

Some companies now offer holidays that combine the glorious beach life of the Kenyan coast with a short cruise from Mombasa to Zanzibar.

Mombasa has a very long history; Roman, Arabic and East Asian seafarers sheltered in its fine natural harbour. For centuries the Old Town saw bloody battles between the Portuguese and the Omani Arabs following the Portuguese seizure of the city in an attempt to break the Arab monopoly of the lucrative spice trade. Modern Mombasa, despite its turbulent history, is a fine city, with a laid-back Swahili culture.

The name itself conjures up exotic fairytale images, and Zanzibar in reality is a bewitching place. This fertile tropical island is clothed in spice plantations and ringed by picture-postcard beaches and perfect blue waters. The capital, Stone Town, is steeped in history; it is a maze of narrow winding lanes and hidden courtyards, minarets and mysterious, massive closed doors. Zanzibar, under the rule of the Omani Arabs, who moved their capital from Muscat, was the world's most important clove supplier. Now, though the sultans and slaves have gone, the spices remain.

THE ASMARA TO NEFASIT STEAM TRAIN

East Africa/Eritrea

The narrow gauge, Italian era steam train from Asmara to Nefasit is a joy, not just for steam train buffs but for anyone finding themselves in Eritrea's delightful capital city. Set high on the Kelbessa plateau, 2,350 m (7,755 ft) above sea level in the Eritrean Highlands, Asmara itself is delightful, but take a day out for this trip and you'll be richly rewarded.

The journey is just 25 km (16 mi) long, but from the moment you clamber aboard, you know it will be fun. Built between 1887 and 1938, this track was the brainchild of Mussolini, also responsible for the fabulous Art Deco and Modernist architecture of the city itself. With his demise, it sank into disrepair, but using the expertise of the old railway workers, brought out of retirement, and most of whom are now in their 70s and 80s, it was rehabilitated in the late 1990s.

Pulling out of Asmara, the train chuffs and puffs along the track. Great plumes of dirty grey smoke rise into the air and urgent tooting alerts the world as it makes its way down the escarpment. The views are spectacular: dramatic mountains, deep valleys and forest. You'll pass traditional villages with orchards of lemon trees, banana plants and the ubiquitous prickly pears, and you'll stop at small stations. This was an amazing engineering feat – the downhill gradient is an almost constant 1 in 28, and the train negotiates its way through some 20 tunnels and over 65 bridges during the course of the journey. Some of the track runs along narrow ledges cut into the mountainsides, with a vertiginous drop to the valley below. These scenes are much as they must have been for hundreds of years.

WORTH A DETOUR:
TThe neo-Romanesque cathedral, with its plaque commemorating its benefactors – including Benito Mussolini himself.

THE BLUE NILE GORGE

East Africa/Ethiopia

The Blue Nile Gorge is one of the world's most spectacular sights, rivalling, if not beating, America's Grand Canyon. The river itself flows south from its source near Lake Tana, and then northwest until it joins the White Nile at Khartoum in Sudan. Then, as the Nile, it flows through Egypt, eventually discharging into the Mediterranean. It is the longest river in the world, and the source of life for millions of people. There are different methods of arriving at and travelling through some or all of the gorge. From Lake Tana, the road drops sharply for well over 300 m (1,000 ft), to the riverbed, with outstanding views in every direction. The closer you get to the bottom, the hotter and more humid it becomes, but the breathtaking views more than make up for this minor problem.

HIGHLIGHTS:

Lake Tana and its island monasteries.
Tis Issat Falls, one of Ethiopia's most famous scenic attractions.

YOU SHOULD KNOW

If you are going to camp in the gorge, be careful not to be too close to the river – remember those crocodiles!

The gorge is glorious, covered in beautiful vegetation including dragon trees and junipers that jostle for space between small, terraced fields of a grain known as teff, used in Ethiopian flatbread, which sways and bows in the light breeze. Frankincense trees are grown as part of a project – they can be tapped for resin up to ten times annually. There are small Amharan villages to be seen, the round houses roofed with grass blending naturally into their surroundings. Baboons bound in and out of view, and birds include lammergeiers, bee-eaters and various raptors. The road is carried on Italian viaducts for part of the way – watch out for crocodiles and hippos down in the river beneath. People here are friendly folk, fascinated by foreigners, the women and girls often nonchalantly balancing huge, beautiful pots full of water on their heads. The climb out of the gorge is exhaustingly steep, but walking here is well worth the effort.

RAFT THE OMO RIVER

East Africa/Ethiopia

The Omo River rises in the Shewan Highlands, and the only easily navigable stretch is in the far south. The entire river valley is archaeologically important, and the earliest known fossil fragments of Homo sapiens were discovered in the southern reaches.

This is a truly remote region, not only rich in wildlife and birds, but also in the many unique tribal peoples, hunters and pastoralists, who inhabit the surrounding areas.

Your raft carries you along the broad, brown river, which by now has levelled out and become quite placid. There are crocodiles sunning themselves upon the banks, and hippos to be seen as you glide through open forest of tamarind and figs. Colobus monkeys chatter and leap, baboons bark in the distance and the birds are magnificent – you will see goliath herons, kingfishers, turacos, fish eagles and more.

The Omo Delta, a maze of islands and marshes, is inhabited by the Dassenach people. Pastoralists who practise flood retreat cultivation, they hunt crocodiles at night, by spearing them from small canoes – a small crocodile makes a large meal.

WHEN TO GO:
November–January.

TIMBUKTU BY BOAT

West Africa/Mali

Though Timbuktu remains a fabled place in the minds of many, today it is quite possible to reach. In order to do so, you can't beat travelling there by boat, along the mighty Niger, Africa's third longest river. The flood plains around Mopti provide a wonderful habitat for birds of all sorts, including many migratory species, and the river itself is home to many fish, some of which will no doubt be caught and cooked for you. You may well see hippos, too – their large, irascible presence alerting you to the relative fragility of your craft. The river is full of activity: local boats carry goods and livestock, fast boats speed tourists to Timbuktu. Children shriek 'toubab' (white man), and wave frantically as you pass, men fish, women wash clothes at the river's edge or pound millet in time-honoured fashion.

Lunch is cooked on board, and at night tents are pitched on the riverbank and dinner cooked over a fire. Gradually the scenery changes: marshlands give way to grasslands and finally, the desert. The trip ends at Korioume, just 10 km (6 mi) along a paved road from Timbuktu.

DON'T MISS
Taking a camel trip to a Touareg village.

THE SIMIEN MOUNTAINS

East Africa/Ethiopia

One of Africa's major massifs, the magnificent Simien Mountains were formed some 40 million years ago by violent seismic activity, erosion produced the dramatic mountain-scapes we can enjoy today – dramatic escarpments, mile-deep gorges, sculpted mountains, plateaux, river valleys and ambas, sheer pinnacles of lava, the last remnants of ancient volcanoes.

Despite the altitude and harsh terrain, villages and terraced fields are dotted about these mountains, linked by rough tracks. The most scenic route takes you down into the Jinbar Wenz Gorge, across the river to Gich village, and up to Gich Camp, which looks across richly forested valleys and mountains bursting with wildlife, including large groups of the Gelada baboon, also known as the Bleeding Heart baboon for the patch of deep red on the chests of the males. Here too are very rare Walia ibex and Simien fox. Hike to the superb viewpoint of Imet Gogo, with its tremendous vistas across a vast canyon to the rock spires beyond. Looking down you might see a Lammergeyer (Bearded vulture) repeatedly dropping its prey onto the rocks far below – a process designed to access the marrow by pulverizing the bones.

HIGHLIGHTS:
Spotting endemic and rare species of mammals, birds and plants.
Axsum, Ethiopia's most ancient city, said to be the hiding place of the Ark of the Covenant and the home of the Queen of Sheba.
Lalibela, and its monolithic, rock hewn churches.
Ascend Rash Dashen, Ethiopia's highest peak at 4,600 m (15,159 ft) and the fourth highest on the African continent.

THE SALT ROAD FROM TIMBUKTU TO TAOUDENNI

West Africa/Mali

YOU SHOULD KNOW
You need to be fit and healthy to undertake this journey, particularly if you are travelling by camel caravan. Daytime temperatures can reach 49°C (120°F), and the nights can be very cold.

Azalai, as the camel caravans travelling from Timbuktu to Taoudenni are known, regularly trek some 800 km (500 mi) across one of the harshest regions of the Sahara desert. They have passed this way for over 1,000 years, ever since salt, which could be traded weight for weight with gold, was discovered in the area.

There is austere beauty in the desert, and little sound other than the soft shoe shuffle of camels moving over hard sand and sharp stones. Sleeping under the stars in the immense silence of the desert is a profound experience.

Days begin before sun up, and the caravan travels doggedly until darkness falls. At night, rice and dried meat is cooked and eaten, with a sprinkling of sand thrown in. Reaching the halfway point of Arouane, a tiny settlement en route, feels like a great achievement. From there on in, the desert is empty – no grass, no trees, just sand stretching to the horizon. There is little wildlife – desert rats, lizards, beetles and, perhaps, gazelles, but you may pass camel bones: bleached by the sun they underline the fact that your life is in the hands of your guide.

HIGHLIGHTS: A night on the mountain – the brightness of the stars and sunrise on the slopes.
Birds include the Cameroon pigeon and the Cameroon francolin.

MOUNT CAMEROON TREK

West Africa/Cameroon

An active volcano (the last eruption was in 2000) Mount Cameroon is is a 'biodiversity hotspot', a scientifically important area with varied habitats and endemic plant and birdlife. The most direct route up, the Guinness Route, is very steep, and can be completed in a day and a half (the runners in the annual Race of Hope manage it in as little as five hours). But spending longer on the mountain is very rewarding and set hikes of several days, starting at Mann Spring or Buea and descending the northwest face by Elephant Opening allow time to appreciate the diverse vegetation, do some bird-spotting and admire the views.

The climb to the summit is demanding: because the mountain starts at sea level, a short climb brings a big change in altitude. The weather is notoriously changeable – even in the dry season trekkers can be engulfed in sudden tropical downpours and, at the summit, the temperature can fall below freezing.

CRUISE THE GAMBIA RIVER

West Africa/The Gambia

Dominated by the Gambia River, which runs from the Atlantic coast inland for some 320 km (200 mi), the Gambia consists of the river and the land to either side of it. The river is the country's lifeblood, providing water and food in an otherwise arid region, and for those who like wildlife, a cruise along all or part of this essential waterway is a treat. Begin your trip at Bintang, a small town some 80 km (50 mi) from the capital, Banjul, and take a pre-arranged boat along the river to Farafenni, passing the renowned Baobolong Wetlands on the north bank. This is The Gambia's first designated RAMSAR site, and the country's largest nature reserve, covering 220 sq km (85 sq mi). It is a maze of small islands with waterways, or bolongs, weaving their way between them. Here you will see ancient mangroves, many over 19 m (60 ft) tall, as well as tidal mudflats and savannah forest.

HIGHLIGHTS:
Baobolong Wetland Reserve
Abuko Nature Reserve
The island of Janjangbureh
Wassu Stone Circles
The beautiful, empty beaches
of Kombo South.

ILE DE GORÉE

West Africa/Senegal

HIGHLIGHTS:
Stay on Gorée in one of the several pleasant hotels and, enjoy the peace.
Sit on the mainland wharf at twilight and watch the low, rocky outline of Gorée fade.

Dakar, a huge, feverish city, brims with life. Here are all the sights, smells and sounds of Africa – noisy markets, great live music, fabulous street-food and exuberant nightlife. The sprawling city swarms with jet-setters, expats, French military types and the grindingly poor. A mere 20 minute ferry ride away lies the meditative calm of the Ile de Gorée.

Europeans first colonized the easily defensible island in 1444; power shifted between the Portuguese and the Dutch until the French took over in 1677. They stayed, with brief periods of British rule, until Senegalese independence in 1960. The colonial legacy is evident in the island's lovely old mansions, flower wreathed balconies and quiet unpaved lanes (there are no cars on the island).

Gorée became a centre of the West African slave trade – the first Portuguese slave house was established in 1536. The trade continued, officially and unofficially, under the French until 1848. Now the island's main draw is La Maison des Esclaves and its 'doors of no return', with its grim basement 'storage rooms' for slaves, the airy quarters for traders above. It has become a place of pilgrimage for African Americans, though it is debateable whether this was in fact a major shipping point for slaves – Gorée is a tiny island, and the Maison has no good moorings. But this site brings slavery's iniquities movingly to life.

MOLE NATIONAL PARK SAFARI
West Africa/Ghana

HIGHLIGHTS: The sounds of the savannah at night. The animals – particularly elephants bathing in the waterhole – they can be approached within a few metres.

Mole, an immense, remote tract of wooded savannah in northeast Ghana, is home to a huge range of animals (over 90 species including elephants, baboons, warthogs and antelope) and birds (300 species recorded, from tiny bee-eaters to vultures and eagles). However, its tourist potential is unrealized – 95 per cent of its area is unvisited even by rangers, which has allowed regular poaching. The game-viewing circuit is limited to a few miles of poor roads around the southeast corner.

The area is best seen on foot and Mole Motel, where the bus arrives, is the only place to stay. The buildings are old and basic, the accommodation far from luxurious, the water supply erratic, but its situation, high on

a steep escarpment above the savannah, is superb, affording views of the untouched wilderness landscape, the glorious sunsets and of two waterholes and the animals which gather there to drink. Outside the hotel grounds, walkers must be accompanied by armed rangers (rifles protect against poachers, not big cats – lions have not been observed for some time). The hotel runs 'walking safaris'. These guided walks allow close-range observation of wildlife and can be tailored to the needs of the group.

HIGHLIGHTS: The 12th-century Koutoubia minaret. Marrakech's famous square, Djema el-Fna, crowded with exotic street entertainers and excellent street food.

MARRAKECH EXPRESS
West Africa/Ghana

Immortalized by the eponymous song, the Marrakech Express remains an iconic journey. Rabat is Morocco's capital. Less famous than other Moroccan cities, it is a delightful place, with a marvellous fortified Kasbah, and an ancient, walled medina, as well as a French-built new town.

The train then follows the coastline southwest to Casablanca. All Morocco's cities pride themselves on their individuality, and Casablanca is no exception. Built mainly in the 20th century by the French, and boasting some fine Art Deco architecture, this is the country's business and financial hub.

Leaving Casablanca, the track veers inland, through the city's fertile, agricultural hinterland, past orange groves loaded with fruit and fields of crops and vegetables. Gradually the green fields are left behind as the train makes its way across a flat, increasingly barren plain. Scoured by the wind and sun for millennia, the deep red earth and rocky outcrops look bleak and under populated.

As the train approaches its goal, the scenery changes again and the magnificent range of the Atlas Mountains, with their snow-capped peaks, come into view.

RIF ROAD TRIP

North Africa/Morocco

HIGHLIGHTS:
The Medersa Bou Inania, Fes.
The view of Fez from the
Merenid Tombs.
Friouato Cave, perhaps the
deepest and most impressive
cave in North Africa.

WORTH A DETOUR:
Ouezzane, a town honoured by
Muslims and Jews alike, busy
with craftsmen.

The highly scenic Rif Mountains stretch across northern Morocco. Entirely separate geologically from the Atlas Mountains, they were originally part of Europe. With the highest of the craggy, limestone peaks rising to some 2,500 m (8,250 ft), this is untamed country, full of hidden valleys, gullies and streams. The only large towns lie on the foothills. It's a lawless area, where much of the forest has been cut and the land put to kif (cannabis) and hashish production.

From the port city of Tangiers, the road climbs to Tetouan, and then on to Chefchaouen, a beautiful town of blue and white houses, nestling on the edge of the wildflower-strewn mountainside. Continuing to Fez, the road twists and turns for 217 km (135 mi), through steep bends and dramatic scenery. Fes is unique: its old town, one of the great medieval cities of the world, contains some of the most spectacular buildings in the country. The narrow, twisting alleys of the souks are extraordinary and thrilling to explore, your senses swamped by sights, sounds and smells that are both alien and bewitching.

Leaving Fes, the road takes a circuit around Jbel Tazekka, a high altitude national park of cork oaks and cedar forests, before reaching Taza. From here you pass over sparsely populated plains and plateaux, the countryside becoming increasingly green and fertile, until you reach Oujda, the capital of eastern Morocco and the gateway to Algeria.

HIGH ATLAS MULE TREK
North Africa/Morocco

Morocco's High Atlas mountain range stretches east from the Atlantic Ocean to the Algerian border. Centuries of erosion have produced rocky peaks that descend to deeply carved, green valleys. Djebel Toubkal, at 4,167 m (13,670 ft), the highest peak in North Africa, dominates the Toubkal National Park. Established in 1942, and situated 60 km (37 mi) south of Marrakech, this remote area is a traditional Berber homeland, and small settlements and villages are scattered throughout, clinging precariously to the mountainsides. Built of pisé (rammed earth), they blend perfectly into the environment.
From Tamatert, the highest village at about 2,000 m (6,600 ft), you set out, with mules and a guide, to ascend to the Tamatert Pass, trekking through terraced fields of wheat and barley, orchards of apples, cherries and walnuts, and finally forests of pine and junipers. Walking or riding is the only way to travel and transport goods in this region, and the undulating tracks, though sometimes rocky, are well maintained.

HIGHLIGHTS:
Djebel Toubkal – you do not have to be a very experienced mountaineer. The lovely Lake Ifni, and its nearby waterfalls. Traditional Berber villages including Sidi Chamharouch, a place of pilgrimage. Ait Ben Haddou, a remarkable fortified village and UNESCO World Heritage Site.

DON'T MISS
Medina of Tozeur – 14th-century decorated brickwork and doors.

FROM TOZEUR TO DOUZ ACROSS THE CHOTT EL-DJERID
North Africa/Tunisia

The Chott el-Djerid is the largest saltpan in the Sahara, covering an area of over 5,000 sq km (1,900 sq mi). Whatever the season, it is incredibly dangerous to walk on. There are terrible local tales of it swallowing whole caravans of camels.
The only way to cross this forsaken land is by using the 250 km (155 mi) causeway. As you leave Tozeur, the road runs through undulating hills where goats and camels graze. The completely straight gypsum causeway plunges you into an eerie otherworld. As far as the eye can see, there is nothing but salt crusts gleaming in the sun against the straight line of the horizon. By the roadside there are lurid pink-tinted crystalline deposits, wherever you look there are shimmering reflections, and Fata Morgana mirages pop up out of nowhere.
Thoroughly disorientated and with some relief, you finally arrive at Douz, the 'gateway to the Sahara' – a date palm oasis inhabited by the Mrazig, a tribe of nomadic desert shepherds. Here you can do something 'normal' – like take a camel ride out into the dunes – to ground yourself back in reality.

Right: High Atlas Mule Trek

JEBEL NAFUSA MOUNTAIN DRIVE

North Africa/Libya

WORTH A DETOUR:
Gharyan, on the edge of the Nafusa Mountains – with extraordinary troglodyte dwellings dug straight down into the ground.

A good way of seeing traditional Libya is to journey from Tripoli to the Jebel Nafusa Mountains and on to Nalut at their western extremity, up by the Tunisian border. Don't hurry to hit the road, though – take a day to explore the exotic capital city and see some of its famous sights.

Then head for the mountains. Apart from the narrow coastal trip, Libya is all Sahara Desert, and this 300 km (185 mi) journey is an ideal way to experience something of the unique atmosphere of that silent sea of sand. Head south from Tripoli through scrubby semi-desert for 80 km (50 mi) to Bi'r al Ghanam, where you meet the Jebel Nafusa Mountains, a harsh landscape of rocky escarpments and barren hills broken by fertile patches where olives, figs, apricots and grain are grown. This is the heartland of the Berber people and remains of their civilization dot the landscape, with ancient stone villages overlooking the plain. Follow the road along the northern foothills past Bi'r Ayyad, Qasr al-Hajj, Shakshuk, Tiji and Al Hawamid until – at the westernmost end of the Jebel Nafusa range, up by the Tunisian border – you reach Nalut. Then you'll appreciate the reason for choosing this destination. It's one of the finest Ghurfa (storage chambers) villages in Libya, in a commanding position with sweeping desert views, atmospheric twisting streets and an old town made up of over 400 extraordinary ghurfas.

WORTH A DETOUR:
Elijah's Basin – a 500-year-old cypress tree marking the spot where Elijah is said to have heard the voice of God.

FOLLOW THE FOOTSTEPS OF MOSES UP MOUNT SINAI

North Africa/Egypt

Perched on the summit of Mount Sinai are both a Greek Orthodox chapel and a Muslim shrine. There are two routes up the 2,285 m (7,500 ft) high mountain. The Siket Sayidna Musa (Path of Our Lord Moses) – 3,750 Steps of Penitence hewn out of stone by the monks of St Catherine's – lead directly up a steep ravine to the summit. Or you can take a gentler, more winding path, the Siket El Bashait (Camel Path) either on foot or by camel. The two paths meet at Elijah's Basin, a sandy hollow where visitors can camp overnight before climbing the final 750 steps to the summit. As you tread the Steps of Penitence, you cannot help but be moved by its mystical connotations. From the summit, the view over Sinai is breathtaking.

WORTH A DETOUR:
Karnak Temple –
the largest temple
complex in the world.

DON'T MISS
Zulu cultural centres
at Eshowe, Empangeni
and Ulundi.

UP THE NILE
North Africa/Egypt

The cruise from Luxor to Aswan takes you through the heartlands of the oldest nation state in the world. As you sail past the timeless agricultural scenery of the valley, flanked by sheer desert cliffs up to 550 m (1,800 ft) high, five millennia of history unfolds before your eyes. Luxor, the ancient city of Thebes, is 'the world's greatest open air museum'. Here is the stupendous Karnak Temple, the tombs of the Valley of the Kings and the Colossi of Memnon. At the great lock at Esna, the Nile is transformed into a chaotic water bazaar as traders in rickety boats besiege the river traffic, proffering scarves, trinkets and souvenirs. The Temple of Horus at Edfu is the best-preserved temple in Egypt, and on the riverbank at Kom Ombu a temple with beautiful relief carving stands as a wondrous reminder of the antiquity of this land.

The charming southern city of Aswan is a riot of new impressions – the vivid colours and smells of the souks, the tall graceful Nubian townspeople, the Nile at its most picturesque – all swaying palm trees, golden dunes and white-sailed feluccas (traditional wooden sailing boats).

OASES OF THE GREAT SAND SEA
North Africa/Egypt

HIGHLIGHTS: Shali Fortress, Siwa
Gebel al-Mawta – Mountain of the Dead, tombs cut into hillside.
Painted houses of Farafra.

The Great Sand Sea is an uninhabitable belt of shifting golden dune ridges up to 100 m (330 ft) high, a natural impassable barrier between Egypt and Libya up to 300 km (200 mi) wide and extending for some 600 km (375 mi) north to south. Human habitation is only possible in the five remote oases at its edge, where mineral springs and waterholes enable life. Siwa, Egypt's westernmost oasis, is the site of the ancient Oracle of Amun, consulted by Alexander the Great. It is an 80 km (50 mi) swathe of date palms, olive trees and salt lakes inhabited by Berbers. The 400 km (250 mi) road along the ancient caravan route to Bahariya, is part rutted sand track, part concrete and part no road at all – just rough driving across the dunes in vaguely

the right direction. From Bahariya, you cross the surreal White Desert with dramatic rock formations like giant mushrooms, to reach Farafra, one of the most isolated places in Egypt.

Compared to this tiny oasis, Dakhla seems huge – 14 villages surrounded by fields of mulberry, citrus, datepalm and fig, overlooked by magnificent pinkish cliffs. The village of Al-Qasr with its medieval architecture is one of the most significant archaeological sites of Egypt's Western Desert.

EUROPE

SNAEFELLSNES NATIONAL PARK

Iceland

HIGHLIGHTS:
Bird colonies along the cliffs.
Badstofa Cave, Hellnar.
Mary's Spring – water
emerging from lava, thought
to have healing powers.
The Midnight Sun.

The whole of Iceland is a geological treasure; and the Snaefellsjokull is the absolute jewel in the crown. A mysterious 1,446 m (4,743 ft) high strato-volcano, with a 200-m (650-ft) deep ice-filled crater, shrouded in a 7 sq km (3 sq mi) ice cap, it has lain dormant for the past 1,800 years; ancient plaits of lava trail down its flanks across the plains of the Snaefellsnes Peninsula to the sea.

From the romantic moonscape wilds of the Budir estuary you walk for 18 km (11 mi) in a surreal fairyland, across a moss-carpeted and rock-strewn lava plain to the picturesque fishing village of Arnarstapi. From here you can walk a further 8 km (5 mi) along a bizarrely beautiful coast of fantastic lava formations and spectacular caves. Fierce Atlantic breakers crash through holes in the rocks, hurling great fountains of spray up into the sky, and the basalt column cliffs are packed with birds – colonies of kittiwakes, fulmars, razorbills and arctic terns. Reaching the sheltered natural harbour by the hamlet of Hellnar you can stand beneath the Snaefellsjokull, only 10 km (6 mi) from the snowline, on the meeting point of the ley lines that supposedly carry currents of transcendental volcanic energy round the planet.

DON'T MISS
Stone Age settlements
and ruined
boathouses on Gimsøya.

LOFOTEN ISLANDS

Norway

A cycling vacation along the Vestfjord route is a most memorable experience – new, breathtaking sights appear around every bend. White sandy beaches butt up against soaring mountain scenery. Archaeological relics and historical buildings satisfy those who seek more cultural pursuits, while for the more active there is ample opportunity to swim, hike or fish. Idyllic little villages of brightly painted wooden houses line the route as you travel from island to island. It is easy to see why locals describe this area as the real Norway and the archipelago features prominently in Nordic art, film and literature. To cover the full 450 km (281 mi) would be to undertake a journey of epic proportions; however good transport links make it possible to get to almost any part of the trail quickly.

Old market centres such as Løvøy and Grøtøy have been faithfully restored, while Steigen is a real hidden gem, teeming with innumerable historical relics. Those who seek more adventure should explore the cave system at Nordskot, while those looking for a more sedate outdoor experience can soak up the sun on the wonderful white sandy beaches near Misten.

TRONDHEIM TO BODØ

Norway

This is an incredibly beautiful journey and, when taken in summer, the light evenings ensure that you miss nothing. The train transports you through pine forests, across foothills and alongside fjords and rivers. This sea of green and blue is broken only by the occasional red wooden farmstead.

It is a curious feeling to head towards something that you will never see, but the Arctic Circle announces itself in many ways. As you head north, the light changes imperceptibly. The snow, which was confined to the mountain tops moves ever nearer, while on the track the wooden tunnels, constructed to protect the line from avalanches, grow more numerous.

As the signs of human habitation thin out and the mountains get more rugged, the landscape becomes ever more hypnotic. Thoughts turn to wildlife watching and there is every chance that you will spot a majestic reindeer in its natural surroundings. The Arctic Circle is heralded not only by a hoot of the train's whistle and two cairns on the side of the track, but by curious rituals on the train. A party spirit suddenly erupts; some partake in illicit drinking, while others share food and sometimes kissing breaks out as though it were New Year's Eve. It does feel significant to have crossed 'the line' and it is always interesting to watch the impromptu ceremonies that mark it.

The final steep descent takes you from Arctic tundra towards the blue Atlantic Ocean. This is as far north as the railway goes and as the charming town of Bodø comes into view, you are left with the feeling that you have taken more than just a train journey.

HIGHLIGHTS:
The journey over three marvellous mountain ranges. If you are lucky enough or stay long enough – the Northern Lights (September–March). Bodø Domkirke – a modern Cathedral in Gothic style. Nordlandmuseet – a museum recording local life.

WHEN TO GO:
Year round; May–August have longer days.

SPIRIT OF NORWAY

Norway

HIGHLIGHTS: The picturesque village of Flåm and the mountains around Sognefjord.
The improbably narrow Naeroyfjord.
The Folk museum at Stalheim – a celebration of Nordic traditions.

It is hard to think of a better trip anywhere in the world that can be completed inside a single day without difficulty. It could be that the Norwegians, ever mindful of their high cost of living, feel that most tourists want to get their money's worth. Several companies operate excursions that whisk you up mountain railways, along precipitous roads and then out to sea, to experience Norway's most famous feature, the iconic Fjords.

The typical journey starts with a ride on Northern Europe's highest-altitude railway line, the Bergen Railway. Exposed to harsh Atlantic weather systems, it is a huge engineering feat just to keep the line open, but you will be glad they do. The mountain views are stunning as the engine hauls you up incredibly steep inclines. From there the roller coaster ride continues as you transfer to the Flåm Railway, a 20 km (12.5 mi) journey from the hill station of Myrdal, which runs alongside the magnificent mountain scenery and tumbling waterfalls.

Beautiful though this all is, you quickly realize that it was merely the hors d'oeuvre. From Flåm the next leg of the excursion is completed by boat. Although the fjords are so obviously a symbol of Norway, one cannot tire of seeing them. These deep-sea gullies, carved by ice, take the breath away and the towering rock faces on both sides make it sometimes hard to believe that you are on water. Legendary, labyrinthine and starkly beautiful, a journey through the fjords leaves you with images that will stay with you for the rest of your life. The last leg of this most fabulous of days out takes you, by coach, along the amazingly winding mountain road to your final destination of Stalheim. From there it is possible to transfer by train back to Bergen.

BERGEN TO KIRKENES
Norway

Large cruise ships ply the 2,000 km (1,250 mi) voyage between Bergen and Kirkenes, but for sheer intimacy it's difficult to beat the more informal service offered by the 'postal' ships that serve outlying Norwegian coastal communities. This odyssey takes you around Norway's breathtakingly beautiful fjord coastline, stopping over thirty times and showing you a side of Norway inaccessible by any other means of transport. The journey begins in Bergen, a harbour town founded by the Vikings almost a millennium ago, when it quickly became a vital hub, handling trade between Northern Europe and the British Isles. As you leave the port, the splendid 14th-century gabled buildings of the seafront slowly dwindle to nothing and your eyes are drawn to the wonderfully rugged coastline.

Along the way you will see glorious fjords, precipitous mountains and quaint fishing villages before crossing the Arctic Circle. Here, as you approach the North Cape, you will experience the midnight sun in the summer. Winter offers the chance to see the Northern Lights – the ultimate light show.

HIGHLIGHTS:
The Lofoten Islands.
The Sor-Varanger Museum in Kirkenes.
Bergen – full of Hanseatic history.
The lovely town of Bodø.

For much of the journey all eyes are fixed on the starboard side, where snow-capped mountains and fjords abound. This is until the vessel meanders between the Lofoten Islands whose stark, craggy beauty hits you from both sides. The trip gives you a true appreciation of this beautiful country and how most of its population clings to the coast. When you cross the Arctic Circle the population becomes more thinly spread and the scenery ever more dramatic. The awe-inspiring Laksefjorden and Tanafjorden lie ahead, before the vessel finally reaches the sheltered port of Kirkenes.

RAUMABANEN RAILWAY
Norway

HIGHLIGHTS: The Brudesløret (the bridal veil) – a spectacular waterfall.
The Kylling turning tunnel – quite a ride.
Lesjaskogsvatnet Lake.

Now over 80 years old, the Raumabanen Railway has always unashamedly been a tourist track. Aside from a brief period when it was used to ferry around the country's gold reserves, it has operated to cater for the cruise ship trade arriving into Romsdalfjord and Åndalsnes. Whereas other railway journeys take you past wonderful sights as if by coincidence, the Raumabanen has a single purpose – to show off Norway at its finest.

This 114 km (182 mi) long marvel of 1920s engineering starts at Åndalsnes, the northern gateway to the fjords. Right from the start the views are spectacular and as the train climbs steadily, hugging the mountainside, you are treated to breathtaking views of the valley below. The imposing peaks of Romsdalhorn and Trollveggen soon dominate the skyline. You are torn between looking up or looking down as the train crosses Kyllingbrua, a startlingly high stone arched bridge which hangs above the Rauma River. It seems scarcely possible to climb any higher, but this is exactly what happens just after you pass Verma, as the train takes you through a corkscrew tunnel under the mountains. This really is a giant fairground ride for grown-ups.

As you approach Dombås, the scenery opens up offering panoramic views of this most remarkable of lands. Here you can either continue to Oslo or Trondheim or, better still, go back and do it all again.

DON'T MISS
The charming little town of Lysebotn.

LYSE ROAD
Norway

The Lyse Road was constructed as a service route for a hydroelectricity station, but that bland description reveals nothing of the experience the road has to offer. It twists and sweeps, clinging precariously to the side of a mountain that rises out of one of Norway's most beautiful fjords, making it the ultimate challenge to your driving skills and a rush like no other.

Built in the 1980s, the 44 km (27 mi) long Lyse Road stands as the critical test for those who have a zest for driving on mountain roads. All along the route you are book-ended by magnificent mountains on one side and the shimmering darkness of Lysefjord on the other – this really is like a scene from a car advertisement. Viewed from above it would seem as if someone had thrown a giant sidewinder onto the edge of a mountain. With 27 hairpin bends, the Lyse is the ultimate brake-tester. The views are always amazing, if at times a little disorienting – and the relative shallowness of parts of the fjord produces a wonderful light. Consideration for other users of the road must be a priority on this often single lane highway, but this is a top rate scuttle if you get a clear run.

HIGH COAST TRAIL

Norway

The Höga Kusten (High Coast) was formed when the region sank under a gigantic mass of ice during the last ice age. When the ice retreated, the land sprang back and it is still rising today. This has left a dynamic landscape of vertical cliffs and craggy outcrops, lined with tranquil sandy coves. Accessibility and flexibility are the watchwords for the exciting 127 km (80 mi) trail that takes you through this terrain. Divided into 13 stages, it offers the hiker a wide variety of challenges, while each stage is handily reachable by car. There are even organized self-guided tours where you can walk between lodgings, while your luggage is transported for you, allowing you to travel light.

This striking area has been given UNESCO World Heritage Site status and the hike takes you through Sweden's highest coastal area. A rich diversity of rivers, lakes, inlets and hills makes it a good test for hikers of all levels. Each day offers varying terrain as well as beautiful views out over the dark blue seas of the Gulf of Bothnia.

Starting near central Örnsköldsvik the trail presents the hiker with compact challenges. Mountains seem more climbable when you know that old-fashioned Swedish hospitality awaits you at the end of each day. Accommodation ranges from simple huts to guesthouses, but for a genuine Swedish welcome, nothing beats staying in a traditional farmhouse, several of which open their doors to tourists in summer.

WHEN TO GO:
Fully accessible from May–October.

HIGHLIGHTS:
The Skuleskogen National Park.
The imposing Slåtterdalsskrevan Gorge.
The suspension bridge near Härnösand.
Surströmming (fermented herring) – a local delicacy certain to greet you at the table at some point.

GOTA CANAL

Sweden

HIGHLIGHTS: The gorgeous lakes of Vättern and Vänern.
The Trollhätte Canal Museum
Birka Viking settlement on Björkö Island.

This marvel of 19th-century engineering stretches 190 km (118 mi) from Sjötorp on Lake Vänern to the Baltic Sea at Mem and is a real crowd-puller. Whether you are travelling on it or cycling alongside it you cannot help but be impressed by its sheer scale. Fifty-eight locks, some of them rising to an incredible 90 m (295 ft) above sea level, carry vessels through a chain of stunning natural lakes.

The canal takes you through the heart of Sweden, passing historic sites, medieval churches, attractive towns and rich green forests along the way. Many steamers ply their trade along it and this gentle form of transport has much to recommend it.

For a more intimate experience there is nothing better than hiring a boat on any one of the stunningly beautiful lakes that grace the waterway, stopping only to have a picnic lunch by the shore. Most journeys are about getting somewhere, whereas riding the Gota Canal invites you to stop and marvel at every point. It offers great fishing, kayaking, Nordic walking and a whole host of other activities. Like one big joyful playground, it has become more than the sum of its parts – a wonderful potpourri of outdoor adventure.

PADJELANTA TRAIL

Sweden

Reachable only by helicopter, the 140 km (88 mi) Padjelanta Trail is nature at its most raw. Padjelanta translates as 'the higher land' and is the summer home to the Sami people who bring vast reindeer herds here to graze. Aside from the mountains of the Sarek National Park, the landscape is relatively flat and open, consisting mainly of rolling hills with a scattering of higher peaks. Located entirely above the Arctic Circle, trees are scarce, though there is a surprising abundance of flora. There are no roads in the area, adding to the feeling of complete isolation, and accommodation is rudimentary. This trek has the motto 'as nature intended' stamped all over it. There is no electricity and water is sourced from fast running streams. Heat comes from wood fires and bathing take place outdoors.

At the centre of Padjelanta lies a succession of four wondrous lakes, the Kutjaure, Sallojaure, Vastenjaure and Virihaure. It is here that the Sami set up their summer camps and invite visitors to sample their unique way of life. You soon get to learn that communal living and interdependence are essential in this starkly beautiful setting.

YOU SHOULD KNOW

You really are cut off from most modern amenities on this trek. You should be fit and have a good knowledge of first aid and some basic survival skills.

WHEN TO GO: The train runs only in summer (June–August).

INLANDSBANAN
Sweden

The 1,067 km (667 mi) Inlandsbanan (inland railway) carries you along the spine of central northern Sweden. Built to serve the logging industry, it has now diversified to cater for the burgeoning tourist trade. The pace of the train is very laid back. As befits a Swedish operation, you are transported at an average speed of 50 kph (30 mph) through magnificent pine and birch forests.

As the train departs Mora on its northbound journey, all eyes are drawn to the deep forest where yellow wild flowers line the track. This is an ideal habitat for bear, reindeer and moose and the train will conveniently slow down if any are spotted, so be sure to have your camera primed and ready. The train passes many water features on the way but the waterfalls at Strorstupet and Helvetesfallet are the most spectacular.

While it is possible to make this gentle journey inside two days, it is best experienced in separate stages with stopovers between. Aside from the wonderful forest surroundings, there is much to enjoy on the way. The first main stop is at Östersund. More associated with winter sports, it takes on a different life in summer. A picturesque little town, it offers historic walks, a heritage museum and the splendid Lake Storsjön is nearby.

The next stop, Vilhelmina, is most worthy of exploration. Surrounded by invigorating fast flowing streams, it is home to many Sami artisans and has many naturally heated pools and an extensive cycleway.

As the train continues steadfastly towards the Arctic Circle, the forest becomes more untamed and the vista ever more beautiful. The train finally pulls in to Gällivare, a town where people successfully combine modern living with a more traditional way of life.

HIGHLIGHTS: Beaverland – a Sami craft gallery located in Vilhelmina.
Swimming in any one of the surprisingly warm mountain lakes along the way.

NORSJÖ CABLE-WAY
Sweden

HIGHLIGHTS:
The Cable-way Museum at Örträsk.
The pretty ski resort of Mensträsk.
The film of how the cableway was built – shown in the cinema in Örträsk.

Originally built in 1943 to ferry ore buried deep in the mountains, the Norsjö Cable-way seemed to have had its day by the end of the 20th century. It was then that the locals, some of whom could recall the great sacrifices that were made during its construction, rallied round to save it. At over 13 km (8 mi), it stands as the longest cable car journey in the world and now ferries tourists between Örträsk and Mensträsk, gliding at a majestic 10 kph (6.25 mph) high above the Västerbotten countryside.

Fourteen cabins ply their trade in each direction, offering the chance to enter a fragile woodland environment accessible by no other means.

Reindeer and moose are common sights and, unlike other forms of transport, the relative quietness of the cable cars does not seem to disturb them too much. As you pass each concrete mast – there are 73 in all – you can't help but marvel at the amazing feat of engineering that produced this modern wonder.

It is a strange experience to be held aloft for so long and the cable-way provides a wonderful bird's-eye view of this splendid environment. After the initial jolt into action, the cable-way provides a real Hansel and Gretel experience, soaring above lakes and forests through a dizzying expanse. All passengers have a window seat and the compact cabins have an intimate feel, each housing just four people. In summer, birdsong provides the perfect soundtrack to your voyage, while in winter snow and ice cling to the trees as if they were sculpted that way.

HIGHLIGHTS: Sønderborg Castle overlooking the dramatic Flensborg Fjord.
Koldinghus – a beautifully restored castle.

THE EAST COAST ROUTE
Denmark

At 650 km (406 mi), the East Coast Route is the longest and most spectacular cycling route in Denmark. Stretching from Skagen to Sønderborg, the route meanders through pretty Danish countryside, taking the rider along fjords, round bays and peninsulas.
The towns that line the route are rich in tradition and culture. Charming fishing villages are to be found along the northern section, while to the south grand castles and sumptuous manor houses grace the rolling landscape.
Of all the towns along the route, Århus, Denmark's graceful and welcoming second city, must be singled out for special mention. Nowhere in Denmark will you find a greater concentration of artists, museums, musicians and historically significant sites.

HÆRVEJEN OXEN TRAIL

Denmark

HIGHLIGHTS: The historic town of Vejen – the only major settlement on the route.
Hairulf Stone – a splendid inscribed standing stone.

If roads could speak this one would recount tales like few others. Throughout history this route, which starts just the other side of the German border and runs down the spine of Jutland, has borne the weight of Danish hopes – as well as their livestock. A source of great pride for modern day Denmark, many of its secrets still lie by the roadside, yet to be discovered. It is probable that the route has been trodden for millennia and an air of historical significance hangs over every part of it.

For much of the way it seems little more than a dirt track, while other sections are more like modern roads. Famous for its magnificent stone bridges, the Hærvejen is ideal for hiking or biking vacations. Whichever mode of transport you choose, you will want to stop and marvel at sights both ancient and modern. Runic stones, burial mounds and monoliths line the route and offer cryptic clues to the regions antediluvian past. More recent history is displayed in the German World War I bunkers and the Froslev Concentration Camp, where Danish Communists were imprisoned during World War II.

The road's elevation of some 92 m (300 ft) in places, gives you excellent wide views of the countryside and the ridge forms the source of Denmark's two longest rivers, the Skjernå and the Gudenå. All in all, this is a journey which can be relished as a trek through the tranquil Jutish countryside, or studied deeply like an ancient text. The choice is yours.

COPENHAGEN WATERBUS

Denmark

HIGHLIGHTS:
Frihedsmuseet – a museum dedicated to those who resisted the Nazis in World War II.
Little Mermaid statue – a perfectly formed landmark.
Trekoner Fortress – an imposing historical monument.
Christianborg Palace – a former royal palace, now home to the Danish government.

Copenhagen is one of Europe's truly great cities. With its perfect blend of old and new, it is a city that demands to be explored. While most cities are only slowly waking up to the fact that their waterways are a vital resource for life, as well as for trade, Copenhagen has always known it. Most of its great sights are visible and accessible from the water and there is no better way to travel around it than by waterbus.

This hop-on, hop-off service calls at all of Copenhagen's major tourist attractions, as well as providing an important transport link for those who like to travel at a more relaxed pace. Several operators ply the route and offer up to 16 drop-off points. So with ticket and timetable in hand, it is time to climb aboard and investigate this wonderfully compact city. With forward planning, it's possible to stroll along the world famous Tivoli Gardens before having lunch in Nyhavn, the old sailors' quarter which brims with fabulous cafés. The afternoon can then be spent lapping up the cultural delights of the Frihedsmuseet and the Amalienborg Palace, before visiting the artists' district of Christiania. This can all be rounded off with a visit to the city's renowned Opera House.

The choice is really yours on this most flexible of tours. It is an excellent way to get to know your way around Copenhagen and for those who already know the city well, it affords a new perspective on this most magnificent of urban landscapes.

HIGHLIGHTS: The view of the bridge from either shore.
Copenhagen – a compact city, worth a day or two's exploration.
Malmö – a city of green open spaces and a pretty town centre.
The university town of Lund – the jewel of southern Sweden.

OVER THE ÖRESUND BRIDGE
Denmark

The people of the southern Swedish territory of Skåne have more in common with the Danes than they do with their fellow countrymen in the north. Even the relatively flat rolling landscape is remarkably similar. It is therefore no surprise to learn that these two areas were linked by land some 7,000 years ago, and now, once again, by a wonder of modern construction, to rival that of the Channel Tunnel.

As you depart Copenhagen, the Öresund has a surprise for you as it starts its life as a tunnel, to avoid interfering with the busy airport. Soon it emerges from the water, as a majestic bridge, providing fantastic views.

The crossing has really opened up this area of southern Sweden and re-attached it to the mainland. Once across, the opportunities to explore are numerous. Outside of the cities the most popular destination is the area around the Falsterbo Peninsula. With its long sandy beaches it draws hikers and sun-seekers from far and wide and transport links connect well with the bridge.

THE KING'S ROAD TRAIL
Finland

HIGHLIGHTS: The Gallen-Kallela Museum – a beautiful building housing a good museum.
Hvitträsk Villa – a fine example of modern architecture.

The Western King's Road that runs from Helsinki to Pohj, takes you on a 100 km (62.5 mi) journey through an area of great natural beauty as well as offering up a superb blend of old and new architecture.

Cycling fits best with the tempo of the region and there is a well-maintained cycle route with good signage. The traveller is taken through forests of silver birch and fir trees, alongside the shimmering Baltic Sea, through picturesque towns and on towards the Russian border.

The King's Road offers a wonderful insight into traditional Finnish life and the route is filled with history and culture. Finland has always been a buffer between east and west and the influences on people, food and places are displayed fully on this trek.

This area has long been a summer playground for Scandinavians and nowhere is this better shown than in Loviisa – with its delightful beaches, framed by subtly coloured wooden buildings, it is a seaside resort with few peers.

THE HETTA-PALLAS WINTER SKI TRAIL
Finland

HIGHLIGHTS: Fell Lapland Nature Centre.
Chance to see the Northern Lights.
The husky farm at Muonio, a short side trip from the trail.

The 55 km (34 mi) Hetta-Pallas Winter Trail is the Finnish section of the 800 km (500 mi) pan-Scandinavian Nordkalottleden Trail. The Trail passes through the Pallas-Yllästunturi National Park in Lapland, an area of fast-flowing rivers, turquoise lakes, lush forests and glacier-topped mountains. It is not an overly demanding trail for the experienced cross-country skier, as it follows mostly the lower slopes, apart from one ravine section where it travels above the tree-line. In summer, the Hetta-Pallas Hiking Trail covers roughly the same route, though at higher altitudes, as the winter trails are too wet to be hiked in summer. The Trail goes through a ravishingly beautiful landscape of birch-clothed fell highlands and steep-sided ravines but, while the area is utterly wild, the trek can easily be undertaken by any reasonably fit and eager walker. Free wilderness huts are available all year round, though they can get crowded at the most popular times, so it is always wise to take your own tent. In this land of the midnight sun, you can, of course, hike all night and find a place to rest in the morning.

HIGHLIGHTS: The 200 or so lakes that surround Tampere.
Helsinki Station – a green trimmed Art-Deco style masterpiece.
Central Museum of Labour – a quirky museum full of interest.

HELSINKI TO TAMPERE
Finland

If you can tear yourself away from the cultural and architectural delights of Helsinki, the train journey to Tampere is one of the real gems of European travel. This sparsely populated land is a place of great natural beauty, where the modern sits well with the traditional. Summer brings never-ending daylight, while the winter landscape has an ethereal elegance often lit up by the hauntingly beautiful Northern Lights. As the majestic red and white train glides through the open countryside, passing lakes fringed by forest, you cannot help but be struck by the serenity of it all. It is hard to think of any other intercity journey in the developed world that passes through landscape of such untamed beauty. The only complaint one could have is that the journey is over so soon. The memory of sumptuous lakes, verdant forests and grand farmsteads is one that will linger long in the mind. The next time you are on the train to work, you will be tempted to close your eyes and try to imagine that you are back on the Helsinki-Tampere Express.

THE POST BOAT ROUTE ACROSS THE KVARKEN

Finland

YOU SHOULD KNOW

A good level of seamanship is required to undertake this trip. If you do not have the skills, it is advisable to engage the services of someone who does.

The passage across the Kvarken has always been inextricably linked with taxation. It is a long way around the Gulf of Bothnia and, in the 17th century, King Gustav II bestowed on the residents of Björkö the privilege of conveying goods over the water. In return they were excused military service and given tax breaks. Even up until the late 20th century, these waters were busy with vessels plying the lucrative duty-free trade. All this has now gone and the Kvarken has returned to a quiet normality.

Björkö, at the head of a handsome archipelago, still makes its living from the sea. The relatively shallow waters of the Kvarken are rich with fish and this is reflected in the local diet. Great hiking is to be found on this island group and all paths inevitably lead to the sea; as you gaze over the Kvarken an urge to cross it awakens in you.

It is still possible, by private charter, to make this historic crossing and as you set out, the full beauty of the island chain becomes apparent. Soon you are in open sea and the glimmering waters of the gulf surround

you, until the imposing landscape of Sweden's High Coast heaves into view. The traditional landing for this journey is Holmön, an ideal place to end a perfect voyage.

Each year, just after the midsummer festival (late June), these superb waters spring to life. A flotilla of white-sailed boats sets out in a faithful re-enactment of the original post boat run – it's a magnificent spectacle to behold and a wonderful event to participate in.

WHEN TO GO:
The relatively mild waters of the Kvarken mean that it is navigable nearly all year round. The worst weather is from November–March.

HIGHLIGHTS:
Kvarken Archipelago – the first UNESCO World Heritage Site in Finland.
The picturesque town of Björköby (on Björkö).
Holmön Island – a nature reserve and the sunniest area of Sweden.

THE CURONIAN SPIT TRAIL

Lithuania

The Curonian Spit is a 98 km (60 mi) long sand bar, a remarkable natural phenomenon created by the combined power of the sea and the wind in a continual cycle of sedimentation and erosion. It is an extraordinarily insubstantial landscape, continually battered by the howling gales of the Baltic Sea, a natural sea-wall of giant shifting dunes up to 60 m (200 ft) tall, held together by pine and birch forests. On its leeward side, it encloses the Curonian Lagoon, acting as a windbreak to ensure a millpond-like calm, in startling contrast to the open sea.

The Spit is less than 4 km (just over 2 mi) across at its widest point and 350 m (0.25 mi) at its narrowest. Only the northern 52 km (33 mi) is in Lithuania; the southern section is Russian territory.

From the old port town of Klaipeda you take a ferry across the narrow channel at the mouth of the Curonian Lagoon to the northern tip of the Spit. From here a bike path runs southwards to Nida, the main town. There are several other picturesque hamlets along the way with old churches and traditional brown- and blue-painted tiled-roofed fishermen's cottages, mostly now inhabited by artists and writers. You find yourself roaming through an eerily beautiful, remote land, crossing endless white-sand beaches and pine-forested dunes, passing old cemeteries where graves are marked by wooden crosses and outdated road signs for half-remembered villages that have been swallowed by the sand. The only sounds are the wind, the sea and the call of birds. A bike ride or walk along the length of the Spit is a wonderfully life-enhancing experience, giving you a heightened awareness of the power of the elements and the fragility of the environment.

HIGHLIGHTS:
Witches Hill – woodland path with beautifully carved wooden sculptures of mythological figures.
Great Dune of Parnidis 52 m (170 ft) high.
Dead dunes near Parvalka – where a whole village was swallowed up.
Thomas Mann's summerhouse and museum.
Traditional weathervanes – unique to the Curonian Spit.

THE BALTIC TO CRIMEA

Russia

HIGHLIGHTS:
St Petersburg – the Hermitage.
Moscow – the Kremlin and Red Square.
Lviv – Ploshcha Rynok, 16th-century market square, a World Heritage Site.
Odessa – Potemkin Steps.
Yalta – Chekhov's house.

WHEN TO GO:
May, when the spring flowers are at their height.

For anyone in love with the romance of train travel, a journey by rail across Russia, Belarus, Moldova and Ukraine, through cities that have affected the course of European history for more than a millennium, is an eye-opening experience. This vibrant region of Europe, which for the greater part of the 20th century has been inaccessible, is buzzing with a sense of hard-won freedom and a youthful appetite for the future. From the fabulous imperial city of St Petersburg, take a train down to Moscow then travel westwards through the eerie haunting beauty of the Belarus steppe to Minsk, an old-style Soviet city that now has a certain nostalgic charm, and then to Brest on the Polish border to visit the stupendous Soviet World War II fortress. Travelling southwards into Ukraine, the largest country in Europe, you cross a timeless land of black-earthed wheat fields, copses of silver birch, flower-strewn pastures, and ancient villages to stop at the wondrous World Heritage City of Lviv. Carry on heading south through the startlingly picturesque but little-visited wine country of Moldova – a landscape of rolling hills, tranquil lakes and whitewashed villages – to Odessa, a magnificent Black Sea city founded by Catherine the Great. Next stop is Yalta, a delightful resort on the beautiful Crimean coast and site of the Livadia Palace where Churchill, Roosevelt and Stalin held their fateful 1945 conference to discuss the post-war shape of Europe. Go to the naval base of Sevastopol, steeped in the history of the Crimean War, and visit Bakhchysaray, the 16th-century capital of the Crimean khanate. Finally, catch a train northwards to bring your journey to an end in the beautiful ancient city of Kiev in the heart of Ukraine.

GOLDEN RING TOWNS

Russia

WORTH A DETOUR:

Rostov – 17th-century
kremlin, an architectural
masterpiece.

The Golden Ring is, a 700 km (440 mi) circular tour of the ancient provincial towns and cities northeast of Moscow. You will see kremlins (fortresses), castles, monasteries, churches and cathedrals dating from the 12th to the 17th century.

The journey makes a refreshing change from the noise and pollution of Moscow. Provincial life is surprisingly un-westernized and you will see a completely different side to Russian culture as you travel from town to town through tranquil countryside of cattle pastures, birch forests, fields and lakes.

There are seven main towns on the route. Nearest to Moscow is Vladimir, the 12th-century Russian capital. Travel on northwards to the rustic tourist town of Suzdal on the Kamenka River, filled with monuments; then to Kostromo on the River Volga, famous for the 16th-century Ipatievsky Monastery. Next is the historic city of Yaroslavl and, heading back towards Moscow, the sleepy little towns of Rostov Velikiy, once known as the 'eternal city', and picturesque Pereslavl-Zalesskiy on Lake Pleshcheveyo. The final Ring-town is Sergiev Posad, the 'Vatican' of the Russian Orthodox Church – a famous pilgrimage centre. The Holy Trinity Cathedral's breathtaking blue and golden domes provide a fitting finale to a journey that casts an entirely new light on the historical fabric underlying this influential corner of Europe.

THE TRANS-SIBERIAN RAILWAY

Russia

DON'T MISS
Ulan-Ude –
historic Siberian town.

The legendary Trans-Siberian Railway is the greatest train journey in the world, an epic endurance test of nearly 10,000 km (more than 6,000 mi) across the vast Siberian steppe. The Trans-Mongolian line across the Gobi Desert to Beijing is the usual tourist route. It is the shortest and most scenic. The classic journey from Moscow to Vladivostok is an entirely different experience. Few people travel the entire length of the line and fewer are foreigners. However, it gives you an authentic experience of this vast country. For those who have the stamina to travel without a break, it is still a relief that the train stops every few hours so you can stretch your legs and stock up on food from the platform vendors. For the first three days, whichever destination you aim for, you cross kilometre upon kilometre of apparently boundless Siberian steppe broken only by intermittent industrialized cityscapes. Whether you end up in Vladivostok or Beijing, the experience will provide you with lasting memories of an incredible journey. This is an epic trip to be undertaken purely for its own sake – for the joy of travelling.

HIGHLIGHTS: Moscow Canal.
Yaroslavl – one of Russia's oldest cities.
Kizhi Pogost – island of World Heritage medieval wooden buildings.
Uglich – churches.

THE VOLGA-BALTIC WATERWAY

Russia

The most memorable means of travelling between Moscow and St Petersburg is a river cruise along the Volga-Baltic Waterway, an extraordinarily complex network of canals, rivers and inland seas covering a total distance of 1,125 km (700 mi) and linking the mighty Volga, the longest river in Europe, to the Baltic Sea. Having moved his capital to the Baltic, Peter the Great dreamed of sailing from his new imperial city back to Moscow in the heart of the Empire. Construction began in 1709 and continued throughout the 18th and 19th centuries, making it possible to sail all the way from St Petersburg on the Gulf of Finland to Astrakhan on the Caspian Sea. With the completion of the 128 km (80 mi) Moscow-Volga Canal in 1937, Russia's capital was finally linked to this intricate system of canals and rivers.

You sail the Moscow Canal to the River Volga, through the Rybinsk Reservoir and the Mariinsk canal system, around Lake Onega and onto the River Svir to the southern coast of Lake Lagoda, the largest lake in Europe, finally connecting with the River Neva, having passed through 21 locks on your way. The tourist cruisers take a roundabout scenic route with wonderful natural and historic sights – Yaroslavl, a 'Golden Ring' city on the banks of the Volga; the red, blue and golden-domed churches of Uglich; the 14th-century Kirillo-Belozersky monastery; the ancient wooden buildings of Kizhi Pogost; the scenic River Svir and beautiful coastline of Lake Lagoda. Finally, you arrive at St Petersburg, a city of haunting magnificence.

HIGHLIGHTS: Kiev – Monastery of the Caves; 11th-century caves and tunnels.
Yalta – Livadia Palace, Swallows Nest Castle and Chekhov's house.

RIVER DNIEPER TO THE BLACK SEA
Ukraine

The third longest river in Europe, only outdone by the Volga and the Danube, the Dnieper is the lifeblood of Ukraine: vital water source for a country dependent on agriculture, massive hydro-electric power generator, and – not least – commercial corridor, transporting an endless stream of river traffic for the ten months of the year that it is ice-free. Passenger boats regularly ply this majestic river on an unhurried journey between Kiev, the 'Mother of Cities', and Odessa, the 'Pearl of the Black Sea', cruising through the heart of the largest country in Europe – a country steeped in a turbulent history of war and suffering that has somehow, against all odds, retained its distinctive culture and spirit.

After seeing the sights in the 9th-century city of Kiev, voyage southwards past scenic forested ravines to Dnipropetrovsk, an old fortress town set in green hills, now a major commercial centre; cruise past the Dneproges Dam – a tour de force of design, and stop off at Zaporizhzhya, home of the Cossacks, the legendary warrior horsemen who dominated the southern steppes for four hundred years.

From the wetlands and backwaters of the river delta around Kherson, the boat strikes out along the glorious Mediterranean-like Black Sea coast of the Crimea to Sevastopol, the historic site of the Charge of the Light Brigade; and Yalta, where the Tsar had his holiday palace and Tolstoy and Chekhov spent their summers. Backtrack across the Black Sea to end your voyage at Odessa, fabled 19th-century city of terraces.

SETTLE-CARLISLE RAILWAY
United Kingdom

WORTH A DETOUR: Delightful Appleby Station – built by the Midland Railway as one of the major stations on the line – spot the water tower and crane that service steam specials.

This was the last great main rail line to be constructed in England, completed in 1876 by the Midland Railway Company, whose builders overcame major natural obstacles to create 116 km (72 mi) of track frequently described as 'the most scenic rail journey in England'. With 14 tunnels and 17 major viaducts a route is created through the magnificent Yorkshire Dales, on through the lush, gently rolling hills of the Eden Valley with its charming villages and traditional market towns to Carlisle, gateway to Scotland.

The full journey actually begins in Leeds, with its connection to the intercity rail network. Also, the so-called 'Lancashire Dales Rail' service runs on many Sundays between the beginning of May and mid-October, offering a through trip from Blackpool via Preston and Blackburn on to Settle and Carlisle. This has associated guided walks and coach trips from certain trains to beautiful parts of the North Pennines and Yorkshire Dales. For those drawn by the romance of bygone travel, charter trains with vintage carriages – pulled by classic steam locomotives – regularly do the Settle to Carlisle run (usually as part of a longer journey). But whichever way you choose to go, it will be an experience to treasure.

THE FERRY TO ORKNEY

United Kingdom

DON'T MISS
The famous waterside stack known as The Old Man of Hoy (take the Scrabster crossing for a sea view).

Sometimes the journey's the thing, other times it's the destination that counts – but when you sail to Orkney you get the best of both. This group of 67 islands is off Scotland's northeastern tip and 20 are inhabited, with most people living on Mainland, the largest island and home of Kirkwall, the administrative centre. Orkney is well served by air, but the way to go is by ferry for a scenic journey on the ocean wave (which, be warned, can be quite high). There is a choice of services.

From Aberdeen (to Shetland, calling at Kirkwall four days a week) a car ferry follows the coast past Peterhead, the gas terminal at St Fergus, Rattray Head lighthouse, Fraserburgh and Kinnaird Head, before heading out to sea. Land is sighted at Wick on the Caithness coast, before Duncansby Head lighthouse and Orkney – passing South Ronaldsay and East Mainland before docking in the Bay of Kirkwall. The most scenic is the 90 minute crossing from Scrabster, near Thurso. The large MV Hamnavoe starts from the low cliffs near Holborn Head lighthouse, before crossing the Pentland Firth, where the Atlantic meets the North Sea head-on. Landfall is at Rora Head on the island of Hoy.

WORTH A DETOUR: Goathland Station – recognize it from regular appearances in the TV drama series 'Heartbeat' (Aidensfield) and Harry Potter films (Hogsmeade).

NORTH YORKSHIRE MOORS RAILWAY

United Kingdom

Lovers of steam will be beguiled by this 29 km (18 mi) line, especially if they also appreciate the Yorkshire Moors. For those who just love wonderful landscapes, it is possible to travel the line in a train pulled by a heritage diesel loco – but how much better to take one of the steam trains that not only delivers scenery, but also nostalgic transport back to a bygone era?

The North Yorkshire Moors Railway (NYMR) runs from Pickering to Grosmont, from whence onward travel to Whitby is now available by steam train.

Pickering station has been restored to 1937 condition, with wonderful period detail. Levisham is in pretty Newton Dale, two miles from the village it serves, and now represents a small North Eastern Railway station from around 1910. Newton Dale Halt is a remote request stop in splendid countryside, mainly used by walkers. Goathland was built in 1865 and is almost unchanged, now restored as a country station from the 1920s. Grosmont represents the British Rail era of the 1950s, where through travellers change for the charming old fishing port of Whitby.

The NYMR timetable is complex, in that not all trains from Pickering to Grosmont have an onward connection to Whitby. However, special Grosmont Day Rover or Whitby Day Rover tickets allow unlimited travel all day, permitting the journey to be broken by anyone who wishes to explore interesting diversions along the way.

LAKE WINDERMERE

United Kingdom

HIGHLIGHTS:

Windermere Steamboats Museum at Bowness, with a collection of craft that tell the story of lake cruising from its inception in the 19th century – don't miss Beatrix Potter's rowboat.

Brockhole Visitor Centre between Windermere and Ambleside, in a mansion with lovely gardens and lake frontage, showcasing the attractions of England's largest National Park.

England's largest natural lake, set within Cumbria's Lake District National Park, has been a popular holiday destination since 1847, when a branch of the Kendal and Windermere Railway was opened. This magical lake set amidst spectacular fells beneath a big sky has never lost its appeal, surely attracting more visitors now than ever it did during its Victorian and Edwardian heyday.

Windermere is a ribbon lake, some 17 km (10.5 mi) long and never more than 1.6 km (1 mi) wide, stretching from Newby Bridge in the south to Ambleside in the north. Ambleside is one of two towns on the lake, the other being Bowness-on-Windermere, halfway along the east bank. Strangely, the town of Windermere does not itself have lake frontage, though it has effectively merged with Bowness, which does. Although there is a road along the eastern shore of the lake, the best way to enjoy Windermere and its impressive surrounds is from the water.

There are any number of cruises on offer from three main departure points – Lakeside in the south, Bowness in the middle and Waterhead (Ambleside) in the north. A wide variety of options are offered, including travelling from end to end, a return journey from Lakeside to Bowness, a circular islands cruise from Bowness, a return journey from Waterhead to Bowness or circular lake tour from any departure point. All types of cruise boats operate, from large lake steamers, through mid-sized modern launches to smaller traditional wooden launches… and even the occasional vintage steam launch. It is certainly a busy stretch of water in summer, but all that marine hustle and bustle – set against the majestic grandeur of the unchanging fells and mountains – seems part of Lake Windermere's timeless charm. Afterwards, visit the Aquarium of the Lakes, a unique freshwater aquarium on the southern shore of Windermere that recreates lake life from around the world.

GLASGOW TO MALLAIG
United Kingdom

HIGHLIGHTS:
Britain's only railway show shed, at Cruach Cutting shortly before the WHL's high point at Corrous Summit on vast Rannoch Moor.
At Banervie, where the WHL meets the Caledonian Canal – the amazing series of canal locks known as Neptune's Staircase.

Scotland's West Highland Line is a mighty fine line, especially for lovers of dramatic scenery. The WHL begins at Glasgow's Queen Street Station and takes a while to get going scenically – trundling through suburbs, Dumbarton and Helensburgh before turning north for Garelochhead. It gets up to landscape speed as it passes along the northwestern shore of Loch Lomond and reaches Crianlarich, where a western branch goes to Oban while the northern branch crosses wild Rannoch Moor before arriving at Fort William.

There beginneth one of the world's great scenic railway journeys, starting near Britain's highest mountain (Ben Nevis), crossing Britain's longest inland waterway (Caledonian Canal), visiting Britain's most westerly mainland station (Arisaig), passing Britain's deepest freshwater loch (Loch Morar), Scotland's whitest beach (Morar) and arriving at Europe's deepest sea loch (Loch Nevis). The train follows the rugged coastline, passing through many tunnels and small stations before reaching Mallaig, 265 km (165 mi) from Glasgow.

It is also possible to marry the romance of steam with that overdose of magnificent Highland scenery, by taking a trip from Fort William to Mallaig and back on The Jacobite, a special service that runs on weekdays between mid-May and mid-October, with added weekend services in July and August. This not only offers the Highland sights, but also the evocative sound of steam... plus a leisurely stop at Glenfinnan where Bonnie Prince Charlie raised his standard in 1745 and time to explore the thriving fishing community of Mallaig.

LONDON TO EDINBURGH ON THE FLYING SCOTSMAN
United Kingdom

WORTH A DETOUR: The King Edward VII Bridge crossing over the River Tyne, between the iconic Metro Bridge and Redheugh Bridge.

The Flying Scotsman is a rail route, train service and world-famous locomotive, in that chronological order. The route is the 627 km (390 mi) East Coast mainline from London King's Cross to Edinburgh Waverley, created by the combined efforts of three different Victorian railway companies.

The train service is the modern incarnation of one that began in 1862 as the Special Scotch Express, a daily train each way simultaneously leaving at 10.00. Renamed The Flying Scotsman in 1924, it began a non-stop run between the two capitals in 1928, a journey that reached luxury heights in the 1930s with on-board hairdressing, cocktail bar and a fine restaurant. World War II ended that, but the service survived rail nationalization in 1948, with journey times falling steadily as first diesels and then electric locomotives were introduced. After privatization in 1994, the Flying Scotsman was seen as a flagship asset and it continues running to this day.

The locomotive was built in 1923 and named The Flying Scotsman in 1924, to gain publicity for the newly acquired and re-titled service of the same name launched by the London Midland & Scottish Railway.

WORTH A DETOUR: The Grey Cairns of Camster – ancient burial chambers that are remarkably well preserved, and almost at journey's end!

LAND'S END TO JOHN O' GROATS
United Kingdom

This is the longest place-to-place journey in Britain. The start point at Land's End is the signpost giving the choice of New York or John o' Groats (most people choosing the latter) and the first decision is whether to leave the West Country by using the main A30 road, or choose one of the longer, hillier and scenic routes on minor roads.

After Cornwall and Devon it's into Somerset, through the Cotswolds towards Birmingham and then Staffordshire, where a strategic decision must be made – head due north on the western route, through the Lake District, or tack across to the Peak District and the eastern route through the Yorkshire Dales. Whichever route is chosen, the intrepid cyclist will cross the line of Hadrian's Wall into the Scottish Lowlands, continue through the scenic Borders and on towards Glasgow (western route) or Edinburgh (eastern route). From there the western route takes in Fort William and the eastern route Aviemore and Inverness (capital of the Highlands) before they converge around Dingwall for the final run up the coast. There aren't too many alternative roads in the Highlands, but those few are all scenic. John o' Groats is a small village and harbour, and nearby Dunnet Head is actually the most northerly point in mainland Britain.

DON'T MISS
The ruined but impressive
White Castle close to
the village of Llantilio.

OFFA'S DYKE PATH
United Kingdom

Offa was the Anglo-Saxon King of Mercia, the great English kingdom that thrived in the Dark Ages, who ruled from 757 to 796. Offa's Dyke is a massive earthwork that roughly follows some of the modern English-Welsh border – but why it was created remains a mystery.

It certainly required effort, being some 103 km (64 mi) long, from Rushock Hill in the south to Llanfynydd in the north – not as once thought stretching from 'sea to sea', completely separating two countries. It consists of a ditch on the Welsh side and rampart on the English side, but patently couldn't be defended like that other great boundary construct, Hadrian's Wall. The best explanation is that the famously belligerent Offa built it because he could. The message to potential enemies was 'look how powerful I am because I can build such a mighty earthwork, so trespass across it at your peril'.

Be that as it may, today Offa's Dyke Path is one of the most attractive National Trails, passing through some of Britain's most beautiful countryside. Although following the full length of Offa's Dyke, it is actually longer than the original, running for 285 km (177 mi) from the Severn Estuary near Chepstow through the tranquil Welsh Marches and on to Prestatyn on Liverpool Bay. Anyone who hikes the Dyke will see high moorland, wide river valleys, lush fields and ancient woodland. Along the way there are historic towns and lonely villages, castles and hill forts, churches and abbeys, together with rich and varied flora and fauna.

WAINWRIGHT'S COAST TO COAST WALK
United Kingdom

WORTH A DETOUR Stopping off at Grosmont Station towards the end of the walk – have a refreshing cup of tea and inspect steam engines being restored by the North Yorkshire Moors Railway.

This 305 km (190 mi) walking trail crosses northern Britain from the Irish Sea to the North Sea. On the way it passes through three National Parks (Lake District, Yorkshire Dales and North Yorkshire Moors) that together offer some of England's finest upland scenery.

The Walk is generally undertaken from west to east, starting at the sea cliffs of St Bees on the Cumbrian coast. The first port of call is the Lake District with its incomparable mountain scenery – and plenty of steep paths. After Shap the route crosses undulating farmland until it reaches the Yorkshire Dales at Kirkby Stephen, after which the hilly terrain returns, though the Pennines are not quite so demanding as Lakeland mountains. After Richmond there is another level march across the Vale of Mowbray to Ingleby Cross and from there on to the North Yorkshire Moors. This undulating last stretch over heather-covered hills leads to the North Sea and on to the bustling fishing village of Robin Hood's Bay.

PEDDARS WAY & NORFOLK COAST PATH

United Kingdom

HIGHLIGHTS: Historic Castle Acre with the extensive ruins of a priory and the castle that gives the village its name. The Wells to Morston stretch of the Norfolk Coast Path.

Peddars Way follows the line of an old Roman Road built in AD 61 to help subdue those troublesome Iceni and their warrior queen Boudicca. The peaceful way-marked route is a pleasing mix of footpaths, tracks and country lanes that runs through Breckland, a uniquely East Anglian area of forest, heathland and shallow river valleys, before crossing rolling wooded farmland to the sea.

Many people walk the whole length of this atmospheric route along North Norfolk's heritage coast, within an Area of Outstanding Natural Beauty.

There are sights such as low clay cliffs that are under constant assault by the restless sea, abundant wildlife, windswept salt marshes punctuated by gutters and creeks, shifting sand dunes, wide beaches and pretty coastal villages notable for their brick-and-flint buildings, quaint quays and harbours. Finally, at Cromer (famed for crabs and classic pier) the journey ends.

PEMBROKESHIRE COAST PATH

United Kingdom

HIGHLIGHTS:
One of the finest Neolithic dolmens (burial chambers) in Wales – Carreg Sampson. The glorious medieval Cathedral and Bishop's Palace at enchanting St Davids – Britain's (and surely the world's) smallest city. Unspoiled fishing villages.

If someone said 'I'm off for a stroll from St Dogmaels to Amroth' few people would know what they were talking about – but those who love wild, unspoiled coastline should find out fast. For those places are at opposite ends of one of Britain's best long-distance walks, the 299 km (186 mi) Pembrokeshire Coast Path in West Wales. For much of the wilder northern section the Path keeps to clifftops, giving marvellous views of beaches, cliffs and offshore islands, plus abundant seabird life. In spring, there is the added bonus of colourful wildflowers. The section from St Dogmaels to St Davids includes the rocky bay of Witches' Cauldron, Whitesands Bay (from where St Patrick set sail for Ireland), the Norman castle at historic Newport, the old harbour at Lower Fishguard and Porthclais (where St David was baptized).

The southern section is gentler, passing along the shores of Milford Haven's great natural harbour (teeming with birdlife) before reaching some of the finest beaches in Wales – Freshwater West, Broad Haven South, Barafundle Bay and Freshwater East. There's also plenty of commanding cliff scenery, especially numerous stacks and arches on the Castlemartin Peninsula.

LONDON RIVER JOURNEY

United Kingdom

DON'T MISS
A ride on the riverside
London Eye for
a bird's-eye view of the city.

Nearly 2 million commuters (a number that is rising fast) now travel to work on London's river each year, using stylish catamarans with on-board coffee bars, airline-type seats and bicycle racks for those who pedal on from boat to office. These frequent scheduled services run up the River Thames from Woolwich (which has a free car ferry across the river to North Woolwich) to Waterloo and Embankment in Central London, and downriver from Putney via Chelsea Harbour and Embankment to Blackfriars. Taking both trips will allow the voyager to see many famous sights.

However, there are some 25 major piers and terminals along the London river, and commuter services are supplemented by a wide variety of tourist boats, most of which offer a running commentary on the sights and history of this vibrant capital city as the Thames weaves its way through the heart of historic London and the chosen journey unfolds.

Some of these sightseeing services extend the distances that can be travelled on the river down to the Thames Flood Barrier and up to Kew (for the world-famous Kew Botanical Gardens) and Hampton Court (Henry VIII's wonderful palace).

LONDON MARKET WALK

United Kingdom

WORTH A DETOUR:
Electric Cinema, Portobello
Road – London's oldest
working cinema.

After a bit of dawdling among the picturesque antique shops, clobber stalls and costermongers' barrows of Portobello, stroll northwards through Golborne Road flea market, where old London scrap dealers, Portuguese pastry shops and Moroccan food stalls vie for trade, and head towards the Grand Union Canal.

Walk eastwards along the towpath and, suddenly, the abandoned concrete cityscape morphs into graceful Victorian villas, brightly painted narrowboats and weeping-willow trees of Little Venice.

Where the Grand Union ends, at the shiny steel wharves and gleaming commercial buildings of Paddington Basin, the Regent's Canal begins. Pick your way across the grimy Edgware Road under railway bridges to emerge into fairyland: gleaming white stucco Regency palaces, rolling lawns and curtains of greenery trailing into the water. Follow the path to skirt Primrose Hill; cut through London Zoo, and along the backs of elegant early Victorian terraces. Finally, dive into Camden Lock, the hippest street market in London.

FERRY ACROSS THE MERSEY

United Kingdom

WORTH A DETOUR:
An extended cruise up the Mersey and Manchester Ship Canal for those interested in this historic waterway.

The River Mersey runs for just 113 km (70 mi) from Stockport in Greater Manchester to the sea in Liverpool Bay, for some of its length now merged with the Manchester Ship Canal.

Its wide estuary is constricted as the Mersey passes between Liverpool and Birkenhead. There, it may be crossed by two road tunnels and a railway tunnel dating back to 1880 – but by far the most famous way of crossing the river is on the Mersey ferry, which runs from George's Landing Stage at the Pier Head in Liverpool to the terminals of Woodside in Birkenhead (opposite the Pier Head) and Seacombe in Wallasey on the Wirral Peninsula bank. There are triangular River Explorer Cruises with informative commentary that take in all three terminals and some of the river towards New Brighton.

But the real experience is the simple Ferry Cross the Mersey, as immortalized in the song by Gerry and the Pacemakers as part of the 1960s explosion of musical creativity in Liverpool known as Merseybeat. The self-same ferries that inspired it are still running today: Royal Iris of the Mersey, Snowdrop and Royal Daffodil (originally Mountwood, Woodchurch and Overchurch after post-war housing developments in Birkenhead when launched in the late 1950s, all renamed after major refits in the 1990s). Ride one of these on the short river crossing and enjoy a wonderful view of the thing that made Liverpool great – its waterfront.

DON'T MISS
The fabulous castle and medieval buildings of Warwick.

LONDON TO BIRMINGHAM BY GRAND UNION CANAL

United Kingdom

Once an important commercial artery endlessly travelled by barge families who lived in cramped quarters aboard narrowboats that transported a huge variety of goods, the Grand Union Canal fell into disuse as the roads conquered all. Happily, this great engineering feat, with 166 locks on the main 220 km (137 mi) waterway (there are also various arms) has been revived by modern leisure interest, and it is now possible to make the signed towpath walk from Little Venice near Paddington in London into the heart of Birmingham. This not only offers a tranquil (and level!) hike through some beautiful countryside, but also passes some splendid canal architecture.

The same scenic pleasures are, of course, available to those who let a narrowboat do the walking, and make the trip in a manner that most nearly recreates the experiences of those old-time bargees. Most canal cruises either do a specific section of the Grand Union, or undertake journeys that include other scenic canals as well, as one thing to remember about canal journeys is that the boat usually has to end up back where it started!

LLANGOLLEN CANAL

United Kingdom

This 66 km (41 mi) route links Llangollen in North Wales to Hurleston in Cheshire, via Ellesmere in Shropshire. The journey is worth it for two aqueducts alone. The amazing 19-arch Pontcysyllte Aqueduct spans the River Dee and 10-arch Chirk Aqueduct crosses the River Ceirog. These were the audacious creations of Thomas Telford and William Jessop in the early years of the 19th century. Pontcysyllte soars above the Dee Valley to a height of 38 m (125 ft) for a distance of 305 m (1,000 ft). This awe-inspiring engineering marvel certainly deserves its status as a Grade I listed Scheduled Ancient Monument. The water is carried by an iron trough that extends to just 30 cm (1 ft) above the water level, and though there is a towpath on one side, the other is unprotected. When travelling by narrowboat, this leads to the extraordinary sensation of floating through mid-air. Chirk Aqueduct is less eye-catching than Pontcysyllte, but an equally clever piece of engineering. From the English end, the Canal passes through lush green countryside with the Welsh hills as a backdrop, then wends its way through ancient woodland before reaching the final stretch to Llangollen beneath limestone cliffs. Narrowboats are available for hire at Llangollen, Whittington, Trevor and Wrenbury.

HIGHLIGHTS:

Horseshoe Falls – a weir and pumping house on the River Dee near Llangollen built to supply the canals with water. Chirk Castle – a magnificent medieval fortress, the oldest castle built by Edward I that is still inhabited.

THREE RIVERS RIDE

United Kingdom

WORTH A DETOUR:
A bottle of locally brewed farm cider from one of the village shops in Herefordshire – rather stronger than most commercial brews!

This is part of Britain's National Bridle Network, a series of cross-country routes that is being developed for long-distance horse riders. The way-marked 153 km (95 mi) Three Rivers Ride through the glorious Welsh Marches starts at Tidbach near Bromyard in Worcestershire, enters Herefordshire at Wolferlow and crosses the Rivers Lugg and Wye before entering Wales at Hay Bluff and continuing through the Brecon Beacons National Park to the third and final river – the Usk – finally finishing at the Mountain Centre (Brecon Beacons Visitor Centre) near the town of Brecon.

This really is a scenic ride par excellence, with stunning views all the way. It is a journey of two halves. The first section in Worcestershire and Herefordshire offers a peaceful ride past cider orchards and through classic English countryside, across the rapidly flowing River Lugg and along the breathtaking Wye Valley. After crossing the Welsh border the second section runs through a sweeping bank of hills, along the Western flank of the Black Mountains, skirting the picturesque Llangors Lake and crossing the River Usk. Some riders do the full journey, while others concentrate on the more dramatic mountain scenery of the 56 km (35 mi) Welsh section. The weather in the Brecon Beacons can be unpredictable, and the path itself is often far from human habitation, so riders are advised to take appropriate all-weather gear and be sure to tell someone their plans before starting out for the day. Don't assume you can rely on a mobile phone to summon assistance if something goes wrong in the remote Welsh hills – there is rarely a signal.

Those who don't have their own horse will find several riding and trekking stables.

YOU SHOULD KNOW
Don't stray over the
border into France without
your passport.

CHANNEL TUNNEL BY EUROSTAR
United Kingdom

A tunnel linking England and France was first dreamed up around 1800, but Napoleon's rampages and invasion fears put an end to that. In fact, it took nearly two centuries for the dream to become reality, with the opening of the Channel Tunnel in 1994. Known in France as Le Tunnel sous la Manche or simply Le Tunnel, this 50 km (31 mi) double rail tunnel runs from Folkestone to Calais and handles both vehicle shuttle trains plus high-speed passenger services.

The latter are run by Eurostar, offering a fast journey at up to 320 kph (200 mph) between the city centres of London and Paris. With the (somewhat belated) completion of the high-speed line at the English end, it is now possible to take a day trip from one great capital to the other, to do business, shop or just look around. From London, this stylish journey begins at the excellent new terminal within the magnificent, refurbished Victorian station of St Pancras. There, travellers find everything they need (such as a ticket office, currency exchange, newsagent, cafés and lounges) and some things that are more about setting the mood (like the Champagne Bar). Passengers may carry baggage straight onto the sleek, ultra-modern trains prior to their journey. After speeding through the English countryside via Ebbsfleet International and Ashford Stations, Eurostar shoots through the Tunnel before racing across France via Lille to Paris Gare du Nord. It's a great railway journey that everyone should do at least once.

There are different classes available – Business Premier, Leisure Select and Standard – and Eurostar regularly wins awards for the all-round quality of service it offers. As a result, the service is heavily used and it is advisable to book in advance to be sure of a seat on the train of your choice.

HIGHLIGHTS:
A great view of the Dartford Crossing high-level bridge over the River Thames.
The old tunnel-boring machine on display near the English end of the Channel Tunnel.
Crossing beneath the English Channel in just 20 minutes (the ferry on the ocean wave above takes much longer!).

ISLE OF MAN STEAM RAILWAY

United Kingdom

YOU SHOULD KNOW

There are other worthwhile railway journeys on the island – the Manx Electric Railway on the east side (Douglas to Ramsey tramway), the Snaefell Mountain Railway and Great Laxey Mine Railway.

Once upon a time there was a considerable network of steam railway lines in the ancient kingdom that is the Isle of Man, but time has taken its toll and only one remains – and that was saved from closure in the 1960s by the Marquis of Aisla, who funded the Southern Steam Railway personally until the Manx Government belatedly took it over as a tourist attraction in the 1970s. A further stretch is currently being restored by enthusiasts, and the Groudle Glen Railway provides a limited summer service along a scenic stretch of line near Douglas.

HIGHLIGHTS:

Milner's Tower on Breda Head, overlooking the bay at Port Erin – built in 1871 to represent a lock in honour of local benefactor William Milner, a safemaker.
Castle Rushen, probably the finest medieval castle in the British Isles.
Ronaldsway Halt – close to the Isle of Man Airport, making this one of few places in the world where one can travel from airport to town by steam railway.

To travel this delightful line is to step back in history – the journey starts at a classic Victorian Station at the end of North Quay in Douglas, and the trains date back to the 1870s (with rolling stock and seven locomotives maintained in the same local workshops that were always used). Britain's longest narrow-gauge steam railway at 24 km (15 mi) runs from Douglas to Port Erin, via Port Soderick, Santon, Ballasalla, Ronaldsway, Castletown, Ballabeg, Colby, Level and Port St Mary. Several of these stations are request stops and passengers can hop on and off as the fancy takes them.

Each train has an open carriage, plus closed first- and second-class carriages. It's a case of 'first come, first served' when it comes to obtaining seating, with no premium fares. The route passes through pleasant countryside with distant sea views, climbing out of Douglas to a summit at Santon Station, before descending steeply towards Ballasalla with good views of sea-cliffs. The line then runs on across beautiful rolling farmland to the delightful seaside town of Port Erin, which has a Steam Railway Museum adjacent to the station.

SOUTH WEST COAST PATH

United Kingdom

First trodden by vigilant excisemen who needed to see into every cove and bay in their unrelenting battle with smugglers, the South West Coast Path is a National Trail that hugs some of the most precious coastline in Britain, recognized by the formal status afforded to much if it – the path goes through World Heritage Sites, National Parks, Areas of Outstanding Natural Beauty, Sites of Special Scientific Interest, a UNESCO Biosphere reserve, past offshore bird reserves... and of course follows a number of designated Heritage Coasts. This is Britain's longest footpath, stretching for 1,014 km (630 mi) from Minehead in Somerset along the coasts of North Devon, Cornwall, South Devon and Dorset to Poole Harbour. As you hike through Westward Ho! you'll be visiting the only place in the British Isles with an exclamation mark in its name.

The number attempting the whole path is small, but many hike individual sections or complete the full length in different visits over the years. Those willing to undertake the ultimate challenge must be fit – with all those undulations, walkers who take on the entire path will climb a total of some 27,000 m (88,500 ft) – that's three times the height of Mount Everest – cross 17 large rivers, 300 bridges, 900 styles, skip up 27,000 steps and pass 2,500 way-marks. The West Country is Britain's most popular holiday destination and – while there is beautiful countryside and many inland attractions – the real draw is the ocean, the dramatic coastline it sculpted and the heritage created by those who sought to make a living from the sea over countless centuries. Those who walk the length of the South West Coast Path will be rewarded by seeing it all – an extraordinary variety of terrain, dramatic landscapes, seascapes, breathtaking coastal vistas, bustling towns, quaint harbours and delightful villages.

HIGHLIGHTS:
Somerset and North Devon
– the Great Hangman
(England's highest cliff),
Braunton Burrows (England's
largest sand dune system)
Cornwall – Tintagel (of King
Arthur fame), St Ives, Polperro
(a classic fishing village).
South Devon – Slapton
Sands (wonderful beach and
adjacent freshwater lake),
Dartmouth (historic port),
Jurassic Coast (fossils in
eroded cliff faces).

THE RIDGEWAY NATIONAL TRAIL

United Kingdom

WORTH A DETOUR: The White Horse of Uffingham, cut into the chalk hillside – the oldest such figure in Britain, dating from over 3,000 years ago.

This chalk ridge path – a National Trail since 1973 – is known as 'Britain's oldest road', having been in use as part of an ancient trade route from the Dorset coast to The Wash since Neolithic times. Following 18th-century Enclosure Acts the Ridgeway – formerly a loose collection of paths heading in the same direction – was consolidated into a single road defined by digging earth banks and planting hedges and trees. The National Trail runs for 139 km (87 mi) through the counties of Wiltshire, Berkshire, Oxfordshire and Buckinghamshire. It starts at Overton Hill near the prehistoric stone circle at Avebury, within a UNESCO World Heritage Site, then follows the high ground across the open, rolling expanse of the North Wessex Downs to the west of the River Thames. It runs alongside the Thames after crossing at Streatley and continues into the secluded beech woods (carpets of bluebells in spring, spectacular foliage in autumn) and gentle valleys of the Chiltern Hills, ending at the top of Ivinghoe Beacon (from whence the Icknield and Peddars Ways continue on to the North Norfolk coast at Hunstanton).

WORTH A DETOUR: A leisurely visit to the on-board boutique to spend a little pocket money on memorabilia.

VENICE SIMPLON-ORIENT-EXPRESS

United Kingdom

Sadly, one of the great rail journeys of all time – the Orient Express between Paris and Istanbul – ended in 1977 after reaching a peak of perfection in the 1930s. The modern Orient Express is less glamorous – a practical, workmanlike sleeper from Strasbourg to Vienna. But happily, the atmosphere of the original may be recaptured by taking the Venice Simplon-Orient-Express, which offers an old-fashioned leisure experience as it conveys pampered passengers from London to Venice in the lap of luxury. The first leg from London Victoria uses vintage British Pullman carriages, and after a swift trip through the Channel Tunnel the journey to Venice continues using original cars from the old Orient Express, clad in distinctive blue-and-gold livery.

As the train makes its way across France, via Paris, passengers relax in private compartments attended by a personal steward, before cocktails and dinner prepared under the direction of a top French chef. Afterwards, passengers congregate in the bar car, listening to the baby grand piano's tinkling ivories and making new friends. Then it's time to return to a compartment that has been transformed into a bedroom. Morning sees the train amidst the Swiss Alps as breakfast is served in the compartment. The morning is spent in the bar car drinking coffee and admiring the passing Austrian scenery as Innsbruck comes and goes, before a three-course lunch is served. The Italian Dolomites appear, before afternoon tea in the compartment. After crossing the Brenner Pass and passing Verona, just as people are thinking they could get used to travelling like this, the Orient Express crosses the Lagoon and pulls into Venice's Santa Lucia Station.

LONDON TO AUSTRALIA

United Kingdom

Since hippies were invented (and gap years became popular), the scenic route from London to Australia has been well trodden. A classic journey involves travelling from London (by public transport or hitchhiking) through France, Belgium, Germany, the Czech Republic, Austria, Hungary, Romania, Bulgaria, Turkey, Iran, Pakistan, India, Nepal, Myanmar, Thailand, Malaysia, Indonesia, East Timord in the end to Sydney. The beauty of travelling alone or with a few companions is the that there are almost infinite possibilities for varying the route and taking interesting side trips – indeed, an essential part of this rewarding experience is remaining flexible and seeing where the fickle finger of fate points.

However, there are also advantages in joining a pre-arranged bus trip. Arrival is guaranteed after a set period (usually three months), and the potential concerns of travelling alone are avoided. It is also ideal for those who enjoy being part of a like minded group, sharing chores, laughs, companionship and anything else that occurs en route. Also, the itinerary will be planned to provide the maximum number of highlights, including exotic places like the Mount Everest base camp that might not be easy for lone travellers to reach.

HIGHLIGHTS:

Dracula's Castle in the Transylvanian Mountains of Romania – once the home of fearsome Vlad the Impaler.

Tabriz in the north of Iran – a city of stunning blue mosques

World-famous Bagan in Myanmar (formerly Burma) – once capital of the powerful Burmese Empire, featuring literally thousands of amazing temples.

Approaching journey's end – Uluru (formerly Ayers Rock) near Alice Springs in the centre of Australia.

CROSS THE ATLANTIC ON A CARGO BOAT

United Kingdom

HIGHLIGHTS:
Sunsets at sea.
Being up on the Bridge.
Spotting a whale.
Entering New York Harbor.

In a post-modern age of counting carbon footprints, freighter-travel is about as eco-friendly as it gets, short of a rowing boat. Cargo ships are the life-line of the global economy, transporting containers of goods all over the world. Although they do carry passengers, freighters don't advertise themselves. To book a passage you must be prepared to do plenty of research and be dedicated to the idea of a cryptic adventure into the unknown.

Of all the trade routes, the transatlantic crossing is perhaps the most romantic, harking back to the belle époque, era of the ocean liner. The prospect of crossing the bleak immensity of the Atlantic without any organized on-board entertainment may seem a challenging one, but if you are self-reliant yet congenial then a freighter is the ideal way to travel.

On the voyage to New York from Tilbury, London's container port, there comes a point, after the ship has weighed anchor at Rotterdam and Le Havre and there is only ocean ahead, when you may fleetingly feel stir-crazy; until the mesmerizing effect of the sea suddenly makes you aware of your own insignificance in comparison to the immensity of nature.

After days of nothing but sea and sky, the sight of the Statue of Liberty is both elevating and humbling. You cannot help sparing a thought for the countless numbers who made this crossing before you.

WORTH A DETOUR: Glendun's magnificent viaduct bridge by engineer Charles Lanyon, built in 1832 – a fine example of the engineering genius required to construct the Antrim Coast Road.

ANTRIM COAST ROAD
Northern Ireland

With an end to the Troubles in Northern Ireland – when Protestant and Catholic activists squaring up to each other frightened away outsiders for several decades – the economy has boomed, especially tourism. It's hardly surprising – Ireland is a delightful country, and the North has its share of fabulous scenery. This is especially true of Northern Ireland's rocky coastline, and the best way to appreciate that is to take a leisurely drive along the Antrim Coast Road, unquestionably one of Ireland's most scenic drives.

This is part of the A2 road, which actually begins in Newry in County Down and runs through Belfast and on to Derry City. The two-lane Antrim Coast Road section was constructed in the 19th century to open up the hauntingly beautiful but then-isolated Glens of Antrim, and is quite an engineering feat. It starts at Larne, then follows the coast through Ballygalley, Glenarm, Carnlough, Waterfoot and Cushendun, where it leaves the sea for an inland stretch before rejoining the water at Ballycastle to complete the journey. However, it is possible to stay with the coast by turning off the A2 at Cushendun and finding Torr Road, a very narrow and winding road that will return you to the A2 at Ballyvoy. This detour delivers truly awesome coastal views, though you will miss the enchanting Ballypatrick Forest Park on the main road. Tough choice!

No denying it, the Antrim Coast Road is stunningly beautiful. Not only does it offer ever-changing vistas of this extraordinary coast, but it also passes glacial valleys, sandy beaches, wooded glens, waterfalls, picturesque villages and ancient sites. Taken together, it all adds up to a very special journey that becomes not only a magnificent scenic drive but also a fascinating voyage of discovery.

BUSHMILLS TO BENONE
Northern Ireland

WORTH A DETOUR: The Giant's Causeway itself – the amazing grouping of interlocking basalt columns that are one of Ireland's most famous features.

This well-marked coastal cycle journey officially begins at the famous Giant's Causeway, just outside Bushmills in County Londonderry. The North Atlantic Coast section of the National Cycle Network Route 93 then runs beside the sea for some 32 km (20 mi) to Castlerock.

Bushmills is the first town along the way, after following the tracks of Northern Ireland's only heritage steam railway. Beware – before continuing along the cycleway it's very tempting to visit the famous distillery and take a glass or two of the finest Irish whiskey.

It's hard not to pause at either Portrush (built out on the peninsula of Ramore Head) or nearby Portstewart (with the wonderful long beach of Portstewart Strand). These two coastal resorts enjoy wonderful natural settings and have a full range of facilities. From Portstewart Route 93 drops down to the large, bustling town of Coleraine at the mouth of the River Bann. There's no avoiding the crowded streets, because this is the first point at which it's possible to cross the impressively wide river, but that's no bad thing – the town has a fine central square. After Coleraine, the cycleway follows the river to the seaside village of Castlerock. The North Atlantic Coast section actually ends here, as Route 93 turns away from the sea towards Limavady, so many cyclists simply return to their start point along the main A2 coast road. However, before doing that it's worth going on through Downhill to Benone Strand, one of the longest beaches in Northern Ireland.

HIGHLIGHTS: Fabulous views from Carrick Island across to Rathin Island and Scotland. Abundant seabird life around the rocky coastline.

CARRICK-A-REDE ROPE BRIDGE
Northern Ireland

Only those with the strongest head for heights should make the swaying journey across the rope bridge at Carrick-a-Rede near Ballintoy in County Antrim. It is at the end of a short footpath that offers wonderful coastal vistas, and crosses a chasm that is 23 m (75 ft) deep (don't look down!) between the mainland and the small T-shaped island. The bridge itself is around 20 m (65 ft) long with a pronounced dip in the middle.

It was traditionally erected by salmon fishermen who laid their nets off Carrick Island but it's now a magnet for visitors – some 140,000 of them every year, drawn by the magnificent scenery and the challenge of crossing the bridge.

The bridge is now taken down around the end of November and not replaced until the beginning of March, depending on the weather, as attempts to cross during windy winter conditions would be both foolhardy and dangerous.

DON'T MISS
The cliff-top mining trail at
Bunmahon, with the
well-preserved remains
of a Cornish-style engine house.

COPPER COAST DRIVE
Eire

This should be in England's West Country, the old centre of tin and copper mining in the British Isles. But it isn't, because Country Waterford also has its mining heritage – its cliffs were mined for lead, silver and copper in the 18th and 19th centuries. Mining finished in 1880, but the name Copper Coast remains. The short journey along this magical road from the seaside town of Tramore offers haunting views of the Comeragh Mountains to one side and the wild splendour of cliffs, beaches, coves and caves to the other. The scenery is indeed magnificent, but that's not all there is to enjoy – the road passes through six delightful villages and each has something to offer. Fenor has peaceful Kilfarrasy Beach, plus forest and lakeside walks and the Bog of Fenor. Annestown is a tiny hillside village, overlooking a scenic valley and wide bay with a sandy beach and rock pools. Dunhill has ancient Stone Age dolmens and a traditional Irish shop and pub that is an ideal refreshment stop, plus a church on the hill – a superb vantage point.

NORTH MAYO DRIVE
Eire

HIGHLIGHTS: The archaeological site of the Ceide Fields.
The glistening Lough Conn.
The stretch around Lackan Bay and Downpatrick Head.

Although only a few hours' drive from Dublin or Belfast, North Mayo feels light years removed from them. The area's population is now lower than it was before the potato famine and those who remain are among the hardiest and most welcoming people to be found anywhere.

The 173 km (108 mi) North Mayo Drive takes you in a loop that starts and finishes in the county's largest town, Ballina. A choice of over fifty hostelries awaits you and good simple food is prepared in most of them. The drive, in essence, links ten communities, each with its own distinct feel. In between there is ample opportunity to visit magnificent abbeys or simply wander along any one of many riverside trails.

Driving counter-clockwise, the road hugs the Atlantic coast before turning inland at Belderrig. From there it travels alongside the picturesque Carrowmore Lough, a perfect place to pull over and have a picnic. As the road swings round and you start the journey back towards Ballina, the peaks of the Nephin Beg Range dominate the landscape and the charming town of Bangor Erris demands that you stop and dwell a while. This drive is a must for anyone who wants to experience the real Ireland. Around every corner there are symbols of martyrdom and sainthood, of suffering and triumph. It is a land of desolate beauty, where the pace is gentle and the Craic is at its most genuine.

THE WICKLOW WAY

Eire

HIGHLIGHTS:
The views from
Croaghanmoira Mountain.
The boardwalk climb up
White Hill.

County Wicklow, just south of Dublin, is one of the most spectacular regions in Ireland. The county contains many large stretches of delightfully unspoilt mountain trails of which the Wicklow Way is the best known. In fact, the Wicklow Way was the first such trail in Ireland, having been formally established in 1980. It begins in Dublin's southern community of Rathfarnham and travels in a southwesterly direction across the Dublin and Wicklow uplands, then it goes through the rolling hill country of southwest County Wicklow to finish in the small, County Carlow village of Clonegal some 132 km (82 mi) later.

SLIGO YEATS TRAIL

Eire

Nothing evokes the spirit of old Ireland better than the sight of horse and rider silhouetted against the setting sun, and there is no better place to ride than the captivating coastline of Sligo, an area steeped in history and blessed with natural beauty.

The preferred option for the experienced rider on the Yeats Trail has to be a self guided tour riding between lodgings. A typical tour starts near the exquisite Streedagh Beach, which is your first chance to slacken the reins and experience the gallop of a lifetime along the wonderful long golden sands. If the tides are right it is possible to ride across to the magical Dernish Island, scene of many a shipwreck.

The next stage takes you along small tracks and down country lanes and then on to the magnificent white sands of Trawbawn. It is then but a small climb to the Cullumore cliffs for an amazing view over Sligo Bay.

Having fed and stabled your horse and done the same for yourself, the final leg of the trip takes you towards Ardtarmon Castle, both sumptuous and rich in history. A ride along Lissadell Beach then takes you on the most challenging part of the trip as you climb steadily up the foothills of Benbulben.

WORTH A DETOUR:
Inishmurray Island – a
monastic settlement founded
about 500 AD.

DON'T MISS
The 2,500-year-old
Staigue Fort.

THE RING OF KERRY

Eire

The Ring of Kerry is the jewel in the crown of Irish tourism. This is a wild and out-of-the-way region, sparsely populated inland but lined with quaint little towns along the coast. Superb scenery bombards the senses at every turn. Starting from Killarney, with the wonderfully named Mcgillycuddy's Reeks (Ireland's highest point) to your left, the first port of call is Killorglin, a town where time has stood still. From here on the views get even more spectacular and the road between Glenbeigh and Kells offers the most magnificent coastal scenery.

The Ring of Kerry provides fascinating glimpses of the ancient heritage of Ireland – Iron Age forts, Ogham Stones and monasteries abound. The route then hugs the coastal road, offering several chances to cross to the Skellig Islands, a paradise for birdwatchers. The loop takes you through the charming towns of Waterville, Caherdaniel and Castlecove, all of which are worthy of exploration.

CONNEMARA COAST TRAIL

Eire

Founded in the late 1980's, the Connemara Coast Trail takes you through a landscape of untamed beauty and serves up the most stunning scenery Ireland has to offer. Refreshed by salty zephyrs from the Atlantic Ocean, the traveller is treated to a wonderful mélange of unspoilt valleys, bogs, shimmering lakes and fabulous mountains.

The trail presents a good challenge for the experienced rider or hiker and has the added bonus of taking you through the Gaelic heartland of Ireland. Even the smallest of settlements is teeming with Celtic culture. At all times the views out to sea and the sight of the brooding Twelve

Bens inland both compete for your attention. But even in a place so consistently beautiful, the stretch of the coast between Roundstone and Moyrus stands out. Rounding the dark recesses of Bertaghboy Bay you are treated to ever changing light as the curving pathway changes the view.

YOU SHOULD KNOW
Storms can roll in quickly and disappear just as quickly. Good waterproofs are therefore a must.

CRUISE THE LIFFEY

Eire

WHEN SHOULD I VISIT?:
River cruises operate from
Easter–September.

HIGHLIGHTS:
A stroll through Trinity
College.
O'Connell Bridge –
a world-class structure.
The nearby fish, fruit and
vegetable markets – great for
people watching.
Dublin Castle – a short walk
south from Grattan Bridge.

No trip to Ireland's resplendent capital is complete without a trip along its iconic river. So much has changed in recent years for this tiger economy of the Eurozone, and nowhere is the transformation better exemplified than along the shores of the Liffey. It was not so long ago that Dubliners referred to their river as 'the slime' and those who walked near it could not help but notice its special aroma. Much effort and money has been put in it to changing this and, as people started to return to living by the water's edge, the river has improved markedly.

Now proud of its river, the city offers cruises through this most magnificent of urban landscapes. Old and new sit side-by-side, offering up a wonderful mix of historical buildings and stunning new architecture. The downstream journey takes you beneath the world famous Ha'penny Bridge while the commentator waxes lyrical on Dublin's past, taking you on a journey through time, from before the Viking invasion to the point where Cromwell first landed through to the present day.

There are great sights to be seen along the way, most notably Trinity College and the Spire in O'Connell Street. However Dublin does not have a waterfront to rival that of London or Paris. To get the full benefit of what the river has to offer, a cruise should form part of a wider walking tour. Using Fleet Street and Abbey Street as your southern and northern boundaries you can cross the Liffey several times and get a most rewarding view of this wonderful city and its fabled river.

HIGHLIGHTS: The heart of the old city around Central Station, for the scenic Amsterdam of canals and tall houses at its best.
Crossing the impressive Enneus Bridge that carries both the IJtram and the only road to and from IJburg.

AMSTERDAM TRAM
The Netherlands

Riding the trams is an excellent way of seeing Amsterdam for those who don't have time for the water tour, and the Combinos with their large windows provide a great view of 'The Venice of the North'. New trams went hand in hand with a major refurbishment and extension of the network, a work in progress, but the first fruit was the introduction of a new route – Line 26 from Central Station to the new housing developments of IJburg on artificial islands reclaimed from the vast (and equally artificial) IJsselmeer inland sea – the former being yet another example of the Dutch genius for turning water into dry land, and the latter of their ability to turn salt water into fresh. Line 26 is inevitably known as the IJtram. This route runs mainly through residential areas, rather than amidst heavy city traffic, and includes the Piet Hein Tunnel. It provides an opportunity to see the on-going work of redeveloping Amsterdam's waterfront.

KEUKENHOF GARDENS
The Netherlands

WHEN SHOULD I VISIT?: Last week in March–mid-May for the Keukenhof Gardens (may vary slightly depending on the weather).

Contrary to its name, Keukenhof has some seven million flower bulbs, which provide an amazing display of spring colour (mid-April sees the daffodils, crocus, narcissi, tulips and hyacinths all in bloom), so is perhaps best described by its alternative name, 'The Garden of Europe'.
A visit may be combined with a cycle journey through the surrounding fields, which together deliver an equally spectacular collection of flowering bulbs. Taken together, the garden tour and cycle ride go a long way to explaining Holland's preeminence in the world of horticulture in general and bulbs in particular.
The gardens are easily reached by bus from Amsterdam, The Hague, Leiden, Haarlem and Schipol Airport.
Cycles are not allowed within the gardens, but may be hired at the main entrance. A number of proven scenic cycle routes are recommended, ranging in distance from 5 km (3 mi) to 25 km (16 mi).
One 'must see' on every cycle tour is the Tulipland Panorama in nearby Voorhout. This mural depicts the bulb fields as they were half a century ago. It is a work in progress, but has already attained a size of some 65 m (215 ft) long by 4 m (13 ft) high. There's only one word for this extraordinary artistic effort and the bulb fields themselves: amazing.

WATERWAY CRUISE

The Netherlands

HIGHLIGHTS:

Fields full of contented black-and-white Friesian cattle.
Mooring up right in the centre of Amsterdam – nip ashore to visit the world-famous Rijksmuseum and the Van Gogh Exhibition.
Loosdrecht Broad, full of uninhabited islands and alive with water birds.
Utrecht – cruise from Amsterdam on the River Vecht, via Loosdrecht, and moor at the quay opposite the Cathedral of Saint Martin.

As serene progress is made along rivers, canals and through lakes, the traditional Dutch picture of big skies, windmills (actually they're mostly wind pumps), dykes and other craft of all sorts is constantly repainted – and there will be plenty of interesting villages, too.

One excellent journey is from Sneek in Friesland to the north, down to Loosdrect south of Amsterdam. Confined only by the length of time for which the cruiser has been booked, the beauty of this trip – and Holland's huge variety of waterways – is that part of the pleasure is planning an interesting individual itinerary with stops and diversions, or simple cruising wherever the mood suggests.

However, the basic route south from Sneek is via Joure (where the world-famous Douwe Egberts trading company was founded in 1753), Ossenzijl (turn off here for the Friesian Lakes), Giethoorn (known as 'Little Venice of the North', with no roads in the old village, which must therefore be explored by water or bicycle), Zwartsluis (home to a fleet of heritage fishing and inland cargo vessels), Strand Horst (a major boating centre), Spakenburg (spot local women wearing traditional costume), and finally Loosdrecht.

NORTH HOLLAND'S HISTORIC TRIANGLE
The Netherlands

YOU SHOULD KNOW

Hoorn is just 30 minutes from Amsterdam by thoroughly modern double-decker train.

WHEN SHOULD I VISIT?:
April–September.

HIGHLIGHTS:
The steam museum in Hoorn – for a splendid collection of vintage locomotives, rolling stock and bygone railway artefacts.
Impressive former Dutch East India Company building in Hoorn and Enkhuizen.
Zuiderzeemuseum in Enkhuizen – reached only by water, this is an atmospheric recreation of a working fishing village from the past.

The 'Historic Triangle' in Noord Holland consists of three small but charming former ports – Hoorn, Medemblik and Enkhuizen. Once fronting the Zuiderzee, since 1932 they have been contained within the freshwater IJsselmeer, the largest lake in western Europe. This area due north of Amsterdam not only offers classic Dutch landscapes of dykes and patchwork fields, but also well-preserved historic towns and villages that grew wealthy in the 17th century as the Dutch East India Company thrived. As always, wealth translated into fine architecture, and there are many splendid buildings from that opulent colonial era to admire.

The classic way of seeing these three is by taking the steam train from Hoorn to Medemblik. With lots of stops and starts for crossings, the preserved 'steam tram' (as the Dutch describe narrow-gauge railways), resplendent in original 1920s livery, chugs and whistles through the countryside, past incurious sheep and cattle and restored stations to Medemblik, complete with period extras that make it perfectly possible to imagine the reality of travelling this delightful line in its heyday. From there, a steamer takes you on to Enkhuizen from whence the 'Historic Triangle' can be completed by returning to Hoorn by the scheduled train service. It is possible to book combined tickets for the train and steamer legs of the trip, with a 'hop on, hop off' option that allows ample opportunity to explore. But do consult a timetable before attempting to undertake this rewarding journey to be sure you won't be disappointed. The steam train doesn't run between December and February, and there is a limited service only in March, October and November. The train does not always operate on Mondays, so a little pre-planning is required.

LUXEMBOURG CITY WALK

Luxembourg

WORTH A DETOUR: A warren of underground casements and tunnels hewn into the solid rock by Spanish and French engineers in the 17th and 18th centuries.

This was one of many tiny fiefdoms that made up the jigsaw of medieval Europe, and the Grand Duchy of Luxembourg has retained its independence to this day. The defensive qualities that made it so important in the Middle Ages are based on its location – high above two rocky gorges at the confluence of the Rivers Alzette and Pétrusse.

An ideal way to appreciate the unique combination of the city's heritage and natural beauty is to take the well-signed Wenzel Walk – a circular stroll around the oldest areas that is boldly billed as 'a thousand years in a hundred minutes'. This journey through European history focuses on the defensive stronghold at the heart of the old city, beginning at the historic Bock Promontory where Count Siegfried built his castle in the 10th century. It then visits the Chemin de la Corniche, old city gates, the Wenzel defensive wall, medieval bridges, the Alzette Valley with its medieval waterside buildings and explores extraordinary Spanish and French military works.

HOW TO GET THERE:
By road from Dieppe
or Le Havre.
WHEN SHOULD I VISIT?:
Any time of year.
TIME IT TAKES:
Fécamp 20 km (12 mi).

YOU SHOULD KNOW

The cliffs are crumbly and rock falls are a hazard.

CÔTE D'ALABÂTRE

France

The Côte d'Alabâtre, or Alabaster Coast is, in fact, a line of chalk cliffs on the coast of Normandy. They are part of the same formation of Cretaceous chalk that makes up the Seven Sisters and the White Cliffs of Dover on the other side of the English Channel. They were formed more than 65 million years ago from billions of fossil skeletons of creatures that lived in shallow, warm seas. Once they covered most of Britain, but still extend as far north as Yorkshire and as far south as the Paris Basin.

The principal towns on the coast are Fécamp and Etretat, where the most spectacular cliff formations are to be found. The western cliff, the Falais d'Aval, has been scoured into an arch, called the Porte d'Aval, by the waves. From its clifftop, visitors can see more rock formations, including *l'aiguille*, the needle, a soaring seastack. At low tide visitors can walk through the arches. In summer it is still bustling with tourists, but in winter it is a spectacular, lonely place to watch the waves crashing into the cliffs.

FLANDERS FIELDS
France

$\mathcal{S}$ome of World War I's most intensive fighting took place in the 'Fields of Flanders'. Medieval Flanders no longer exists, but loosely corresponds to the Flemish area in southern Belgium. Around 550,000 soldiers were killed there, with countless more wounded. There are still plenty of reminders of those dark days and a tour of Flanders Fields gives some idea of what that awful conflict was like – though it's hard to equate today's peaceful countryside with the vast expanses of liquid mud, shattered trees and ruined towns that characterized the hellish battlefields.
The place to start is Ypres (in Flemish, Ieper), the medieval city that became the centre of fighting in Flanders. It doesn't have one building more than 85 years old, as the place was reduced to rubble during 1915. The Flanders Field Museum is on the second floor of the rebuilt Cloth Hall and it provides real insight into the nature of the conflict and the lives (and deaths) of the soldiers who fought hereabouts.
Battlefied maps are available and it is possible to make a reflective journey alone. The hardest moments will be in one or more of 200 beautifully maintained cemeteries containing war dead of all nationalities, known and unknown. Passchendaele was the sight of one of World War I's bloodiest battles in 1917, reflected in Tyne Cot Cemetery, where 12,000 lie. The Sanctuary Wood Museum has thousands of artefacts and photographs, plus a preserved section of battlefield. The eerie Hill 60 is another historic battlefield.

WHEN SHOULD I VISIT?:
May or June for those symbolic poppies – they're still to be seen everywhere.

PARIS

France

YOU SHOULD KNOW

Route 38 follows in famous footsteps – Porte d'Orléans is where General LeClerc, greeted by ecstatic flag-waving crowds, entered Paris to liberate the city from German occupation in 1944.

An excellent way of conserving shoe leather, while seeing Paris, is to ride L'autobus 38 from south to north through the centre of this romantic capital city. As the delightful journey unfolds, the traveller will not only see famous sights but also the hustle and bustle of everyday Paris.

The ancient southeastern gate of Paris, Porte d'Orléans, is the starting point of Route 38's green single-deckers. From there, they pass the Church of St Peter of Montrouge and the superb Metro entrance at Mouton Duvernet. Observatoire de Paris, with its lovely gardens, was created at the behest of Sun King Louis XIV, and appropriately the first map of the moon was made there. Note the chic La Closerie des Lilas in passing – a restaurant once frequented by the likes of Verlaine, Lenin and Ernest Hemingway.

Route 38 passes the 17th-century Luxembourg Palace and Gardens, built for a homesick Italian Queen. A short distance away is the Panthéon, where many of France's greatest citizens are interred and the Sorbonne, where most were educated. Break the journey at Saint michel – the square and boulevard are famous meetingpoints – then wander over the River Seine to the Ile de la Cité, enjoying a wonderful close-up of Notre Dame Cathedral before catching a Route 38 bus in front of the historic Palais de Justice, passing the grand Hôtel de Ville and reaching the terminal at rue de Victoria. Half the buses stop here.

Those that continue go through what Emile Zola described as 'The stomach of Paris' – Les Halles market area (now the Forum shopping centre). Then it's the George Pompidou Centre and the triumphal arch of Porte Saint-Martin before Route 38 nears journey's end, reaching the magnificent Gare de l'Est and terminating at another piece of splendid Victorian railway architecture – the Gare du Nord.

HIGHLIGHTS:

The unostentatious monastery shop at avenue Denfert Rocherau, opposite rue Cassini, for a wide range of hand-made goods produced throughout France by monks.

Climb the Eiffel Tower – day or night offers spectacular views of the city.

The Musée de Cluny in its 15th-century building at Boulevards Saint michel and Saint-Germain – a fabulous collection of medieval artefacts and pictures.

The 136 statues of the great and the good from French history on the façade of the Victorian Hôtel de Ville.

Interesting passages (small covered streets) between Boulevard de Strasbourg, rue du faubourg St-Denis and rue du Faubourg St-Martin.

TIME IT TAKES:

This is not a bus journey to take in one go – allow at least half a day to get off and explore along the way… or better still, make it a day.

Right: The Eiffel Tower, Paris

GORGES DU VERDON

France

Provence in summer is magical, with superb weather that sets off magnificent landscapes and ancient villages to perfection. One of the most dramatic geological features in the region is the Verdon Gorge, a 25 km (15 mi) long ravine that ranges from 6 m (20 ft) to 100 m (330 ft) wide at the base, 200 m (660 ft) to 1,500 m (4,920 ft) across the top and 300 m (990 ft) deep. Carved from limestone by the turquoise Verdon River, this is the world's second-largest gorge – one French

name is Grand Canyon du Verdon. It is also, by general agreement, the most beautiful in Europe.

There are hiking routes within the Gorge, but most people prefer to enjoy its unique charms by driving or cycling one of two winding rim roads. The northern route from Castellane follows the D952 road to Moustiers-Sainte-Marie. The south side may be seen to great advantage by leaving Aiguines on the D71, twisting and turning towards the spectacular Corniche Sublime, one of the very best scenic sections overlooking the Gorge.

WORTH A DETOUR:
The Museum of Prehistory at Quinson – celebrating primitive man's presence in the area, in a thoroughly modern building designed by English architect Norman Foster.

HIGHLIGHTS: Another 'up and away' outing from Chamonix – on the old funicular Montenvers Railway to the Mer de Glace glacier.
An elevator ride up another 42 m (138 ft) at the summit of the Aiguille du Midi – to the top terrace with even better views.

AIGUILLE DU MIDI CABLE CAR

France

Once, only a very few people could enjoy the sensational views from the top of the Aiguille du Midi, a sharp-topped peak in the Mont Blanc Massif in the French Alps. Nowadays, the panorama may be enjoyed by anyone who rides up from the centre of Chamonix by cable car, in two stages, enjoying terrific mountain scenery all the way. The pre-war Téléphérique fell into disuse but it was rebuilt, extended and reopened in the 1950s, for many years offering the world's most elevated cable car journey. It has lost that distinction, but still delivers the world's highest vertical ascent, from 1,035 m (3,400 ft) up to 3,842 m (12,608 ft), with the first stage to the Plan de l'Aiguille at 2,300 m (7,500 ft). The second stage traverses the Pelerins Glacier before rising up the mountain's North Face. The famed Vallée Blanche ski run begins here, and the nearby Cosmiques Refuge is the starting point of a climb to the summit of Mont Blanc. In summer only, there is another cable car – the 5 km (3 mi) Panoramic Mont Blanc route, open from mid-March to September – across the Geant Glacier to Helbronner Point on the Italian side of the massif.

TIME IT TAKES:
It took Napoléon six days, but
he didn't have a car – allow
one day, including stops (five
hours non-stop).

ROUTE NAPOLÉON

France

You may be forgiven for thinking the 'N' in Route N95 stands for Napoléon, especially when you keep passing gilded imperial eagles on stone plinths bearing the legend ROUTE NAPOLÉON. Actually, it stands for National as in Route National, but there is a strong connection with the Great Emperor (or Little Corporal, depending on your point of view).

For this 325 km (200 mi) journey from the French Riviera to Grenoble is the route travelled by Napoléon Bonaparte upon returning from Elban exile in 1815, determined to overthrow Louis XVIII. What followed is history – one hundred days that culminated in the Battle of Waterloo, which finally ended the Napoleonic era. He may have had other things on his mind as he journeyed north, but the comeback kid must surely have appreciated the rugged beauty of the mountainous landscape as he went, using a remote route unlikely to bring him into conflict with hostile Royalists.

Starting from Golfe-Juan, Route Napoléon passes through Cannes, where Napoléon's party spent the first night, and up to Grasse with its sweeping coastal views. From there, the road winds to Séranon, where they slept. They proceeded via Castellane to Barrême through heavy snow on day three. On the fourth day it snowed again but they pressed on, taking lunch at Digne-les-Bains before following the River Bléone to Malijai. On the fifth day they progressed through Sisteron (another mandatory French lunch stop!) and Tallard to Gap. The next day saw them complete the demanding stretch over the Col Bayard to Corps, from whence they proceeded via La Mure to a triumphal entry into Grenoble on the final evening. Today N95 is a scenic through road – but in Napoléon's time it was no more than a series of mule tracks and rough trails.

LA MÉRIDIENNE SCENIC ROUTE

France

WORTH A DETOUR: The exhibition centre and (after a climb) the overview that gives a tremendous view of the Millau Viaduct.

France's vast and rugged range known as the Massif Central traditionally made communication difficult and isolated southern France from the more economically advanced north. A railway was built through the mountains in the 19th century, but it was not until the end of the 20th century that a really good road was constructed.

The autoroute A75 runs from Clermont-Ferrand to Pézenas, a distance of 340 km (240 mi) and is a work in progress, with the final short section to Béziers still under construction. For all those who head for the Languedoc each summer (and the rather fewer number that use this spectacular road at other times of the year) this extraordinary constructional feat has proved to be a real blessing, offering an alternative route to the old and slow A6 road which became choked with traffic every summer.

Known officially as La Méridienne Bonne Route, the new A75 delivers a wonderful scenic drive as it snakes through the mountains, for much of its length at a height of 800 m (2,600 ft) or more. Along the way there are five mountain passes, three tunnels and eight major bridges or viaducts. Undoubtedly the most impressive engineering (and design) feat is the Millau Viaduct, designed by Norman Foster and appearing impossibly delicate as it crosses the Tarn Valley, reaching a greater height above ground than the Eiffel Tower.

WORTH A DETOUR: Taking the cable car from Le Chable up the mountain to Verbier – incredible views as you relax, recharge the batteries and let the winding gear take the strain.

CHAMONIX-ZERMATT HAUTE ROUTE

France

Why go on foot or skis when there's a car or public transport available? Actually, if the journey rather than the destination is the thing it makes perfect sense to give a simple answer – 'because I can'. In the case of the Chamonix-Zermatt Haute Route, that reply really means something – this is one of Europe's ultimate physical challenges, and anyone who successfully undertakes this 180 km (110 mi) traverse through the Alps from Chamonix to Zermatt (bridging the spectacular gap between those two iconic Alpine mountains, Mont Blanc and the Matterhorn) can feel proud indeed – around half fail, especially in winter.

The summer walking route, pioneered by 19th-century English mountaineers, crosses Alpine meadows, passes shining lakes, skirts glaciers, goes through forests and visits picturesque mountain villages. There are variations allowing for a personal itinerary. In the case of a summer hike, the basic choice is between the original 'high' route and a lower-level option that avoids collapsing glaciers that have made the high route even more difficult. Along the original route hikers mostly stay at mountain huts.

HIGHLIGHTS: The pretty station at Villars-sur-Var.
The thermal baths that put 'les-Bains' into Digne-les-Bains – but
don't think you're the first to find them (the Romans were here first).

LE TRAIN DES PIGNES
France

This 150 km (130 mi) rail line, up through the mountains from Nice to Digne-les-Bains, is a nostalgic reminder of a bygone era of railway travel. It is the sole survivor of the Train des Pignes network built during the late 19th century, once consisting of four narrow-gauge lines. Even with the benefit of modern rolling stock the train bounces and rattles as the track follows rushing rivers through steep-sided mountain valleys.

The section from Nice to Plan-du-Var is busy, but once the route follows the Var River into the rugged Vésubie Gorge the landscape improves dramatically. The train continues along the river, stopping at delightful old-fashioned stations until it finally parts company with the Var, climbing more steeply up the beautiful Vaire Valley, going through tunnels and looping back on itself to gain the necessary height to continue into the mountains, passing through a 3.5 km (2 mi) tunnel between Méailles and Thorame. The next stage is along the wide Verdon Valley, before another long tunnel carries the train beneath the Col des Robines and along another lovely valley. The final stretch follows rivers through the mountain park of Trois Asses and curves through gentler terrain to Digne-les-Bains, completing this scenic journey par excellence.

Picnic sites and walks are signed from many stations and there are plenty of historic villages to explore. For those with steam tendencies, there is a section of the line (between Puget-Théniers and Annot) where like minded enthusiasts run a service pulled by old steam locomotives at weekends between May and October.

RHÔNE CRUISE
France

DON'T MISS
Crussol Castle – one of the most impressive sights in the entire Rhône Valley.

The mighty River Rhône rises in the Swiss mountains, flows through Lake Geneva and on into France. Joined by the River Saône, this fickle river used to be hazardous, with fierce currents, unexpected shallows and sudden spates. It was tamed in the 20th century with the construction of locks and other major works – a process that both improved navigation and created several hydro-electric plants.

End-to-end cruises start at Chalons-sur-Saône, to offer an entrée to wine country in the form off those splendid Beaujolais and Mâconnais vineyards, all within easy reach of Bordeaux. Below Viviers, the boat traverses the extraordinary Bollène Lock and cruises down to Avignon, home of 14th- and 15th-century Popes and Antipopes. It then continues to Arles, the important Roman city that retains many well-preserved reminders of that era. From there, you have a choice of route as the Rhône splits, its two arms (Grand Rhône and Petit Rhône) forming the fabulous Camargue Delta.

RIVIERA CORNICHES

France

La Turbie on the Grand Corniche – the symbolic border between Gaul and Ancient Rome, with an impressive Roman colonnade.
On the Middle Corniche – the view of Cap Ferrat from the elevated Villefranche Neck, and (upon exiting a tunnel) the appearance of the dramatic village of Eze, perched high on its rock.
On the Base Corniche – Cap Ferrat... and of course Monte Carlo, where you definitely won't break the bank.

The French Riviera may be a playground for the rich and famous, but there's much more to the Côte d'Azur than casinos, exclusive villas and harbours stuffed with billion-dollar yachts. This delightful coast stretches from St Tropez to Menton on the Italian border, with Fréjus, Cannes, Antibes, Nice and Monaco along the way. There couldn't be a better way of appreciating the natural beauty and diverse character of this special place than by driving the three spectacular coast roads known as corniches, with each of these parallel highways delivering a different perspective on the Riviera.

The Grand Corniche (La Grande Corniche) is a 31 km (19 mi) cliff-top road, rising to a height of some 450 m (1,475 ft) as it passes above the Principality of Monaco. It was built at the beginning of the 19th century (following the line of the Roman Via Julia Augusta) to facilitate the movement of Napoléon's troops to Italy, and as such does not pass through many interesting places. No matter – the road itself is the star of the show, offering sensational far-reaching views. It is by far the most satisfying way of entering and leaving Nice, and the drive from there to sober Menton is unforgettable.

The 33 km (20 mi) Base Corniche (La Corniche Inférieure) along the shoreline is an altogether different experience – slow-moving and traffic-choked, it was built by a Prince of Monaco and visits each and every place on the Côte d'Azur in turn. This is the way to go if you're interested in the hothouse social and commercial street life of the Riviera. The Middle Corniche (La Moyenne Corniche) runs between the other two roads, clinging to the escarpment's rocky backbone as it winds through the Mediterranean landscape, offering wonderful views of the coast and the Riviera's towns and villages below.

VOSGES WINE ROUTE

France

WORTH A DETOUR:
The red-roofed l'église Sainte Colombe in Hattstatt, begun in the 11th century with a 15th-century Gothic choir and 18th-century furniture.

Much of Alsace looks as though it has been created as the backdrop for a Hansel-and-Gretel fairy tale… or maybe a Disney film. The picturesque medieval villages with their brightly painted half-timbered houses vie with each other to put on the best floral display, as they sit in an undulating landscape beneath rocky crags topped with romantic ruined castles, surrounded by terraced vineyards that produce the region's famous white wines.

The 200 km (130 mi) Route du Vin runs through the foothills of the Vosges, following the western edge of the wide Rhine Valley from Marlenheim west of Strasbourg to Thann, near Mulhouse. It winds from north to south and biking is an excellent way of fully appreciating this delightful area, though fitness is required – there are plenty of thigh-sapping hills. For car drivers with a discerning palate, the journey can be a battle against temptation – there are free roadside dégustations (wine tastings) at almost every turn.

ECHOES OF RIMBAUD & VERLAINE

France

WHEN SHOULD I VISIT: September or October for the splendid autumn foliage.

The names of Jean-Nicholas-Arthur Rimbaud and Paul Verlaine may not mean all that much to today's world citizens, but these 19th-century literary giants are French national heroes. The poet Rimbaud made an enormous impact in his home country, and the older Verlaine was an eminent Symbolist poet who invited Rimbaud to Paris, where the pair soon started living a Bohemian life of hashish- and absinthe-fuelled excess. Rimbaud was from the Ardennes, the region of rolling hill country and extensive forests that is mainly in Belgium and Luxembourg, but extends into France. He returned there after his relationship with Verlaine ended badly (the drunken Verlaine shot him in the hand), walking endlessly through the countryside and writing poetry. He then travelled extensively, working in many exotic parts of the world, before he died at the age of thirty-seven in Marseilles and was interred in the family vault at Charleville. Ironically, Verlaine also spent time in the Ardennes after Rimbaud had departed, working as a teacher.

Today, it is possible to follow in their footsteps through this beautiful region by taking the Route Rimbaud-Verlaine. This 150 km (95 mi) pilgrimage from the Old Mill in Charleville-Mézières to the Auberge du Lion d'Or in Juniville has been devised as a themed route that includes places where the poets lived, worked and caroused, and has therefore been well mapped and described for the would-be traveller. It is a journey that may be made on foot, bicycle or by car.

RIVER CHARENTE CRUISE

France

HIGHLIGHTS:

Angoulême – a lovely old town with fine 17th- and 18th-century streets, plus Cathédrale de St Peter with its stunning Romanesque façade, a grand château and cartoon museum.

It doesn't take long for a tamed river to revert to the wild, and that's pretty much what happened to the River Charente in western France after commercial traffic ceased in the 1950s. It rises in the Haute-Vienne and flows into the Bay of Biscay near Rochefort, just south of La Rochelle, once forming a major transport artery that brought prosperity to the Cognac region.

Happily, the Charente's fortunes have been restored by the arrival of waterborne tourism, with major works restoring navigability. It is now possible to sail down from Angoulême via delightful towns like Jarnac, Cognac and Saintes to the bustling ship building port of Rochefort.

And this process is still new enough to ensure that the Charente isn't solid with boats from bank to bank all summer long.

That said, small (for up to eight people) boats are available for hire at many marinas along the Charente (by the day or for longer) and navigation is easy. The popular choice is a cruise that allows leisurely exploration of the chosen area. For those with deep pockets, an end-to-end trip from Fleac near

Angoulême to Rochefort would deliver a dream holiday – along all 170 km (105 mi) of navigable water, passing through 21 locks on the canalized section as this idyllic river meanders through its beautiful valley.

Anyone who undertakes this journey will appreciate why so many put France at the top of their holiday wish list, because such a cruise ticks all the boxes that make the French countryside such a special destination – incomparable pastoral landscapes, a timeless river, ancient villages and towns with traditional markets, vineyards, fine churches and splendid châteaux, history everywhere.

THE LOIRE VALLEY

France

The Loire Valley is known as 'The Garden of France and Cradle of the French Language'. The lush landscape combines with architectural and cultural heritage to make this an area of outstanding natural and cultural excellence. High on everyone's list of special attractions are the numerous châteaux along the river – around a thousand remain in the Loire Valley out of a total that was once much greater, with some 300 along the river itself. The reason for this over-abundance of great houses is simple – just about every one of the country's serious movers and shakers – from kings on down – built here over the centuries. The Valley between Chalonnes-sur-Loire and Sully-sur-Loire is classified as a UNESCO World Heritage Site, and this is an ideal section for an extended cycle tour. Starting at Chalonnes and heading east, the route follows the river to Angers, Saumur, Tours, Amboise, Chaumont-sur-Loire, Blois, Beaugency, Orléans, Châteauneuf-sur-Loire and finally Sully. The distance is around 300 km (185 mi). The riding is not too hard, and this is a splendid way to see and appreciate the best that the Loire Valley has to offer – which is very good indeed.

What an experience – the banks of this delightful river are ablaze with sunflowers and home to the finest examples of the castle-builder's art, from imposing medieval fortresses like Angers and Amboise to Renaissance masterpieces like Chambord and Chenonceaux and spectacular gardens like Villandry. This is also the home of great white wines, with the vineyards of great domaines everywhere, so there will be plenty of opportunity to sample fine vintages and enjoy the distinctive local cuisine (river fish a speciality!).

NORMANDY BEACHES
France

It's easy to jump into a car and whiz along the Normandy Coast from the mouth of the River Orne to the Varneville Dunes on the Cotentin Peninsula. Nothing hints at the drama played out here when Allied troops stormed ashore on D-Day – 6 June 1944 – to begin a fight to liberate France that saw 100,000 dead and dozens of Normandy's towns and villages destroyed. Little evidence of the furious battles that raged here survives, though the sheer size of these beaches makes it easy to imagine the enormous scale of operations. Some traces are left – like remains of the astonishing Mulberry Harbour that was towed across the Channel to Arromanches and many German bunkers, notably at Pointe du Hoc on Omaha beach, where cliffs are pitted with shell holes. Also, nearly every town has a D-Day museum and war memorial that helps to bring the reality of the savage fighting that took place along this coast to life, as do numerous Allied and German war cemeteries. It's a drive that's well worth making – a journey of solemn remembrance.

WHEN SHOULD I VISIT?:
April–September.

WORTH A DETOUR: Saint Malo – this dramatic walled port city is worth a day of anyone's time, with many splendid sights to see, including Chateau Saint Malo, Cathédral de St Vincent and the Solidor Tower.

BRITTANY'S EMERALD COAST
France

Brittany is a jewel in France's coastal crown, as the soubriquet 'Emerald Coast' suggests. The Breton coast is a wonderland of cliffs and seascapes, magical islands and estuaries, beaches and coves, fishing villages and ports... and a gastronomic delight for lovers of seafood and rich regional cuisine. It's possible to spend a lifetime exploring this endless coastline but an excellent introduction to the sort of delights to be found is provided by a round-trip cycle ride from Saint Malo via Dinan to Dinard and back. This offers excellent seascapes, sandy coves, fishing villages and (as a bonus) some lush Breton countryside.

The easy journey (no steep hills!) starts beside the River Rance at Saint Malo (cycle hire available), setting off in an easterly direction along the D201 coast road that hangs above the sea, through Rothéneuf to Cancale – the picturesque fishing village famed for its delicious oysters. From there, head south to Les Portes Rouges and pick up the D155 – the spectacular Rue du Bord de Mer that hugs the coast to Le-Vivier-sur-Mer. Stay with the D155 as it turns south to Dol-de-Bretagne, then turn onto the D676 and ride to the walled town of Dinan, high above the River Rance. This last stretch provides an opportunity to enjoy rolling Breton countryside.

JONTE RIVER GORGE

France

The Cévennes Mountains are in the southern part of the Massif Central, a place described as 'being between land and sky' – an assessment that's easy to appreciate when standing on high ground beneath a big sky, looking out over wooded hills that roll away into the far distance. This area has been accorded National Park status and is an unspoiled wilderness, but this land of dramatic moors and gorges, rivers and forests, medieval towns and little villages that cling to hillsides is a well-kept secret as far as mass tourism goes.

To get a feel for this special area, cycle the round trip along the short Gorge de la Jonte from Le Rozier to Meyrueis – but be warned that you will have to make a serious physical effort to earn those scenic rewards. The Jonte River rises in the Massif du Mont Aigoual within the Cévennes National Park and runs into the Tarn River at Le Rozier. The Jonte Gorge may not be quite as spectacular as the nearby Tarn Gorge, but it has a romantic charm all of its own.

For a ride to remember, this takes some beating. The outward journey from Le Rozier is the hard part. It's just 19 km (12 mi) long, though this is a demanding climb. But with the help of gravity the run back down from Meyrueis to Le Rozier makes all that effort worthwhile, as the narrow road snakes above the blue river, within the V-shaped Jonte Gorge with its rocky sides rising to the high plateau of the Grandes Causses. This really is a journey through breathtaking scenery – a genuine case of 'seeing is believing'. And if you duly like what you see, over 200 km (125 mi) of dedicated cycle paths await within the National Park.

HIGHLIGHTS:

Be sure to stop and enjoy one of the very best viewpoints on the entire route – the Belvédère des Terrasses.

A side trip to the fabulous limestone cave of Aven Armand between Meyrueis and Saint Enimie.

The 16th-century Château de Roquedols near Meyrueis – a sturdy 15th- and 16th-century castle in the forest that doubles as an information centre for the National Park (castle open July and August only, grounds all year).

The bizarre Le Rozier Museum in a former priory – an extraordinary collection of miniature buildings loving created using tiny blocks of the region's natural stone (open June–September).

YOU SHOULD KNOW

Birdwatchers flock to the Jonte Gorge for the rare opportunity to see three species of vulture circling (Black, griffon and Egyptian vultures).

CATHAR CASTLE WALK

France

YOU SHOULD KNOW

Whisper it if you dare – some 'Cathar' castles were actually built in the Middle Ages, long after the Cathars had been wiped from the face of the earth.

The Sentier Cathare is a 250 km (155 mi) trek from Port-La-Nouvelle on the Mediterranean near Narbonne, through the breathtaking Languedoc countryside. It is so called because – in crossing the Corbières and Pyrenean foothills of the Aude en route to Foix, in Ariège – the walk passes nine ruined Cathar castles. These 'castles in the sky' are picturesque ruins built high on rocky pinnacles by the Cathars, a Christian religious sect with mystic links to the Holy Grail that emerged in the 11th century, before being crushed as heretical by the Catholic Church in the bloody Albigensian Crusade of the early 1200s that is said to have cost over a million lives.

As a result, France acquired lands that were more Catalan than French, and it is through this wonderful terrain that the Sentier Cathare passes. The trail is way-marked with red-and-yellow signs (combining the colours of Languedoc and Catalonia), and is divided into manageable daily stages of around 20 km (12 mi). The trail is well maintained and – while there are some quite steep and rocky sections – it can be safely tackled by anyone who is fit. It might best be described as a challenging hike rather than demanding mountain trek, and there are rest houses and *gites d'etape* where travellers can bed down at the end of each day.

HIGHLIGHTS: The Malpas Tunnel, the world's first-ever canal tunnel, under Ensérune Hill.
A typical canal-side village – a fine example is Capestang with its stone bridge.

CANAL DU MIDI

France

In the 17th century boats provided the most efficient way to carry goods. The 235 km (145 mi) Canal du Midi, connecting Toulouse on the Garonne River to the Mediterranean port of Sète opened in 168. It was a monumental engineering achievement with over 300 significant structures, including more than 100 locks, many bridges, several dams and a tunnel.

The Canal du Midi goes through stunning countryside and time has been kind, mellowing the canal to the point where it seems like a graceful extension of the landscape as it meanders through Cathar country, passing towns and villages that have preserved their traditional character and charm. It is possible to travel from end to end (either way) on cruise boats, which usually offer additional sightseeing opportunities along the way. This journey can also be done by hire craft. Most people prefer to focus on a section of the canal (often one with no locks!) and proceed slowly, opting for one of the many different types of craft on offer from numerous boat-hire establishments and enjoying a truly relaxing holiday in wonderful surroundings.

Right: Canal du Midi

LE PETIT TRAIN JAUNE
France

WORTH A DETOUR:
A tour of Villefrance-de-Confluent, an unspoiled medieval town within its original walls… don't miss sensational views from Fort Liberia above the town.

The Languedoc-Roussillon Region's Little Yellow Train – operated by the French national rail company SNCF – runs from Villefrance-de-Confluent over a 63 km (39 mi) route that climbs steeply to Bolquère in the Catalan Pyrenees – the highest station in France at a giddy 1,593 m (5,225 ft). From there, le Petit Train Jaune crosses the plateau beneath the brooding presence of the Cerdagne Massif to Latour-de-Carol, where it connects with two mainline services – to Barcelona and Toulouse.

In summer, these quirky red-and-yellow narrow-gauge trains are much appreciated by tourists, as they run through dramatic mountain scenery, passing through many tunnels and over viaducts and bridges. In winter (with a snow plough fitted to the front) the reduced twice-daily service carries skiers and acts as a lifeline for the isolated communities along the line.

This service has been running for over a hundred years, and (much to the dismay of purists) the characterful original rolling stock – which is becoming increasingly difficult to service and repair – has now been supplemented by modern units, though heritage trains still run all summer long. Both types are 'multiple units', where electric motors are spread along the length of the train to permit the train to climb (and more importantly descend!) steep inclines safely – until this was developed around 1900, a rack-and-pinion system would have been the only option for le Petit Train Jaune.

Things to watch out for along the way are the mountainside village of Olette (spot the tall houses jutting precariously over the river), the fortified village of Mont Louis and the futuristic 'solar oven' at Fort Romeu… and of course the mountain scenery, which speaks for itself.

YOU SHOULD KNOW

Emergency rations are essential – one of the main difficulties in walking the HRP is that food supplies cannot be replenished every day.

PYRENEAN HAUTE ROUTE
France

This 800 km (500 mi) trek runs from Hendaye on the Atlantic to Banyuls-sur-Mer on the Mediterranean. It takes the high line along the spine of the mountains, avoiding centres of human activity. Though it rarely strays too far from useful facilities, the Haute Route Pyrénéenne (HRP) from one end of the Pyrenees to the other is not always well marked (good maps are essential) and there is little prospect of rescue in case of difficulty. It is therefore an undertaking reserved for adventurers experienced in demanding backpacking, as the sheer length of the journey precludes professionally guided trips. That said, many people choose to hike shorter sections of this superb mountain route alone or with an organized party.

The HRP is one of Europe's classic hikes and is definitely the highest, most beautiful, dramatic and challenging walk the Pyrenees can offer, as it weaves to and fro across the French-Spanish border. Although not waymarked, the path is generally well defined, and there are a number of refuges along the way that allow the intrepid walker to 'stay high' and rarely descend into the valleys. The true joy of walking the Pyrenees – apart from the rugged mountain scenery – is the fact that this is one of Europe's last great wilderness areas.

CORSICAN MULE TRAILS
France

WORTH A DETOUR:
A short side trip to the summit of a 'lookout mountain' – Paglia Orba with its stunning panoramic views.

As its rises abruptly from the Mediterranean, with pink granite peaks that soar to a height of over 2,500 m (8,200 ft), Corsica is often described as the 'mountain in the sea'. What's more, many aficionados of the long-distance hike say that Corsica's Haute Route GR20 (GR stands for Grandes Randonnées) from coast to coast is Europe's finest mountain walk. There may be other contenders, but there can be no denying the fact that this is a supreme physical challenge.

Paths are well defined – most are former mule trails – and clearly marked. But they are often rough underfoot with many steep ascents and descents. It is rarely possible to progress for more than 16 km (10 mi) in eight hours of demanding hill walking. From south to north, the GR20 follows the high mountains that divide the island's two regions, starting among the soaring pinnacles around Conca.

The path goes through woods and alpine meadows, crossing high ridges, bare granite slopes and deep gorges. Fitness is a must!

VIA DE LA PLATA, SANTIAGO DE COMPOSTELA PILGRIM ROUTE

Spain

Santiago de Compostela, the 'Jerusalem of the West' was Europe's first tourist destination. Ever since the 9th century, when skeletal relics supposedly belonging to St James (Santiago's namesake) were discovered, people have been flocking here on the premise that the Way of St James pilgrimage cuts in half the time to be spent in purgatory. The Via de la Plata is one of the least-travelled of the Ways of St James – an uplifting 1,000 km (625 mi) physical and spiritual trek for anyone who would prefer to walk in contemplative solitude rather than socialize with the throngs of wayfarers along the much better known Camino Francés. It follows the path of the old Roman Road from the orange groves of Seville to the northern market town of Astorga, where it merges with the Camino Francés east-west route. Much of the path is a reminder of how it must have been two thousand years ago, with Roman bridges and ruins, original paving and ancient milestones. You walk across open country of fields and olive groves, woods and moors, passing through some of Spain's most beautiful cities and stopping off at pilgrim refugiós.

The road runs through the hills and plains of the Extremadura taking you to Mérida, one of the richest Roman sites in Spain, and Cáceres, an intact medieval walled city, through the pastures and highlands of Salamanca, along the Duero River to the Romanesque city of Zamora, and into the verdant woodlands of Galicia. The final triumphant step of your pilgrimage is onto the carved scallop shell inscribed into the pavement of Santiago Cathedral, a ritual that supposedly purges you of your sins.

HIGHLIGHTS:

Cáceres – city walls.
Zamora – Romanesque churches.
Salamanca – Plaza Mayor.
Santiago de Compostela Cathedral.
Pilgrims wearing a 'uniform' of cloak and wide-brimmed hat and carrying a walking stick, a gourd (for drinking from wells) and a scallop shell (the St James pilgrim symbol).

A CORUÑA TO MADRID

Spain

WORTH A DETOUR:
Tower of Hercules, A Coruña – the oldest lighthouse in the world, dating from the 2nd century with magnificent views from the top.

Considering how long Spain has been a major tourist destination, its magnificent hinterland has remained remarkably undiscovered. There is no better way to see the interior of this beautiful country than catching the train from the lovely city of A Coruña, on the Galician coast, to Madrid – a 740 km (460 mi) scenic journey that takes you through a sparsely populated rural backwater of historic hill villages and ancient agricultural landscapes with breathtaking Mediterranean and Alpine views.

Leaving the dramatic coastal cliffs and bays of A Coruña behind, the train travels through the lush valleys and verdant woodlands of Galicia, up to the desolate romantic moorland around the city of Ourense on the banks of the River Miño, and through the virtually uninhabited borderlands of Spain and Portugal towards Zamora, across a mountain wilderness of rugged heath and forest where wolves still roam. Passing through countless tunnels, you cannot help thinking about the forced labour that built this section of the railway – half-starved Republican political prisoners of the 1940s and 50s, hacking their way through the mountain rock in pitch-darkness.

From Zamora, known as a 'museum of Romanesque art' for its 12th- and 13th- century churches, the railway meanders through the vineyards of the fertile Duero Valley and cuts across the ancient farmlands of the Tierra del Campo. The last leg takes you up past olive and citrus groves, oak and pine forests into the highlands north of Madrid. Finally you descend to the plain of Castilla-La Mancha and arrive at Spain's impressive capital city, by which time your head will be full of splendid scenic impressions and your appetite whetted to explore more deeply into this world away from the usual hackneyed tourist itineraries.

GREEN SPAIN

Spain

WHEN SHOULD I VISIT?:
April–October.

HIGHLIGHTS:
Bilbao – FEVE Railway
station,a period masterpiece.
Guggenheim Museum.
Santander – Magdalena
Palace and period
architecture.
Churches and monuments of
Oviedo.

TIME IT TAKESS:
19 hours minimum.

The railway system that runs across northern Spain is a mere 1m (3 ft) wide, originally designed for transporting coal from the mines of the Cantábrican Mountains. The network runs for 800 km (500 mi) through the exuberant terrain of 'Green Spain', the fertile coastal strip between the stormy seas of the Bay of Biscay and the misty slopes of the Cordillera Cantábrica, from the French border town of Hendaye to the Atlantic port of Ferrol, near the pilgrim city of Santiago de Compostela.

Travelling on the little electric railway lines that weave their way along the coasts of four provinces – the Basque country, Cantabria, Asturias and Galicia – is an enchanting way of seeing the little-known Celtic face of Spain. You pass through magical landscapes of brooding mountain peaks and white-water rivers, verdant estuaries and craggy shorelines, vibrantly green valleys and luxuriant woods. There are more than 250 stops along the way – historic provincial capitals, market towns, fishing villages and remote hamlets in the heart of the countryside – with several changes en route. You are unlikely to encounter many other tourists as the train trundles through the back of beyond. Your travelling companions will be a miscellaneous assortment of commuters – local fishermen, housewives going to market, teenagers off for a day trip in the city, and the odd village priest.

Although the whole journey can be undertaken in one long day, it is far more fulfilling to take your time,

seeing the city sights in Bilbao, Santander, Oviedo, Gijón and Avilés, branching off to visit the Gothic city of León and the gorges of the Picos de Europa, and spontaneously stopping at any number of picturesque seaside towns or country villages, spending the night at tourist guesthouses.

An alternative means of exploring Green Spain is by taking an 8-day rail-cruise on El Transcantabrico, a FEVE Railway luxury tourist train which stops for sightseeing.

HIGHLIGHTS: Madrid – Prado Art Gallery.
Zaragoza – Cathedral of San Salvador.
Barcelona – Parc Güell and Sagrada Familia Church.

The Alt Velocidad Española, better known as the AVE ('bird' in Spanish), is a high-speed train capable of travelling at 350 kph (220 mph) – the Spanish super-equivalent of the French TGV. AVE trains have been running between Madrid and the south of Spain since 1992 but, until recently, it still took more than six hours to get to Barcelona, Spain's second most important city.
The Madrid-Zaragoza-Barcelona line was finally inaugurated in February 2008 with seventeen trains in each direction per day. It is one of the world's fastest trains covering a distance of 660 km (410 mi) in just 2 hours 38 minutes. This brand-new self-driving, high-speed train may well live up to its acronym and make air travel obsolete. The AVE takes hardly any longer than the plane once you include check-in times and the journey to and from the airport, and is far less hassle and much more comfortable.
Madrid's Atocha Station looks more like an airport terminal than a station, its huge central atrium decked in palm trees. The AVE glides away from the platform and is soon whizzing across the beautiful countryside of Aragon and Catalonia. But it goes so fast, the view from your window is a blur.

EL GRECO WALK, TOLEDO
Spain

HIGHLIGHTS: The Alcázar (Castle).
Toledo Cathedral – one of the largest in the world.
Puerta Bisagra – main entrance gate to the Old City.

Known as the 'city of three cultures', the World Heritage city of Toledo was renowned in medieval times for intellectual and religious tolerance. . Wandering through the twisting medieval streets and narrow covered passages, you feel as though you have been time-warped into a mysterious fairytale past.
Toledo itself, perched on a rocky hill enclosed on three sides by the deep ox-bow gorge of the River Tajo, appears in many guises as a favourite background in his paintings and is the subject of one of his most iconic – and haunting – works ('View of Toledo').

If you cross the 13th-century five-arched Puente San Martin to the south bank of the Tajo and walk along the Carretera de Circunvalción, following the bend in the river all the way along the gorge to the restored Roman Puente de Alcántara, you can see the amazing views that were the inspiration for El Greco's Gothic masterpiece.
The time-scoured city walls of earth-brown brick emerge from the hill in perfect harmony with the golden landscape, dark green olive groves contrast with the parched hills and the spire of the Cathedral, like a raised sword, stands guard over the land.

MONTSERRAT RACK RAILWAY
Spain

HIGHLIGHTS: Old Monistrol Vila Station exhibition. El Rosari Monumental – a series of sculptures by Gaudi and others along the path to the Santa Cova shrine.

A railway to the legendary monastery of Montserrat was first opened in 1892, built for the increasing number of pilgrims who trudged up the mountain to make obeisance at this centre of Catalan faith and culture, the home of La Moroneta (the Black Madonna).

From the town of Monistrol de Montserrat, the modern train makes a brief but thrilling, sometimes near-vertical journey along the original 5 km (3 mi) route through tunnels and across bridges with amazing views of the bizarrely shaped granite teeth, for which Montserrat is so famous, outlined against the sky.

You plunge into the darkness of the recently constructed La Foradada tunnel then across the 480 m (1,574 ft) long Pont del Centenari – an awesome engineering design of steel lattice supported by eight pillars – to arrive at Monistrol Vila Station. Here the rack rail section of the line begins and the cog-wheel kicks in to haul you further up the mountain. Suspended between mountain and valley you continue your ascent in and out of tunnels to make one final spectacular upward heave to Montserrat Monastery, a gargantuan 19th-century complex of buildings, complete with basilica and museum, resting on a broad ledge enclosed by steep cliffs that soar skywards.

LA PEDRIZA
Spain

HIGHLIGHTS:
Castillo de Manzanares.
16th-century Church of Nuestra Señora de las Nieves.
Panoramic view from La Ermita de Nuestra Señora de la Peña Sacra.

Less than an hour's bus ride north of Madrid, you can breathe pure mountain air and escape the crowds in the wilderness of La Pedriza. This 32 sq km (12 sq mi) granite massif, a spur of the Sierra de Guadarrama, is a mind-blowing landscape of golden-pink granite spires and domes, veined with streams. Crazily complex rock formations sprout out of the woods, with names like El Pájaro (the Bird), La Foca (the Seal), and La Tortuga (the Tortoise). Wild goats roam among the granite slabs and falcons and vultures whirl through the sky.

La Pedriza is incredibly popular among Madrileños for the hiking and climbing here but it's not often frequented by tourists. There are numerous romantic legends and anecdotes attached to the area. It is all too easy to lose one's way among the granite cliffs and slabs, making it a haven for 19th-century bandits and later a Republican hideout in the Spanish Civil War. At the foot of La Pedriza lies Manzanares el Real, a faintly bohemian village inhabited by artisans, artists and musicians.

Right: La Pedriza

LA RIOJA

Spain

HIGHLIGHTS: Rio Oja Valley.
Romanesque architecture on Camino de Santiago.
San Millán de la Cogolla – World Heritage Site.
13th-century Yuso and Suso Monasteries.

La Rioja is practically synonymous with wine. The economy of the Alavesa hills around the River Ebro has relied on wine production since Roman times and produces some of the most famous vintages in the world. The region is only 150 km (90 mi) long and 50 km (30 mi) wide, almost completely encircled by mountains, ensuring a perfect micro-climate for grape growing. It is brilliant cycling country – kilometre upon kilometre of quiet country road, sleepy villages, historic monuments and dozens of bodegas (wineries) where you can sample the wares on your way.

Laguardia, the heart of Alavesa, is a walled medieval hill-town with 320 cellars dating back to the late 18th century. From here you cycle along the banks of the Ebro, passing the historic towns of El Ciego and San Vicente de la Sonsierra, to Haro, where the 15th-century monastery has been converted into a winery. Then, skirting the Ebro, wind your way through vineyards to reach the atmospheric town of Briones, cut almost vertically into the hillside.

Many of Spain's monasteries and convents are hidden in the mountains of the Sierra de Demanda, the southwestern boundary of La Rioja.

WHEN SHOULD I VISIT?:
March–June when the flowers are at their best, or September–October.

RUTA DE CALIFATO

Spain

The remains of Andalucia's golden age as a centre of culture a thousand years ago are to be seen in the incredible Moorish monuments of the cities and startlingly picturesque architecture of the hill villages. Setting out from Córdoba for Alcala La Real, 125 km (78 mi) away, you drive through the olive groves, vineyards and fields of the Guadalquivir Valley, stopping at whitewashed villages bedecked with petunias, and admiring the rugged scenery of the Sierra Subbéticas. From Alcala, an ancient strategic stronghold dominated by its magnificent Moorish castle, you can either take the direct 50 km (30 mi) route to Granada, through the village of Pinos Puente, where Queen Isabella is said to have granted permission for Christopher Colombus to sail the Atlantic, or add a few kilometres to your journey by touring the Vega, frontier territory between the Moors and the Christians, where medieval fortified villages are dramatically perched on craggy outcrops of the Sierra de Huétor, guarding the plains. As you approach Granada, the snow-capped peaks of the Sierra Nevada, the highest mountains in Spain, gradually loom into view.

THE RAPIDS OF THE NOGUERA PALLARESA RIVER
Spain

WHEN SHOULD I VISIT?: The best time is May and June when the river is in full flood but you can raft any time between April–September.

The 146 km (90 mi) long Noguera Pallaresa River is the most powerful river in the Pyrenees – a major source of hydro-electric energy. Its turbulent waters pour down from the 2,000 m (6,550 ft) high Val d'Aran in the Pyrenees through the beautiful lake and mountain scenery of the Pallars Sobirà. The reliable flow and relative safety of the unpolluted white water rapids make the Noguera Pallaresa perfect for rafting and kayaking.

There are charming cobble-stoned villages up- and downstream, from any of which you can take a dramatic river journey through breathtaking countryside. You can run a 45 km (28 mi) stretch of water from the village of Escaló through Sort, the main sports centre for the area, to the Collegats Gorge. Or, for novices, the 14 km (9 mi) stretch between Llavorsi and Rialp, with eight rapids along the way, is a brilliant introduction to the joys of river navigation and a lot less dangerous than it feels: despite unpredictable rapids and a lot of boat-bumping as you swirl downstream, the worst that can happen is a good soaking. From Sort, you make a jaw-dropping descent down the fastest rapid of the entire river and float through the spectacular rock formations of the Collegats Gorge, an epic climax to a journey of thrills and spills. Whether you decide to test your solo oarsman-ship in a kayak or cling with several others to an inflatable raft, you will experience an exhilarating buzz of adrenaline.

CROSS THE STRAIT OF GIBRALTAR
Spain

HIGHLIGHTS: Monastery of Poblet.
World Heritage monuments of Tarragona.
Seu Vella, Lleida – 12th–15th-century Cathedral.

The ferry ride across the Strait of Gibraltar is a startling journey of contrasts and culture shock. You suddenly realize how incredibly close Europe and Africa really are. The Strait is very narrow indeed – only 13 km (8 mi) at its narrowest point, and 50 km (31 mi) separate Algeciras from Tangier.
Algeciras, a sprawling industrialized city on the Bay of Gibraltar, at the bottleneck between the

Mediterranean and Atlantic, is one of the busiest ports in the world. But, for that very reason it is a peculiarly exciting city, with the highly charged, chaotic atmosphere that invariably pervades a port. Looking back to catch a last glimpse of the Rock of Gibraltar from the boat, you feel a quite extraordinary sense of loss, only to be overwhelmed minutes later by the thrill of sighting the minarets of Tangier in the distance. Tangier has a curious, fading grandeur about it and while it's by no means a typical Moroccan city, it is an exciting and idiosyncratic introduction to an extraordinary continent.

TARRAGONA TO LLEIDA

Spain

When you have had your fill of the hedonism of the Catalan coast, it is time to head inland, to explore the agricultural heartlands of Catalonia where the villages have their own folklore, culture and customs, local festivals rooted in medieval tradition, and magnificent regional food and wines. The people of this fiercely independent, semi-autonomous province have a strong sense of nationalism. They are Catalan first and Spanish second, their identity clearly visible in their preference for speaking in their native tongue, a language very different from the Castillian Spanish spoken elsewhere.

Inhabited since prehistoric times, Tarragona, on the Costa Dorada, was the base from which the Romans set out to colonize Iberia. It is beautifully situated on a rocky outcrop overlooking the sea with a walled old quarter and impressively intact Roman remains both in and around the town. A 115 km (70 mi) cycling tour of the back roads to the pleasant inland town of Lleida on the River Segre gives you an insight into Catalan rural culture as you meander through the pretty farmlands from village to village, winding along country lanes, passing dry-stonewalled terraces of fruit and olive groves, visiting ancient chapels and monasteries, old farm buildings and windmills along the way.

WHEN SHOULD I VISIT?:
October for the olive harvest.

You pass the vineyards of Montsant and see the olive oil factory at El Soleras at work, the famous olive villages of Les Garrigues and the historic curiosity of the old oil mill at Albatàrrec before ending your bike ride glowing with well-being at the gateway to the Pyrenees.

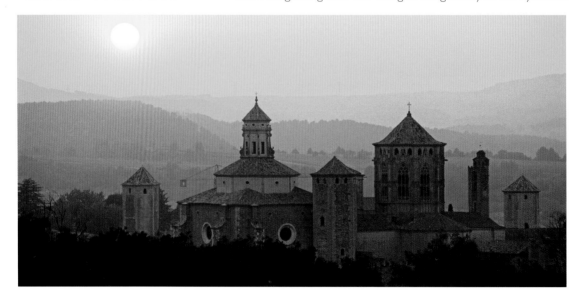

MOUNTAINS OF MAJORCA

Spain

The reality of Majorca belies its reputation as a high-rise hell of commercialized tourism. Apart from the narrow coastal strip along the Bay of Palma and the grim east coast resorts, the island is startlingly beautiful, particularly in the Serra de Tramuntana, the rugged mountains of the northwest. Here are soaring peaks interspersed with valleys of olive and citrus groves, sheer cliffs plunging into the sea, and charming mountain villages tucked away in the hills.

By far the most enjoyable way of travelling to the mountains is to catch the quaint little antique train from Palma to Sóller, originally built for the orange merchants of Sóller who needed a more efficient means of getting to the island capital than the long circuitous haul across the mountains by horse and cart. The train has been running since 1912 and its mahogany panelled, brass-fitted wooden carriages take you a step back in time as you make the 28 km (17.5 mi) journey along a narrow-gauge track through staggeringly beautiful countryside.

The train winds its way northwards across the plain of Palma and climbs into the mountains across enchanting valleys thick with citrus groves. It stops at villages along the way and there are some astounding views as well as scarily long sections of tunnel.

Sóller is a lovely mountain town, built on a slope around a main square with several cafés and bars. The town has retained a genuine, un-touristy atmosphere about it and you stroll through sleepy narrow streets of 18th and 19th-century stone houses with huge wooden doors and wrought iron rejas (screens). It is a brilliant base for hiking expeditions or you can take an old-fashioned tram down to the coast.

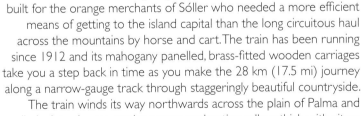

HOW TO GET THERE:
By train.
WHEN SHOULD I VISIT?:
April–May or September.
TIME IT TAKES:
1 hour 20 minutes.

YOU SHOULD KNOW

The Serra de Tramuntana is brilliant walking country with well-marked trails to suit all levels of ability.

199

THE WHITE VILLAGES OF LA ALPUJARRA IN THE SIERRA NEVADA

Spain

WHEN SHOULD I VISIT?:
March–May for the wild flowers or September–October for the autumn colour.

After the official expulsion of the Moors from Spain in 1492, refugees retreated into La Alpujarra, an inaccessible region of steep valleys in the southern Sierra Nevada, where they survived in isolated pockets for a further 150 years by cultivating the fertile silt washed down from the mountains. Today some 70 'white villages' are testimony to the Moorish cultural roots of the inhabitants. On a hike through this beautiful rugged country the Moroccan Berber influence can be seen all around – in the inimitable terracing of the fields, intricate irrigation techniques and cubic architecture.

The land is so steep that the quaint whitewashed houses with flat roofs and crooked clay chimneys seem to be piled on top of each other, each village an idiosyncratic jumble of narrow streets. The beautifully tended terraces of olive, fig, mulberry and nut trees are constantly watered by melting snow, directed down the mountains along *acequias* (irrigation channels). A network of ancient walled trails and mule paths takes you along ridges dotted with cacti, down into rocky wooded gorges, through almond groves and wildflower meadows, always with breathtaking views of the snowy peaks of the Sierra Nevada.

DON'T MISS
Levada of 25 Fontes – where you will find 25 springs cascading into a lake.

WALKING THE LEVADA DO CALDEIRAO VERDE IN MADEIRA

Portugal

In the early 15th century, Portuguese settlers found an uninhabited, densely forested, mountainous island, which they named Ilha de Madeira, meaning 'Island of wood'. They found that the south – the best agricultural land – was dry for much of the year.

This led to the building of levadas, a huge system of irrigation channels that divert the excess water from the mountains to the rest of the island. Today the 2,000 km (1,250 mi) long system is still being expanded, and the footpaths alongside the levadas, essential for maintenance, are now a favourite destination for walkers, and a perfect way of exploring the stunning interior of the island.

The levada of Caldeirao Verde (Green Cauldron), built in the 18th century, is a beautiful, steep walk, beginning at Queimadas Forestry Park, at an altitude of 890 m (2,900 ft). The path first takes you up through the forest of laurels, beeches, Japanese cedars and junipers, soon providing spectacular views of the terracotta roof tiles of the villages below. The route winds through four different tunnels, the second of which is 200 m (660 ft) long, each carved by hand, after which you will soon see the Caldeirao on your left – a natural, mossy rock bowl containing a waterfall-fed lake. All along the narrow path, moss, ferns and lichen growing to either side, you will see dramatic mountain scenery, and by the time you reach the Caldeirao you'll be glad to have a rest, with just the sounds of splashing water and birdsong for company.

WORTH A DETOUR: The Ethnographic Museum of Vilarinho da Furna, dedicated to the eponymous village that was 'drowned' to make way for a dam in 1972. If the water levels drop dramatically, the village begins to reappear.

PENEDA-GERÊS NATIONAL PARK
Portugal

Little known, Peneda-Gerês National Park is located in northern Portugal, part of a system of mountain ranges along the border with Spain. It is a glorious, unspoilt region of mountains, valleys, forests, lakes and rivers speckled with small, traditional farming communities linked by ancient footpaths, old paved tracks and even the remains of a Roman road.
The sense of wilderness is strong – tourism is light, and you will often find yourself alone for hours at a time, despite almost always being within easy reach of a village. The dense woodland includes birch, juniper, holly and several species of oak and silver birch at the rivers' edge. Peneda-Gerês is a rare refuge for both golden eagles and wolves, both of which were hunted remorselessly until recently, but there is more chance of seeing roe deer, otters or wild boar. There are birds, too – red kites, buzzards, falcons and many more.

TUA RAILWAY
Portugal

WORTH A DETOUR: Vila Real, with its Roman site at Panoias, and 18th-century palace of Solar de Mateus.

The historic, narrow-gauge railway line that runs from Tua to Mirandela is thought to be not only the most spectacular train journey in Portugal, but also of the entire Iberian Peninsula. The 54 km (34 mi) track clings to the rocky edge of a gorge as it carries you up into the Trás-os-Montes ('beyond the mountains') region, following the course of the Tua River valley. This major feat of engineering was completed in 1887, after three years of difficult, dangerous work, requiring vast quantities of dynamite to blast a track through these rugged mountains. From the Douro River at Tua, the lime green and white diesel locomotive quickly leaves the town behind and begins to climb north towards Abreiro, the halfway point.
For a while the main Douro line from Porto to Pocinho, of which this is an off-shoot, is visible beneath you, but you rapidly reach the most dramatic part of the journey, which takes you through narrow tunnels and over bridges, with exceptional views across the river on your left, which itself drops further and further away. Sometimes, looking out of the window, there appears to be absolutely nothing between you and a vertiginous drop of hundreds of metres to the water below, tumbling along at speed, over granite boulders, between the rocky walls of the gorge.
After Abreiro the incline lessens as the train reaches the Trás-os-Montes plateau and its olive groves, before finally pulling in to Mirandela.

VICENTINE COAST

Portugal

HIGHLIGHTS:
Sagres – The unusual,
43 m (142 ft) diameter wind
compass at the fortress.
Cape St Vincent and its
lighthouse, sacred to Romans
and Christians alike.
Surfing the beaches around
and north of Cape St Vincent.
The stunning sunsets.

YOU SHOULD KNOW
The Atlantic coast has strong
currents and big waves.
Whether you are experienced
or not, take advice as to the
safest places to swim or surf.

In 1995 a large stretch of Portugal's Atlantic coast was designated The South-West Alentejo and Vicentine Coast Natural Park. Consisting of a remarkably well-preserved landscape of outstanding natural beauty, this region is a remote and unusual area to explore by car or bike, though easily reached from either Lisbon or the Algarve. Sagres in the south is well known throughout Portugal as it was here, during the 15th century, that Prince Henry the Navigator not only made his home, but also started his school of navigation. All the great Portuguese explorers of the age studied here, including Vasco da Gama and Magellan. From the beach halfway between Sagres and Sao Vicente, newly designed ships set sail into the unknown, thus launching Portugal's colonial empire. The town itself was damaged first by Sir Francis Drake and again during the earthquake in 1755, but it is still dominated by Prince Henry's impressive fortress.

The scenery along this coast is wild and exciting: towering cliffs, secluded, sandy coves, sand dunes, estuaries, rocks and islets provide many different types of coastal habitat. You will find rare, even unique, wildflowers that have adapted to life in sand or rocky crevasses, while inland are orchards of fig, orange and almond. This is a major migration route for birds of prey as well as a multitude of seabirds. You may see Bonelli's eagles, kites and fishing eagles, as well as rock doves and white storks, making their untidy nests on rocky pinnacles by the sea.

En route you'll pass through small villages of gleaming, white houses, where you can enjoy delicious seafood, and take walks along tracks through flower-filled fields to the sea. Zambujeira do Mar, a pleasant, seaside village with a splendid beach, makes a convenient end point.

LISBON TRAM LINE 28

Portugal

WORTH A DETOUR:
The Gulbenkian
Museum, a superb
collection of treasures.

Lisbon's Tram Line 28 takes you across four of the seven summits upon which Lisbon stands, in the course of a classic journey through some of the most interesting areas of this historic city. The trams make their way up the Mouraria hill to Largo da Graca, before trundling down through Alfama, the oldest, most beautiful and best-known part of the city. The next port of call is Baixa, the lower city, which was rebuilt in French neo-classical style after the earthquake of 1755, by the Marques de Pombal. Climbing uphill again, the trams pass through the old city centre, the Bairro Alto and the Bica, haunt of writers and artists. Rattling and clanking their way up and down the hills, through narrow streets, the trams pass many important sites, including handsome churches, the Parliament building and the Cathedral, before finally reaching the Cemitério dos Prazeres, Cemetery of the Pleasures, where members of Lisbon's noblest families are buried.

VIA FERRATA HIGH ROUTE

Italy

The first via ferrate, iron roads, were built in the Dolomites during World War I. These high mountain routes consist of fixed steel cables, ladders and bridges, forming long trails through the mountains that are available to walkers and climbers of varying experience and ability.

Originally built to help high altitude troop movements taking place in very harsh, winter conditions, these routes have not only been renewed and restored, but many others have been added, enabling access to much of the high Dolomites.

A great many towns and villages give access to via ferrate, but one of the most popular routes is Alta Via Uno. Beginning at Pragser Wildsee, near Toblach, this 120 km (75 mi) hike, ending at Belluno, takes days to complete and carries you through some of the most unforgettable scenery in the 'Pale Mountains'. The routes are all very well signed, and

WHEN SHOULD I VISIT?: May–mid-September.

there are frequent refuges in which to stay, providing simple, inexpensive meals and beds for hikers. It is also possible to take a much shorter, weekend trip that ends at Passo Falzareggo.

AMALFI COAST ROAD

Italy

Winding its way between Sorrento and Salerno, on the ankle of Italy's boot, is the famous Amalfi Coast Road. This heavily used stretch of tarmac, carved into the mountainsides, is renowned for its stupendous views and extraordinary hairpin bends. The route, along with the charming villages and towns along the way, has been one of Italy's major tourist attractions for decades.

Sorrento, situated on cliff-tops, overlooks the whole of the Bay of Naples. From here you can see Naples itself as well as Vesuvius and the island of Ischia. Steps and lifts drop down 45 m (150 ft) to the sea, where swimming is from wooden jetties rather than a straightforward beach. From here, the road twists around the rocky peninsula to Positano, where pastel hued houses of pink, peach and apricot, enhanced by brightly coloured flowers, seem to cling precariously to the mountainside, up which they scramble from the small beach below. The road soars and descends, through occasional tunnels, curling round frightening bends where one false move could send you hurtling off into the sparkling blue sea, hundreds of metres below – these spectacular, dizzying views are unparalleled. Visit Amalfi, set at the foot of Monte Cerreto, and admire the magnificent 9th century cathedral, built when the town was a major maritime republic. Make the trip up to the stunning medieval hill town of Ravello, a tranquil gem of a place, boasting palaces, villas, gardens, narrow, cobbled lanes and a view which writer Gore Vidal rated as the most beautiful in the world.

From Amalfi, the road passes through Vietri, known for its ceramic production since the 15th century, and a mere 5 km (3 mi) further, head into the bustling port area of Salerno, an historic town with a wealth of splendid palaces and churches.

WHEN SHOULD I VISIT?:
April–June or September–November; during the high summer months (July and August) the area suffers from too many visitors and far too much traffic.

HIGHLIGHTS:
Amalfi's Wednesday market. The Grotta dello Smeraldo, a swimming spot accessible only by boat from Amalfi or Positano. The gardens of the Villa Cimbrone in Ravello.

TIME IT TAKES:
About three hours, but you'll find it far more rewarding to spend two or three nights in different places along the way.

YOU SHOULD KNOW
The Amalfi Coast is a UNESCO World Heritage Site.

Right: Amalfi Coast Road

GREAT DOLOMITES ROAD

Italy

WHEN SHOULD I VISIT?:
April–September.

HIGHLIGHTS:
The breathtaking views in
every direction.
The South Tyrol
Archaeological Museum,
home to the 5,000-year-old
mummy known as 'Otzi the
Iceman'.
Bolzano's Gothic cathedral,
started in 1184 and
completed in 1382.
The Tyrolean village of
San Genesio, known for its
celebrations, where
the locals wear traditional
Tyrolean costume.

There is no doubt that the journey along the Great Dolomites Road between Cortina d'Ampezzo and Bolzano is one of Europe's great road trips. It twists and turns, switchbacking around some of the highest peaks in the range, and passing through ski resorts and mountain villages along the way.

This astonishing feat of engineering was built between 1895 and 1909, and provides a true feast for the eyes of those who travel along it.

From Cortina d'Ampezzo, a chic, expensive ski resort during the winter months, surrounded by magnificent peaks dotted with cable cars and funicular railways, the road ascends sharply to the high pass of Passo Pordoi. During the winter, when the mountains are covered with thick snow, the road may sometimes be impassable without chains, but in spring and summer the scene is verdant and the slopes are covered with a million wildflowers – buttercups, rhododendrons, Alpine poppies and more. The narrow road twists past the Stella mountain group, which looms above you and there is a superb view of Sassolungo thrown in.

As you descend towards Canazei, an attractive town in its own right and the halfway mark, you find yourself at the base of the area's tallest peak, the mighty Marmolada. At 3,342 m (10,000 ft) the mountain, with its pristine white glacier, is known affectionately as the Queen of the Dolomites. As the road drops down to Bolzano it passes through an amazing canyon, near vertical walls rising on either side. The town itself is enchanting: its historic centre rich with notable buildings, Hapsburg era churches and narrow, cobbled streets ensuring its enduring popularity as a tourist resort.

CINQUE TERRE

Italy

The Cinque Terre are five little, coastal villages set in steep valleys surrounded by rugged, mountainous terrain. This region remained isolated until roughly 100 years ago, when a railway line was built, but the area's unique landscape and culture has been well preserved, and it's now a UNESCO World Heritage Site.

The Cinque Terre region is characterized by a multitude of terraces carved into the hillsides over hundreds of years. Vineyards and olives groves are cultivated here, and the villages are linked via a maze of footpaths. The main, coastal path, or Sentiero Azzuro, is the most direct, but there is another, more difficult ridge path too, and many shorter, ancient tracks up to the village sanctuaries.

Starting in the west, at Monterosso al Mare, the cactus lined trail climbs through terraces to Vernazza. This is the toughest section of the coastal path, but Vernazza is stunning – rose and ochre painted houses nestle at the base of the mountain, jutting out on a promontory beside a natural harbour, with the ruins of an ancient castle high above. Corniglia offers the Gothic-Ligurian style church of San Pietro (1334) while Manarola, situated beside a stream, is known for its wine. The famous 'Lovers Walk' starts here: a paved path through vineyards to Riomaggiore, the most easterly of the five villages. Here a picturesque cascade of pastel houses tumble down to the small dock below.

Whether you decide to walk the coastal path directly, or stay in one or two of the villages on the way, this is a magical place. The air is fragrant with wild herbs, the views inspiring, the wine and food delicious. Take your time, walk and swim, drink local wine in the sunshine, visit some beautiful churches – this is a splendid place for a break.

HIGHLIGHTS:
Vernazzo – Santa Margherita di Antiochia.
Manarola – San Lorenzo.
Riomaggiore – San Giovanni.
Battista Riomaggiore –
The Sanctuary of Madonna di Montenero.
The renowned local pesto –
a sauce of basil, garlic, pine nuts, olive oil and pecorino cheese.

WHEN SHOULD I VISIT?:
April–November. Avoid July and August crowds.

SENTIERO DEL VIANDANTE
Italy

YOU SHOULD KNOW

On 2007 Lake Como was reported as being too polluted for swimming. Check on the situation before you dive in.

Lake Como, in northern Italy close to the Swiss border, has attracted visitors for centuries. The lake, shaped like an inverted 'Y', boasts a delightful, sub-tropical climate, and the resulting vegetation, olive and citrus groves, bougainvillea and palm trees, looks remarkable against the backdrop of snow-clad mountains. The Sentiero del Viandante, or Wayfarer's Trail, is an ancient mule path connecting the villages along the lake, originally used for bringing goods both from Milan, to the south, and the northern plains. Nowadays it is a little piece of hiker heaven, with orange signs marking the route.

Starting at Lierna, a lovely medieval town with two of the lake's best beaches, follow the path up towards Ortanello, through the forest to the 13th-century church of St Peter. This is a perfect spot for a picnic. A sunny, grassy space – complete with fountain, tables and even barbecue equipment – spreads out around the church, and by now you'll need a break.

Follow the trail through Ortanello and soon you'll be heading down to Varenna. You are now high over the lake and this is the trickiest part of the hike, but the views over the sparkling blue lake and the mountains are glorious. Visit the ruins of Vezio Castle – from the top of the tower you can see over the entire lake. Varenna, perhaps the most picturesque town on Lake Como, has steep, narrow lanes that wind down to the harbour, past lovely houses, their balconies a mass of colourful flowers.

HIGHLIGHTS: The Vatican City and St Peter's. Rome's famous ruins, such as the Colosseum and the Catacombs. Exploring Mount Etna.

ROME TO CATANIA
Italy

This is a rare journey where the train boards a ship to cross the sea. Leaving Rome's main station in the morning and heads for Naples, its shabby, colourful tenements strung with washing, the line turns to run parallel to the coast. You'll catch a glimpse of the island of Capri and the Sorrentine peninsula, and soon the landscape becomes one of bare, rocky hills, abandoned villages, with an occasional sprinkling of modern houses.

The beach too, looks somewhat abandoned: with few people and just the odd fishing boat out to sea. Finally, the train pulls into Villa San Giovanni, where the carriages, uncoupled, are rolled onto the ferry, and taken across the Straits of Messina, where they are rolled back onto tracks and re-assembled.

HIGHLIGHTS: Siena's annual medieval horse race, the Palio, which takes place in the Piazza del Campo.
The Romanesque church of Santa Maria a Chianni.
Castelfiorentino – The Baroque church of Santa Verdiana and Benozzo Gozzoli's frescoes.

Originally going south to Bari, the launching point for Jerusalem, the Via Francigena is an ancient pilgrim trail stretching all the way from Canterbury to Rome. Much of the trail is relatively undeveloped and the paths are sometimes overgrown – thus allowing walkers to meditate on an enchanted landscape in peace. One of the loveliest sections of the trail takes you through the Tuscan heartlands. Starting at Castelfiorentino, a fortified town in the Valdesa Valley with a superb Baroque church, the path follows the course of the River Elsa to Certaldo. Like many Tuscan towns, it rests upon a hill, 129 m (426 ft) above sea level, and from its walled, medieval centre you can see the modern section spreading out beneath, surrounded by fecund vineyards.

Visible in the distance are the towers of San Gimignano.

The path continues through Poggibonsi: set on a small hill, its crucial position between the old states of Siena, Volterra and Florence provoked centuries of invasions and uprisings. A further 11 km (7 mi) and you reach San Gimignano, an almost perfectly preserved, absolutely gorgeous hilltop town. During the 10th-century San Gimignano prospered from pilgrims and traders travelling the Via Francigeno, and art flourished in the many churches and monasteries. The magnificent frescoes in the Duomo are just a taste of the treasures to be found here.

Monteriggioni, the next fortified village en route, boasts almost intact 13th-century walls, encompassing fourteen towers that are the largest of their kind in Tuscany. By now you are only some 15 km (9 mi) from Siena, the region's capital. On reaching the Piazza del Campo, one of Italy's most sublime squares, and the Piazza del Duomo, dominated by an astonishing cathedral, you can vividly imagine a medieval pilgrim's awed response to his surroundings. Your own will doubtless be much the same.

The recent revival of interest in long distance walks and pilgrim trails has prompted the Italian government to plan to upgrade the route, which is less well known and less travelled than the trail to Santiago de Compostela. Check travel websites for updates.

UMBRIA HILL TOWNS

Italy

HIGHLIGHTS:

Todi, with its ancient walls.
Civita – an artist's paradise,
built on a pinnacle and
attached to the wider world
by a narrow bridge.
Collevalenza – with its unique
Sanctuary, built in 1965.
The church of Santa Maria
degli Angeli, outside Assisi,
which encloses another
tiny church that was the first
Franciscan friary.
Orvieto – Tempio Belvedere,
the last above-ground
Estruscan temple
in Italy.

A tour around the medieval hill towns of Umbria makes for the most pleasant of journeys. Pottering along the small back roads, amidst spreading chestnut trees and luxuriant elms on the hillsides, through valleys and beside clear sparkling streams, you are in a landscape captured by many a master painter. The popularity of nearby Tuscany has allowed Umbria to remain relatively unscathed.

Perugia is both beautiful and lively – home to the University for Foreigners and topped by the 16th-century Rocca Paolina, Italy's largest fortress; the July Jazz Festival is colourful and exciting, thousands of people speaking hundreds of languages throng the streets and piazzas, enjoying free concerts late into the night.

Assisi, reconstructed after the shocking earthquake of 1997, is crowded with pilgrims coming to visit the Basilica of St Francis. He was born here in 1181. From the magical castle of Rocco Maggiore look out across the glorious Tiber Valley, which so inspired him. There are treasures to be found everywhere – countryside and town alike: Spello's ancient walls date back 2,000 years, and its 13th-century church is illuminated with Pinturicchio's fabulous frescoes.

CRETE SENESI

Italy

HIGHLIGHTS:
The Bravio delle Botti, an annual event occurring on the last Sunday in August, when competing teams push large wine casks up the hill.
Asciano, a small walled town in the heart of Crete Senesi, with mixed Romanesque and Gothic architecture.
San Quirico and Bagno Vignoni, popular for their spring water even in Roman times.
The Abbey of Monte Oliveto Maggiore and its famous frescoes.
The glorious landscapes through which you travel and the views from the hill towns.

WHEN SHOULD I VISIT?:
April–October.

Cycling through the lovely landscapes of Crete Senesi is possibly the best way to see the part of Tuscany to the south of Siena. Meaning 'Siennese clays', the name refers to the greyish beige colour of the clay soil, which is used in the production of terracotta tiles and splendid, large olive jars.

Leaving the Val d'Orcia, its green, undulating hills occasionally interrupted by eroded gullies, make your way to Montepulciano. Topping a ridge, its superb views stretch out for miles. At the foot of the hill is the Renaissance church of San Biagio. Designed by Antonio da Sangallo, this is an exceptional building. The road from the church up to the town, however, is steep, and you'll need a glass or two of the excellent, local red wine by the time you get there.

Wheel along through vineyards and olive groves on unpaved roads that wind up hill and down vale. Catch glimpses of fortified hilltop villages and ancient farmhouses, and notice the vines giving way to fields of wheat and sunflowers swaying in the welcome breeze, Cyprus trees standing sentinel against the deep blue sky. Arriving in 15th-century Pienza, you find a treasure trove of Renaissance architecture, built by order of Pope Pius II, whose birthplace it was. The piazza, with the Pope's family palazzo and a splendid cathedral, is a glorious sight.

Leaving Pienza, you head for Montalcino. Set on a hilltop overlooking the valleys beneath, the town has been settled since Etruscan times, though today it is far better known for its exceptional Brunello wines than for its historic architecture. Make sure you visit the nearby Sant'Antimo Abbey: started in the 9th century, it is a sublime example of monastic architecture. The mellow stone glows in the warm light of the surrounding countryside, forming a perfect, harmonious scene.

ITRIA VALLEY TRULLI

Italy

WHEN SHOULD I VISIT?: May–October. Try to see the 'Processione della Grata, a candlelit procession of up to 6,000 people that takes place on the second Sunday of August, going from the Sanctuary della Grata, outside Ostuni, into the centre of town.

Until recently, Puglia, the easternmost part of the heel of Italy's boot, remained largely unknown, but today things are changing, and the region is recognized as a fascinating place, rich in architecture and lovely to behold. Farming is still the mainstay here – ancient, gnarled olive trees and verdant vines, luscious figs and almond trees emerge from the intense red soil, and deep green pines clothe the low hills.

Begin your journey at Monopli on the coast, with its defensive walls and towers that protect a once important harbour, dominated by an ancient castle. The pedestrianized centre is a charming maze of narrow streets, and there are imposing palaces and a splendid Cathedral to be seen. It's an easy ride from there to Conversano, inhabited since Palaeolithic times. Built by the Normans, part of the megalithic walls form the foundation of the trapezoidal castle, which today houses Paolo Finolglio's 16th century frescoes.

Now ride through the gently undulating landscape of the Itria Valley, with its old fortified farmhouses, masserie, standing amidst the cherry trees and olive groves, to the UNESCO World Heritage Site of Alberobello, and its 1,500 14th-century trulli houses. Unique to this area, trulli are small, circular buildings made of limestone blocks, with conical roofs, originally constructed without mortar. The town is, of course, heavily visited, but more trulli are dotted around the countryside.

YOU SHOULD KNOW

Don't try to do this trek on your own – you really won't know where you are and could get into serious difficulties.

SELVAGGIO BLU TREK IN SARDINIA

Italy

Said to be the toughest trek in Italy, as well as one of the most beautiful, Selvaggio Blu is a 45 km (28 mi) hike around the Gulf of Orosei on the east coast of Sardinia, the Mediterranean's second largest island.

In the late 1980s, Peppino Cicalo and Mario Verin, two Tuscans, conceived the idea of finding and linking a network of shepherds' and charcoal burners' paths, long unused, around the Gulf, keeping as close to the sea as possible.

The trek to Cala Gonone takes you through a wild, lonely landscape of rock and stone, through ancient forests of oak, canyons, rock gullies and limestone arches. There is no sign of human habitation, and in parts you'll need to use ropes to climb or abseil, you'll walk along narrow ledges beside high cliffs, with the sea roaring hundreds of metres beneath you.

GRAND CANAL
Italy

WHEN SHOULD I VISIT: All year round, though there can be floods from November to March. June to September get crowded.

Venice is certainly one of the wonders of our world. An archipelago of 118 islands formed by 150 canals within a marshy lagoon on the Adriatic, it relies on waterways for transport, with the Grand Canal as the highway. Almost 200 remarkable buildings, most of which rise straight from the water, form the 'banks' of the canal in an extraordinary sequence of façades, their reflections rippling below. This was the most expensive and sought-after area in the city, and these fine palazzi were built by aristocrats and wealthy merchants between the 13th and 18th centuries.

The canal winds through the heart of Venice in an inverted 'S' shape, and the vaporetto zigzags across it to stops on either side, passing under three bridges, the 16th century, marble Rialto, the Academia, made of wood (1854) and the stone Scalzi (1858). This is a breathtaking voyage, varied, colourful and surprising. You'll pass fifteen splendid churches, museums and galleries such as the Guggenheim Collection, housed in the Palazzo Venier dei Leoni. You'll even see postmen delivering mail by gondola.

VENICE TO PATRAS DAGI
Italy

HIGHLIGHTS: Venice in all her glory.
Sunbathing on deck in the middle of the Adriatic.
Patras Carnival – the largest of its kind in Greece, it starts on January 17th and continues until the Monday before Lent.

Travelling overland from Italy to Greece is a lengthy and expensive trip. If time is of the essence, take the ferry from Venice to Patras, thereby spoiling yourself with a mini-cruise into the bargain. Even a short stay in Venice can be exhausting, with so much to see, but a couple of days crossing the Adriatic will boost your energy levels.

Many ships leave from Venice port – large cruise liners as well as ferries head off in all directions. There is a frequent service to Patras.

Patras itself has a long and distinguished history. Built on the slopes of Mount Panachaikon, its old town is charming, full of neo-classical buildings, churches, monuments, narrow lanes and steps. Greece's third city and second largest port after Piraeus, Patras is large, lively and a good base for exploring.

RIVIERA DAY TRAIN

Italy

The ancient city of Genoa is situated on the Ligurian Sea, on Italy's northern coast, not far from the border with France. Taking the train along the Italian and French Rivieras has been a classic journey ever since the railway arrived in the late 1800s. Prior to that, the coastline was largely unknown to the wider world, but the railway brought an influx of foreign visitors, including European royalty and artists who came for the climate, the lovely scenery and the clear, sharp quality of the light. To best enjoy the trip, make sure you find a seat on the left side of the train, so your view of the dazzling green-blue sea is uninterrupted. The windows on the right look out mainly at high walls and lines of drying laundry. The train is heavily used, by people going to work, school or college, as well as by day-trippers and more serious travellers, and it stops at every little station along the way. From the windows you will see the gorgeous Mediterranean countryside, decked with flowering shrubs and palm trees swaying in the warm breeze. At Ventimiglia, close to the border, there's an addictive Friday morning market, which many French people come to each week. Once in France, gawp at Monte Carlo, home to the famous casino and principal town of the tiny, sovereign state of Monaco, its harbour bursting with millionaires' yachts. The train passes in and out of dark tunnels, making you blink each time you emerge into the golden sunlight. Look out for Eze, perched 400 m (1,300 ft) high above the sea, Beaulieu-sur-Mer, Villefranche and finally, Nice, the undisputed Queen of the Côte d'Azur.

HIGHLIGHTS:
Genoa – historic centre, the largest in Europe.
The aquarium, the second largest in Europe.
Nice – the Cours Saleya Flower market and the Matisse Museum.

WHEN SHOULD I VISIT?:
From September–June to avoid the high season crowds.

WORTH A DETOUR: The 'corkscrew' of the waterjet of Trummelbach Falls in Lauterbrunnen Valley: inside the mountain, and accessible by lift installed in the rockface, the Jungfraujoch meltwater pumps 20,000 litres (4,399 gallons) per second through smooth-bore chutes.

LAUTERBRUNNEN TO SCHILTHORN
Switzerland

T he classic image of Switzerland – dramatic snow-capped peaks, icy torrents crashing down the sombre grey of sheer cliffs, emerald meadows studded with the white, gold and pink of wild flowers, and endless vistas of Uhland-green forests and turquoise lakes beneath a swollen arc of sky – belongs to Mürren in the Bernese Oberland. Mürren is a car-free cluster of ancient wooden chalets, an eyrie set on a ledge 800 m (2,100 ft) straight up (literally) from the Lauterbrunnen Valley floor. You reach it on a cog railway from Lauterbrunnen, itself impossibly pretty, and as the train passes Grutschalp it leaps the valley wall, opening up the best views bar none of the entire Jungfraujoch. It really is the ultimate: only from Mürren do you get the slanting range of the Eiger, Monch and Jungfrau heaving their rocky mass out of the forests and meadows of their flanking valleys. It's like looking through a cross-section of natural beauty, of wilderness and domestic pastoral.

You can ascend much higher than Mürren, on the cable car from Stechelberg to the dizzy heights of Schilthorn (2,970 m/9,742 ft). If anything, the panorama – from Bern to Mont Blanc – is even more magnificent, but from the summit you see an exclusively Alpine world of peaks and skyscapes. The softer valleys and lakes that from Mürren balance earth with heaven are lost in this airy empire. On the other hand, when you regain your powers of speech, you can enjoy a drink in the revolving restaurant on Schilthorn's summit – made famous by the James Bond film *On Her Majesty's Secret Service*. Equally stunning in summer or winter, Lauterbrunnen to Schilthorn is the best railway journey in Switzerland.

BERNESE OBERLAND HIKE
Switzerland

The Bernese Oberland is home to the great peaks, glaciers, forest valleys, vivid green pastures, rugged gorges and mare's tail waterfalls that form the composite quilt of Switzerland's most potently attractive image. There is a discreet network of trails and paths that enables you to go just about anywhere within its sphere of mythic mountain splendour. Follow the angry Reichenbach torrent up the densely wooded flank of the Haslital to the Falls. At Kaltenbrunnen you burst out of the trees to get the first, exquisitely framed view of the snowy mountains. Every little valley here is another Shangri-La of flower-strewn meadow, bubbling stream, forest, and soaring cliff-faces; but ahead and behind, the view gradually gets bigger

and bigger. Suddenly, you stand on the Grosse Scheidegg Pass itself. From 1,962 m (6,434 ft), with the Wetterhorn to one side close by, you look down across the upper Grindelwald glacier to the wisps of cloud hovering above the valley.

WORTH A DETOUR:
Riding a sledge or velogemel (snow bicycle) at night, in winter, from Grosse Scheidegg to Grindelwald down the 7 km (4 mi) ice-covered, snow-banked road.

HIGHLIGHTS: The oldest alpine resort of Burgenstock, a place of utter calm and peace set on the low hills of a wooded peninsula, seemingly set on the water.
William Tell's chapel, near Flüelen.

LUCERNE TO FLÜELEN
Switzerland

Lake Lucerne is also known as 'Vierwaldstadtsee', the Lake of the Four Forest Cantons through which it winds. On its southeastern shore lies the Rutli Meadow, traditional site of the founding of the Swiss Confederation, and it is lined by many of Switzerland's oldest communities like Vitznau, Brunnen and Treib. From Lucerne to Flüelen, at the foot of the Lake's wildest and most remote arm, these ancient villages and towns are oases of highly picturesque domesticity set against dramatic peaks. The unlikely combination is even more impressive when you enjoy it from one of the fin-de-siècle paddle steamers that turn the journey to Flüelen into a stylish rite. The historic boats seem appropriate to the grandeur of the waters they patrol. They fit into a scenario that includes castles on promontories, timber-framed villages huddled round 12th-century stone-quoined ports, waterfalls cascading down sheer granite cliffs, mountain meadows folded into rock-filled ravines, and the brooding menace of mountains like Rigi, forever changing mood, reflected in the sparkling water. Other boats might reach Flüelen more quickly; the steamers add grace to breathtaking landscapes that seldom look quite the same twice.

WHEN SHOULD I VISIT?:
June– September, when the
alpine wild flowers are at
their best.

ALPINE PASS HIKE

Switzerland

The Alpine Pass route is one of the great European hikes. It crosses Switzerland from Sargans in the east on the Lichtenstein border, to Montreux in the west on Lac Lèman. It crosses sixteen passes along its 354 km (220 mi) length, and completing it involves climbing and descending a total of 19,500 m (63,960 ft), the equivalent of going up and down Mount Everest more than twice! The Hike is usually divided into fifteen stages, and with bad weather and rest days, it's generally regarded as a minimum 19 to 20 day journey. The important thing is to give full scope to your sheer enjoyment of the landscape. You'll pass the Wetterhorn, Eiger, Monch, Jungfrau, Gspaltenhorn, Blumlisalp and Les Diablerets – mountains of consummate grace and charisma. You'll cross huge glaciers in the high wilderness, traverse grassy saddles of alpine meadow, and drop deep into steep valleys of velvet emerald pasture. The Bernese Oberland rises in majesty, and the Alpine Pass route weaves over, round and through the best of it. Ancient villages like Meiringen, Grindelwald, Mürren and Kandersteg typify regional variations in decorative architecture, cooking and local tradition.

YOU SHOULD KNOW

1. Pre-conditioning on similar terrain is valuable if you intend to spend more than 2 days at a time walking; and even in high summer you'll need clothing suitable for the unreliable temperatures.

2. Taking a guide is highly advisable in the remoter sections like Griesalp-Kandersteg-Adelboden. In any case, guides' intimate knowledge of mountains and folk-lore adds a whole dimension to the hike.

GOLDEN PASS PANORAMIC EXPRESS
Switzerland

WORTH A DETOUR: The super-privileged view from the very front of the train (beneath the driver's elevated cab), going up the giant horseshoe curve out of the gorgeous Simmental.

The Golden Pass offers travellers a means of exploring the heart of Central Switzerland between Lucerne and Montreux without doubling their tracks.

From Lucerne you can take a paddle steamer across the Lake to the cog railway up Rigi, the artist J.M.W. Turner's 'mountain of infinite mood'; or plunge into the gloomy splendour of the gorges leading to the dramatic Reichenbach Falls. At Interlaken, you can take one of several funiculars or mountain railways into the soul of the Bernese Oberland – even to the top of the Jungfrau itself. The onward journey is always magnificent, past the lakes of Brienz and Thun, through Spiez to the Simmen Valley, guarded at Wimmis by a fairytale 15th-century castle. At Zweisimmen, you change trains to the special gauge Golden Pass

Panoramic train designed by Ferrari's Pininfarina for the best possible views. The train climbs slowly enough to see the intricate and elaborate carvings typical of the region's chalets.

These designs change radically from the steep-sided alpine pastoral valleys above Gstaad, to the gentler landscapes of French-speaking Switzerland near Chateau d'Oex (where a perfect sheltered microclimate makes it a world centre for hot-air ballooning).

DON'T MISS
The tunnel at Furka – with its viaduct and staggering ravine views, a technological triumph.

GLACIER EXPRESS
Switzerland

The Glacier Express is the last word in panoramic luxury. In just eight hours it traverses the heart of Switzerland's highest mountain ranges. The journey starts at the foot of the twisted pyramid of the Matterhorn and skirts the Bernese Oberland, following the valley floors where the Rhône and the Rhine begin, and just below the line where glaciers spill out from the high passes. The landscape is a roll call of iconic names. The snow-capped summits of Schilthorn, Jungfrau, Monch and Eiger pass in distant backdrop, and the high peaks close in around the climbing train. Soaring viaducts arch above cloud-filled chasms, carrying it up and over the 2,033 m (6,668 ft) Oberalp Pass. Edging round sheer precipices, across 291 bridges and through 91 tunnels, the Glacier Express brings you so close to the mountains you can actually see the occasional chamois looking outraged at having to share the elemental magnificence of its perch.

WORTH A DETOUR:
The beautiful mountain
Lake Oeschinen above
Kandersteg, and the Lotschen
Valley, one of Switzerland's
most remote and pristine.

LÖTSCHBERG

Switzerland

The Lötschberg Line connects the UNESCO World Heritage city of Bern with the Jungfrau-Aletsch-Bietschore. It's a grand Euro-train, powering through the Simplon Tunnel to Italy, where Domodossola is effectively a terminus of the Swiss Railway system. Here the Lötschberg transfers its passengers to the delightful blue and white carriages of the narrow-gauge Centovalli Railway, which takes them back into Switzerland at Locarno, at a fraction of the pace but with scenery every bit as magnificent as the Aletsch Glacier north of the mountains. In just five hours, you see some of the very best pre-alpine landscapes – utterly different north and south – either side of the Bernese Oberland. The miniature-scale Centovalli Railway always connects with the Lötschberg, but it runs many more trains on its dedicated section. The route potters for 20 km (12.5 mi) to its highest point at Santa Maria Maggiore (830 m/2,722 ft), before dropping dramatically to Valle Vigezzo and leaving Italy at Ponte Ribellasca. Dense chestnut forests, studded with tranquil, ancient stone-built hamlets fill the web of steep valleys. Slowly inching across deep ravines on seemingly precarious viaducts and bridges, and through 22 short tunnels, the route offers staggering views of Mediterranean Alpine scenery as it cuts across some of the 'hundred valleys' between Camedo and Locarno. The 'panoramic' carriages of the Express are worth the supplement – but the region's incredible beauty is best appreciated if you stop (for lunch, a drink, a short hike or some other local activity) and breathe it in before catching the next train onwards.

ANDERMATT TO GRINDELWALD
Switzerland

HIGHLIGHTS: The melodious tinkle of big cowbells, answered by the frequent triple horn of the bus – the sound of alpine Switzerland. Stopping for a meringue at Meiringen, where it was invented.

The yellow livery of the Alpine Postbus Network is a national institution in Switzerland. They even have a special, triple-toned horn based on a sequence from Rossini's opera William Tell. A series of Express routes covers the most spectacular roads across and between the high passes, and among the best is the 'Romantic Route'. It starts from the rustic village of Andermatt at the foot of the St Gotthard Pass, and climbs a terrifying sequence of hairpins rising 1,000 m (3,280 ft) in 18 km (12 mi).

Most people fall silent as the Postbus weaves past gentle reservoir lakes, dropping over 1,500 m (4,900 ft) to Meiringen on the Reichenbach Valley floor. This is where every dream about the Bernese Oberland is fulfilled. Rugged mountain drama yields to lucid green meadows in their summer glory of wild flowers; and the climb back up to Grosse Scheidegg, on to Grindelwald itself, is a landscape of the kind of beauty that robs you of speech. Every hamlet, farm, cow and cowbell seems in its proper firmament – and that's why the journey is called 'Romantic'. In fact, there's a lot of romance about: the route is so popular that double-decker Postbuses are used. If even that's not good enough, historic Postbuses are available for private charter.

JUNGFRAUJOCH COG RAILWAY
Switzerland

HIGHLIGHTS: Using the big permanent telescopes at Kleine Scheidegg to watch climbers on the North Face of the Eiger. Posting a letter at Europe's highest post office, next to Jungfraujoch Station.

The Jungfrau Railway leads to the highest railway station in Europe, at 3,454 m (11,333 ft). It is literally the zenith of a circular route from Interlaken round the heart of the Bernese Oberland, connecting its most famous resorts and providing access to the very best of the region's incomparable scenery and topographical splendour. The train engages its sturdy cog-wheels at Lauterbrunnen, ready to climb parallel to the fabled Lauberhorn Downhill World Cup course past pretty Wengen to Kleine Scheidegg, 2,061 m (6,762 ft) up at the foot of the fateful North Wall of the Eiger.

As you travel on, in every direction, mountains pierce the clouds in the valleys far below, and in the intense blue clarity of the sky you can see as far as the Vosges Mountains in France, and the Black Forest in Germany. Here on the Jungfraujoch – the saddle connecting the Eiger, Monch and Jungfrau peaks among others – the Aletsch Glacier begins, the longest (22 km/14 mi) river of ice in the Alps. In summer, there are husky-drawn sleigh rides at Jungfraujoch.

WHEN SHOULD I VISIT?:
May–October. The roads
over the St Gotthard are not
always open during winter.

VAL TREMOLA
Switzerland

The St Gotthard is the most historic of all Alpine passes. It opened to regular foot traffic in about 1200, and the first vehicle crossed in 1775. Take the autoroute if you're in a hurry to reach Bellinzona and Milan. But better by far is the much quieter old cobbled road that branches off just after Andermatt. You get a taste of how spectacular (and how worryingly lonely) Alpine travel must have been – until you reach the wild and windy top of the Pass, where you meet the new road, and where a

new hotel and the old St Gotthard Hospice building (now a museum) sit by a small lake. From here the buses and nearly all the traffic follow the new road down to Airolo. Instead, find the old road which restarts behind the hotel. Now virtually deserted after centuries, it switchbacks in broad hairpins down the Val Tremola (the 'Trembling Valley'). The slick cobbles, hammered and rutted with use, cling to the steep green hillside, with some of its 38 bends propped up by precarious retaining walls. Passengers will be absorbed in the astounding vistas first, down into the heart of the valley; then along the length of the Ticino Valley (here called the Val Leventina) as it opens up below.

THE SPREE AND HAVEL RIVERS
Germany

HIGHLIGHTS: The hauntingly romantic vision of Potsdam's palaces, lawns, parks and colonnaded avenues dripping icicles and stilled by a shroud of snow.
The hidden corners of Old Berlin, seen from the waterways.

The Spree River joins the larger Havel at Spandau. It brings Berlin most of its water – and the opportunity to float through the heart of Germany's capital. The Havel continues to the palaces and pleasure grounds of Potsdam, Germany's former royal capital, and onwards west and north. It bulges with lakes, leading eventually to the forested seclusion of the Shorfeide-Chorin UNESCO Biosphere, but it shares its enchanting natural wonders with evidence of Germany's most illustrious history. The Elector's Castle at Oranienburg, and Brandenburg an der Havel, the medieval town set on three islands in mid-river, are just two of hundreds of jaw-dropping surprises.

Using the Landwehrkanal linking the Upper and Lower Spree (at Schlesisches Tor and Charlottenburg) you can visit the Reichstag and the very centre of the reunited city. But you can also see the 19th-century elegance of lovely Nikolaiviertel, and the thirty historic ships still working at Berlin's oldest quarter, the old harbour of Fischerinsel in Kreuzberg. Berlin is veined with waterways based on its two rivers, and the options are endless.

BERLIN WALL BIKE TRAIL

Germany

WHEN SHOULD I VISIT?:
Year-round. Berlin Wall
Bike Trail guided tours
are only scheduled from
May–September, but can
be arranged with most tour
agents throughout the year.
So can the information packs,
bike rentals and anything
else you need for
a self-guided tour.

HIGHLIGHTS:
Just think – you're riding the
path used by heavily armed
DDR Customs, Police and
Army patrols 24/7 throughout
the Wall's existence. About
3,200 people were arrested
trying to cross it; and 270
died trying to get over, under
or through it.
The wackiness of having this
parkland 'highway' through
a major capital city – in it,
and very much of it, but still
utterly distinct from it.

It appeared in 1961 without warning, and disappeared just as suddenly in 1989. Now, the very few fragments of the original Berlin Wall still in situ are themselves protected by fencing from souvenir hunters. Once an embarrassment, the Wall is now regarded as the defining icon of the reunited, reconstructed and re-born capital of Germany. Recently, Berliners completed a bike trail that follows its path for a meandering 106 km (66 mi) across the city and its suburbs. Where railway lines or reconnected streets forced long detours, tunnels and bridges now link the obstructed sections; and as nature has reclaimed the open spaces originally cleared to make a 'killing ground' along its length, the Wall is now represented by a ribbon of green in a grey urban landscape. This chilling 'death strip' was 5–100 m (16–330 ft) wide – big enough to get lost in the sprouting birch trees and thick underbrush if you miss one of the grey 'Mauerweg' ('Wall Trail') signs at intersections.

The Trail provides a privileged green access corridor to the heart of Berlin and the best of its sights and amenities. But every inch of it is also a confrontation with some of the city's – and Germany's – worst historical nightmares. Bravely, modern Berliners embrace the past as inevitable. They've rescued one piece of their history, the Brandenburg Gate, from isolated sterility in former no-man's-land, but kept the flaking concrete pillbox watchtower column behind it, from which guards sniped at and killed dozens who made their pitiful dash for freedom. The Trail helps explain how optimism triumphed over the institutionalized violence implicit in the Wall's graffitied concrete and its associated artefacts. It is gut-wrenchingly successful, and a brilliant introduction to modern Berlin.

Endlessly fascinating, this is one of the great bike trails in the world, combining the exercise with the highest standard of visual, cultural and historical interest. What it reveals about the Cold War remains a work in progress, of relevance to all of us.

Right: Fragment of the Berlin Wall

BRIDGES CYCLE ROUTE
Germany

HIGHLIGHTS: The ancient battle site of Kalkriese (aka. 'Varus battle'), near Bramsche, where Roman legions suffered a devastating rout in 9 AD at the hands of Germanic tribes and never got this far again.

The web of rivers, lakes and canals spread across the flatlands of Germany's northwest corner is cycling heaven. Easy riding leaves you plenty of energy to enjoy the succession of nature reserves, moors and wetlands that stud the rich loam of Lower Saxony's northern farmland. Isolated now, the region's small villages and towns once stood on some of Europe's busiest trade routes. The Bridges Cycle Route follows one of them, from Osnabrück to Bremen.

Osnabrück's market place and old town comprise one of the most beautiful survivals of urban medieval architecture anywhere; while still evident behind Bremen's bustling modernity is the equally ancient city of Roland, who held the pass at Roncesvalles for his King, Charlemagne.

Between them, Dummer Lake is home to every kind of watery recreation, besides providing sanctuary to a huge variety of waterfowl and bird species. Goldenstedt has an ingenious tunnel to introduce you to moorland ecology; and the historic wonders of Diepholz, Löhne and Vechta are matched by the megalithic tombs and historical monuments of the Wildeshauser Geest.

WHEN SHOULD I VISIT?:
April–September. Come for one of the big festivals or annual religious parades.

THE BENEDICT TRAIL
Germany

The Benedict Trail is a six-day biographical bike tour round the heart of rural Upper Bavaria. It's a circular route 'in the footsteps' of Pope Benedict XVI. Joseph Ratzinger was born, raised, educated, and found his vocation in the region. After his clerical studies, he (and his brother) celebrated their 'Primiz' – the first Mass of a newly consecrated priest – in Traunstein; and at his Papal inauguration in the Vatican he was handed a special memento of the 'Black Madonna' of Altötting, to whom he had proclaimed devotion as a boy. She has been venerated for 500 years as special to Bavaria, and is one of Germany's greatest centres of pilgrimage. It is as much a compliment to this most devout region of ultra-Catholic Bavaria, where Benedictine educational tenets have been entrenched for centuries, as to the Saint, that the Pope chose Benedict's name for himself.

The scenic marvels – rivers, forests, ancient hamlets still toting their manorial loyalties on banners and chivalric regalia, massive fortresses, needle-spired churches and capitals of forgotten dukedoms by lakes – unfold forgivingly on the eye. These are landscapes familiar from 15th–17th-century oil paintings, and not a lot has changed on the Trail's constantly stimulating historic byways. Pope Benedict's life inspires a rare intimacy between visitor and place, bringing the region's history, living, into the present.

THE ROMANTIC ROAD

Germany

Beloved by Germans as one of their favourite holiday routes, the Romantic Road starts by the River Main at the Prince-Bishopric fortress town of Wurzburg. Picking its way through rural backwaters of stunning beauty, it seeks out some of Germany's least-famous but most magnificent castles, palaces, old towns and topographical curiosities; crosses the Danube at Donauwörth, and follows the bubbling torrent of the alpine Lech River all the way to King Ludwig II's 19th-century fairytale extravaganzas of Neuschwanstein and Hohenschwangau. Finally, it crosses the Alps in a flourish of jagged peaks to the Austrian Tyrolean city of Innsbruck. It's a route that is archetypically German, a visual poem of misty, chivalrous romance.

Across Francony, Swabia and western Bavaria you pass through the topography of feudalism in all its degrees. Commanding each valley, river junction, or broad plain, a huge castle-palace proclaims the regional duke of yore; a cathedral lends him spiritual authority; in nearby towns, lesser towers and imposing manors announce his fiefs; and his borders are marked and guarded by gigantic fortresses. In each city, town and village, this hierarchy is repeated on a half-timbered domestic scale of wonderful subtlety, their buildings and services ranked according to the medieval or Renaissance priorities when they were built.

The discovery makes the journey entrancing. The system may repeat itself, but even within short distances, the landscapes and styles change completely. Vagaries of history mean you encounter Baroque, medieval, Renaissance and Gothic styles at random, just as you cross ranges of hills, river gorges, and meadow plains before the journey's dramatic finale among Alpine peaks.

HIGHLIGHTS:

Making the rounds with the night watchman in the walled Gothic town of Rothenburg.
The medieval city centre of Landsberg, set romantically in bed of the River Lech.
Neuschwanstein Castle's Music Room, a great hall on the top floor, its ceiling painted the dark blue of night, set with a thousand stars.
The magnificent mountain landscapes on the Austrian side, near Imst.

MIDDLE RHINE VALLEY

Germany

The Middle Rhine Valley from Strasbourg to Koblenz is a slow crescendo culminating in Germany's most iconic geographical feature. By car, train, bicycle or boat, your path runs between the Black Forest and the more rugged Pfälzerwald to the west. The river broadens and unwinds lazily into the wetland sanctuaries downstream around Worms and Mainz. Gaining momentum with the added mass of the river Main, it fusses its way to Bingen before unleashing itself into the 65 km (43 mi) gorge twisting north to Koblenz. Celebrated in painting, poetry, music and the grandest of opera, the Rhine Gorge here is a byword for wild, dramatic beauty – but in fact it is a cultural landscape fashioned not by Nature but by Man.

HIGHLIGHTS:

Listening to German composers like Beethoven, Brahms, Mendelssohn and even Wagner, while contemplating their dramatic inspiration of precipitous cliffs, ruined castles and half-timbered villages.

Life in the Middle Ages, through the prism of stupendous Marksburg Castle (not a ruin), near Braubach.

The cobbled prettiness of Bacharach, especially Castle Stahleck, and Castle Pfalz, imposing and complete on its island in mid-river.

With a railway and two roads (upper and lower) on each vineyard-terraced bank, the Rhine's importance as a highway for commerce and tourism is undiminished in 2,000 years – and we visitors are participants in the continuing process. The Middle Rhine Valley is the gateway to central Europe. The castles, towns and villages perched on its jagged rocks, unable to expand and unwilling to modernize the genuinely historical 'look' that helps to stimulate the mythic notions called 'Rhine Romanticism', have become their own industry. By boat, there are no tollgates but your fare contributes to the river. In a car or on a bike, you tap more directly into the symbiosis of trade and beauty that remains so attractive.

WORTH A DETOUR: The ceremonial coach and treasures of the Furstenberg family, at their 1723 Schloss in Donaueschingen. In 1806, everything passed to Baden-Wurttemberg, so the coach looks particularly forlorn.

HELL VALLEY RAILWAY
Germany

Höllental (Hell Valley) is a 'V'-shaped gash 9 km (5.4 mi) long in the rocks of the Black Forest in southwest Germany. Its imposing slopes are 600 m (1,970 ft) high, pulled into a gorge so narrow that at one point, a bronze statue high on a crag commemorates a stag that famously escaped its hunters with one gigantic bound right across it. The Valley was typical of the dense impenetrable forest of legend until just 150 years ago, when the only mule track became a narrow road, inspiring the Railway of 1889–1901 that connects Freiburg with Donaueschingen.

Modern locomotives now pull double-decker carriages to cope with the number of travellers. The 'Hirschsprungfelsen' is one of several rock formations that make whole mountains look sculpted, but the natural landscapes are enhanced by nine tunnels and a series of impossible viaducts – like the Ravennaschlucht, 222 m (728 ft) long and 42 m (138 ft) high – that carry you up to Doeggingen. Without overt fuss, in the middle of a 535 m (1,755 ft) tunnel, the line crosses Europe's principal watershed, and drops you, blinking in the bright light, in the beautiful high woods where the River Danube springs forth.

THE ALPINE ROAD
Germany

WORTH A DETOUR: The classic quality of the hairpin sections of the highway – if you've ever enjoyed driving, this is the thrill you've always imagined (and with a safety margin on the road's width).

The German Alpine Road belongs to the heyday of motorcar 'Touring', when Bugatti battled with Daimler-Benz on road rallies like Italy's Mille Miglia. The Alpine Road was built in the 1930s to stimulate the new mobility, but Hitler, ambitious to impress, annexed the project. Germany's Alpine Road was to be altogether more grand, more sweeping and more beautiful than anyone else's – and 26,000 labourers were to build 105 bridges, 15 tunnels, and 10 viaducts to make it so, joining Lindau on Lake Constance with Berchtesgaden in the heartland of the Bavarian Alps. In fact, it was only completed in 2002. Now it carves boldly through some 450 km (281 mi) of Germany's loveliest mountain scenery. Through the Allgau and up into the Alps it winds past 21 turquoise and lapis lakes, 25 castles, and brooding dark green forests cut with

secret valleys, where ancient moss soaks emerald in angry waterfalls. Imperiously the Alpine Road swings back and forth, cresting precipices and swaying round the long corniches.

The road owes its sublime pleasures to its natural magnificence. From the grand, Italianate, gabled houses of medieval Lindau, prettily reflected in the lake, the landscapes are composed of drama and varied history, and each little town has a facet to add to its regional culture.

RENNSTEIG TRAIL
Germany

HIGHLIGHTS:

The satisfaction of the first day, walking far above Blankenstein, looking back across the Saal and its lakes spread below.

The highest section of the ridge, Beerberg (982 m/3,221 ft), part of the astonishingly lovely view from Schmucke.

The summer toboggan run at Brotterode – just off the Rennsteig, but worth the detour for its 12 steep curves to the racing kilometre.

Although the term 'rennsteig' ('racing steep') has been applied to many of Germany's ancient trade routes, 'The Rennsteig' refers exclusively to the famous high altitude trail through the Thuringian Forest. For 168 km (106 mi) it follows a ridge connecting the highest peaks between Blankenstein on the Upper Saal River, and Horschel near Eisenach. The path has served as a geographical and political border as well as a highway for over 1,000 years, but it has been relatively inaccessible until recently. That has helped revive its natural ecology, and the region has become a wildlife haven despite its popularity with summer crowds. Known as the 'green heart' of Germany, an upland corridor of emerald forest some 20 km (12 mi) broad stretches 60 km (37 mi) northwest, (roughly) from Greiz to Eisenach. This highland plateau includes the Thuringian Forest's most dramatic, unspoilt and beautiful natural scenery. Its hills are bounded by fault lines, rising in steep scarps from the spruce and broadleaf woods whose canopy is broken only by a few open pastures close to the smallholdings of ancient hamlets. Within the forest, the highest peaks are only about 985 m (3,230 ft), but they are geological marvels of gneiss, porphyry and granite. The Rennsteig weaves between them, taking in the best vistas of its pastoral idyll, and occasionally opening up superb panoramas on either side to one of the peaceful, romantic villages folded into hollows.

DON'T MISS
Walking through the woods between Binz and Sellin (the train stops at both).

RASENDE ROLAND
Germany

Rugen, the Baltic island close to Germany's northeast border with Poland, has been a popular holiday resort for generations of visitors. Rasende Roland has been one of its greatest attractions for over 100 years. It's a vintage, steam-puffing, narrow-gauge train service that connects Putbus with Rugen's southeast resorts of Binz, Sellin and Göhren. Its track is only 750 mm (2 ft 6 in) wide and 24 km (15 mi) long, and its immaculately maintained engines and carriages – to the same scale – reinforce its appearance as an overgrown children's toy.

Rugen's southeast corner is a region of peninsulas, small islands, hooked spits and sand bars; and it includes the Granitz Forest, the Mönchgut peninsula, and Vilm – a small island whose oak and beech forest has remained untouched for centuries, and whose unique flora can only be visited by appointment. Dogged and unobtrusive, Rasende Roland runs just inside the Reserve's edge. Thirteen stations provide access to the many natural wonders and variety of sights and entertainments. At Sellin, you can take a little funicular to the beach and pier below. Get off at Baabe for biking round leafy lanes and blueberry woods, or Göhren, to cycle through the coastal forest to Thiessow, where you can sit near a small café to watch the waders and waterfowl in the marshy lagoons. From Göhren you can also cycle back to Binz by way of long strands of white beach, ice creams and swimming.

THE EAGLE'S NEST
Europe/Germany

WHEN SHOULD I VISIT?: May–October – the bus service does not operate at any other time.

The 'Eagle's Nest' is the nickname given by the American occupying forces of 1945 to Hitler's lodge on the 1,834 m (6,017 ft) peak of Mount Kehlstein, pressed against the Bavarian Alps' border with Austria.

Getting there is a unique journey. There is only one way: you must take the bus from Obersalzberg, From Obersalzberg to the top, the road is designed so that in a 700 m (2,296 ft) vertical ascent over 6.5 km (4 mi), there is only one bend, and you cross the steep northwest face of the Kehlstein twice.

At the top, an ornate, brass-frilled and ornamented lift whisks you up to the inside of the Eagle's Nest buildings in just 41 seconds. The walls are a metre thick, and the place is a fortress. The conference and domestic rooms and the terraces would be mundane except that imagination is in full flow, reconciling extraordinary location and engineering with all the rest. You set out joking, excited. You come back speechless.

SOUTHERN WINE ROAD

Germany

HIGHLIGHTS:

Federweisser (featherwhite) wine – 'a cloudy, sweet, bubbly almost-wine' still in the process of fermenting, and much more potent that it tastes.

Walking from Deidesheim across the 'Pfalz balcony', with the hills rising on one side and stunning vistas across the Rhine plain, full of ancient and beautiful wine estates.

A towering stone archway called the Weintor ('Wine Gate') marks the beginning of Germany's Southern Wine Road, at the French/German border town of Schweigen in the Pfalz (Palatinate). From here, the Road curls through the small river valleys carved out of the foothills of the Pfälzerwald, a huge UNESCO Biosphere Reserve of upland forest, moors and sandstone crags; then emerges into the broad reaches of the Rhine, where an almost Mediterranean climate makes the low hills ideal for viticulture (the Romans introduced the vines, along with the almond trees, figs, lemons and kiwis which grow here). It is scenic, gentle countryside, set with small castles on promontories and little villages of intricately carved, half-timbered antiquity. Only Neustadt a.d.Weinstrasse, the regional centre, reveals the industrial aspects of the massive wine industry, but its giant silver tanks offer more promise than offence.

The Southern Wine Road continues north as far as Durkheim, September site of the world's biggest wine festival (held around the world's biggest wine-barrel). Durkheim is the centre of a marvellous

loop hike through especially picturesque and historic villages, but the Road to Neustadt and Landau is in any case a sybarite hiker's dream – wonderful landscapes, welcoming towns and villages and festivals of some sort in every one. The trip is more intense in the hills between Landau, Bergzabern and Schweigen. Each valley is more isolated and each tiny town more distinct. Filled with flowers and vines trailing across narrow streets and ancient buildings, hamlets like Dörrenbach, Gleiszellen-Gleisorbach or Oberotterbach nevertheless have characters as different from each other as their wines. Dramatically placed between steep terraces of vines, or huddled under cliff faces (so the higher ground is free for vineyards) they demand that you sit and drink in what makes them special.

CASTLE ROAD

Germany

HIGHLIGHTS:
Horneck Castle at
Gundelsheim – the
headquarters and city of the
13th-century German Order
of Chivalry.
The thousand-year-old
town of Kulmbach, with
12th-century Plassenburg,
the fortress remodelled
as a residence for its
Hohenzollern rulers.
The towers and ramparts of
medieval Guttenberg Castle,
built in the Staufer period and
never destroyed, and owned
since 1449 by the Counts of
Gemmingen.

Travelling on Castle Road across Germany to the Czech Republic feels like leafing through a storybook. One day might be a chivalric adventure of knights-at-arms. The next, a Renaissance romance of courtly manners, or a poetic extravaganza of Baroque magnificence, or the military reminiscences of a Roman soldier. There are more than sixty notable castles and palaces between Mannheim and Prague, each one with a 500–1,000 year-old history written into its fabric. Individually fascinating benchmarks of power, strength, wealth and pleasure during many eras, they tell an even more absorbing collective tale of German cultural evolution and of its contribution to a shared European heritage.

Castle Road is roughly 1,000 km (625 mi) long, with Nuremberg approximately halfway. Its byways wind through local, provincial and regional capitals from the Neckar Valley to the magic sylvan tranquility along the course of the Jagst and Tauber rivers. It crosses the green, picture-perfect range of Franconian Switzerland and the Main River into the crags of Francony's huge forest and the Fichtelgebirger, with Bohemia beyond. Like the natural landscapes, the castles and great houses range in style and setting from the graceful, gentle and elegant, to the sophisticated, imposing and grand. Some swagger with brooding magnificence. Others inspire frightful awe. After Bamberg (a UNESCO World Heritage Site of breathtaking historical magnitude), the terrain is wilder, and huge fortresses at Coburg and Kronach, along with a dozen medieval masterpieces further on, show how might was usually found to be sufficiently right. Castle Road passes through whole medieval towns, like Rothenburg, Schwabisch Hall, or Kirchberg on the Jagst, where town and castle clearly show the Rennaissance and Baroque additions on their medieval origins. Castle Road's real achievement is to combine the roll call of towns and the disparate virtues of their unique structures into a single fanfare for Germany's richest history.

THE ROUTE OF EMPERORS AND KINGS

Germany

HIGHLIGHTS:
Discovering Regensburg to be one of Germany's most complete remaining medieval cities.
Tulln – with its baroque old town.
Brooding medieval magnificence and baroque exuberance – the hallmarks of the Danube's royal cities and towns.

For more than 1,000 years, the Danube has been the principal highway for the exercise of power in central Europe. It connects major capital cities east and west. Between Regensburg and Budapest especially, its banks are studded with the towns, abbeys, fortresses, palaces and cathedrals built to demonstrate the temporal power of bishops, princelings, dukes and oligarchs whose shifting allegiances raised Kings and lowered Emperors. The gorges of the Danube still echo hallowed names – Charlemagne, Attila, Wittelsbach, Hohenzollern, Hapsburg, Esterhazy – whose assaults and confrontations have left their stamp. Journeying along it now from Germany to Austria, Slovakia and Hungary you could feel that little has changed in centuries – except that modern travellers do so in much greater comfort. Most go by boat, which certainly offers a unique visual perspective on the Danube's natural wonders as well as its sights. Rounding a curve to your first sight of the Benedictine Abbey at Melk, in the UNESCO World Heritage Cultural and Natural Heritage Site of leafy Wachau Valley, is just one of the princely landscapes you can't see any other way. Even so, lots of people choose to travel the Danube by bike. You can speed or tarry at will, and because the special bike route follows the old towpath, the going is flat the whole way. If you're prepared to use an agent to smooth your path, you can combine bike and boat, either for excursions in Passau, Linz, Durnstein, Vienna and Budapest, or as alternative transport through the woods, terraced vineyards, orchards and meadows between stops like the venerable towns of Aggspach, Spitz and Weissenkirchen.

Like the emperors and kings who have preceded you, allow plenty of time, however you travel. The wealth of history, culture and giddy-making surprises is too rich, and the Danube too beautiful, to rush.

'LIMES' ROUTE

Germany

DON'T MISS
The reconstructed
Roman fort at Saalburg,
near Bad Homburg.

The longest heritage route in Germany immerses you in the oldest period of German history. From Bad Honningen near Koblenz to Kelheim outside Regensburg, the 550 km (344 mi) route – all of it a UNESCO World Heritage Site – marks the line of forts, watchtowers, earthen palisades and stone walls which 2,000 years ago formed the border between the Roman Empire and the Germanic tribes Romans called 'barbarians'. 'Limes' is the Latin for 'border defences': this route is part of Roman 'limes' stretching over 6,000 km (3,750 mi) round the Middle East, North Africa, Spain and France, at the moment of the Empire's greatest expansion in circa AD 150. The Upper German and Rhaetian 'Limes' meet at Aalen on the upper

reaches of the Kocher River. In fact, for a short way the trail is shared with the 330 km (206 mi) Kocher-Jagst Cycle Route, a delightful circular riverside ramble through the meadowlands of the Kocher and Jagst – but evidently not topographically attractive to Roman commanders. Working its way from the Rhine-Westerwald nature reserve to the solid walls of Regensburg's Porta Praetoria ('Guardian Gate') in Bavaria, the route is a constant scenic surprise.

WORTH A DETOUR: The UNESCO World Heritage site of Reichenau – Germany's oldest monastery complex and repository of its historic Benedictine soul.

GERMAN AVENUES: NORTH TO SOUTH

Germany

Germany's longest scenic route picks its way from the dazzling wall of pure white cliffs at Cape Arkona on the Baltic island of Rugen, to the flowered gardens of Reichenau. For 2,500 km (1,562 mi) between Poland in the extreme north and the southern borders with France and Switzerland, it wends through central Germany's most vivid scenery. It's a leisurely road, but it is not random. Its path is determined by the avenues of trees that line what used to be trade routes and super-highways, and are now forgotten byways. The trees provide an almost unbroken, leafy canopy of continuous charm that crosses eight of Germany's federal states – a magical path that brings travellers close to some of the country's finest cities and landmarks, without ever losing its own transcendental quality of peacefulness.

ZILLERTALBAHN

Austria

The little steam train that chugs up the Zillertal (Ziller Valley) in the heart of the Tirol runs on a track only 760 mm (2 ft 6 in) wide. It is the most famous narrow-gauge railway in Austria; as well as being a means of transport it's a visible reminder of the valley's history. The railway was built in 1901–2, in the days when the local inhabitants depended on agriculture, mining and forestry for their living. They desperately needed a freight line to transport timber and minerals down the valley, to replace a thoroughly inadequate road – a tortuous track that was only negotiable by mule. Although the railway's prime purpose was to ensure that the existing economy prospered, it had the secondary unforeseen benefit of opening up the valley to tourism.

Throughout the 20th century the Zillertal grew in popularity, attracting skiers, climbers and walkers with the allure of its unspoilt natural surroundings. The picturesque agricultural villages along the railway are now charming little resorts.

The Zillertal inclines gently southwards towards the Zillertaler Alps, enclosed by the Kitzbüheler Alps to the east and the Tuxer Mountains to the west. It is not only the largest valley branching from the Inntal but also the loveliest – a scenic delight of alpine pastures and forests surrounded by mountain peaks. The railway runs for 32 km (20 mi) between Jenbach, on the River Inn, and Mayrhofen, under the Hintertux Glacier, with 14 stops on the way. The train is pulled by a heritage steam engine at a maximum speed of 35 kph (22 mph). It takes you on a romantic journey back in time, in a classic passenger car, listening to the soothing repetitive clickety-clack of the wheels and the intermittent hissings and puffings of the engine, while you admire the unspoilt pastoral beauty of the valley all around you.

HIGHLIGHTS:

Classic steam engine and antique railway carriages. Beautiful mountain views. Hintertux Glacier – for year-round skiing. Zell am Ziller – once a gold mining town.

THE ARNOWEG

Austria

YOU SHOULD KNOW

Some sections demand the use of crampons, ice-pick and harness.

In 1998, the 1,200 km (750 mi) Arnoweg long-distance hiking trail was established to celebrate 1,200 years of history, dating from the Vatican's decision in AD 798 to raise the status of the city of Salzburg by creating an archbishopric. The trail is named after Archbishop Arno, a friend of the Emperor Charlemagne, who was the first appointee to the post. The route combines several well-established alpine trails in a circuitous tour around Salzburgerland with 60 signposted stages and alpine huts along the way. It cuts through three national parks, climbs to heights of over 3,000 m (9,800 ft) and passes innumerable sites of cultural significance.

The Arnoweg is a challenging hike through some of the most beautiful scenery in the world. You hike along mountain ridges, past the medieval town of Hallein to the Hohenwerfen fortress for a spectacular view over the Salzach Valley, then into the lush valleys and glaciated peaks of the Hohe Tauern National Park where eagles and bearded vultures circle the skies. Visit the 16th-century gold mining town of Rauris and the famous 19th-century spa town of Bad Gastein, and see the medieval Mauterndorf fortress – hunting castle of the Archbishop. Stroll through the gently contoured landscape of the Grasberge and Nockberge seeing marmots, mountain hares and herds of chamois, and scramble up scree crags in the Niedere Tauern. Hike across gentle hills in the lower Alps to reach the last leg of the trail through the lakes region to the historic city of Salzburg – and return to the real world exhausted but fulfilled.

HIGHLIGHTS:

Hohensalzburg Fortress – the largest medieval fortress in Europe.
Krimml Falls – the largest waterfall in Europe.
Grossglockner – the highest mountain in Austria at 3,798 m (12,460 ft).
Neukirchen – a beautifully situated village.
Dürrnberg Salt Mine – the oldest in the world.

GROSSGLOCKNER HOCHALPENSTRASSE

Austria

DON'T MISS
Hochmais – a 1,850 m
(6,068 ft) viewing point
over the impressive glaciers
of the beautiful Feirleiten Valley.

The Grossglockner High Alpine Road was first opened in 1935, specifically constructed as a tourist attraction – 48 km (27 mi) of death-defying hairpin bends winding far above the snowline with breathtaking views over the idyllic pastoral landscapes of the Hohe Tauern National Park.
The road runs across the highest pass in the Austrian Alps, between the village of Bruck on the edge of the Hohe Tauern and Heilgenblut at the foot of the Grossglockner, climbing through pastures and forests to craggy snow-covered mountain peaks. The landscape is especially striking in early summer when fingers of un-melted snow from the previous winter still reach down into the green valleys.
From Bruck the road heads southwards towards a 10 per cent incline. Make a detour up the steep little side road leading to Edelweissspitze for a mind-blowing panoramic view over the pass before heading up to Fuscher Törll, from where you get your first sighting of Grossglockner, the highest mountain of the Austrian Alps at 3,798 m (12,457 ft). From Hochtor, the highest point of the road at 2,504 m (8,213 ft), descend to Kaiser-Franz-Josef-Hohe, the most dramatic lookout of all – Grossglockner towers directly in front of you.

SEMMERING RAILWAY

Europe/Austria

The 160-year-old World Heritage Semmering Railway is the most scenic route in Austria, running for 41 km (26 mi) across the Semmering Pass in the mountains between Vienna and Graz. Built between 1848 and 1845 in the pioneering days of railway construction, it became the prototype for all high-mountain railways. It is an inspired feat of engineering with sixteen viaducts, fifteen tunnels, and a gradient five times greater than anything that had been built before.
The line runs from the country town of Gloggnitz in the Schwarza Valley up to Semmering, a charming 19th-century ski resort that today has a distinctly quaint feel about it. The highest point of the railway is 898 m (2,945 ft). It then descends the southern slopes of the mountains to Mürzzuschlag, a small provincial town. The dramatic landscape of sheer gorges, craggy mountains and forest makes for a hair-raising ride.

HIGHLIGHTS: Kalt Rinne Viaduct.
Gloggnitz Castle, originally an 11th-century Benedictine monastery.
Südbahn Kulturbahnhoff – Railway museum at Mürzzuschlag.

GERLOS ALPENSTRASSE

Austria

The main road from the old gold mining town of Zell am Ziller in the Tirol to the lakeside town of Zell am See in the province of Salzburg is a favourite among cyclists and motor-bikers. It is a winding route along a panoramic stretch of road, crossing the Gerlos Pass at an altitude of 1,530 m (5,020 ft) and descending through enchanting mountain countryside, with an amazing view of the Krimml Falls.

WORTH A DETOUR:
Krimml Falls – highest
waterfall in Europe, and one
of the top eight in the world.

The history of the road goes back to the 17th century, when gold was discovered in the Ziller Valley. Rather than risk transporting the precious metal through what were then the foreign states of Bavaria and Tirol, the prospectors widened the mule track over the Gerlos Pass so that cartloads of gold could be carried into the safe territory of Salzburg for smelting.

The present road zigzags its way up from Zel am Ziller in the Ziller Valley to the high moorland at the top of the pass, then descends through the Salzach Valley alongside the innaccessible narrow wooded valleys and fissured gorges of the Pinzgau Mountains, along the edge of the Hohe Tauern National Park. The Krimml Ache River flows through just such a valley, making a sudden plunging drop of 380 m (1,250 ft). Tons of water thunder down in three great cascades, sending clouds of mist into the air.

THE BRINE TRAIL

Austria

The Salzkammergut, the old salt mining region of Austria, is one of those rare parts of the world where mankind has managed to leave its mark without blighting the natural environment. Now designated as a World Heritage Cultural Landscape, the region is not only scenically breathtaking but also architecturally beautiful. Historic palatial buildings and picturesque villages nestle around clear-watered lakes under the silver crags and green forested slopes of the Dachstein Mountains as though they belonged naturally as an integral part of the landscape.

Of all the many charming villages, the old salt mining town of Hallstatt is the most enchanting – a cobble-stoned lakeside town straight out of the pages of a picture book. Its fairytale 16th and 17th-century houses are squeezed into every square metre of space on a precipitous mountainside, expanding upwards on terraces and outwards into Lake Hallstätter, on piles driven into the lakebed. The 10 km (6 mi) walk from Hallstatt to the quaint market town of Bad Goisern follows the course of a historic pipeline used for transporting brine from the salt mine to the trading town of Ebensee on Lake Traunsee, 40 km (25 mi) away. The path, known as the Soleweg (Brine Trail), is cut into the rock face 200 m (650 ft) above the western bank of the lake. As you amble through romantic countryside of woods and pastures, spotting wildlife and breathing pure mountain air, you are accompanied by a heart-stopping view of the opposite shore – the towering crags of the Sarstein Ridge mirrored in the water. The beauty of the pastoral surroundings induces a sensation of mild euphoria.

HIGHLIGHTS:
A tour of Hallstätt salt mine.
Gosauzwang Bridge – impressive 38 m (125 ft) bridge built on enormous stone piles over the rushing torrent of the Gosau River.

MOZART CYCLE PATH

Austria

This 450 km (280 mi) cycling route in the borderlands of Austria and Bavaria is a wonderfully relaxing way to unwind, dawdling along through enchanting pastoral scenery of rolling fields, mirror-like lakes and alpine meadows with the snowy peaks of the mountains always in the background. From Salzburg you cycle north to Oberndorf, the site of the 'Silent Night Chapel', where the world's best-loved Christmas carol was first sung in 1818, and into the Chiemgau region of Bavaria. Pass the Waginger See, a pretty oxbow lake set in rolling farmland, and cycle along the shore of Bavaria's largest lake, the Chiemsee or 'Bavarian Sea'. The route continues past the Seeon Benedictine Monastery to the lovely old market town of Wasserburg, sited picturesquely on a bend of the River Inn, and follows the course of the river before heading on.

HIGHLIGHTS:
Salzburg – Mozart's birthplace.
Herrenchiemsee – island in the Chiemsee with fairytale castle.

WHEN SHOULD I VISIT?:
May–June – to see the waterfall at its most dramatic.

WILD WATERS HIKE TO THE REISACH WATERFALL

Austria

Squeezed between the glaciated peaks of the Hohe Tauern and the limestone spires of the Dachstein, the landscape of the Niedere Tauern is a gorgeous district of lakes and tarns set in rounded mountains and plateaux veined with rivers and streams, reminiscent of Scotland. The Hochgolling, a great stone giant of a mountain, juts out at the end of the range at a height of 2,863 m (9,390 ft), towering over the mountains around the old Styrian mining town of Schladming in the Upper Enns Valley.

Schladming is superb walking country – pastoral mountain scenery of rivers, pastures and woods with tumbling streams and a network of over 500 km (300 mi) of hiking trails. The 12 km (7.5 mi) Wild Waters Trail leads from the town up through the steep Untertal valley, passing a quaint old mill and through a nature reserve, alongside a river that flows in intermittent bursts of rippling cascades. It is fed by two creeks: the Steinriesenbach, from the direction of Hockgolling, and the Reisachbach. Following the course of the Reisachbach, the valley gets ever steeper and narrower until you reach the Reisach, the longest waterfall in Styria – a violent avalanche of water that pounds down through a cleft in the rocks and drops a distance of 140 m (460 ft) over two steps. Carry on up the steps of Höll, a steep mountain path, and across a perilous suspension bridge to the Reisachsee, a tranquil alpine lake where you can sit and relax, admiring the silver peaks of the Dachstein Mountains in the distance.

CARNIC PEACE TRAIL – VIA ALPINA

Austria

HIGHLIGHTS: Medieval villages. Lienz – beautiful historic town. Traces of trenches, battery positions and bivouacs from World War I.

The Via Alpina is a network of trails traversing the Alps all the way from Trieste on the Adriatic to Monaco on the Mediterranean. It was established in 2005 to create a single cohesive route out of the countless existing trans-Alpine paths. The main artery, known as the Red Trail, is some 2,400 km (1,500 mi) long, broken down into 161 manageable stages.

The summit trail along the ridge of the Carnic Alps in eastern Austria has been integrated into the Red Trail. It was the front-line between the Austrians and Italians in World War I and, in the 1970s, the supply paths used by the troops were linked up and given the symbolic name of the 'Carnic Peace Trail' in remembrance of the devastating loss of life here – as many soldiers died from the freezing weather conditions as were killed by the enemy.

Easily as beautiful as anywhere else in the Alps, the Carnic Peace Trail is one of the less touristy sections of the Via Alpina. You enter a timeless country of traditional villages and flower-strewn pastures, make hair-raising 750 m (2,500 ft) ascents and scramble across valleys, wash in sparkling mountain water and wake each morning in a different mountain hut but to the same inevitable tinkling of cowbells and chorus of moos.

A hike through the Austrian Alps really is the perfect way of getting away from it all: walking through some of the world's most beautiful scenery, spending the night in the shelter of spartan but adequate huts, and living on the staple alpine diet of cured ham and un-pasteurized cheese, you cannot fail to be satisfied.

THE BOHINJ RAILWAY

Slovenia

WHEN SHOULD I VISIT?:
April–early November. If you ride the train only part of the way, you can link the journey to one of the spring or summer festivals that abound in the region, or to one of many natural attractions in the Triglav National Park.

The Bohinj Railway is an authentic classic steam train trip on a historic line through some of Europe's loveliest mountain scenery. It runs between Jesenice, just inside Slovenia's border with Austria, to Gorizia in Italy, along what used to be the Austro-Hungarian 'Transalpina' railway from Vienna to Trieste, inaugurated in 1906. Although the service is scheduled (at roughly fortnightly intervals), it's definitely an excursion train. You can get on or off at any of the stops, and rejoin it after your own sightseeing, but the full trip incorporates a bus tour to the Friuli vineyards, staff in period uniforms, tour guides for railway enthusiasts, and entertainment staff to make sure travellers match Slovenian standards of enthusiastic merrymaking.

Partying aside, the Bohinj Railway takes you through countryside so beautiful it will twang your heartstrings. From Jesenice, you steam along the Sava River past the alpine dreamscape lake at Bled (where, if you started your journey in Italy, the medieval castle will be your vineyard-equivalent lunchtime goal). After Bohinj itself, the jewel of Slovenia's alpine crown, a 6.33 km (3.93 mi) tunnel cuts through the Bohinj Mountains to the southern side of the Julian Alps, and skirts the Triglav National Park until it turns southwest along the Soca Valley at Most na

Soci. The bridges, viaducts and gradients must have represented extraordinary engineering at the time they were built, and they are still spectacular. The most famous bridge of all is at the Gorizia end of the line.

The Solkanski Most features the longest (220 m/721 ft) stone railway arch in the world, with 4,533 chunks of limestone in the principal arch. Bohinj Railway staff have been known to tease travellers by testing their memory for these important facts – after the vineyard visit. The fun is deemed essential to the journey.

VRSIC PASS ROAD

Slovenia

WORTH A DETOUR: The glorious concentration of rarities in the Juliana Alpine Garden, set at 800 m (2624 ft) at the southern foot of Vrsic Pass, in the valley where the mild Mediterranean climate still has influence.

Triglav National Park fills the northwest pocket of Slovenia, where it meets both Austria and Italy. It protects Slovenia's Julian Alps, returned to their pristine remoteness since their mutilation during some of the bloodiest and longest battles of World War I. Only one road remains across it from which to gauge the stunning landscape of winding glacial valleys, torrent-filled gorges, forested ridges and stark mountains. It follows two of the most beautiful valleys of all. From Bovec, on the Park's southern edge, it traces the milky turquoise Soca River up the last of the narrowing Upper Trenta Valley to the alpine watershed of the Vrsic Pass. The road seems to end before a towering ridge of forest that rises high beyond the treeline to the snowy peaks of Jalovec (2,645 m/8,676 ft) on one side, and Slovenia's highest mountain, Triglav

(2,864 m/9,394 ft) on the other; but it twists its way steeply to Vrsic itself, Slovenia's highest pass at 1,611 m (5,284 ft). A short walk to one side leads you to the Soca's source – a cave from which, in spate, a torrent jets out.

From the top of Vrsic, the hairpin descent is dizzying. So is the panorama, of one the most picturesque of all alpine valleys. Zgornjesavska is a Hollywood dream alpine set of meadow, mountain, snow, stream and forest; and its fame is global thanks to the World Cup skiing venue of Kranjska Gora on its far side.

WHEN SHOULD I VISIT?: May–October/November (depending on the weather). Come for the Lent Festival, when throughout June Maribor's left bank district celebrates its oldest traditions.

RAFTING DOWN THE DRAVA RIVER

Slovenia

Born as a mountain torrent in the Julian Alps in Austria, the River Drava is significantly broad and deep by the time it flows through Dravograd into Slovenia, through which it runs for 102 of its total 720 km (450 mi). There are two ways to go rafting on the Drava. If you're determined and lucky, you can raft from Dravograd all the way to Maribor or even Ptuj, passing through the most beautiful section of the entire river's course, camping or sleeping in hotels as your own pace dictates. Otherwise, you join a raft at Koblarjevzaliv (an artificially wide but very pretty section of river near Maribor) with anything from five to forty others. Unfortunately, each raft promises to send '2 rafters plus a rafter's girl' with you, and their function is not just to steer, but to sing you their selection of hearty Slovenian folk songs, and stuff you full of (quite good) wine.

THE AMBER TRAIL
Hungary

HIGHLIGHTS:
The wooden church at Lestiny, built without a single nail; and the wooden rugmaking looms in Malatina. Both villages are typical of the Chocsky and Oravsky Hills.

For 1,000 years, amber has been traded between the Baltic and Hungary. Soaring pinnacles on cathedrals, palaces, and public buildings reveal the complex bargains of Church and State at Esztergom, Banska Bystrica, Orava and Kracow.

The revived Amber Trail is now an outstanding example of central European co-operation: three countries (Hungary, Poland and Slovakia) reserving a corridor across some of their loveliest hills, rivers, and plains for international enjoyment. The Danube Valley and the Great Bend, the Fatra and Tatra sections of the Carpathian Mountains, and the Northern Plain in Poland, include magical landscapes of every variety; and the Trail route follows the smallest back roads. There are wetland meadows as well as mountain beech forests and river gorges.

HORTOBAGY GREAT PLAINS
Poland

WORTH A DETOUR: Visit 'Puszta Otos' ('Great Plains Five') – when a csiko (horse-herder) stands with one foot on each of two horses, while driving three others, unyoked, before him, at a full gallop.

Unless they are actually cowboys, even experienced riders like their comfort on a long journey, so the most popular way to ride Hungary's 'Puszta' (Great Plains) is to ride from place to place, but to stay in hotels rather than camp. It's possible, but difficult, to do it any other way. And you do need to be experienced for a journey across northern Hungary's vast grasslands to its greatest vineyards at Eger and Tokaj. Depending on your choices, you could take seven–fourteen days, riding steadily with long canters, for five or six hours. There's scarcely a fence or man-made obstacle to bar the way through hundreds of kilometres of woods, shrub-studded hills and

a horizon of stirrup-high grasslands. You get to feel the Puszta intimately; and the only people you're likely to see will be herders, practising inbred equine traditions going back 600 years. If you're lucky, they might show you some of their astounding accomplishments with horses.

POZNAN TO WARSAW SCENIC ROAD

Poland

HIGHLIGHTS:
The annual Classical Music Festival in Poznan.
Smielow Palace, late 18th century, it is set in a large nature park.
Goluchow Castle, where you can see Polish bison in the grounds.

The drive between the two major Polish cities of Poznan and Warsaw can, of course, be made on a multi-lane highway. It's much better though, if you have the time, to take the scenic route, a lovely trip through the Weilkopolska lakelands, passing a variety of pretty small towns, old churches, castles and palaces.

Poznan itself is a historically significant city on the Warta River. At one time the capital of Greater Poland, it contains the oldest cathedral in the country, built in the 10th century. Today it is the region's administrative capital, and a commercial and industrial centre. Just a few miles to the south, and a slight detour off your route to the village of Kornik, lies the Weilkopolska National Park, a peaceful area of forests and lakes, cut

with a few, well-signed trails. Set on a lake, Kornik boasts a splendid, moated castle, with a landscaped arboretum that includes trees and shrubs from around the world. At Rogalin, not far away, stands a beautiful 18th-century palace, with 3 protected oak trees in the grounds that are over 1,000 years old. The journey takes you to several more castles and palaces before eventually reaching the city of Kalisz, generally considered Poland's oldest city as it was mentioned as being a trading post by Ptolemy in 200 BC.

Avoiding heavily industrial Lodz, travel south to Piotrkow, site of the first Jewish ghetto in the country, built in 1939. Outside the town is the infamous Rakow Forest, where memorials stand testament to the 600 Jews massacred here in 1942, and to the 7,000 Polish and Russian prisoners also killed here.

Now you are about an hour's drive from Warsaw, Poland's lively capital city. Remarkably, brilliantly rebuilt after World War II, its historic old town is inscribed on the UNESCO World Heritage List.

GALICIAN CARPATHIANS

Poland

HIGHLIGHTS:

Wolosate village, where there is a breeding station for Hucul mountain horses – you can hire these horses in nearby villages and ride in the Park. Sanok Historical Museum, which contains the largest collection of 14th–18th-century icons outside Moscow.

Tucked away in the far south-eastern corner of Poland is the Bieszczady National Park. Located in the Carpathian Mountains, which rise in Slovakia and stretch through Poland, Ukraine and into Romania, the Park protects the Bieszczady Mountains, in the eastern section. It has been enlarged four times since its creation in 1973, when this unique region became the world's first tripartite International Biosphere Reserve, encompassing areas of Slovakia and Ukraine. The mountains comprise three zones: foothills forested with willow, ash, sycamore and grey alder, ancient beech forests interspersed with firs and maples at about 900 m (3,000 ft) and high pastures, known as poloniny, from 1,050 m (3,500 ft). This gorgeous, Alpine-type grassland includes scree and rocks covered with rare lichen and mosses. Elsewhere, endemic wildflowers as well as Alpine and sub-Alpine species carpet the mountain meadows. Bieszczady National Park has 132 km (83 mi) of marked trails, providing hikes of relative ease. One of the best is the hike to the top of Mount Tarnica, at 1,364 m (4,500 ft) the Park's highest peak. Starting at Ustrzyki Gorne walkers can follow the red path through the forest, which probably looks at its best when decked in autumnal colour. If you start early enough you may see deer, but these forests are rich with flora and fauna, including wolves, bears, elk, lynx, wildcats, wild boar and beavers, which have been successfully introduced into the creeks and streams. As the trail leaves the forest for the poloniny, the landscape opens out around you, the wind ruffles through the grasses, and an extraordinary range of raptors can be seen – honey buzzards, goshawks, sparrow hawks, perhaps even a golden eagle. On reaching the top of Mount Tarnica, the 360-degree views over the whole Park are quite something to behold.

DUNAJEC GORGE

Poland

HIGHLIGHTS:
Czorsztyn Castle, a partially
restored ruin.
Niedzica Castle, beautifully
maintained this is a hotel as
well as housing an interesting
museum.

Way down in the south of Poland, on the border with Slovakia, is the little-known Pieniny National Park, through which the Dunajec River flows. An important tributary of the Vistula, the river cuts through the narrow Pieniny Mountain range, and over the centuries its waters have gouged a splendid gorge through the limestone crags. For 18 km (11 mi) the river forms the border with Slovakia, and since both countries joined the European Community in 2004, rafting downstream has become a popular jaunt for tourists from many destinations.

The Flisaki raftsmen have been active on the Dunajec for centuries, transporting goods, fishing for the salmon that were once plentiful here, and steering log-booms. In 1832 tourism began on the river, and just over 100 years later, the Flisaki registered as an organization. Today some 500 men work about 250 wooden rafts, each carrying ten passengers, and accompanied by two raftsmen, wearing traditional round-brimmed, black felt hats, usually decorated with white cowry shells or embroidery. Starting from the marina in Sromowce-Katy, the rafts set out on their voyage, bobbing down through rapids which give onto more placid stretches of water, and finding their way around seven loops in the river, changing direction by more than 90 degrees many times over the whole course. On the way they pass

through wonderful limestone scenery – 500 m (1,600 ft) cliffs, partially tree-clad, forests and fields, even two formidable castles, one on either side, built as strategic fortresses during the 13th and 14th centuries. The Flisaki are knowledgeable guides as well as being very experienced raftsmen, and they delight in educating their passengers about the mountains and their folklore. The trip ends in Szczawnica, a charming mountain resort in the Grajcarek Valley, with vistas towards the highest peaks of the Pieniny range.

HIGHLIGHTS: Troja – Baroque Troya Chateau in its formal gardens, and the pleasant Prague Zoo.
The Charles Bridge is an impressive medieval engineering feat; at each end stand fine towers; Baroque statues line the walkway.

Since the advent of cheap flights the ancient and magnificently beautiful city of Prague has become a popular destination for short and long breaks From the river, Prague Castle, the best-known image of the city, occupies the heights of the Left Bank. The long, almost blank palace façade is crowned by the irregular Gothic spires and pinnacles of the St Vitus Cathedral. Below are the narrow, hilly streets, steep roofs, towers and cupolas and terraced gardens of Mala Strana, 'Little Quarter'. To the south rises the big, wooded hill of Petrin with its funicular railway. On the Right Bank, several of the imposing buildings of Stare Mesto, 'Old Town', can be seen. From here down to Vysehrad, 'High Castle', with the spires of the neo-gothic St Peter and St Paul, the river side of Nove Mesto is lined with fine mansions and commercial buildings.

GUSTAV MAHLER CYCLE TRAIL
Czech Republic

DON'T MISS
The Gothic Cathedral of St Barbara is spectacular.

This cycle trail, one of a number of well-planned and mapped tours in the Czech Republic, runs from Jihlava in the heart of the Bohemian-Moravian highlands northwards to Kutna Hora in Central Bohemia, west of Prague. The trail covers about 83 km (52 mi) of track, with short country road sections, through wooded, rolling hills, river valleys, villages, and two charming towns with Mahler connections.

In medieval times this was a wealthy and important silver mining region. Jihlava was founded by King Wenceslas in the 13th century and prospered. However, it never recovered from the ravages of the Thirty Years' War, though it still has many fine medieval and renaissance buildings. In 1865 the Mahler family moved here; Gustav attended the grammar school and learnt music; his love of Czech folk tunes was life-long. His parents are buried in the Jewish cemetery.

Humpolec is another old town with a history of silver mining, though it became better known as a centre for the cloth trade. The art nouveau Town Hall houses a museum with a Gustav Mahler gallery. The hilltop village of Kaliste, with its lovely views over the countryside, was Mahler's birthplace. The tiny cottage has been reconstructed and is visited by music lovers from all over the world.

For a change from Mahler, a restored castle above the Sazava River bridge at Ledec nad Sazavou offers a collection of handicrafts, weapons and coins.

ISLAND HOP ALONG THE DALMATIAN COAST
Croatia

WORTH A DETOUR: Split – Diocletian's Palace. Built for the Emperor's retirement, the walls of this UNESCO World Heritage Site enclose Roman buildings converted over the centuries.

Dalmatia's dramatically beautiful coastline is fringed by hundreds of small, enticing islands. Those south of Split are easily reached and, despite their popularity, peaceful. They offer fine cycling – quiet roads through fertile, hilly, well-wooded countryside, tiny coves, pretty villages, and no long distances. Combined yacht and cycle trips are becoming popular, but bike rental is available in many places and the bike fares on the car ferries are modest. Split is a big, hectic, vibrant city centred on an old town built around and into the

massive remains of Diocletian's Palace. The regular ferry connecting Split and Dubrovnik calls at Brac, Hvar, Korcula and Mljet. Wooded Solta and rugged, remote Vis are easily reached from Split but not by the connecting route.

Brac produces good wine and its lustrous white building stone is prized worldwide. The south coast has several seaside villages, including Bol, famous for its lovely beach and for its windsurfing.

Ancient little harbour towns nestle in the deep bays of Hvar's green, indented coastline, but, with its harbour and fortress, Renaissance square and Gothic palaces, Hvar Town is the main attraction.

HIGHLIGHTS:
Views from the battlements over the whole of Budva, Saint Nikola Island and Sveti Stefan.
The little port village of Przno for a sunset drink.

BUDVA RIVIERA
Montenegro

The beautiful Budva Riviera, with its azure water, background of mountains and string of bays, coves and fine sand beaches, runs only about 35 km (23 mi) from Budva to Petrovac. Some of the settlements that punctuate the coast date back to Roman, Greek and even Phoenician times, though little archaeological evidence remains. A walk along the Riviera, either on the beaches, by the coast road or on the peaceful hillside path parallel with the old road, allows breaks or overnight stays at irresistible beaches and exploration of the inland villages and old, frescoed monasteries.

Budva old town was built on a headland and is surrounded by 15th-century walls. This busy tourist town offers old buildings, churches and museums, festivals and a lively nightlife. Southwards, a promenade walk follows the bay round to Becici beach. Milocer, once a royal holiday spot is, with its two beaches – King's and Queen's – and lush parkland setting, a fashionable resort. Sveti Stefan is reached by a causeway; built on a tiny island as a fishermen's village in the 15th century, it is now an exclusive and hotel complex.

Right: Budva Riviera

DAJTI EXPRESS CABLE CAR
Albania

HIGHLIGHTS: There are some good restaurants, including one with fish straight from its own pools.
In the late spring, alpine strawberries grow among the trees.

This spacious and easily accessible National Park is a favourite excursion and escape for city-dwellers in Albania. It has been inhabited from early times and the name could be linked with the ancient cult of Diktynna, a mother goddess venerated around the Mediterranean. Until 2005 the only approach was by road, passing through the city outskirts and fashionable new housing, winding along the contours of the mountain. Inside the Park, low-key tourist developments are built around restaurants and the road finishes at a large, green area which is used for picnics and barbecues. This is also the terminus for the Dajti Express Cable Car, an Austrian-built enterprise which runs from the edge of town. The 4 km (2.5 mi) ride up to 1,230 m (3,998 ft) takes just fifteen minutes.

From the Dajta Field, paths lead through attractive beech woods and areas of pine and fir. These quiet wooded slopes are home to many flower and plant species and to small mammals including red squirrels.

HIGHLIGHTS: The enormous baptistery is a building of great beauty and tranquillity.
Sunset on Saranda's waterfront, when Corfu seems to drift in a haze.

CROSSING LAKE KOMANI
Albania

Lake Komani was formed when the River Drin was dammed in 1970 as part of a huge hydroelectric scheme. It winds, fjord-like, from the huge Vau i Dejax dam near Shkodra to the Fierza Dam. The memorable ferry ride is the best way to reach the remote and spectacular Tropoja region – the road is dreadful.

Another ferry plying the waters is the local waterbus, a ramshackle-looking craft created by welding an old bus onto a hull. This takes about four hours – twice as long as the car ferry – but it provides links for the remote dwellings of the lake and offers a unique insight into the life of the area. A night in Shkodra (old Scutari) makes catching this early ferry bus possible.

The ferry journey is superb, following the twists and turns of the lake whose deep, still, jade-green waters reflect the precipitous tree-clad gorges. In places the deciduous woods have been cleared, the ground terraced to allow those whose homes are clustered high above the lake to scratch a living. Bajram Curri is a windy, ugly little town set in magnificent scenery. Named after a key figure in the liberation of Albania from Ottoman rule, it is a good base for exploring the huge lakes and towering mountains.

THE ALBANIAN COAST FROM CORFU
Albania

HIGHLIGHTS:

Shkorda – Rozafa Castle, a medieval/Venetian fortress high above the confluence of three rivers.

The Phototheque a selection of photographs from a huge 19th-century archive, a unique record of historical and everyday life in Northern Albania.

An easy trip from Bajram Curri is to lovely Valbona Valley with its plunging waterfalls.

WHEN SHOULD I VISIT?: Late April–October.

TIME IT TAKES: It's possible to complete the trip in one day, but much better to make it a jaunt of at least three days.

The southern Albanian coast is very close to Corfu and, since the 7th century BC when Greece established colonies in what was then Illyria, strong trade and cultural links have existed. Now regular short ferry and hydrofoil crossings from Corfu make it easy to reach Saranda and the remarkable UNESCO World Heritage Site at Butrint. It is just possible to make a day-trip of it.

Sunny Saranda is an attractively situated port and seaside town, a pleasant place to stay. An ancient city, it has Roman and Byzantine remains, though little archaeological work has been undertaken. On the Butrint road south lie the interesting ruins of the Byzantine Monastery of Shen Gjergi, a lovely spot with views of the Adriatic and good birdwatching in the marshes. Further south, the pleasant beach-resort of Kasmili makes an alternative base.

Butrint is one of the most exciting sites in the Balkan Peninsula. Set against a background of hills and largely bounded by water (ancient Butrint was effectively an island), this extensive and complex site has remains dating from periods covering 2,500 years. The excellent guide to Butrint by Neritan Ceka is essential for serious exploration. The massive perimeter walls, some dating from the 5th century BC, shelter Roman baths, a Venetian tower, a Greek lustral well, fragments of early Christian buildings and a large complex known as the Tri-conch Palace. Finely carved gates pierce the walls, two opening onto the lakeshore, where the ancient harbour lay. The inner fortress contains temples and baths, a gymnasium, a Roman house, Greek theatre and acropolis and an early Christian baptistery. Many of these have fine mosaic floors.

DRACULA'S TRANSYLVANIAN TOUR
Romania

DON'T MISS
Cross the mountains by Red Tower Pass.

Transylvania, part of Hungary and then of the Ottoman Empire, became Romanian in 1918. The name now is synonymous with spiky mountains and castles, dark forests, werewolves and Dracula the Vampire Count. In reality, Vlad Tepes, the Impaler, son of Vlad Dracul, was a fierce fighter and ruthless ruler.

The inhabited, fortified citadel Sighisoara was the birthplace of Tepes; with its jagged skyline of battlements and spires, it looks the part. The tour-bus magnet though is Bran, south of Brasov. 'Dracula's Castle', perched on a crag and bristling with turrets, may have inspired Stoker, but was never inhabited by Vlad. The sprawling hilltop castle in nearby Rasnov is more atmospheric.

This north-south journey ends in Bucharest, but a westward loop back to Sighisoura passes the brooding, little-visited Poenari Castle where the Impaler spent years in refuge before escaping the Turks aided by the villagers of Arefu. The Saxon city of Sibiu was briefly his home, and the cathedral contains the tomb of his son, Mihnea the Bad.

WORTH A DETOUR: The Tabula Traiana (a carved stone with Roman inscriptions) was laid in AD 103 to mark the start of construction of the road and of Trajan's famous bridge, the first across the Danube.

THE DANUBE GORGE
Europe/Romania

The Iron Gate, Portile de Fier, now refers to the 117 km (73 mi) stretch of the Danube from Moldova Veche to the huge dam upstream of Drobeta-Turnu Severin. This section of the Danube Bike Trail passes through four gorges. Bazias is a convenient point to join the route. At the little port of Moldova Veche the waters divide around an island and flow into the Golubac Gorge. Though the town here was submerged, some castle ruins remain. The second gorge, Gospodin Vir, is, like Golubac, about 15 km (10 mi) long and as little as 220 m (715 ft) wide. Kazan Gorge remains spectacular; here the cliffs tower to 700 m (2,300 ft) and the twisting chasm narrows to just 150 m (492 ft). The Romans built an extraordinary planked road here, inserting supporting beams into the rocks. Upstream from Orsova on the Serbian side a plaque commemorates this road and Trajan's Bridge.

KOM EMINE TRAIL

Bulgaria

HIGHLIGHTS:
Access from Sofia passes the spectacular Iskar Gorge. Brown bears and wolves are still found in the Stara Planina, which is home to many rare birds including golden eagles.
The road to Emona gives glorious and welcome views of the sea.

Between Mount Kom on the Serbian border and Cape Emine on the Black Sea coast stretches the Stara Planina (Old Mountain) range along which runs the Kon Emine Trail, part of the trans-European E3 trek. The whole walk – about 700 km (438 mi) will take about a month. The railway and road which follow the southern contours permit breaks in interesting, historical towns and villages where, as well as rest and provisions, information and advice on routes and day walks can be obtained.

The western and central sections of the range contain the highest peaks – many over 2,000 m (6,500 ft) – and the most demanding terrain. From the ridge the views are superb – south over green undulating foothills, north over sheer rock walls and deep gorges. Large areas are National Parks, rich in birds and wildlife. The weather is fickle; spring is particularly wet.

The trail begins at Berkovitsa, in the northwest – a lovely area of deep wooded valleys and remote monasteries; it can also be reached from Sofia in the south. The Troyan Pass (a link between provinces in Roman times) gives road access, as does the Shipka Pass. Here, the road south leads to Kazanlak, the 'capital' of the rose-growing region and the 'Valley of the Thracian Kings', with many burial mounds. The pleasant town of Slivan is the start of shorter walking trails.

Sleepy, attractive Kotel is a good starting point for the Eastern section where the range is still a dominating north/south barrier.

ATTIC COAST ROAD

Greece

YOU SHOULD KNOW

Highway 91, with its sharp curves and unheeded speed limits, is a dangerous road.

WHEN SHOULD I VISIT?:
All year; but avoid weekends and July and August.

HIGHLIGHTS:
Sunset at the Cape – the views over the islands and sea are sensational.
Vouliagmeni Lake – the warm sulphurous water has brought relief to rheumatism sufferers for years.
Anavysos – a lively little town, with fish sold from the boats in the harbour.

Cape Sounion is the windy southern tip of Attica, 69 km (43 mi) from Athens. Here on a rocky cliff-top spur high above the Aegean stands a Doric temple to Poseidon, god of the sea. It was built in 444 BC, the same time as the Parthenon, and its brilliant white columns have been a welcome landmark to seafarers ever since. The marble, quarried at nearby Agrileza, contains no iron and retains its whiteness over centuries. Of the original 34 slender columns, 15 survive; Lord Byron set an unfortunate precedent in 1819 when he carved his name on one of them. The sacred site was sealed by massive walls; these can be followed down to the bay and the remains of ancient boathouses, which later became a pirates' lair.

The coast road along the Attic Riviera passes many busy and commercialized beaches and resorts. South of Vouliagmeni and Varkiza with their marinas and luxury clubs, the road is lined with quieter coves and tavernas and exclusive villas. There are regular buses from Athens to Sounion, and it is a popular outing – an early morning visit avoids some of the crowds. It is possible to drive back round the Cape and a little north to the rather desolate town of Lavrio. The Mineralogical Museum is a reminder of its wealthy past as a silver mining centre. A loop inland rejoins the coast road at Anavysos.

YOU SHOULD KNOW

Walkers should be fit and used to long walks over rough terrain. Beware of falling rocks.

SAMARIAN GORGE HIKE
Greece

The Samarian Gorge is a long – 16 km (10 mi) plus 3 km (2 mi) to the coast – and gruelling walk. Wardens, donkeys and helicopters are on hand – every year injured walkers are rescued – and flash floods are not uncommon early and late in the season. But this is an exciting trek, with magnificent scenery and remarkable flora and fauna. The Gorge is home to hundreds of bird species and to the shy and elusive kri-kri, the Cretan ibex. Herbs scent the air, and Cretan dittany, used medicinally since ancient times, grows on the rocks.

Organized trips usually arrive early (the Gorge opens at 6.00 am), with boats from the bottom of the gorge to the waiting coaches at Hora Sfakion. This can be done independently, by public bus. A south to north walk is quieter, but uphill, and against the tide of trekkers coming down.

THE PIRAEUS TO SANTORINI FERRY
Greece

HIGHLIGHTS: While the ferry is moving slowly, dolphins may swim alongside and play for a while.
The extraordinary thrill of entering the great bay of Santorini.

Sailing the Aegean between the Isles of Greece may be a dream, but the ferry journey from Piraeus to Santorini is a pleasant reality: a day of sea travel with glimpses of interesting islands.

The ship leaves the chaotic sprawl of Piraeus, heading southeast, and sails round either the rocky north or the greener south of Syros, into the handsome port of Ermoupoli. This, the largest town in the Cyclades, was, in the 19th century, Athens' main port. Its opera house is based on La Scala! On two hills behind the harbour are a medieval quarter and a fine domed church.

The ferry runs south to Paros whose single central peak is ringed by fishing villages, beaches and little bays. The busy harbour at Parikia is the hub of inter-island transport, but behind it, ranks of tightly packed square white houses rise gently to an old kastro. Just an hour west, Naxos is big, beautiful and, unusually, very fertile. Fishing boats and restaurants crowd the harbour and narrow, ancient alleyways climb through stone archways to the fine mansions of the fortified Venetian town. Midway between Naxos and Santorini, the little 'party island', Ios, has one of the prettiest harbours in the Aegean: linked by a stepped path to the port at Yialos, hilltop Santorini (Thira) was part of the Minoan civilization until (probably around 1640 BC) a cataclysmic eruption when its high centre sank to form a deep lagoon around which the island – actually the partial rim of the crater – curves.

PATRAS TO MESSOLONGHI

Greece

HIGHLIGHTS:
The fine Castle of Morea, the
moated fortress at Rio.
The view from the bridge
– lush hillsides, towering
mountains and the water,
busy with shipping, far below.

A short ride east by back roads from Patras, the attractive port village Rio is the southern entry point for the Charilaos Trikoupis Bridge. Named after the 19th-century statesman who first suggested a bridge here, it was opened in 2004 at the time of the Olympic Games. The overall length is 2,880 m (9,449 ft) and its cable-stayed suspended deck is the longest in the world. Designed to improve road communications between mainland Greece and the Peloponnese it has, in addition to toll-paying traffic lanes, a bicycle/pedestrian lane which offers, for those with a head for heights, a spectacular crossing of the Gulf of Corinth.

A ferry still runs between Rio and Antirio – both villages still have the forts which guarded this, the 'Little Dardanelles', the narrowest point in the Gulf. On both sides, fertile coastal plains, backed by mountains, are dotted with small seaside resorts. Just east of Antirio is Nafpaktos, ancient Lepanto, where in 1571 the sea battle that ended Turkish domination of the Mediterranean took place. To the west the road passes through coastal villages and over flat swampland to the serene area of salt marsh, reeds and calm waters (a protected biodiversity zone) of Kolsova Lagoon. On its banks lies Messalonghi, once a collection of stilted fishermen's huts, now a lively modern town, usually visited for historical reasons. Lord Byron came here to join battle in the struggle for independence, but died of fever in 1824. His death brought the war to international attention. In 1826 after a bitter siege the townspeople abandoned their fallen city by the Gate of Exodus, which still stands. Most were recaptured and killed. The town was awarded the honorary title of Hiera Polis (Sacred City) for its heroic part in the War of Independence.

DON'T MISS
Stavroupolis is a lovely
village with traditional
stone houses and
a shady square.

NESTOS VALLEY
Greece

The Nestos River, which forms the boundary between Macedonia and Thrace, rises in the lofty Rodopi range in Bulgaria. It flows south through craggy mountains, gorges and deep forests to spreading fertile plains and a wetland delta fed by dozens of tributaries. The valley makes a glorious mountain bike ride; some of it is tough going, some uses well-marked donkey tracks, old roads, or paths alongside the railway line.

The mountain road from Drama to Xanthi crosses the valley at the village of Paranesti, from where it is possible to cycle a 'there and back' loop into the remote mountains, a region of hidden waterfalls, thick flower-scattered woodland, a refuge for many animals and birds. From Paranesti downstream the river runs through forested foothills and fields of sunflowers, past isolated villages.

South, the thick beech woods are full of birdlife. Now the river flows into The Narrows, a remarkable protected landscape of seven successive hairpin bends. The railway and the track cut along above the river and allow views of the tight meanders and the lush, undisturbed – there's no road access – wildlife habitat.

HIGHLIGHTS: The two original steam engines are displayed, one at each end of the line.
Kalavryta Museum is a dignified, undramatized and moving memorial to the 1,436 men who died.

VOURAIKOS GORGE RAILWAY
Greece

Diakofto is a peaceful village on the Gulf of Corinth. It has a small beach and a background of steep mountains, olive groves and citrus orchards and it is the end of the remarkable Vouraikos Gorge Railway. The short – 22.5 km (14 mi) – journey is memorable and enjoyable; the track climbs 700 m (2,275 ft) using a rack-and-pinion system for traction over the steep gradients. The best view of the mechanism is from the front of the train; the very back gives wonderful views of the scenery.

After a gentle ascent through the lush landscape of the valley, the line criss-crosses the river; the gorge narrows and the train enters the first of fourteen tunnels, then runs along a ledge above the river. The only stop is at the picturesque settlement of Zahlorov – there is accommodation and good walking here. The journey continues beside the river in the shade of plane trees, and over open country to Kalavryta. This is a delightful spot. At 756 m (2,457 ft), with fresh air, bubbling springs and tree-shaded plateia (town square), it is a favourite with Athenians for weekends. Some miles south of the village the deep Cave of the Lakes has fine stalactites and a chain of deep stone basins which run with water in the spring. Little Kalavryta is famous nationwide – the War of Independence started officially here in 1821, and in 1943 it saw one of the worst atrocities of World War II when the Nazis executed all the men of the area.

IOANINNA TO MÉTEORA ROAD
Greece

WHEN SHOULD I VISIT?: May–early July, September. In spring, the snow-melt clothes the slopes of the Pindus with wild flowers.

Ioaninna, a lively and attractive town on the shores of Lake Pamvotis, is the capital of Epirus. During Ottoman rule the city prospered; it was at this time that the famous Crafts Guilds of Epirus were started by those driven by poor land to practise skills from silversmithing to baking. The old, walled Turkish town is built on a headland and the despot, Ali Pasha, made it his capital.

The scenic road northeast climbs steadily to the Katara Pass through the Pindus Mountains. This massive range, snow-capped from October until May, stretches to the Albanian border. Below the pass lies Metsova, still the 'capital' of the Vlachs, mountain-dwelling shepherds who speak a dialect of Latin. Metsovo also flourished under Turkish rule and later those who grew rich elsewhere re-invested in their home town. Here, stone lanes wind between fine old houses and many of the traditional crafts survive.

WORTH A DETOUR: Boat trips visit painted cave-shrines, old monasteries and the 15th-century Panayia Eleoussas, a rock church deep in a chasm.

PRESPA LAKES FROM KASTORIA
Greece

Set on a promontory in Lake Orestiada and surrounded by mountains, Kastoria in western Macedonia is one of Greece's loveliest towns. Its name means 'place of beavers' and it has long been a centre of the fur trade. After the beavers became extinct in the 19th century, the trade continued with imported fur. The town is architecturally outstanding. Many of the 17th and 18th-century merchants' mansions survive and there are 54 Byzantine and medieval churches. Panaghia Koumbelidhiki has an unusual tall, drum-shaped dome; 10th-century Aghia Anarhyri overlooks the lake.

A side road 36 km (22 mi) north leads through fertile meadows to the Prespa Basin where Greece's borders with Albania and the Republic of Macedonia run through the two Prespa Lakes. This was a politically sensitive, little visited place, but now the Prespa Lakes National Park is a Transnational Park and though still remote this beautiful and serene area is more accessible. The huge Megali Prespa has steep, rocky shores interspersed with lush wetlands; Mikri Prespa and its encircling reed-beds is a protected area – among the many birds breeding there is the endangered Dalmatian pelican.

SACRED WAY

Greece

The Sanctuary of Apollo at Delphi took shape from the 8th to the 7th century BC, on a temple guarding the centre of the world, the Omphalos (Navel), the chasm of the Oracle. Here Pythia, the priestess, perched above the void and spoke the words of the god; a priest interpreted the often-ambiguous pronouncements to the waiting supplicants. From the 6th to the 4th century BC, Delphi was the spiritual and international political centre of the ancient world, for warriors and kings joined the worshippers.

Great wealth and power were amassed – in addition to ritual cleansing and sacrifice, those seeking advice paid tribute. Individuals and cities erected dedications to Apollo – statues and small buildings (treasuries) and the Sanctuary grew. Under Roman rule, the power of the Oracle declined, and in the Christian 4th century it was declared defunct.

Delphi spreads over a natural amphitheatre of rocks and cliffs in the foothills of Mount Parnassus. The Sanctuary – the Sacred Precinct – is part of a larger complex that includes a gymnasium, stadium and sanctuary to Athena. The entrance is through the Roman agora; the Sacred Way, a paved path, zigzags up the terraces and slopes. The lower section is flanked by plinths and niches, which once held more than 3,000 votive statues, and the remains of the treasuries.

Above these, the Spring of Gaia and the Rock of the Sibyl pre-date the building of the temple.

The Athenian Stoa acts as a gateway to the Temple, which now consists of foundations and a re-erected line of Doric columns.

The Sacred Way ends at the 5,000-seat rock-cut theatre, which still has remarkable acoustics.

HIGHLIGHTS:

The Museum – with a superb collection of the sculpture, friezes and artefacts.

The stadium where the Pythian Games took place every four years still has a starting line of marble slabs with grooves for toes.

The Tholus, or Rotunda, a very beautiful construction in the Sanctuary of Athena, the postcard image of Delphi.

The views – beyond the grey crags, green valleys studded with olives roll down to the sea.

MANI PENINSULA

Greece

HIGHLIGHTS:
Areopolis – several of the
churches have been restored;
the frescoes are superb.
Vathia – the most spectacular
of the tower villages; the
narrow towers cluster in a
maze of cobbled streets. It is
almost deserted.
Asomati Bay – as well as
the rather dull 'entrance to
the underworld', there are
scattered remains of an
ancient settlement.

The middle of three rocky fingers extending from the Peloponnese, the Mani is a mountainous, harsh region. Outer Mani, south of Kalamata, is watered by streams from the thickly forested Taiyetos Range. Inner, or Deep Mani, is barren, rock-strewn, starkly dramatic – blank tawny hills bristling with tower-villages, scattered with tiny churches, tangled with prickly pear. Until Greek independence in 1832, Maniots lived in chieftain-led clans, in villages of almost windowless towers, defence against invasion and blood feuds. Until recently no roads penetrated the mountains; now the little ports, then so vital, are ghost towns. Christianity was not accepted until the 9th century, and then zealously; many of the tiny Byzantine chapels and churches are strikingly frescoed and carved.

Areopolis, named for the god of war, is the chief town of the Inner Mani. From here to Cape Matapan, southernmost point of mainland Greece, about 36 km (22 mi) of very scenic road follows the western 'shadowed' coast, linked by a network of unmetalled roads and stone tracks to villages and churches in the foothills of the mountainous spine and the coves and bays of the jagged rocky coast. From Pyrgos Dirou, where a track leds to the famous Diros Caves, the road runs south to Gerolimenas, a sheltered harbour and fishing village with accommodation. The road onwards crosses the coastal plain to Alika, climbs steeply past Vathia, hugs the cliff edge and turns east to Porto Kayio.

Right: Mani Peninsula

AUSTRALASIA & PACIFIC

GREAT OCEAN ROAD

Australia

WHEN SHOULD I VISIT?:
Year-round. Be warned that on the more exposed cliffs you can get stiff winds off the ocean at any time of year.

HIGHLIGHTS:
A round of golf on the course at Anglesea, where you will share the fairways with a mob of kangaroos.
A helicopter flight – for a different perspective on the Twelve Apostles.
The rock arch known as London Bridge.

The Great Ocean Road belongs in an élite group of classic coastal drives, which includes California's Pacific Highway and Italy's Amalfi Coast Road. It runs 285 km (180 mi) along Victoria's south coast, west of Melbourne between the towns of Torquay and Warrnambool. Constructed originally to open up a previously inaccessible coastline for commerce, the Great Ocean Road has now become a major tourist attraction in its own right. Started in 1919 with the labour of ex-servicemen and completed 13 years later, this engineering marvel clings precariously to sheer cliff faces, snakes around inlets, crosses narrow gorges and passes through tunnels blasted out of solid rock. Leaving the lively seaside resort of Torquay with its world-famous surf break at Bells Beach, the road hugs the shoreline as it passes through the pretty little towns of Anglesea and Lorne. As you negotiate sharp corners and descend into protected bays you are presented time and again with stunning views of the Southern Ocean, endless expanses of virgin sands and rugged cliffs stretching off into the distance. After Apollo Bay the route bears inland and crosses Otway National Park, part of the Otway Ranges, an area of dense temperate rainforest which offers one of your best chances of seeing a koala in the wild. These shy creatures are notoriously hard to spot, thanks to their camouflage and inertia during the day. Appropriately enough, the highlight of this trip comes towards the end. Just 70 km (45 mi) before Warrnambool the Twelve Apostles rise proudly from the sea, like giant sentinels guarding the coast.

These majestic limestone stacks, up to 45 m (150 ft) high, are the result of coastal erosion and they provide a justly famous spectacle at sunrise and sunset.

GIBB RIVER ROAD

Australia

HIGHLIGHTS:
Waterfalls in full flow in the gorges – but you need to go early in the summer to see them.
Walking along beautiful Bell Creek and into the Gorge.
Swimming in a gorge pool (crocodile-free!).

Running straight across the heart of the Kimberley region in Australia's remote northwest, the Gibb River Road remains one of the country's great off-road driving adventures, There is still a real sense of achievement as you motor into the small towns of Derby at the western end or Kununurra at the eastern end, saddle-sore after 700 mostly bone-shaking kilometres (440 mi). 'The Gibb', as the road is known locally, is serious 4x4 terrain. Apart from a short sealed stretch east of Derby, it is a red dirt and gravel track, fairly wide and smooth for the most part but badly corrugated in places from the effect of other vehicles and 'wash outs' from the wet season. All this might still be negotiated in a conventional car but what you really need the high clearance of a proper 4x4 vehicle for are the even rougher side tracks you must take in order to visit the main attractions along the route. Involving detours of up to 50 km (30 mi), places such as Bell, Adcock and the Manning Gorges showcase the natural features for which this ancient and rugged landscape is famed: narrow sandstone gorges, waterfalls, hidden creeks and tranquil pools. Most travellers tackling the Gibb choose to camp along the way but there are accommodation options for those wanting more comfort. You can drive the road in either direction but as the majority of the big sights are in the western half you might prefer to start from the eastern end and save these delights for later.

THE INDIAN PACIFIC RAILWAY

Australia

HIGHLIGHTS: Experiencing something of the hard life of the miner on an underground mine tour in Broken Hill.
Early morning sightings of kangaroos and emus beside the line.

This classic long-distance rail journey crosses the Australian continent from the Pacific Ocean in the east to the Indian Ocean in the west. Running twice weekly in each direction, trains are hauled by huge diesel locomotives and can be up to a kilometre (over half a mile) in length. From Sydney the journey provides an inspiring overview of many of the country's most distinctive landscapes: the lush, heavily forested slopes of the Blue Mountains give way to the sprawling rural heartland of New South Wales which in turn is succeeded by the bleak outback scenery of the Broken Hill mining region. Crossing into South Australia gives you fine views of the Flinders Ranges with their dramatic ridges.

After an extended stop in Adelaide the Indian Pacific heads northwest along the Spencer Gulf to Port Augusta before embarking on the most forbidding part of the journey, across the vast and featureless Nullarbor Plain (which means literally 'empty of trees') – 1,200 km (750 mi) of red earth, low scrub and nothing else, which includes the longest straight stretch of railway track in the world (478 km/300 mi). The bustling gold mining centre of Kalgoorlie returns you to human activity with a jolt before your last night on board conveys you the final 600 km (375 mi) for a morning arrival in the West Australian capital of Perth. The Indian Pacific is run by the same company that operates the Ghan Railway, and it offers the same range of travelling options.

HIGHLIGHTS: Waking up on your first morning to the reds and ochres of the vast central desert.
Dining on the train under the stars of the desert sky.

THE GHAN

Australia

The Ghan takes two days to bisect the Australian continent from Adelaide on the Southern Ocean to Darwin. Over its 3,000 km (1,900 mi) course it crosses three distinct climate zones, from the fertile coastal plains of South Australia through the vast dry desert of the Red Centre to the luxuriant vegetation of the tropical Top End. The Ghan takes its name from the Afghan camel drivers who with their animals opened up 19th-century trading routes into the interior.

The company running the Ghan manages quite a trick spoiling you with all the benefits of modern rail travel in comfortable, air-conditioned carriages and the highest standards of on-board service, while at the same time imparting a real sense that you are blazing an adventurer's trail as you travel across one of the world's harshest, least hospitable terrains. As you gaze out from the window of your compartment over the endless expanses of red earth and spinifex grass, the flat horizon only rarely broken by sandstone outcrops, you have ample time to reflect on those early pioneers, as well as the indigenous peoples who have sustained themselves for centuries in this very environment.

YOU SHOULD KNOW
If you fancy something a little more exclusive you can rent your own houseboat to take out on the river.

PADDLE STEAMER ON THE MURRAY RIVER
Australia

The presence of Australia's principal river, the Murray, has been a key factor in turning the southeast of the country into its most productive and heavily populated area. The American writer Mark Twain hailed the Murray as Australia's Mississippi, although in a country where water has always been a limited resource it lacks the flow of its mighty American counterpart. Like the Mississippi the Murray offered a means of navigation for the early European settlers to reach the rich pastoral country inland; and for over 50 years from the 1860s it reigned unchallenged as the main transport artery for the region, carrying livestock and produce downriver to the coast and bringing supplies back to the sheep and cattle stations.

As in America the paddle steamer was the dominant means of river transport in these years. Where once they had a strictly commercial, utilitarian role these elegant vessels now ply their trade on the Murray as leisure boats. There is no better way to enjoy the varied sights of this riverscape – the mighty cliff-faces, the stands of towering red gums, the wetlands with their abundant wildlife – than from the deck of a paddle steamer as you glide by in sedate comfort. At the historic river port of Mannum, on the Murray's lower reaches you board the Murray Princess for an extended cruise upriver to the first lock near Blanchetown and back again, sleeping on board in well-appointed cabins. The rewards for opting for this slower and gentler form of transport are many, not least the grandstand views it gives you of the river's spectacular birdlife – pelicans, black swans and egrets are all commonly seen here.

HIGHLIGHTS:
Watching the birds and animals as the riverbank comes to life in the early morning.
Taking a guided nocturnal tour to seek out the varied wildlife that emerges after dark.
The ancient rock carvings at Ngaut Ngaut Aboriginal Reserve.

THE NED KELLY TRAIL

Australia

The short and violent life of Ned Kelly, Australia's most famous outlaw, or 'bushranger', has long since gained iconic status. You can compare the legend with the more humdrum realities of a life spent in rural poverty in this driving tour around its key locations. By Australian standards it is a relatively compact affair – some 650 km (400 mi) in a round trip from Melbourne – since Kelly never strayed far from his roots in the 'high country' of Victoria's northeast.

The Hume Highway, the main Melbourne to Sydney road, conveniently connects many of the Kelly sites. Beveridge and Avenel, an hour's drive north of Melbourne, were two of Ned's childhood homes; his ex-convict father John 'Red' Kelly died when Ned was twelve and is buried in Avenel. Ned robbed the bank in nearby Euroa, while the town museum in Benalla has a number of Kelly-related exhibits. Glenrowan marks the heart of the Kelly story. Here Ned and his gang made their famous last stand in the local inn. While the other gang members all died in the police siege, Ned himself was wounded when trying to break out wearing a suit of homemade armour.

A country drive brings you to Beechworth, the furthest point on the tour, where you can still see the gaol in which the fifteen-year old served his first sentence. There are fine views of the King valley and mountains on the journey back to Mansfield, which takes you via Power's Lookout and Stringybark Creek; an atmospheric walk through blue gums and blackwoods leads you to the site where Ned achieved notoriety when the gang shot three policemen dead; their graves and a memorial can be seen in Mansfield.

HIGHLIGHTS:

The green silk sash in Benalla Museum given to the ten-year-old Ned as a reward after he had saved a boy from drowning; the sash bears the marks of his blood as he was wearing it when he was wounded and captured at Glenrowan.

Kate's Cottage and Ned Kelly Memorial in Glenrowan, a replica of the Kelly home.

DON'T MISS
Watching the sunset
with a beer at Karumba
Point – journey's end.

MATILDA HIGHWAY
Australia

The Matilda Highway is the main north-south route through the interior of the state of Queensland. Starting in Cunnamulla, the first town after the New South Wales border, it runs for 1,700 km (1,060 mi) in a north and northwesterly direction until reaching the Gulf of Carpentaria at Karumba. This is a classic drive through the great Australian outback, and if you like your roads straight and empty and your vistas boundless then you will enjoy this experience. But you should be warned that the landscape can be dauntingly unvarying: wide open expanses of grassland and low scrub, extending for kilometre after kilometre in every direction. Only as the highway approaches the Gulf in the north does it change somewhat to feature a coastal habitat of cracked saltpans – and to become, if anything, even flatter.

Many of the key towns of the Queensland outback line the route of the Matilda. Places such as Winton, Longreach and Charleville developed in the 19th century as supply and transportation centres for the vast and isolated sheep and cattle stations that cover much of the area.

The Highway takes its name from the region's associations with 'Waltzing Matilda', Banjo Paterson's ballad which has become Australia's unofficial national anthem. You can visit the Combo Waterhole, the supposed setting for the story, outside Kynuna on the highway south of Cloncurry. The North Gregory Hotel in Winton is where 'Waltzing Matilda' is said to have had its first performance in April 1895 (although the hotel has since been rebuilt following a fire).

SYDNEY TO MELBOURNE COAST ROAD

Australia

....

HIGHLIGHTS:
Mogo, site of a former gold mine where there is a reconstructed mid-19th-century gold-rush town.
Take a trip out to sea to spot whales on their annual migration (June–November) at places like Jervis Bay, Narooma and Eden.
Croajingolong National Park in the far east of Victoria, over 100 km (62 mi) of isolated, unspoiled coastline with excellent bushwalking opportunities.

The direct route linking Australia's two largest cities is the inland Hume Highway, but the coast road is unquestionably the more rewarding option, and the distance involved is not much greater. Known as the Princes Highway, this route follows the New South Wales coastline south from Sydney to the state border with Victoria, at roughly the halfway point on the 1,050 km (655 mi) journey. It then heads east across the Gippsland region towards Melbourne. Leaving Sydney the Highway skirts Botany Bay, site of Captain Cook's famous first landing in 1770, before reaching the industrial city of Wollongong. The road then passes through a succession of small fishing villages and relaxed seaside resorts that stretch all the way down to the state border. Here you are rarely more than a few kilometres from the shoreline and there are regular opportunities to turn off for wonderfully secluded beaches. These, together with outstanding surfing and all manner of water sports, including diving and game-fishing, constitute the area's main attractions, but inland there are also easily accessible national parks, such as the Royal National (the second oldest national park in the world, after the USA's Yellowstone), Morton and Ben Boyd Reserves, which contain spectacular upland scenery and some of Australia's best-preserved remaining temperate rainforests.

After the old whaling station of Eden, the Princes Highway strikes inland across southern Victoria and the fertile dairy-farming region of Gippsland. This is a land of gently rolling hills and forests of tall eucalypt. You brush the coastline once more briefly at Lakes Entrance, which as the name suggests is a good base for exploring the Gippsland Lakes, the country's most extensive network of inland waterways. And if you are after a bigger adrenalin rush, Ninety Mile Beach (which you can drive along!) is never far away.

THE BRUCE HIGHWAY

Australia

Running between the state capital, Brisbane, and the bustling city of Cairns 1,720 km (1,075 mi) to the north, the Bruce Highway is Queensland's principal transport artery, connecting most of the main towns and cities of Australia's second-largest state.

On this road you are rarely more than a few kilometres from the Pacific Ocean, so it is easy to relieve the tedium of highway driving with a short detour to chill out on a clean, deserted beach. Inland you are accompanied much of the way by views of the foothills, escarpments and plateaux of the Great Dividing Range.

On leaving Brisbane the Highway runs up the Sunshine Coast, more relaxed and less developed than its famous Gold Coast cousin. You cannot miss the striking profiles of the Glass House Mountains to your left, while to the north you will be hard put to resist the seductive seaside charms of Noosa. These coastal plains are rich agricultural country and intensive cultivation is evident throughout the journey: pineapples around Gympie, mangoes around Bowen, huge sugarcane fields in the Mackay region. At Rockhampton, self-styled 'beef capital' of Australia and a great place for a steak, you enter the Tropics and notice the vegetation becoming thicker and lusher as hills and rainforest edge ever closer to the coast.

A number of coastal towns north of Mackay provide excellent bases for exploring the Whitsunday Islands lying offshore and for longer trips to the Great Barrier Reef itself. Townsville is the region's main city; you certainly know you are in the Tropics wandering along its attractive promenade. And as you cover the final 300 km (190 mi) to Cairns you would be well advised to have some energy in reserve for the vast array of adventure activities offered by your destination city.

YOU SHOULD KNOW

Deadly box jellyfish, populate the tropical waters north of Agnes Water from October–April), so you are strongly advised not to swim in the sea during this period.

ALICE SPRINGS TO COOBER PEDY
Australia

HIGHLIGHTS: Staying in an underground hotel in Coober Pedy. Seeing the desert sun rise over the MacDonnell Ranges from a hot-air balloon above Alice Springs.

This trip follows the Stuart Highway, named after Scottish-born John McDouall Stuart, one of Australia's pioneering explorers who in 1862 finally succeeded, on his third attempt, in blazing a trail from the south to north coast. This feat paved the way for the construction just ten years later of the Overland Telegraph Line linking Adelaide with Darwin.

On leaving the lively town of Alice Springs, boundless stretches of flat highway extend to the horizon and are punctuated by occasional tiny roadside settlements like Kulgera and Marla, whose sole function is to

service the needs of long-distance travellers. All the while you are surrounded by unbroken vistas of the great central Australian desert, one of the world's harshest, most arid environments. Amazingly, the earliest known evidence of animal life on the planet was found not far south from here, at Lake Torrens. And if you are lucky enough to be on the road following a desert rainstorm you will see the landscape transformed by a sudden profusion of wild flowers.

WHEN SHOULD I VISIT?:
March–May and September–November are the most pleasant times.

SIX FOOT TRACK TO THE BLUE MOUNTAINS
Australia

Easily accessible from Sydney, the Blue Mountains have been inspiring visitors since the early days of European settlement. They really do look blue, thanks to the mist given off by the ubiquitous eucalypt trees; it was this mist, indeed, which kick-started the tourism industry, when the first intrepid visitors came to savour the therapeutic benefits of the mountain air at the end of the 19th century.

The Six Foot Track, so named from the original specification for a track six feet wide, was created as a bridlepath back in the 1880s. Hiking its 42 km (26 mi) length from Katoomba to the Jenolan Caves remains one of the best ways to immerse yourself in the varied natural splendours of the area. There are several energetic climbs on a route that takes you up along high ridges and down into steep-sided valleys, dense with spreading ferns. The rewards for your efforts are panoramic views of distant canyon walls and sudden variations in habitat which increase your wildlife-spotting opportunities. Campsites at strategic locations along the way mean that you need not exert yourself to the extent of the doughty runners who compete every March in the Six Foot Track Marathon, billed as Australia's toughest off-road race.

HIGHLIGHTS: The Horseshoe Bend, a 180-degree curve which marks the start of the climb out of the coastal plain to Kuranda. Stoney Creek Bridge on its three tall trestle piers.

KURANDA SCENIC RAILWAY
Australia

Prolonged and torrential rains during the wet seasons in the early 1880s were making life very difficult for the tin miners of North Queensland. It became imperative to improve supply lines to their camps up on the Atherton Tablelands inland from Cairns, and so the line now known as the Kuranda Scenic Railway was born.
You can join the train at Freshwater Station in the northern suburbs. Each carriage is equipped with an audio-visual commentary on the route to enhance the unrivalled views of mountains, precipitous cliff-faces, waterfalls and a World Heritage rainforest. And if you are lucky your train might be drawn by the 1720 Class Diesel electric locomotive that has been painted to depict 'Buda-dji', the legendary carpet snake whose story from the Aboriginal Dreamtime you will hear during your journey.

PORT PHILLIP BAY
Australia

HIGHLIGHTS:
The high-rise skyline of downtown Melbourne viewed from Hobson's Bay. The revelling in Melbourne's Alexandra Gardens where the 'Around the Bay in a Day' event ends.

Australia's passion for pedalling comes to a grand climax during October every year with 'Around the Bay in a Day' – the country's greatest mass cycling event, when up to 15,000 cyclists gather in Melbourne to ride around Port Phillip Bay. Distances on offer are 50 km (31 mi), 100 km (62 mi), 210 km (130 mi) and 250 km (155 mi).
Port Phillip Bay, with Melbourne at the top, is almost land-locked – access to the Bass Strait is via the narrow Rip between Port Lonsdale and Point Nepean. The Bay has an irregular coastline of some 265 km (165 mi) and the full circumnavigation by road is somewhat shorter. It has many inlets and beaches, with the western shore being somewhat swampy and the eastern shore characterized by sandy beaches. For those planning their own ride there are numerous options, though there is increasing suburban development and consequent road traffic around the Bay, especially on the eastern shore. A full circumnavigation at a sensible pace to include recreational stop-offs and side trips could take a few days.
Clockwise from Melbourne, the route passes through the suburbs to Frankston and follows the water to Sorrento, where a ferry crosses the Rip to Queencliff. Then the road goes through Geelong before travelling back up the more sparsely populated western shore to Altona Beach and back to Melbourne.

SKYRAIL RAINFOREST CABLEWAY

Australia

HIGHLIGHTS:
The panoramic views of the Coral Sea.
The Ulysses butterfly, a true Australian star with its electric blue wings.
Kuranda, with its laid-back atmosphere and huge array of arts and crafts stalls.
The Barron Falls in full flow (wet season only – December–March).

The World Heritage-listed tropical rainforests of north Queensland are the oldest continually surviving rainforests on earth. The opening of the Skyrail Rainforest Cableway outside Cairns in 1995 has given visitors an entirely new perspective on this dazzlingly lush environment. From the safety and comfort of your enclosed gondola cabin you gaze down on a previously inaccessible world as the cableway carries you silently over the dense, verdant rainforest canopy. And with much of the natural activity taking place in the heights of the trees, you have a good chance on your trip of seeing sights that are simply unavailable from the forest floor up to 60 m (200 ft) below.

Skyrail connects Smithfield, a northern suburb of the coastal city of Cairns, with the small inland town of Kuranda, 330 m (1,100 ft) up on the edge of the Atherton Tablelands. At 7.5 km (4.5 mi) it is one of the world's longest cableways and can carry up to 700 passengers per hour. Not only is it an enjoyable way to travel, it is also good for the planet; Skyrail's operators pride themselves on its low environmental impact, which has been recognized in numerous ecotourism awards. There are two stops on the route, at Red Peak and Barron Falls. Both give you the chance to get off and explore the rainforest at ground-floor level along boardwalks and with the help of knowledgeable local rangers. Here you may well see a brush turkey foraging on the forest floor, while from your gondola you should catch flashes of brightlycoloured parrots, lorikeets and cockatoos; and although you are unlikely to see them, you can listen out for the whip-crack call of the whipbird and the cooing of the Wompoo pigeon, among the most distinctive sounds of the rainforest.

FRASER ISLAND TREK

Australia

WORTH A DETOUR:
The Southern Lakes Drive covering features including Lakes Boomanjin, and McKenzie with its white sand and blue water.

Sand-based Fraser Island off the southern coast of Queensland extends to 123 km (76 mi) from north to south and is 26 km (16 mi) across at the widest point. It has a variety of habitats – from pristine rivers to freshwater lakes, lush subtropical rainforest to eucalypt forests, mangroves to melaleuca swamps, heaths and – of course – endless beaches. All are inhabited by wildlife, including over 200 species of bird and a variety of reptile life, with migrating whales frequently spotted. Even 4x4s get marooned in Fraser's soft sand and a surer way of seeing this enchanting island is to make the Fraser Island Trek – a hike that follows the continuous beach up the eastern coast with possible detours into the interior, starting at Hook Point on the island's southern tip. The first stop is Dilli Village, where accommodation can be booked in advance. From there, the hike continues to the outpost of Eurong and on to the island's main settlement, Happy Valley.

THE HEYSEN TRAIL

Australia

Any super-fit backpacker with two months to spare can achieve the ultimate prize – an end-to-end certificate and badge to prove that they've tackled and beaten one of Australia's toughest official long-distance hikes, also recognized as one of the world's great long-distance walks.

The Heysen Trail runs from Parachilna Gorge in the Northern Flinders Ranges down to Cape Jervis on the southern tip of the Fleurieu Peninsula, passing Adelaide along the way. It traverses some of South Australia's most breathtaking landscape, providing an incredible variety of stimulating sights to reward determined hikers who follow the distinctive red-and-white markers with their stylized representation of the Trail crossing hills and valleys.

The Heysen Trail takes in rugged gorges, native bushland and scenic coastal areas, also passing through rich farmland, vineyards and historic towns. The northern part through the South Flinders Ranges offers rocky landscapes, ridges, gullies, pines and gum-lined creeks.

DON'T MISS
The stunning Wilpena Pound in the South Flinders Ranges.

CAPE YORK PENINSULA

Australia

The northernmost point of the Australian continent, lonely and remote, Cape York Peninsula has been described as one of the last great wild places on earth. The so-called 'Trip to the Tip' is a challenging one whichever mode of overland transport you choose. If you have the stamina and confidence, one of the best ways to encounter a landscape largely untouched by human hand is by mountain bike. Cairns is the place to organize your own transport or else sign up for an escorted tour. If you travel independently you should bear in mind that accommodation options are limited, so you need to take basic camping equipment as well as appropriate spares and supplies.

Most of the 1,000 km (625 mi) from Cairns to the Cape is on dirt tracks and unsealed roads. Whilst you have to be on constant alert for potholes and the heavy corrugations that form on many surfaces, you will find your progress is often not much slower than fellow travellers in motor vehicles. And your greater lightness and flexibility will give you the advantage when negotiating the many creek crossings with their swift-flowing streams and steep-sided banks.

The route from Cairns takes you up the coast through the Daintree Rainforest and on to Cape Tribulation and Cooktown, before heading inland across Lakefield National Park to join the main road running up the spine of the peninsula.

The 160 km (100 mi) from the Wenlock River north to the Jardine River, which follows the route of the old Overland Telegraph Line, is a particularly exciting section. After a ferry crossing of the mighty Jardine River it is a relatively straightforward ride, via the small Torres Strait Islander town of Bamaga to Cape York itself, where a sign confirms you are at the tip of mainland Australia.

HIGHLIGHTS:

The huge abundance and variety of wildlife.

Camping beneath the paperbark trees on the bank of the Archer River.

The detour to the Iron Range National Park on the east coast of the peninsula, which protects a rainforest ecosystem of world-wide importance and where you have your best chance of spotting a cassowary.

Visiting Thursday Island in the Torres Strait by ferry – still Australia but a different world.

YOU SHOULD KNOW

For a less strenuous option than pedal power you can do the trip by 4x4, in which case you should allow one week, including breaks and detours. Make sure you have the right equipment and spares as paying for repairs and breakdowns in remote areas can be very expensive.

WHEN SHOULD I VISIT?:
September–May to avoid the
hottest desert conditions.

PERTH TO ADELAIDE ROAD TRIP

Australia

Billed as 'Australia's Ultimate Road Trip', the journey from Perth in Western Australia to Adelaide in South Australia lives up to its name. This epic route stretches for 3,200 km (1,900 mi) along Australia's southern coastline, delivering an ever-changing drama of striking landscapes, soaring cliffs, azure sea – and the mesmerizing desert that is the Nullarbor Plain. It's a largely empty land, with few significant towns along the way, but there's plenty to see. That emptiness also requires pre-planning, with a need to carry spare fuel and adequate emergency water supplies, just in case.

From Perth, the journey begins with a sortie down the coast along Highway 1, passing through Bunbury to the South Coast at Walpole, then along to Albany and the charming seaside settlement at Esperance, where the road turns north and runs up country to Norseman. Alternatively, it's possible to head inland from Perth along the Great Southern Highway, with a quick stop in the small town of York with its 19th-century buildings, before continuing through the small settlements of Aldersyde, Gorge Rock, Hyden and Forestania. From Norseman the long-distance Eyre Highway begins a long straight run parallel with the coast through the fearsome Nullarbor Plain to Eucla, the largest place on the Plain. Between the tiny settlement of Nullarbor and Eucla there are half a dozen lookout points that offer superb views of the impressive cliffs of the Great Australian Bight. After Eucla one of the longest stretches of tarmac road in Australia follows the coast through Nullarbor National Park to Ceduna, from whence the Flinders Highway continues.

PINNACLES DESERT WALK

Australia

DON'T MISS

A spring display of seasonal wild flowers around the desert area.

Within the Nambung National Park in Western Australia may be found an extraordinary natural phenomenon – the Pinnacles. These surreal limestone monuments have become one of Australia's major attractions, and it's easy to see why.

The Pinnacles were formed over millions of years to create a unique landscape that contains over 4,000 sculpted monuments, scattered across a vast and arid desert landscape of rippled quartz sand dunes. They have been likened in appearance to fingers, termite mounds or even tombstones, but one thing is certain – Pinnacles come in all sizes and shapes and every single one is different, ranging from tiny spikes to sturdy monoliths that rise to over 4 m (13 ft) in height.

There's a loop track from the end of the access road that can be driven but is much better walked, as this allows for exploration of interesting groups of stones, with every twist and turn opening up new vistas.

To make the very most of the Pinnacles, it is sensible to arrive early in the morning or late in the day. Then, the desert becomes an eerie wonderland of contrasting colours and extended shadows when viewed in dawn light or at dusk against the purple and orange hues of a big sky. Photographers become ecstatic whilst the rest merely marvel.

WORTH A DETOUR: The short walk through the narrow Echidna Chasm, with its towering walls and tall palm trees – one of the most mysterious places in Australia.

PURNULULU NATIONAL PARK
Australia

Lots of Australia is pretty remote – and Purnululu National Park is more remote than most. This stunning place lies in Kimberley, the empty northeastern corner of Western Australia that is often described as 'Australia's last frontier'.

Although Aborigines lived in the area for countless generations, it only became generally known in 1982 when a TV crew 'discovered' the extraordinary landscape of orange-and-grey-striped beehive sandstone formations (called the Bungle Bungles), cliffs, tropical pools, plunging chasms and gorges with elegant fan palms adorning the rocks.

The best option is to get in among the real thing on foot, for a day hike or camping trip, though this requires more effort than merely turning up and tramping the terrain. The only way in is along the unmade Spring Creek Track.

TASMANIA COAST TREK
Australia

YOU SHOULD KNOW
Some of the deadliest snakes on the planet lurk along the way – they tend to be shy, but carry anti-venom in the First Aid kit, just in case!

A trip across the Bass Strait to Tasmania seems like a visit to another country. This island is the most distinctive of Australia's states, with its self-proclaimed status as 'The Natural State'.

Those who wish to underline Tasmania's eco-credentials – and prove their own advanced self-sufficiency qualifications – should undertake the marathon hike along the connecting South Coast and Port Davey Tracks in the vast Southwest National Park. Your pack must contain everything needed for two

unsupported weeks. That includes food and camping gear (there are basic campgrounds at regular intervals), plus all-weather clothing. Any hike in Tasmania involves battling against mud. The 84 km (52 mi) South Coast Track has plenty of it, plus two mountain ranges to cross where the coast is impassable and shoreline sections where the waves can be dangerous. The route is Cockle Creek, South Cape Rivulet, Granite Beach, New River Lagoon, Deadmans Bay, Louisa River, Cox Bight and Melaleuca. The demanding 80 km (50 mi) Port Davey Track begins at Melaleuca and goes inland via Spring River, Watershed Camp and Junction Creek to Scott's Peak.

HELICOPTER RIDE OVER FRANZ JOSEF GLACIER

New Zealand

WHEN SHOULD I VISIT?:
Any time of year.

TIME IT TAKES:
A typical helicopter-dropped guided glacier walk on Franz Josef takes two hours.

HIGHLIGHTS:
The Lake Wombat Walk from Franz Josef township – up through lush ferns and rimu forest with abundant bird life to the lake named after the 19th-century gold prospector known as Wombat Jack. The coastal walkway near Harihari – one of the West Coast's most scenic short hikes with great views of coastline, mountains, rivers and forests.

YOU SHOULD KNOW

The weather around the glaciers can be changeable, so walkers should be prepared for all conditions and let someone know where they intend to go.

The Franz Josef Glacier and its near neighbour, the Fox Glacier, are extraordinary natural phenomena on the West Coast of the South Island. Descending from the Southern Alps, they terminate less than 300 m (985 ft) above sea level in verdant rainforest. Classification of both glaciers and the surrounding Westland National Park as a UNESCO World Heritage Site is well deserved. Due to heavy snowfall, Franz Josef is one of the few glaciers in New Zealand that is still growing. It is around 12 km (7.5 mi) long and terminates just 19 km (12 mi) from the Tasman Sea.

The glacier is one of the country's top attractions, with the former mining township of Franz Josef catering for visitors. It is some 5 km (3 mi) from the glacier's face and from there it is possible to hike up to the glacier, either solo or as part of a guided group (basic mountaineering equipment required). However, this is a fairly demanding walk that terminates at the first icefall – a frozen near-vertical slope.

By far the most popular way of experiencing this extraordinary place is to take a helicopter tour from the heliport in Franz Josef. It is possible to take a scenic ride that shows the glacier in all its glory from the comfort of a helicopter seat, or alternatively, a longer trip that is extended to include the Fox Glacier.

But most able-bodied visitors prefer to set foot on the ice – the helicopter drops its passengers between the first and second icefalls on Franz Josef Glacier, where they have a guided tour of awe-inspiring glacial landscape – a wonderland of pinnacles and brilliant blue ice with sensational views of surrounding mountains. This is undoubtedly one of the world's most spectacular glacier experiences – or perhaps the most spectacular.

WALKING THE KAURI COAST

New Zealand

For those who prefer to see their landscape from two feet rather than four wheels, and enjoy a bit of an adventure at the same time, walking the old Waoko Coach Road on the North Island is an ideal challenge. This historic route is an example of pioneering road building, dating back to the early years of colonial New Zealand. The Coach Road was once the only link between Hokianga and Kaipara Harbour on the sparsely populated West Coast, and remains isolated.

It extends to 22 km (13 mi) between Taheke and Tutamoe, with the northern entry at Waima and the southern entry at Tutamoe. It is certainly the shortest route between the two points – the distance between the two ends of the Coach Road by the modern State Highway is 90 km (56 mi).

Along the way the old road passes through the Waima and Mataraua forests, which are impressively preserved examples of the kauri forests that used to cover the coastal area hereabouts. Hikers will have the forest pretty much to themselves – the route is not well marked and little used, so it is essential to take good maps, food, water and wet-weather clothing... and wear stout boots. The journey goes up hill and down dale to a maximum height of 700 m (2,300 ft) but the gradients were chosen to allow horses to pull up fully laden wagons, so are never too steep.

The weather can be unpredictable and anyone who gets caught in one of the occasionally violent rainstorms on the high plateau can head for the public shelter halfway along the Coach Road. For anyone who likes their adventures organized, there are guided trips that offer accommodation and transport along with the scenic tramp.

WORTH A DETOUR:
The interesting side leg to Wekaweka Valley near Weimamaku.

WORTH A DETOUR: Chartering a boat at Opua (with or without a skipper) to explore the beaches and coves of the offshore islands.

TWIN COAST DISCOVERY HIGHWAY
New Zealand

Discovery Highway is a stunning circular route which provides a superb scenic drive through New Zealand's Northland, starting at Auckland, travelling up the North Island's East Coast before returning down the enchanting West Coast. The first stretch up the East Coast ends at the vibrant Northland centre of Whangarei, with its wealth of activities and strong cultural aspect. Then it's on to the Bay of Islands area, where hundreds of coves, beaches and islands are waiting to be found. This is also the place to explore New Zealand's heritage, especially at Waitangi and Russell, a former whaling port once known as the 'Hell Hole of the South Pacific', though happily it's now a charming waterside village. Another mandatory stop is at the seaside settlement of Paihia, known as the 'Jewel of the Bay of Islands.

WHANGANUI RIVER JOURNEY
New Zealand

HIGHLIGHTS: Meeting indigenous Tieke people beside the river at Tieka Kainga (if they're there!) and taking part in a traditional powhiri (Maori welcoming ceremony).

Here's a novelty – a walk that's undertaken by canoe. The Whanganui River Journey is officially classified as a 'Great Walk', underlining its status as one of New Zealand's great outdoor adventure trips. The mighty Whanganui River is situated in the southwestern part of the North Island, winding down in pristine splendour from the volcanic plateau near Mount Tongariro to the Tasman Sea.

The upper reaches run through dense rainforest. In the middle reaches its rocky banks are crowded by broadleaf woodland that forms the heart of Whanganui National Park, before it passes through rolling farmland on the last stretch to the sea. The whole area is rich in Maori tradition and from the 1890s to the 1950s a riverboat service used to support Europeans who had settled along the banks.

The landscape is young in geological terms, formed a million years ago of soft sandstone and mudstone (papa) from the seabed and since eroded into dramatic ridges, deep gorges, sheer cliffs and plunging waterfalls.

LAKE WAIKAREMOANA

New Zealand

DON'T MISS

The view from the top
of Panekire Bluff at the
southern end of Lake
Waikaremoana.

A natural gem in the North Island's East Coast/Hawke's Bay Region is the remote and rugged Te Urewera National Park, which preserves some of the country's most magnificent scenery. Tucked away in the southwestern corner of the Park is the Lake Waikaremoana Great Walk – one of the nationally designated 'Great Walks' managed by the Department of Conservation, indicating that they are New Zealand's finest tramping tracks.

This 46 km (29 mi) hike loosely follows the lakeshore after which it is named, offering superb lake views when it strays from the water. The going is fairly easy and the Great Walk isn't that long, but the idea is to take it easy, stopping overnight and enjoying recreational opportunities such as swimming and fishing offered by Lake Waikaremoana as you go. There are five huts and campsites and prior booking is mandatory throughout the year – even in winter this is a popular trek, though the Great Walk is occasionally closed as a result of heavy snowfall that brings down overloaded tree branches to block the track.

Most hikers drive in to Aniwaniwa on the gravel-surfaced State Highway 38 that links the East Coast with Central North Island. From there, there are well-signed roads to both walk entrances, though most prefer to park securely at Aniwaniwa and take one of the regular shuttle buses or water taxis that service each end of the walk. They will also return hikers to their vehicles after completing the Great Walk.

THE SOUTHERN SCENIC ROUTE

New Zealand

WORTH A DETOUR: A trip from Invercargill to beguiling Stewart Island – a National Park where it's still possible to see kiwis in their natural habitat.

The natural beauty of this wonderful country never ceases to amaze, but nowhere is it more impressive than along the aptly named Southern Scenic Route. The U-shaped journey takes you from Te Anau to Dunedin, skirting Fiordland National Park (part of the Te Wahipounamu World Heritage Site) and passing

through Manapouri and Tuatapere to the coast at Te Waewae Bay, where the road swings east to Orepuki, Colac Bay and Riverton before turning south into Invercargill. Heading east again, the Route goes through Fortescue into the rugged Catlins, a sparsely populated area that contains New Zealand's southernmost tip, Slope Point. The next ports of call are Owaka and Balclutha. Here 4x4-drivers can take a detour along rough roads through Kaitangata, though the official course is along State Highway 1 to Milton and Lake Waihola. From there, the last leg crosses the Otago Coast Forest to Taieri Mouth before continuing through Brighton and Green Island to Dunedin.

WORTH A DETOUR: A trip along the winding Queen Charlotte Drive from Picton to Havelock – it's like cruising the spectacular Marlborough Sounds without a boat!

THE CLASSIC NEW ZEALAND WINE TRAIL

New Zealand

New Zealand wines are high on the list of challengers to the great established wines. Your exploration starts in Napier on the North Island and continues via Hastings, Waipukurau, Norsewood, Dannevirke, Woodville, Pahiatua, Eketahuna, Masterton and Martinborough to Wellington. From there, the Cook Strait is crossed by ferry to Picton on the South Island, before the Trail goes on to end at Blenheim. This 485 km (300 mi) road trip passes through three major wine-growing areas and five regions – Hawkes Bay, Tararua, Wairarapa, Wellington and Marlborough – that together offer the bonus of some great scenery. And many of the vineyards to be visited along the way not only offer fine wines, but also excellent meals. The Wine Trail starts in the Hawkes Bay wine-growing area, the heart of New Zealand's red wine country. Next comes Martinborough, the country's first great stronghold of the Pinot Noir grape. Then it's on to the sunny skies of Marlborough, where the claim to fame is undoubtedly superb Sauvignon Blanc.

TARARUA MOUNTAINS SOUTHERN CROSSING

New Zealand

WHEN SHOULD I VISIT?:
Any time (June–August
for the possibility of
a snow crossing).

HIGHLIGHTS:
A magnificent panoramic
view from Field Peak near
Kime Hut – west to Otaki,
north along the Tararua
Range, east to Mount Hector
and south to the Hutt Valley
and Wellington.
The undulating ridge route
over the humps and bumps
of the aptly named Beehives.
A dramatically steep path
down from Alpha Hut into the
scarily named Hell's Gate.
A short side trip after fording
the Tauherenikau River to see
Cone Hut – one of the best
examples of bush carpentry
in New Zealand.

YOU SHOULD KNOW
Kime Hut is named in
memory of E.J. Kime, who
lost his life attempting the
Southern Crossing.

The North Island has a mountainous spine that stretches from the East Cape to Wellington, parallel to the sea. The southernmost part is formed by the Tararua Range, spanning 80 km (50 mi) from Palmerston North to the Hutt Valley, which runs down to Wellington Harbour.

Within sight of Wellington is one of the country's best-known hiking routes – or tramping tracks, as New Zealanders prefer to say. The rugged Southern Crossing goes over the bare peaks of the southern Tararuas from Otaki Forks (reached by single-track unmade road – drive with care!), past Mount Hector and on to Kaitoke. It is no picnic stroll – New Zealand's unpredictable weather presents an ever-present and often-realized threat and there have been several fatalities over the years. But this is a challenge that will be relished – and met – by the well-prepared and experienced hiker, who will be rewarded with sensational panoramic views of mountains and sea.

There are huts along the route, providing both accommodation and bad-weather shelter. But there is only one hut – Kime Hut – on the exposed tops between the bush lines above Field and Alpha Huts, the latter pair being the usual places to overnight during the Crossing (nights one and two respectively). The climb to Field Hut is relatively short, so some hikers continue and stay at Kime Hut on their first night, though this is technically a bad-weather refuge. But the standard approach on Day One is a three-hour walk up to Field Hut, just below the bush-line, followed by a truly awe-inspiring eight-hour tramp along the tops to Alpha Hut on Day Two, with the Crossing being completed by a less dramatic eight-hour exit via the Marchant Ridge on Day Three.

A winter Southern Crossing in good snow conditions is one of the most exhilarating hikes in New Zealand (alpine equipment and crampons essential!).

PUNAKAIKI HORSEBACK RIDE

New Zealand

DON'T MISS
With luck – spotting
Hector's Dolphins
disporting themselves just
off Pancake Rocks.

Between the towns of Westport and Greymouth on the South Island's West Coast is Paparoa National Park, alongside State Highway 6. This is a land of extraordinary coastline, lush coastal forests, canyons and limestone cliffs, caves and underground streams.

It begins with an atmospheric ride into the Punakaiki Valley, fording the river and passing through native bush to view huge limestone bluffs topped with temperate rainforest. Abundant birdlife is a feature of the Park, and birds seem less cautious when the watchers are on horseback. Species to look out for are white-breasted native kereru (pigeons), the bright pukeko, inquisitive weka, paradise duck, spur-winged plover and harrier hawk. Returning to the coast and riding along Punakaiki Beach, your horses will be strolling through the seething white water at the water's edge. The climax of the ride is simply sitting and marvelling as the powerful sea crashes into the Pancake Rocks and erupts through the blowholes.

WORTH A DETOUR: Break away from the Coast Track near Mutton Point to visit Separation Point, where fur seals breed.

ABEL TASMAN COAST TRACK

New Zealand

The Abel Tasman National Park on the north shores of the South Island is in the Golden Bay area. It contains one of the country's 'Great Walks' – the Abel Tasman Coast Track. The Coast Track runs from Marahau to Wainui through wild and stunning coastal scenery, of which New Zealand has an almost indecent abundance. It crosses numerous watercourses and estuaries along the way. Rivers and streams are bridged, but some estuaries can only be crossed for an hour or two either side of low tide, and both bridges and estuaries can become impassable after heavy rain. As the name suggests, the Coastal Track follows the sea, though often detouring inland to cross saddles that separate bays, However, most climbs are rewarded with sensational sea and coastal views from those hard-earned vantage points. Down at sea level, there are many interesting coves to be found and estuaries to be explored, so it's best to proceed at a leisurely pace, planning an itinerary that involves overnight stops at the campsites and/or huts to be found at regular intervals (camp passes required). The route goes from Marahau to Apple Tree Bay, Yellow Point, Torrent Bay, Anchorage Bay (hut and campsite), Bark Bay (hut and campsite), Tonga Quarry, Onetahuti Bay, Awaroa Inlet (hut and campsite), Waiharakeke Bay, Goat Bay, Skinner Point, Totaranui (major campsite complex), Anapai Bay, Mutton Cove, Whariwharangi Bay and finally on to Wanui Inlet.

WORTH A DETOUR: The view of Mount Madeline reflected in the lake from Alabaster Hut. **WHEN SHOULD I VISIT?:** September–May (winter is best avoided).

FIORDLAND LONG DISTANCE WALK
New Zealand

In the southwestern corner of the South Island lies the country's largest National Park. Fiordland protects coastal landscape that typifies New Zealand's natural splendour. It is a wonderland of mountains, glaciers, beech forests and waterfalls that tumble into the sea – and of course the sculpted fiords that give the Park its name.

However, those experienced and super-fit individuals who look for a seriously demanding physical challenge will head straight for the Hollyford Track. They know they've got it right when they see the sign at the start of this 112 km (70 mi) return trip from the route's dead end at the sea. It reads: 'Warning: The Pyke Valley is a difficult track. It is subject to flooding and is suitable for fit, experienced trampers'. This becomes a wilderness trip par excellence, travelling through wild, untamed landscape.

For utterly determined and super-fit adventurers who prefer not to retrace their steps and can take the pain, there is an additional 60 km (37 mi) route from the end of the Hollyford Track that returns to the starting point at Alabaster Hut. The isolated and testing Pyke Route is the ultimate test!

THE TRANZALPINE TRAIN
New Zealand

WORTH A DETOUR: Riding a while in the open-sided viewing carriage that really lets you feel close to – and photograph – the beautiful surroundings.

The sleek blue TranzAlpine runs for a distance of 224 km (140 mi) right across the South Island, westwards from Christchurch on the east coast to the small town of Greymouth (and vice versa).

Before long, the train leaves populated parts altogether – reaching the foothills and starting the long climb through the valleys and plunging gorges of the rushing Waimakiriri River. It then continues into the Southern Alps, crossing girder bridges and going through short tunnels amidst fabulous scenery. After crossing a grassy plateau the TranzAlpine stops at Arthurs Pass Station, with its backdrop of misty mountains, before going through the 8.6 km (5.3–mi) Otira Tunnel and starting the descent through a deep valley, criss-crossing the Grey River and passing waterfalls and lush beech rainforest.

HALEAKALA HIGHWAY

Hawaii

WHEN SHOULD I VISIT?:
Any time of year.

HIGHLIGHTS:
Getting to the summit at dawn to view one of the best sunrises you'll ever see.
The fabulous view into the crater from the Kalahaku Overview below the summit.
Science City at the summit – an astrophysical complex that takes advantage of the clear, dry atmosphere and absence of serious light pollution that makes this the perfect location for ground-based telescopes.
A strenuous 15 minute hike to the top of nearby Pa Ka'oao (White Hill) for a sensational panorama.

YOU SHOULD KNOW
The rocks can be slippery and dangerous when wet.

Aloha – welcome to Maui, 'The Magic Isle'! And of course there's one journey you must take – the scenic drive from Kahului along the Haleakala Highway to the top of the massive shield volcano that forms more than three-quarters of the island's mass. The road is a modern two-lane highway, but it twists and turns alarmingly on the way to the 3,055 m (10,023 ft) summit with many blind bends, and is frequently close to sheer drops. To add to the risks, wildlife and cattle often stray onto the road, especially at night.

But the effort is well rewarded – there are great views over the island and surrounding sea during the drive and the sight that awaits at the summit is awesome – a vast crater that is around 11.25 km (7 mi) long, 3.2 km (2 mi) across and 800 m (2,600 ft) deep, with steep walls and a scattering of volcanic cones around the barren interior.

Actually, despite every appearance to the contrary, the summit crater of Haleakala is not volcanic in origin. It was formed when the walls of two erosional valleys merged at the volcano's summit and is technically a depression rather than a crater, but the distinction is too fine for all but vulcanologists, so crater it shall be. The volcano is active, but has not erupted since the 1600s and is considered dormant, soon to become extinct.

Haleakala National Park surrounds the crater, much of it is wilderness. Rainforest cloaks the windward slopes of the mountain, though the dry forest that once covered the leeward side has been drastically reduced. The Park contains Kipahula Valley, one of the most complete rainforest ecosystems in Hawaii. Visitors should look out for the rare silversword plant that only grows here, a strange member of the sunflower family.

Right: Haleakala craters

EXPLORING VITI LEVU

Fiji

Fiji's principal island of Viti Levu, the Pacific's third largest, contains most of the Republic's population. The majority live in the towns and villages that ring the coastline, as the centre of the island is forested and largely undeveloped. Main economic activities are sugarcane production, cattle ranching, gold mining and tourism – with holidaymakers attracted by resorts along the Coral Coast in the southwest and in the locally named 'Burning West'. These offer classic Pacific ingredients of offshore islands, white sand, reefs, emerald lagoons and palm trees.

Viti Levu is divided by a mountain range that makes it an island of two halves – with heavy rainfall and lush green vegetation on windward slopes to the east and drier brown landscape to the west. Most visitors who do explore Viti Levu hire a car and take the paved coast road that circumnavigates the island, with side-trips down tempting tracks. For adventurous souls who like to experience the culture of the places they visit, Viti Levu's busy Sunbeam Bus network offers endless possibilities. One of the most interesting journeys is through the undeveloped interior from Nausori in the southeastern corner of the island through the highlands via Vunidawa up to Tavua on the north coast, crossing Viti Levu's mountainous spine and skirting the country's highest mountain – Mount Tomanivi (formerly Mount Victoria).

YOU SHOULD KNOW

Fiji has a recent history of coups and political instability.

MOUNT KOGHI RAINFOREST TREK

New Caledonia

WHEN SHOULD I VISIT?:
Any time of year.

TIME IT TAKES:
Allow one day for the longest marked rainforest trek at Mount Koghi.

HIGHLIGHTS:
Spotting a cagou – the white flightless bird with a large crest and strange barking call that is a national symbol of New Caledonia.
A guided botanical tour from Mount Koghi station for insight into the unique local flora.
The Museum of New Caledonia in Nouméa, for an overview of the ethnology of these fascinating islands – includes a magnificent collection of Melanesian artefacts.

'New Caledonia – now where exactly is that?' is a common reaction when this French overseas territory is mentioned, because the scenic island chain deep in the South Pacific is something of a secret in tourist terms. It is certainly less well known than destinations like French Polynesia or Fiji, though it has all the qualifications of a Pacific paradise – offshore coral islands, blue lagoons and white-sand beaches.

To that may be added a certain *je ne sais quoi* – that indefinable element of stylish living that nobody does quite so well as the French. The island of Grand Terre is at the centre of New Caledonian life, and the capital of Nouméa has a refined ambiance with fine colonial architecture, tree-lined squares, open-air cafés, casinos, boutique shopping and fine dining the norm. But wait! There is another Grand Terre – dismissed as *la brousse* ('The Bush') by sophisticated townies. Much of the eastern end of the island is undeveloped and remains the domain of the indigenous Kanak people. This is a land of rainforest and fabulous scenery that includes imposing landscapes, bare mountains, unusual rock formations and dramatic cliffs that plunge into the sea.

Every visitor to this magical island should venture into the ancient rainforest, which has survived untouched for millions of years – ever since New Caledonia was part of the lost continent of Gondwana. Just 20 km (12 mi) from Nouméa is one of the most accessible yet rewarding options – a trek through the rainforest of Mount Koghi with its towering trees and lush foliage, alive with tropical birds. There are a number of recognized hikes of various lengths on offer, with or without guides. When the chosen trek is over, relax at the Mount Koghi station and enjoy the splendid views down over the spectacular Dumbéa Valley, Nouméa and the lagoon.

The New Caledonian Lagoon on the west coast is the world's largest, encircled by a 1,600 km (1,000 mi) reef that is second only to Australia's Great Barrier Reef in length.

RAPA NUI TOUR

Easter Island

YOU SHOULD KNOW
Several of the islets
have already succumbed
to rising sea levels.

WORTH A DETOUR:
Two Windows Cave –
accessed through a narrow
passage that opens out into
a cavern with two tunnel-like
openings that run out to the
cliff face above the sea.

There can be few more recognizable images in the world than the mysterious stone heads and torsos on Chile's overseas territory of Easter Island, carved by the Rapa nui people. These monumental statues are moai some of which are 10m (33 ft) tall. This remote Polynesian outpost is in the southeastern Pacific Ocean and it's one of the world's most isolated inhabited islands, so relatively few people have seen those famous stones at first hand. Most of the island is protected within the Rapa Nui National Park.

Easter Island was deforested long before the first Europeans visited in the 18th century and is now mainly open grassland, but there is much to see. There is a single circular road from the only settlement, Hanga Roa in the southwest of the island, but there are also many dirt roads that allow a complete tour.

It is impossible not to be deeply moved by the sense of timeless history in this extraordinary place. Most of the moai are located around the outside of the island, looking inwards, many of them set on beautifully constructed ahus (ceremonial platforms), but hundreds at various stages of construction remain where they were abandoned in the quarry at Rano Raraku. There are also caves such as Ana Tai Tangata with red-and-white bird paintings. And it's all set in an atmospheric landscape dominated by three volcanic peaks.

THE KOKODA TRACK

Papua New Guinea

There's a little spat regarding the most famous hike in Papua New Guinea (PNG) – should it be called the Kokoda Track or the Kokoda Trail? Also in the mix are historic names such as 'The Buna Road' and 'The Overland Mail Route'. But whatever the name, the trek's the same – a demanding slog that runs in a straight line across isolated country for 60 km (37 mi). The Track crosses terrain that can only be accessed on foot, demanding serious physical effort. This single-file walking route runs from Ower's Corner in PNG's Central Province, 50 km (31 mi) east of capital Port Moresby, to Kokoda Village in Oro Province. The Track passes through rugged mountainous country of rainforest, fern jungles and streams tumbling into steep valleys, reaching the lung-testing height of 2,200 m (7,220 ft) as it skirts around the peak of Mount Bellamy. It can be hiked either way, with general agreement that Kokoda to Ower's Corner is the slightly easier direction. This is definitely the way to go for those who want a guide or porter, as there are plenty of experienced locals to choose from in Kokoda. There are rest houses along the route, some in villages and others at traditional staging points. From Kokoda, the Track passes a number of unspoiled villages on the way to Ower's Corner – Kovolo, Hoi, Isurava, Alolo, Kagi, Efogi Creek, Menari and Naoro. Despite hostile terrain, burning days, freezing nights, intense humidity, capricious tropical rainfall and the ever-present risk of contracting endemic diseases such as malaria, the Track is a popular trekking challenge – especially for Australians. In 1942 Australian troops inflicted World War II's first military defeat on Japanese land forces along the Kokoda Track, which now has iconic status for Australians.

HIGHLIGHTS:
Much evidence of surviving World War II Japanese and Australian defensive works at various points.
Villages where friendly Koiari or Orokaiva peoples will offer tempting seasonal fruits.
The memorial overlooking Kokoda Valley – in WWII Australians defied superior enemy forces here for four days, marking the beginning of the end of the Japanese presence.

ARANUI CARGO BOAT

French Polynesia

There's romance in the idea of island hopping in the Pacific aboard a freighter – especially when the journey begins in Tahiti and continues through the remote and unspoiled Marquesas, French Polynesia's most spectacular island group. Creature comforts are supplemented by the extraordinary thrill of a working boat being welcomed by excited islanders everywhere she calls – her regular visit is a highlight of life in the remote villages she serves. The route encompasses two ports of call in the Tuamotu Islands and fourteen on the six inhabited Marquesas, following this course – Tahiti, Fakarava, Ua Pou, Nuku Hiva, Hiva Oa, Fatu Hiva, Hiva Oa again, Tahuata, Ua Huka, Nuku Hiva again, Ua Pou again, Rangiroa and back to Tahiti.

Despite the heat and humidity, the Marquesas are magical – with jagged coastlines and soaring volcanic peaks shrouded in mist, black sand beaches and emerald lagoons, coconut groves and lush forests, bougainvillea and frangipani.

HIGHLIGHTS:
On Hiva Oa – visiting Paul Gauguin's grave and the House of Pleasure where he spent his last years.
On Nuku Hiva – the beautiful Notre Dame Cathedral in Taiohae Village, capital of the Marquesas.

HIGHLIGHTS: Observing one of the penguin colonies with tens of thousands of breeding pairs that have no fear of man.
The hut used by Captain R.F. Scott's ill-fated polar expedition.

CRUISING THROUGH THE ANTARCTIC

Antartica

Those who make this journey join the relatively tiny number of people who have ever visited this very special place, and are rewarded by a land of icebergs and soaring snow-covered peaks that rise from the sea, glaciers and ice shelves – a hostile land that nonetheless nurtures abundant wildlife that includes penguin colonies, giant albatrosses, six species of seals and different whales. And – perhaps best of all – no humans to spoil it!

Antarctic ships, mostly small by cruise standards, are designed to withstand severe conditions. Usually there are no more than a hundred passengers (fewer for unusual trips). A wide variety of cruises is offered, allowing considerable personal choice for those lucky enough to be able to afford this unique (and expensive) journey.

Most of these specialist voyages commence in Argentina, with passengers flying in to Buenos Aires before transferring to the port of Ushuaia and joining the ship. From there, most cruises take in additional sights on the way to the Antarctic, such as Cape Horn, South Georgia, the Falkland Islands and South Shetland Islands. But the main attraction is always Antarctica, and almost all the visitors actually get to step ashore and gain first-hand experience of the white wonderland that is this magical continent first hand.

Right: Antarctic cruise boat

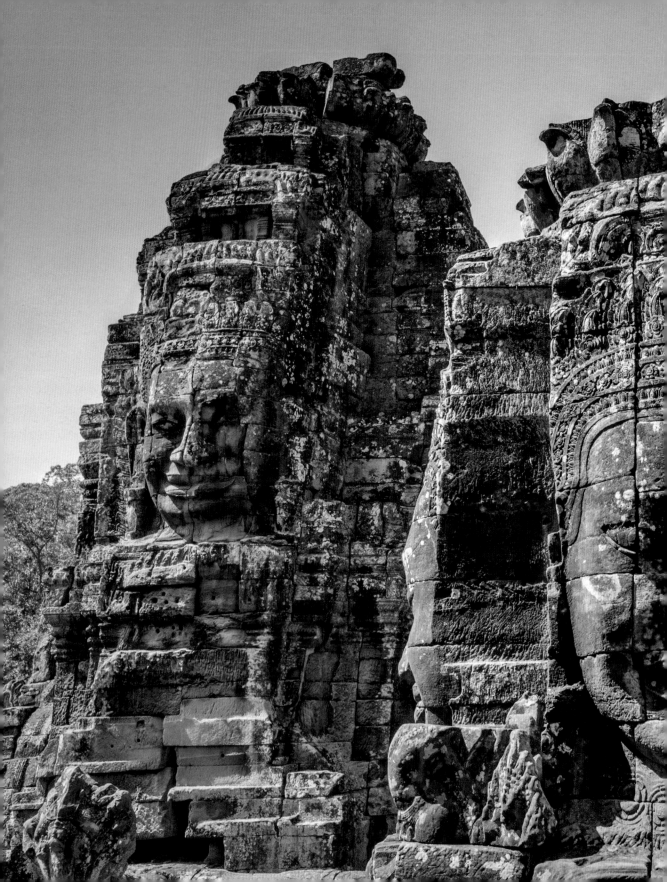

ASIA

RIVER LENA CRUISE

Central Asia/Russian Federation

A voyage along the River Lena is an eye-opening cultural and ecological adventure, taking you to the shores of the Arctic Ocean through a vast tract of virgin territory, only recently opened to tourists.

From its source in the Baikal Mountains of Central Asia, the Lena flows for 4,400 km (2,800 mi) through Siberia. It is among the ten longest rivers in the world, a huge waterway, up to 25 km (15 mi) wide, that is an indispensable transport route through the inaccessible Sakha Republic (Yakutia).

This sparsely populated region of northeastern Siberia contains the largest area of permafrost in the world – where deep-frozen woolly mammoths have been uncovered, perfectly preserved. For most of the year it is a silent frozen land wrapped in snow and darkness, but come spring, a magical transformation takes place – the ice thaws, the river flows and the tundra suddenly bursts into life.

In the 17th century, the first Cossack adventurers to sail along the Lena discovered a wilderness inhabited by semi-nomadic horsemen, cattle breeders and reindeer herdsmen. Little has changed. You voyage through a timeless land of desolate beauty; disembarking at picturesque riverside villages, you will observe the fascinating world of a self-contained shamanic folk culture.

As you approach the Arctic Ocean, the huge river starts to break up into an increasingly complex labyrinth of channels, islands and streams as it gradually spreads into a 400 km (250 mi) wide delta – a 60,000 sq km (37,500 sq mi) lush summer wetland, the largest nature reserve in the Russian Federation. This unique habitat is a vital breeding ground for millions of birds, fish and sea mammals.

HIGHLIGHTS:

Yakutsk – coldest city on earth.
Kyusyur – cultural centre inhabited by native hunters and reindeer farmers.

WHEN SHOULD I VISIT?: Mid-June–mid-August unless you like sub-zero temperatures and ice roads.
WORTH A DETOUR: Mikhailo-Arkhangelskaya Museum, Chita – 18th-century church now a museum dedicated to the Decembrist anti-tsarist revolutionaries.

THE AMUR HIGHWAY

Central Asia/Russian Federation

The Trans-Siberian Highway has to be one of the world's ultimate road trips, along an 11,000 km (7,000 mi) network of roads all the way from St Petersburg to Vladivostok. The infamous 2,200 km (1,375 mi) Amur Highway runs between Chita, historic city of revolutionary exiles, and Khabarovsk on the River Amur, carving its way through the inhospitable, swamplands of eastern Siberia and the impenetrable taiga forests of Russia's Far East, closely following the route of the Trans-Siberian Railway. It is a prestigious engineering project, bulldozing its way across savage terrain regardless of the natural obstacles in its path. Gradually, the road is evolving into a four-lane superhighway, but it is still one of the world's great adventure drives.

TREKKING IN THE GOLDEN MOUNTAINS OF ALTAI

Central Asia/Russian Federation

HIGHLIGHTS:
Sighting a snow leopard.
Crossing the Karatyrek Pass.

Straddling the borders of China, Mongolia, Kazakhstan and Siberia, the Altai ('golden') is a rugged wilderness, a remote land of snow-capped mountains, torrential rivers, glaciers, lakes and waterfalls where wild animals roam in the pastures and forests, and humans are few and far between.

The Altai is not easy to reach. A four-hour flight from Moscow gets you to the pleasant provincial city of Barnaul, then you spend another two days on a bumpy bus ride through the steppe.

Taking ancient herdsmen's trails, you tramp through sweet-scented pine forest and climb across jagged ridges above the treeline, scrambling over moraine and rambling through remote valleys full of wild flowers. Wonder at primeval stone mounds that mark the hilltops as you get closer to Mount Belukha. This sacred twin-peaked mountain towers 4,506 m (14,780 ft) high clothed in snow and half-hidden behind its veil of clouds. According to shamanistic tradition, you are in Shambhala – the mythical kingdom of Tibetan scripture that holds the secrets of the Earth.

CIRCUM-BAIKAL RAILWAY

Central Asia/Russian Federation

WORTH A DETOUR: You can also explore the railway line on foot, going through disused tunnels and over viaducts as you hike along the lakeshore.

A journey along the Circum-Baikal Railway line is an incomparable cultural, historical, technical and scenic experience. It is one of the most complex railway lines in the world, running for 89 km (56 mi) along a narrow mountain shelf.

Lake Baikal, the world's deepest lake, lies directly in the path of the Trans-Siberian Railway and, before the Circum-Baikal was built, trains had to be uncoupled and transported across the lake by ferry. Yet the Circum-Baikal became redundant in the 1950s when a hydroelectric project necessitated flooding a section of line and building a bypass. Today it is a quiet back-route, serviced by excursion trains that trundle along at

25–30 kph (15–20 mph), stopping every so often for passengers to look at the incredible engineering – all the more incredible for having been built without the aid of machines. The railway runs through a region of outstanding natural beauty with breathtaking views of Lake Baikal's astounding scenery. It is a spectacular testament to Russian skill in engineering and design, quite unlike any other railway journey in the world.

HIGHLIGHTS: Zhirovskye and Viluchinskye hot springs.
Kurilskoye Lake – see brown bears and sea eagles.

KAMCHATKA RING OF FIRE TREK

Central Asia/Russian Federation

Barely touched by man, with only a single rough road, Kamchatka is one of the world's greatest ecological treasures – a rugged wilderness in a constant state of geothermal flux containing some of the world's most spectacular volcanoes. It is one of the most active regions in the Ring of Fire belt that girdles the Pacific.

A journey into Kamatchka is like entering a dreamland – a surreal world of elfin cedar trees and giant savannah grasses; boiling mud pots and blue-algae lakes; blackened lava desert and dense primeval forests; steaming sulphur springs and swirling icy rivers. Brown bears roam in the woods, the rivers are stuffed with salmon and the surrounding seas are rich fishing grounds where whales, sea-lions and sea otters flourish.

You trek through highlands and lowlands, scrambling down steep ravines and wading through rivers, wandering through the woods and along the seashore, camping by clear-watered streams, bathing in hot springs and climbing to the summits of snow-capped volcanoes. At the rim of the Mutnovsky Volcano, you peer down into the caldera through a sulphurous veil of fumaroles to glimpse a sparkling wall of ice crystals – an incredible climax to an awesome eco-adventure at the very edge of the world.

LAKE ISSYK-KUL TREK
Central Asia/Kyrgyzstan

Lake Issyk-Kul, the 'Pearl of the Tien Shan Mountains' in northern Kyrgyzstan, is one of the world's highest (1,610 m/5,280 ft) lakes. Yet despite being fed by the icy water of 118 rivers and streams, and the melt-water of the soaring peaks that surround it, it never freezes, because of the slightly saline springs bubbling up in its centre. This quirk, combined with Issyk-Kul's huge size (its shore is 700 km/437 mi long), has resulted in a microclimate that has transformed the adjacent mountains. They should be barren, rugged, windswept and bitterly cold. Instead, below a snowline consistently higher than 4,000 m (13,000 ft), the Tien Shan Mountains here are a hiker's paradise of thick forests, small lakes of vivid colours in rolling alpine pastures, waterfalls and torrents gurgling along valley floors. The lake itself is edged with sandy beaches and, the most unlikely of all, flower-filled meadows.

Issyk-Kul's extraordinary climate has made it a favourite resort for visitors from Bishkek and Alma-Ata – but only the north shore has been heavily developed. The best trekking routes are based on Karakol (formerly known as, and still often referred to as, Przheval'sk, after the Russian explorer), at the lake's eastern end. Typically, 7–14 day treks cherry-pick the region's best two to three day hikes, driving up to 150 km (95 mi) between the most scenic landscapes. From the Dzhetyoguz Valley you cross the Tilety Pass and clamber up the Karakol and Keldyke gorges to beautiful Ala-Kul Lake, from which you can look along the magnificent 5,000 m (16,400 ft) plus peaks of the Terskei Ala-Too range. More remote, and lovelier in all its variety is the Sarydzhaz river valley to Mertsbakher Lake trek.

HIGHLIGHTS:
Staying in a yurt, the traditional collapsible and portable nomadic dwelling, made of felt stretched over a birch lattice framework. Drinking Kymyz (mare's milk) in a yurt camp, listening to the guide/shepherd's stories about the beautiful red rocks known as 'Seven Bulls' and 'Broken Heart' in the Sarydzhaz Valley.

THE FERGANA VALLEY

Central Asia/Tajikistan

HIGHLIGHTS:
Khujand medieval citadel.
Kokand – Palace of Khudayar Khan.

Known as the 'Golden Valley', the Fergana is a 22,000-sq km (8,500-sq mi) wedge of rich arable land enclosed by the Tien Shan and Pamir Mountains. As you travel up the valley from Khujand, an important Tajik city on the Syr Darya River, you will find yourself drawn into an intriguing cultural adventure. The diversity of customs, costumes and language is fascinating and

you may often be surprised by the contradictions between ancient and modern, Islamic and communist ideals. Head northeast through cotton and wheat fields, orchards and vineyards into Uzbekistan, to the historic capital of Kokand; and Margilan, a market town famous for its silks. Admire the faded 19th-century grandeur of the elegant tree-lined streets in Fergana town, and visit Andijan, the city where Babur was born. Cross into Kyrgyzstan, a remote mountainous country of breathtaking natural beauty, ending your travels in fairytale surroundings of sparkling alpine lakes, wild walnut orchards and snow-capped mountain peaks.

HIGHLIGHTS:
Views from the Ak-Baital Pass, 4,655 m (15,270 ft).
Bathing in the Garm-Chashma and Bibi Fatima hot springs.

FOLLOW THE FOOTSTEPS OF ALEXANDER ACROSS THE OXUS

Central Asia/Tajikistan

Crossing the Oxus into Afghanistan, one of the most wonderful countries in the world, is a lot easier now than it was two millennia ago when Alexander the Great's armies floated across the fast-flowing river by clinging onto their leather tents converted into makeshift rafts. In 2007, an imposing 670 m (2,200 ft) long bridge was opened, a vital link in a 21st-century 'Silk Road' that aims to connect landlocked Central Asia to the Indian Ocean port of Karachi.

The legendary River Oxus (nowadays known as the Amu Dariya) separates Tajikistan and Afghanistan. The people on either side share the same ethnic bonds but for decades they have been divided by political turmoil and the barrier of the river itself, which was crossable only by an intermittent ferry service. The spanking new bridge seems utterly incongruous in comparison to its surroundings. As soon as you cross it, you are hurled back through time into a biblical landscape – a startling contrast to southern Tajikistan where the intensively farmed fields and ancient remains of the historic Hissor and Vakhsh Valleys all testify to millennia of civilization.

THE PAMIR HIGHWAY

Central Asia/Tajikistan

The Pamir Highway is one of the highest, most thrilling, least-travelled routes in the world. Here, at the meeting point of the Tien Shan, Hindu Kush and Karakoram mountain ranges, is some of the most extraordinary and beautiful terrain on the planet, an eerie empty land of parched ochre rock, hot springs and turquoise glacial lakes set among the magnificent snow-capped peaks of the world's highest mountains.

Built by the Russians as a Soviet supply road, the Highway runs for some 1,250 km (780 mi) from Dushanbe to Osh along an ancient Silk Road route across the Pamir Plateau. Subject to erosion, earthquakes and landslides, the road is in a constant state of disrepair, making for a journey full of sudden hazards. You will also stumble upon plenty of monuments – petroglyphs, ancient temples, Buddhist stupas and ruined fortresses.

The Highway runs eastwards from Dushanbe across the plains, winding steeply upwards through rugged mountains to Khalaikum. You pass rusting hulks of abandoned Russian tanks and lurid signs warning of minefields as you manoeuvre your way through old landslips and uncontained streams sloshing across the road. At the frontier, the road turns northwards up to Ak-Baital Pass at 4,655 m (15,270 ft) before descending to the hauntingly beautiful Lake Kara-Kul, through the lush pastures and dramatic gorges of the Alai Valley in Kyrgyzstan, to end this epic road trip at the colourful city of Osh.

HIGHLIGHTS: Tajikistan – 18th-century Hissor Fort. Ajina-Teppa – 7th-century Buddhist monastery complex. Balkh – medieval ruins and early Islamic monuments.

ORKHON VALLEY

Central Asia/Mongolia

HIGHLIGHTS:
Galloping across the steppe.
Staying in a traditional
ger camp.
Ruins of Kharakhorum –
Ghengis Khan's capital.

Mongolia is the most sparsely populated country in the world, a vast untamed expanse of mountain, forest, desert and plateau.

An expedition by horse to the Orkhon Valley will open your eyes to a way of life that is utterly unfamiliar. The Orkhon is the cradle of Central Asian nomadic societies, where the inhabitants live in harmony with nature, continuing pastoral traditions and shamanic religious practices. A camping trek of some 200 km (125 mi) along the river valley and up into the Khangai Mountains, through verdant, volcanic plains and forested gorges to the dramatic cascade of the Orkhon waterfall is a liberating escape from the complexities of the post modern age. Incredible as it may seem, you are travelling through the heart of the largest empire in the history of the world. At its height in the 13th century, the Mongol Empire stretched across Central Asia and Ghengis Khan held sway over more than a 100 million people from his capital city of Kharkhorum in the Orkhon Valley.

GOBI DESERT TREK

Central Asia/Mongolia

HIGHLIGHTS:
Bayan Zag flaming cliffs.
Hongor Sands.
Yol Valley glacier.
Staying with local herdsmen
in a ger village.

The largest desert in Asia and the fourth largest in the world, the Gobi is a cold desert of high plateau and mountain where it is not uncommon to see frost. From Dalandzadgad, a town 540 km (336 mi) south of Ulaanbaatar, you can ride either by camel or jeep through the stunning landscapes of Gurvansaikhan National Park where three mountain ridges rise up to 2,600 metres (8,500 ft). The dramatic scenery is extraordinarily varied – rocky and sandy desert, precipitous cliffs and ravines, oases and saltpans. You can climb to the top of Hongor Sands, a giant 180 km (110 mi) long 300 m (1,000 ft) high sand dune, explore the glaciated Yol Valley, and wander in the other-worldly terrain of the Bayan Zag 'flaming cliffs' – a vast red sandstone amphitheatre of weirdly eroded pillars, rock canyons and ridges, where in 1923 Roy Chapman Andrews famously discovered dinosaur remains and fossilized eggs.

HIGHLIGHTS: Altan Ulgii – highest mountain of the Khentii.
Ulaanbaatar – Gandan Monastery, a functioning Buddhist monastery.
Ruins of the Gunjin Monastery.

INTO THE KHENTII MOUNTAINS
Central Asia/Mongolia

From a lush marshland veined with rivers and streams, where bizarrely shaped granite outcrops rise dramatically from meadows strewn with wild flowers, you clamber through a glorious mountainous landscape of wooded hills and valleys. This is Terelj National Park. As you climb from the meadows into the mountains you can watch birds of prey patrolling the huge skies, see wild horses, red elk, moose, wolves and even spot a brown bear. Walk along the banks of clear-watered rivers, catch fish in Khagiin Khar, a 20 m (66 ft) deep glacial lake, and dip a toe in the Yestii hot water springs. Climb to the top of Altan Ulgii, at 2,646 m (8,680 ft) the highest mountain of the Khentii, for wonderful panoramic views and wander round the spooky Gunjin Sum Monastery, deep in the larch forest. Only the outer walls are intact but many old tales are attached to it that will send a shiver down your spine.

LHASA-GYANTSE-XIGATSE SCENIC DRIVE
Central Asia/Tibet

HIGHLIGHTS: Khumbum Pagoda.
Lhasa – Jokhang Temple, the holiest shrine in Tibet.
Yamdrok Lake.

Tibet, for so long closed to outsiders, is the world's largest and highest plateau, a land of snow-clad mountains, turquoise lakes, rolling pastures and cobalt skies – the Shangri-La of western imaginings. However, Lhasa is not at all the 'Place of the Gods' that you expect. The ancient city has long since been engulfed by concrete and commerce. You have to look hard to find the prayer wheels, exotic temples and cymbal-clashing saffron-robed monks that you pictured. You must leave the city to discover Tibet – an enchanting pastoral world of nomad tents and yaks, wild plateau horsemen, brightly costumed women leading pack-mules, and everywhere pervaded by the mysteries of an ancient shamanic Buddhism. The road southward from Lhasa crosses the Yarlung Tsangpo (Brahmaputra) River and climbs through the scenic Kyi Chu Valley to the 4,794 m (15,725 ft) Ganba Pass, where prayer flags flutter in the wind. Below you is the sacred Yamdrok Lake – a truly breathtaking sight. You carry on through a ravine up across the Karo Pass, more than 5,000 m (16,500 ft) high, seeing lakes and glaciers, and descend to Gyantse, a charming traditional market town in a fertile valley 265 km (165 mi) southwest of Lhasa. Here you will find the Palkhor Monastery and the staggering 32 m (105 ft) tall Khumbum Stupa, one of the most magnificent buildings in Tibet. The Tashilhunpo Monastery is a breathtaking complex of golden-roofed buildings where you can see the incredible 35 m (115 ft) high Thangka Wall, built by the first Dalai Lama in 1468.

MOUNT KAILASH KORA

Central Asia/Tibet

WHEN SHOULD I VISIT?:
May–June or
September–October.

TIME IT TAKES:
Seven days – four days 4x4
journey from Lhasa and three
days walking.

HIGHLIGHTS:
La Chu glacial valley.
Gori Kund frozen lake.
Milarepa's Cave.
Lake Manosarovar.

A massive peak, more than 6,600 m (21,700 ft) high in the remote Gangdisé Shan mountain range, Kailash is not only revered in the shamanistic Bön religion of Tibet but equally among Buddhists, Hindus and Jains. It is believed to be the sacred centre of the world and, among Hindus, the home of Lord Shiva.

Pilgrims travel for days through the wilds of western Tibet to make a kora (ritual circumambulation) of Mount Kailash in the hope of a better life. The more circuits that are completed, the more auspicious it is. Thirteen is considered especially lucky, while 108 rewards you with instant nirvana. Exceptionally devout believers prostrate their way around the circuit – flinging their entire body flat out on the ground with every step.

The 52 km (32 mi) circular walk starts and finishes at Darchen, a nondescript mud brick village in a tranquil plain of grazing yaks. It is a mortal sin to set foot on the mountain itself.

The pilgrim trail leads round the edge through green valleys and narrow gorges to the Drolma Pass at 5,600 m (18,370 ft). This is the high point of the kora where celebrating pilgrims chant, prostrate themselves at stone chortens (stupas) and tie their prayer flags, adding to the myriad of multicoloured tattered cloths torn into shreds by the howling wind that buffets the trail.

As you descend round the other side, the view of the striated north face of the mountain is dazzlingly perfect – alternate lines of black rock and shimmering ice, rising to an unsullied glistening cone of snow outlined by the deep blue of the Tibetan sky. There is something extraordinarily uplifting about walking with pilgrims. The intensity of their faith creates an inspirational atmosphere and joyful spirit of shared endeavour as you make your personal kora.

YOU SHOULD KNOW
There are 30–40 small earthquakes in the Tien Shan each year, and snowmelt in spring can cause mudslides.

ROOF OF THE WORLD EXPRESS

Central Asia/Tibet

WHEN SHOULD I VISIT?: May– June or September–October
HIGHLIGHTS: Xining – Kumbum Monastery, one of the most important Buddhist sites in China.
Lhasa – Johkang Temple.
Tanggula Pass.
Qinghai Lake – largest lake in China.

The world's highest railway line, the 'Roof of the World Express' was opened in 2006. It runs for 1,142 km (710 mi) between Lhasa, capital of Tibet and Xining in China, crossing the Tibetan Plateau more than 5 km (3 mi) above sea level. It reaches its highest point at the Tanggula Pass (5,231m/17,158 ft) and goes through the Fenghuoshan, the highest tunnel in the world at 4,905 m (16,093 ft). There are 675 bridges and 45 stations along the line, and more than half the track is laid on permafrost in a miracle of engineering.

The railway is the fulfilment of China's long-term ambition to join its western province with the rest of the country, to promote economic progress and cultural unity. The Tibetans view it rather differently – as yet another threat to their ancient indigenous culture; and environmentalists are concerned about the disruption to the region's delicate ecology. Whatever the rights and wrongs, it cannot be denied that it is both an incredible journey and an inevitability in a globalized economy. Most of the journey is at an altitude of over 4,000 m (13,000 ft). The carriage windows are tinted to block out harmful ultra-violet rays and every berth has a personal oxygen canister in addition to the oxygenated air that is pumped round the train. As you cross the desolate treeless Tibetan plateau – the 'Rooftop of the World' – you enjoy a spectacular moving picture of the surreal scenery. You pass the highest lake in the world, see yak, wild antelope and donkeys grazing and watch golden eagles cruising through the sky. Puffy white clouds hang in the cobalt blue Tibetan sky above a vast moonscape of yellows, ochres and browns, and a skyline of sharply etched snow-capped peaks glows golden in the sun. This is the train ride of a lifetime.

SACRED VALLEYS TREK

South Asia/Bhutan

HIGHLIGHTS: Thimpu, Bhutan's capital city.
The colourful festivals that take place in spring and autumn.
Thanbi Temple, founded in 1470.

First opened to the world in 1974, the present King's policy has been tailored to keep Buddhist Bhutan's traditional culture and pristine environment untouched by outside influences and so far, so good.
Bumthang is a complex of four, beautiful valleys, lying at about 2,600 m (8,500 ft). Buckwheat, barley, potatoes and apples grow in profusion, and this tranquil landscape is Bhutan's sacred heart, containing many of its most revered temples. Trek alongside the Chamkhar River, famed for its trout, visit Thamshing Lhakang Temple, built

in the 7th century, and Membar Tsho (Burning Lake) where Guru Rimpoche, who brought Buddhism here from Tibet, hid some sacred scriptures.
Walk through traditional villages of unique architecture, meet delightful local people, marvel at gorgeous handicrafts, climb up to Phephela Pass through serene forests of miniature bamboo, rhododendrons and pine. Follow the course of the river up to the base camp of Gangkhar Puensum. Bhutan's highest mountain at 7,570 m (24,000 ft) is the world's highest, unclimbed peak. Mountaineering is now forbidden because of local religious beliefs.

WHEN SHOULD I VISIT?:
March and April for the rhododendrons.

BARSEY (VERSHAY) RHODODENDRON SANCTUARY TREK

South Asia/Sikkim

The landlocked state of Sikkim is small, but due to its position tucked into the Himalayas, its climate, flora and fauna is very varied, with elevations that range from 280 m (900 ft) to the summit of Kanchenjunga, the world's third highest mountain standing at an impressive 8,598 m (28,208 ft).
One of the loveliest treks here takes you through the Vershay Rhododendron Sanctuary. Starting from Rinchenpong, a small market village, climb through well-cultivated land, past fruit orchards and plots of rice, maize, millet and vegetables, to the attractive village of Hi Barmoik.
Climbing higher, the trek takes you through mixed forest to Barsey, where the altitude goes up to 4,100 m (13,500 ft), producing habitats that support everything from bamboo to Alpine wild flowers. This is a wonderful area for birds — over 200 species have been recorded here, and mammals include leopard, marten, civet, barking deer and red panda. Barsey lies on a huge ridge, covered with silver fir, hemlock, magnolia, orchid and, of course, rhododendrons. In spring, the sheer quantity of millions of brilliantly coloured rhododendron flowers, (from thirty different species), is overwhelming.

Right: Kanchenjunga mountain

ANNAPURNA CIRCUIT TREK
South Asia/Nepal

HIGHLIGHTS: The walk between Chame and Manang via Upper Pisang with its stupendous, inspirational views. The Hindu and Buddhist temples at Muktinath.

The Annapurna circuit, stretching for 300 km (187 mi), is one of the classic Nepal Himalayan trails. It is a gruelling, exhilarating, life-enhancing trek through some of the most spectacular mountain scenery the world has to offer.

From Besisahar, at about 500 m (1,600 ft), you ascend gently through brilliant, green rice paddies and numerous small streams. As you climb higher, you'll see marijuana fields, goats at pasture, apple and apricot orchards and barley, as well as small villages scattered among the terraced farmland. After a few days the trail becomes steeper and you find yourself passing through temperate and coniferous forests, alpine meadows before finally climbing beyond the tree line.

The air is thin up here and altitude sickness can be a problem – but by now you are living in a different world, where the sound of rushing water from streams and waterfalls replaces that of cars and machinery. The villages become more Tibetan the higher you go, and Buddhism takes over from Hinduism.

By the time you reach Thorong La pass and make the descent to Muktinath, an important religious site, you will have seen the most extraordinary, panoramic views of the snow-laden Annapurnas, crossed high suspension bridges, waded through rivers, and eaten masses of dal and vegetable curry. At Tatopani, relax in the welcome hot springs.

WORTH A DETOUR: The Limbus' famous – and welcome – alcoholic drink tongba. Made from fermented millet seeds, it is served in a tall wooden pot and drunk through bamboo straws.

KANCHENJUNGA TREK
South Asia/Nepal

In remote, northeastern Nepal, on the borders of Sikkim and Tibet, the magnificent mountain Kanchenjunga rises to the sky. At 8,598 m (28,300 ft), this is the world's third highest peak, now part of a conservation area. A climate of high rainfall, humidity, and snow together with isolation, has created a region of unique mountain ecosystems, supporting snow leopards, black bears, goral, blue sheep, yak and red panda. The long, arduous trek takes you from the village of Taplejung, gradually ascending through fertile, cultivated hillsides – rice and cardamom – before entering forests of oak, Himalayan larch, rhododendron and pine. There are 69 varieties of orchid to be found amongst the 1,200 species of flowering plants, and the numerous waterfalls are testament to the heavy monsoon rains.

You will camp in villages, mostly populated by Limbu people, recognizable by their topi hats, which are larger and more colourful than those worn by most Nepalis. The Limbus, along with the Rais, make up the famous Gurkhas of the British and Indian armies. As you climb higher, you'll camp in ever more remote locations, in the midst of magnificent mountain scenery.

FLY OVER THE HIMALAYAS
South Asia/Nepal

YOU SHOULD KNOW
A UN climate report states that global warming could melt the Himalyan glaciers by 2035, causing flooding followed by drought in many Asian countries.

The Himalayan Mountains are the highest in the world. Of the thirty-one summits over 7,600 m (25,000 ft), 22 rise in Nepal, including Everest and seven other great giants that are over 8,000 m (26,000 ft). If you have limited time here but still wish to see some of the highest peaks and do a little trekking, one option is to take the mountain flight from Pokhara to Jomson, where you can take a short trek into the Annapurnas.

Pokhara is the second largest tourist centre after Kathmandu, beautifully situated beside Lake Phewa, and several flights leave here every morning for Jomson. Within 30 km (19 mi) of the town, the elevation changes drastically from 900 m (3,000 ft) to 8,000 m (26,000 ft), and as the small plane takes off it rises sharply, giving you a view of the white, hilltop World Peace Stupa at the edge of town. The flight is short but spectacular, passing through a narrow corridor between Dhaulagiri, 8,167 m (27,000 ft), and Annapurna, 8,019 m (26,500 ft). You also have wonderful views of Manasulu, Nilgiri and Machapuchere, with its instantly recognizable fishtail peak. These mountains are seen at eye level, and on a clear day you can see folds and ravines in the rock face as well as a perfect view of the snowline. Sometimes it can be cloudy, but even then you'll suddenly see a towering snow-capped, glacier-draped pinnacle looming majestically beside you.

On sunny days the plane's shadow races along the bare, brown rock face beneath you. Scattered mountain villages, paths and rivers snaking through deep valleys are clearly visible. Suddenly the plane dives steeply into a valley, making alarmingly tight turns as it aligns itself to the runway. Don't worry – moments later you'll be breathing the pure, crisp air of the high Himalayas.

HIGHLIGHTS:
The superb views of some of the Himalayas' most majestic mountains.
The fortress town of Kagbeni.
Muktinath, a place of pilgrimage and a major religious site.

WHEN SHOULD I VISIT?:
March–May and late September–end November.

TIME IT TAKES:
About 30 minutes.

DON'T MISS
Trekking in the Annapurnas.

SWAT VALLEY

South Asia/Pakistan

WHEN SHOULD I VISIT?:
April–June and
September–October.

Although the country of Pakistan was only created in 1947, it was born from a culture that goes back thousands of years, as is evident from the ancient remains, historic monuments, beautiful architecture and the dignified demeanour of its people.

Swat, the 'Switzerland of Asia', was an independent princely state ruled by the Wali of Swat until 1969, when he ceded his authority to the central government. People have lived here for more than 2,000 years and there are plentiful remains from the Gandhara Buddhist civilization (and plenty of people claiming to be descendants of Alexander the Great). Situated in the foothills of the Hindu Kush, it is a spectacularly beautiful region where snow-capped mountains enclose small enchanting valleys, each a magical s elf-contained world of lakes, forests and waterfalls.

Battered Suzuki jeeps ply the main valley, piled high with passengers hanging onto the tailgate, and they career along in a cavalier fashion that, at first, is frankly terrifying. But, have faith – your driver knows every twist, turn, bump and pothole of the narrow road. Only an attitude of oriental fatalism will enable you to appreciate the captivating scenery as your vehicle whizzes alongside the River Swat taking you from the charming main town of Mingora to the villages of the upper valleys. As the road winds upward, the mountains start to close in and the river becomes increasingly turbulent. Steep verdant slopes, terraced with fruit orchards and poppy fields, reach up to deep green forest and a skyline of glistening icy peaks. The mountain village of Kalam is secreted 100 km (60 mi) up the valley, in the depths of the forest beside a tumultuous river swollen with glacial water. The comparison with Switzerland is belittling. This is an altogether greater, wilder and more mysterious land – a sort of savage Paradise.

TRAVELLING THE GRAND TRUNK ROAD

South Asia/Pakistan

WHEN SHOULD I VISIT?:
September–April.

TIME IT TAKES:
As long as you like.

HIGHLIGHTS:
Qissa Khawani bazaar
(Bazaar of the Storytellers) in
Peshawar.
Badshahi Mosque in Lahore.
Bazaars of Rawalpindi.
Wah Garden at Hasan Abdal.
Greco-Buddhist ruins
in Taxila.

According to Rudyard Kipling, the Grand Trunk Road was 'such a river of life as exists nowhere else in the world', the lifeblood of the Indian sub-continent along which the ideas that have shaped its culture have flowed for more than 2,000 years. The Buddhist, Hindu, Jain and Sikh religions sprang up around it, Alexander the Great marched his army across the Indus on it and the Mughals spread the might of their empire along it. Known to 17th-century British travellers as the 'Long Walk', the Grand Trunk Road runs for 2,400 km (1,500 mi) between Kabul and Kolkata, passing through the historic cities of Peshawar, Islamabad, Rawalpindi, Lahore, Amritsar, Delhi, Agra and Varanasi. From the romantic Mughal city of Lahore, the heart of Pakistan, whether you travel northwards towards the Afghan border or south into India, you get swept up in the life of the road. The stream of traffic moves at a cracking pace as motley bullock carts, bicycles, auto-rickshaws and battered 1950s cars play chicken with the psychedelic trucks and buses. These dazzling works of art on wheels are practically a national symbol of Pakistan, each exquisitely painted carriage work a unique story, telling of the owner's region, ethnic origin, interests and personality in emblematic form of brilliant colour and calligraphy.

In the shade of the wayside trees are street vendors and caravanserais (truckstops), men lolling on charpoys (string beds), children playing in the dust, loose livestock wandering into the traffic, graffiti and garish advertisements on every inch of wall. It feels as though the entire world is on the move. As you cross the Jehlum River, where Alexander defeated the armies of Porus in an epic battle of 326 BC, you are exultantly aware of your own small part in this endless sea of humanity.

SNOW LAKE TREK

South Asia/Pakistan

Said to be the 'Most Beautiful Place in the World', Snow Lake is certainly one of the most remote. This is the land of the yeti, an icy mountain wonderland, a week's trek from the nearest human habitation. Snow Lake belies its name – it is not a lake at all but a huge ice-basin, 16 km (10 mi) wide and thought to be around 1.6 km (1 mi) thick, enclosed by the stupendous 6,000 m (20,000 ft) peaks of the Karakoram Mountains. It lies at the head of the Biafo and Hispar glaciers, which spread down from the 5,151 m (16,895 ft) high Hispar Pass to form the longest glacier system outside the polar regions, a massive ice highway connecting the ancient mountain kingdoms of Baltistan and Hunza.

From Skardu, capital of Baltistan, a jeep takes you on a white-knuckle ride through the Braldu Gorge where hairpin bends are too tight to take in one go and the wheels constantly threaten to slip over the edge of sheer precipice. Thrilled to be alive, you reach Askole, gateway to the highest mountains in the world – a medieval village in the middle of nowhere. Over the next fortnight, you will trek 120 km (75 mi) through an enchanted land of blue ice pinnacles, deep glacial caves, gorges, crevasses and hanging glaciers – up the Biafo Glacier to Snow Lake and across the pass to descend the Hispar Glacier into Hunza. Climbing 300 m (1,000 ft) a day, camping in remote valleys, scrambling over rocky moraine and using ropes to cross crevasses, you test your stamina to the limit – to collapse, exhausted but elated, amid terraced orchards and lush wild flower meadows.

HIGHLIGHTS:

Braldu Gorge drive.
Pinnacles of the Paiyu Mountains.
Ogre Mountain – sheer walled mountain in the Latok massif.

THE KARAKORAM HIGHWAY
South Asia/Pakistan

HIGHLIGHTS: Hunza Valley market town of Karimabad. Balti Fort and picturesque Kashgar – Id Kah Mosque.

The Karakoram Highway is perhaps the 'ultimate' road. A marvel of civil engineering, long considered impossible, it was a joint construction project between Pakistan and China across the highest international pass in the world in a region of hazardous weather and high tectonic activity, with constant risk of landslides.

The Highway covers a distance of some 1,300 km (800 mi) connecting Islamabad to Kashgar in China – a daunting but thrilling scenic drive by way of the Karakoram and Pamir Mountains. You roller-coaster up the Indus Valley through barren foothills until quite suddenly, without any apparent gradation, you are enclosed by craggy, ice-covered peaks. A mellow stretch through the beautiful scenery of the Hunza Valley takes you up to one of the highest altitude national parks in the world – an icebound wilderness that is the hideout of the elusive snow leopard.

Wind your way up hairpin bends, passing spectacular glaciers that practically drop into the road, to the Khunjerab Pass at 4,730 m (15,500 ft) and across 120 km (75 mi) of desolate no-man's land into China.

THE PALACE ON WHEELS
South Asia/India

HIGHLIGHTS: Ram Ganj Bazaar in Jaipur. The Taj Mahal – even more majestic during a full moon. The 'Lake City' of Udaipur.

The Palace on Wheels train, which runs from Delhi through Rajasthan, is perhaps the most audacious feat of recycling in transport history. In 1981, the former royal train was faithfully restored with the aim of bringing a regal experience to a much wider audience. Although replaced with a newer model some ten years later, it still provides a feast of luxury living for those who travel on it. With its bars, restaurants, personal attendants and even a library, the Palace on Wheels pampers the traveller like no other train journey.

The journey starts and ends at Delhi's Safdarjung Railway Station and takes you to some of the finest sights that there are in this northwest corner of India. The first stop on the week-long excursion is the magnificent 'Pink City' of Jaipur, offering a chance to stretch your legs while marvelling at the astonishing architecture of Rajasthan's capital city. The many bazaars within the city give the traveller a real feel of the tastes, colours and smells of India.

The train then continues on its way, allowing you to sample the delights of Jodhpur, the 'Sun City', and Udaipur, the 'Venice of the East'. More colours feast the eye as the train heads back towards Delhi and the vibrant red city of Fatehpur Sikri awaits you. This is a journey that leaves the best to last. The contrast between the industrial city of Agra and its world famous monument – the Taj Mahal – could not be greater.

DARJEELING HIMALAYAN RAILWAY

South Asia/India

YOU SHOULD KNOW

The area around Darjeeling is subject to periods of unrest, which can cause the line to be closed.

WHEN SHOULD I VISIT?:
Avoid the monsoon season (June–September). Otherwise the climate is good year round.

HIGHLIGHTS:
The views of Khanchenjunga – the world's third highest peak.
The Happy Valley Tea Estate – well worth a visit to see how they produce their highly-regarded tea.
Giddapahar Mandir – a temple dedicated to Lord Shiva, just outside Kurseong..

The Darjeeling Himalayan Railway is the most fascinating of all the 'toy train' routes in India. With a 610 mm (2 ft) gauge, it's the narrowest to be found on the subcontinent and it has the unique attraction for a mountain railway of having no tunnels – thus allowing passengers an uninterrupted view of the beautiful Himalayan landscape. Starting from New Jalpaiguri, this wonderfully preserved steam train meanders its way along an 86 km (54 mi) route, making a dozen or so stops along the way before journeying through picturesque tea plantations, and finally reaching the charming hill station of Darjeeling. Aside from the marvellous views, the climb itself is something to behold. Starting at an altitude of 100 m (330 ft), the train reaches an elevation of 2,000 m (6,600 ft) by the time it arrives at its destination. Several hair-raising bends greet you along the way, as the train seems to cling to the hill face like a mountain goat. At the aptly named 'Agony Point', the tightest bend on the line, the train seems to change direction completely in the blink of an eye.

While this journey can be taken in one go, there are several places along the route that are worth exploring. Most notable are the village of Tindharia, which houses a railway workshop, and Ghum, the highest station in India and home to a railway museum.

Having taken this amazing trip, it's easy to see why railway enthusiasts often list it in the world's top ten journeys. This diminutive railway was declared a UNESCO World Heritage Site in 1999, and while many stations are little more than wooden shacks, the sheer effort that has gone into keeping the line open is evident in its well maintained track, burnished engines and comfortably upholstered seats.

KULLU VALLEY TREK

South Asia/India

HIGHLIGHTS:
The Dhoongri Temple – a magnificent wooden structure near Manali.
The charming little village of Jagatsukh – a perfect place to stop for a while.
Old Manali, with its stone and timber buildings.

The Kullu Valley in the northern state of Himachal Pradesh is far removed from the stereotype of India as a country of heat and dust. For many Westerners the valley is merely part of the hippy trail, but to Indians it is a highly productive agricultural area. Freshened by the glacial waters of the Beas River, the valley is home to a major apple-growing industry and is flanked by paddy fields during the monsoon season and wheat fields for the remainder of the year. With conifers and rhododendrons lining the upper slopes, the Kullu Valley is one of the most sumptuous parts of India.

Several operators offer guided tours tailored to meet all requirements and abilities, but a better experience may be gained by hiring a cook and a guide in Manali and venturing out in a smaller group. Engaging locals ensures that you will see the best the area has to offer. Since travelling in nearby Kashmir has become too dangerous, more people are choosing the Kullu Valley as a safer option. However it is still possible to escape the crowds at higher elevations, where you can enjoy the fresh pine forests and the stunning mountain scenery. Walking over mountain passes and between remote villages, you cannot help but be struck by the beauty of the area. At the higher altitudes craggy outcrops replace the lush vegetation and the snow-capped peaks of the Himalayas frame every scene. There are hot springs to warm you and mountain streams to cool you down. The area is also a hive of outdoor activity, including rock climbing, skiing, rafting and paragliding.

YOU SHOULD KNOW

A reasonable degree of fitness is required to attempt the higher passes of the Kullu Valley. Weather conditions can deteriorate rapidly, so allow extra time when tackling the more difficult stretches of the trek.

MANALI TO LEH
South Asia/India

DON'T MISS
Moray Plains – an astonishing plateau, surrounded by white peaks.

WHEN SHOULD I VISIT?:
The Rohtang Pass is only open from May–early November, weather permitting.

It is difficult to comprehend the sheer magnitude of the Himalayas – while most of the world's great mountain ranges can be traversed inside a day or two, the Himalayas fill the horizon like a giant cumulous cloud – indomitable, magnificent and often impenetrable. The 3,900 m (12,800 ft) high Rohtang Pass, closed to traffic for most of the year, springs to life when the thaw arrives. It provides a vital lifeline for remote communities, as well as the most memorable of bus journeys. On leaving Manali, the road starts its long ascent towards the pass; beneath you are forests and mountain pasture, while ahead lies the permanent snow of Solang Nala. A temple sits at the crown of an escarpment, and the bus usually stops here to allow passengers to gain sustenance and acclimatize to the thin air. From this vantage point the panoramic views over the Beas Valley are simply stunning.

The next couple of hours provide the most spectacular scenery of the entire journey. As the bus negotiates its way along the inclines of the valley, you see soaring peaks and suspended glaciers. You are now well above the treeline and surrounded by the most amazing green and red scree, as the bus continues ever upwards. After an overnight stop at Sarchu Serai and an early start, the bus ascends to a head-spinning 5,328 m (17,475 ft) and the brilliant white of the snow-capped peaks surrounds you. Patches of green return, in land fed by the Indus River, as you gradually make the descent into the beautifully tranquil town of Leh, once the capital of the Himalayan kingdom of Ladakh.

HIGHLIGHTS: The general buzz on the train.
The Lookout Points – short walks take you to 38 observation
points to view the stunning valley below.
Charlotte Lake – an area of tranquillity near Mathera.

THE MATHERAN HILL RAILWAY

South Asia/India

Opened in 1907, this narrow-gauge railway is a charming and rather eccentric example of early 20th-century engineering enterprise. Traversing difficult mountainous terrain, the train chugs along a track that has over 200 sharp bends and crosses 120 bridges. With a sometimes-cramped capacity of 100, it links the foothill town of Narel to the beautiful little hill station town of Matheran, covering a distance of 30 km (18.6 mi) at an average speed of 15 kph (9.3 mph).

The atmosphere on board is at times one of barely organized chaos, as food vendors and rhesus monkeys climb on board and vie for your attention. The former try to sell you pastries and the latter immediately try to steal them – you can't help but admire the symmetry of the situation.

As it's the only motorized form of transport that is allowed to enter Matheran, the train enjoys a privileged position, but at times the pace is so sedentary that walking would be a quicker option. Matheran translates as 'jungle at the top' and this becomes ever more real to you as the train struggles to climb the very steep tropical terrain. The views from the train are incredible, with wide-open valleys to one side and steep, mountain faces to the other. The ozone produced by the numerous waterfalls is refreshing even on the sultriest of days.

When the train finally pulls into Matheran you realize that the relaxed pace of the journey was entirely appropriate. The town is all about taking it easy, and there's a peaceful, unhurried air about the place. There is no finer feeling than relaxing with your evening tipple on the verandah of your hotel while marvelling at the sunset over the densely forested hills.

KALKA TO SHIMLA ON THE 'TOY TRAIN'

South Asia/India

HIGHLIGHTS: The Gurkha Castle at Solan – a reminder of the area's former rulers.
Shri Sankat Mochan Temple – a beautiful Hindu temple located 5 km (3 mi) outside Shimla.

This important rail link was built in 1924 and its 'toy trains' still do a roaring trade running on an improbably small 760 mm (2 ft 6 in) narrow gauge set of rails. The construction was an incredible feat of engineering – the track passes through more than 100 tunnels and over 960 bridges, up into the stunning mountain scenery of the Himalayan foothills.

Immaculately maintained stations line the route and the arrival of the train elicits intense interest from locals at every stop along the way. The charming station at Solan marks the halfway point on this stately excursion, and it is from here that you catch the first sight of Shimla high in the distance. The snow-capped peaks of the

Himalayas appear in all their majesty as the forest thins to reveal ever more spectacular vistas.

When the train draws serenely in to Shimla at an altitude of 2,420 m (7,940 ft), it becomes immediately apparent why the British chose the town as their summer capital. While Delhi swelters in the summer sun, Shimla delights in a near perfect 20 °C (68 °F). The town itself is worthy of a day or two's exploration – with its striking Victorian architecture surrounded by magnificent mountain scenery.

DON'T MISS

The 1,100-year-old granite Brahma Temple in Khajuraho.

TEMPLE CITY JOURNEY

South Asia/India

Starting in Gwalior, with its imposing hilltop fort, you enter a region rich in history and legend. This lively city has changed hands countless times over the centuries and its history is etched in the buildings and the faces of the people. The Tuscan and Corinthian style architecture, mixed with more traditional Hindu Mogul temples, makes Gwalior worthy of thorough exploration. From here it is a 120 km (75 mi) journey to Orchha, founded in the 16th century. After a further 160 km (100 mi) you reach Khajuraho, the 10th-century religious capital of the Chandela dynasty and a town now so rural and isolated that it's hard to imagine that it was once a thriving metropolis. Of the 80 or so temples built there, 22 remain and bear testimony to the city's cosmopolitan, multi-faith past.

SAPUTARA SCENIC ROAD

South Asia/India

Saputara's location, 1,000 m (3,280 ft) up on the edge of a plateau, coupled with its congenial climate, pure air and breathtaking views of beautiful scenery, has resulted in some modern luxuries being brought to this picturesque hill station. For more than a century Saputara has offered an increasing number of visitors a respite from the often-oppressive heat of Mumbai and it now boasts first class accommodation and several tourist attractions.

Buses to Saputara run from the main metropolitan centres of western India, but a journey undertaken by car or motorbike allows you to create your own unique experience of this lovely area. The 50 km (30 mi) journey from Waghai is short but rewarding, and there is much to distract the curious tourist with time on their hands. You can stop to breathe in the ozone by one of the many waterfalls or linger at a particularly enchanting lookout spot. The whole area is home to many traditional Gujarati villages, whose masked dances and handicrafts are renowned throughout India.

Ancient mixed forests start to crowd in as you near Saputara. Barely touched by human intervention, the forests provide a wonderful habitat for a wide range of wildlife. The dense growth makes a good home for tigers, leopards, pangolins, pythons and four-horned antelope as well as for a great variety of birdlife. The deep forest is also reputed to offer refuge to higher beings – legend has it that the Hindu deity Lord Rama spent 11 years of his exile here.

Whether you start your journey in Mumbai, 265 km (166 mi) away, or from Waghai, the area has such a magnetic quality that you are always left with the feeling that there was so much more to see.

YOU SHOULD KNOW

While the Saputara-Waghai road itself is in relatively good shape, if you want to make detours to see any of the neighbouring attractions it is advisable to hire a car suitable for off-road driving.

WHEN SHOULD I VISIT?:

The area has a good climate all year round. It is best experienced during the monsoons from March–November when the waterfalls are at their best.

TIME IT TAKES:

Two hours driving without stopping (from Waghai), but allow at least a week to explore the area.

HIGHLIGHTS:

Pushpak Ropeway – India's longest cableway, offering a 10 minute ride across the valley.

Sunrise Point – there are great views from here at any time of day, but, as its name implies, they're even better in the morning.

Vansda National Park – a small but thriving wildlife park (entry permit required).

The spectacular Gira Falls – 1 km (0.6 mi) off the Waghai-Saputara road.

Unnai Mata Temple (near Waghai) – a fabulous temple with hot springs.

THE SOURCE OF THE GANGES

South Asia/India

HIGHLIGHTS: The temple at Mukteshwar Mahadeva – a shrine to the goddess Ganga.
The breathtakingly beautiful azure Gangotri Glacier.
The Golden Temple – a focal point in Varanasi.

There are times while making the climb towards the source of the Ganges when you wonder whether the two-day trek to Gaumukh from Gangothri is really worth it. As you climb up the steep hills, your mind is more focused on the ascent than on the astounding mountain scenery. But the Ganges is no ordinary river and to view its source is to witness the birth of the earthly manifestation of a god. It is said that the goddess Ganga was sent down to earth after a heavenly feud, that her descent was broken by Lord Shiva's matted locks and that she finally reached earth as seven streams.

The forbiddingly beautiful Shivling Mountain hangs 6,543 m (21,470 ft) above the blue-green Gangotri Glacier, which marks the emergence of this great river. When looking at the Ganges here in its purest state it's hard to imagine how mighty and muddy this holiest of rivers will become downstream. To journey down it is not only to follow the path of a geographical feature, but also to look deep into the heart and soul of India. Millions come to her to wash their bodies and to wash away their sins. Rivers are central to Hindu culture and they play pivotal roles in life and death; this trip takes you through some of India's most significant holy places.

After journeying back to Gangotri you can travel by road to the hallowed cities of Rishikesh, Haridwar, Garh-Mukteswar and Prayag, before finally arriving at the most sacred city in India – Varanasi.

Once there, the true significance of this great river becomes apparent, as worshippers line its steps and magnificent temples, forming a procession along the riverbanks. Few rivers, if any, are granted such high status and the sheer power of the Ganges to draw you and thousands of others towards it is awe-inspiring.

HIGHLIGHTS: Saint Paul's Cathedral.
New Market – a market of 2,000 stalls specializing in silk and silver.
Eden Gardens – a nice park and home to the test cricket stadium.
Paresnath Jain Temple.

KOLKATA HERITAGE CITY WALK
South Asia/India

To the outsider, Kolkata (formerly Calcutta) may conjure up images of Mother Theresa nursing the poor, and to the casual visitor it often seems to be an amorphous urban sprawl with poor signage. Thankfully an organization was set up in the early 1990s to change these perceptions.

There are two main tours; the first is a short affair focusing on the city centre. Starting at Dalhousie Square, the visitor is taken around fifteen or so historical buildings, including the impressive Writers Building, the Town Hall, St John's Churchyard and the celebrated Metcalfe Hall. But for a taste of the 'real' Kolkata, the North Calcutta Walking Tour is a must. With the aid of a local guide it is possible to venture into areas otherwise inaccessible to most visitors. There are slums and shanty towns and the streets do seem to be totally covered in litter in some places, but there are hidden gems to be found. Several wonderful secluded courtyards as well as the House of Rabindranath Tagore and the Marble Palace stand out in this old mercantile quarter.

CYCLE IN THE CARDAMOM HILLS
South Asia/India

WORTH A DETOUR: Sri Ayappan forest shrine at Sabarimala – off the beaten track but worth the effort.

A cycling tour in the Cardamom Hills reveals India at its simple best. The slow pace of travel through these fabulously pretty hills on two wheels provides a vacation filled with exploration and discovery of an India that, through increased industrialization, is fast disappearing.

The Cardamom Hills form a long narrow chain at the southern end of the Indian sub-continent. Their ridge

acts as the boundary between the states of Tamil Nadu and Kerala, extending from the Palghat Gap in the north and running 280 km (175 mi) to Cape Comorin in the south. Aside from the crop from which they take their name, the hills are renowned for tea production, and the plethora of the other spices produced in the area provides a wonderful gift for your sense of smell.

The region is also home to a wide variety of wildlife, most notably elephants and some big cats and it is very likely that you will encounter the former. Cats, however, are shy of human contact, so the best chance of seeing them is in one of the local nature parks. Life here is conducted at a slower pace than in much of the rest of India.

HOUSEBOAT CRUISE THROUGH THE KERALA BACKWATERS

South Asia/India

HIGHLIGHTS:
Periyar Wildlife Sanctuary
Rajamala National Park.
The Dutch Palace at Cochin.
Kerala is home to Ayurvedic
massage.

There can be few more relaxing journeys than floating along the waters of Kerala in a traditional houseboat. The backwaters of Kerala are a labyrinthine network of lakes, canals, and the estuaries and deltas of the 44 rivers that drain into the Arabian Sea. It's a wonderful ecosystem teeming with life – over a quarter of India's plant species are found here. There is such an abundance of flora and fauna, nourished by the tropical sun and generous rainfall, that it's easy to understand why Kerala is sometimes called 'God's Own Country'.

The houseboats, known as kettuvallam, are magnificent creations that blend in perfectly with their

environment. They are made with only the locally grown renewable resources of bamboo and coconut fibre – no nails are used in their construction. They were originally designed to carry crops to outlying communities, but since that trade has now sadly all but ceased, many of them have been converted into luxury houseboats for the tourist trade.

With nearly 1,000 km (625 mi) of navigable waterways at your disposal, you are spoiled for choice of routes to take, but wherever you go you will see a traditional India, not visible from any other means of transport.

HIGHLIGHTS: Udagamandalam (Ooty) – the 'Queen of Hill Stations', with its rose garden.
Idugampalayam Aanjineyar Temple at Mettupalayam.

NILGIRI MOUNTAIN RAILWAY

South Asia/India

If trains have personalities, and there are some people who think they do, the engines that ply the Nilgiri Mountain Railway are redoubtable little fighters. Now over 100 years old, this 'toy train' route is an engineering achievement that almost defies gravity. So steep is the gradient that a system of racks and pinions was developed to stop the train sliding back down the track.

The line never really paid its way as a carrier of goods, but thankfully it has been kept open. For safety, the train travels at an average speed of less than 10 kph (6.25 mph), making it the slowest train in India. Linking Mettupalayam near Coimbatose with the celebrated hill station of Udagamandalam (Ooty) in Tamil Nadu, the train's sedate tempo allows travellers to take in the captivating beauty of these seemingly endless hills. At every point on its steadfast journey, you are surrounded by lush mountain vegetation, as the train meanders its way around spine-tingling curves, through tunnels and alongside deep ravines.

THE BEACHES OF GOA

South Asia/India

WORTH A DETOUR:
Canacona Island – a ferry
ride from Palolem Beach.

Goa is India's good-time Riviera, renowned for its sun-kissed beaches, vibrant markets and an energetic nightlife unrivalled anywhere on the subcontinent. The 120 km (75 mi) coastline is interrupted only by the seven rivers that flow into the Arabian Sea. Starting at the ruggedly beautiful Harmal Beach in the north and journeying to the wonderfully secluded Palolem Beach in the south, you are taken on an odyssey of high contrast. Near the capital, Panaji, the noise of the water gives way to the hubbub of people. Venturing south again takes you to Colva, the most popular beach in southern Goa, where golden sands are lapped by the azure sea, while traders, fishermen and visitors give the whole area a wonderful market feel.

HILL COUNTRY SCENIC TRAIN RIDE – COLOMBO FORT TO BADULLA

South Asia/Sri Lanka

WHEN SHOULD I VISIT?:
December–March.

The train to Badulla showcases some of the loveliest landscapes the island has to offer. Starting at the crack of dawn from Colombo Fort, it sets out towards the hills, running alongside the Muthurajawela Marshland, a protected area teeming with birds. Before long you enter the first of the journey's 46 tunnels and begin the ascent, through lush hardwood forests, to Kandy, the spiritual and cultural centre of the Sinhalese. As the native forest gives way to pines and eucalyptus, you'll notice that the temperature is cooler and more pleasant. Glossy green tea plantations cover the hillsides, and brightly dressed Tamil women pick the leaves into baskets carried on their backs. From time to time you'll see

splendid waterfalls and, as the train climbs slowly up towards Nanu Oya, the dramatic, triangular point of Adam's Peak, 2,243 m (7,400 ft), can be seen to the south. Higher still, tea gives way first to vegetable gardens and then more forest. Now you are on a fascinating piece of line, known as the 'Lizard's Spine' where, between tunnels, you can see both north and, more spectacularly, south – way down to the coast. One last treat comes at Demodara, where the line loops around a steep hill with two stations, one 27 m (90 ft) above the other.

SRI PADA (ADAM'S PEAK) PILGRIM'S ROUTE

South Asia/Sri Lanka

HIGHLIGHTS:
The spectacle of dawn breaking from the top of Adam's Peak.
Visiting nearby tea estates.
Kandy and the Temple of the Sacred Tooth.

While Adam's Peak, at 2,243 m (7,400 ft), is not Sri Lanka's highest mountain, its sharply triangular silhouette and religious importance makes it the country's most famous landmark. A place of pilgrimage for over 1,000 years, the mountain resonates in four major religions and, as a result, the thousands of pilgrims who make their way to the top each year are an eclectic mix of nationalities and ages.

The purpose of the pilgrimage is not just to see the Sacred Footprint at the summit, but also to see the dawn break over the mountain. Moments later, the sun produces a unique phenomenon called irasevaya, throwing a perfect shadow of the cone onto the clouds. As the sun rises, this shadow retreats down and across the valley below, before disappearing at the base of the peak.

Leaving Dalhousie before dawn for the 7 km (4 mi) climb – the shorter of the two main routes – you join many pilgrims walking beneath the stone arch that marks the start. Soon you reach steps – over 5,000 of them must be climbed – making this a hard slog. Helpfully, there are rest stops and teahouses en route, and the trail is strung with lights that snake ahead of you up the mountain. The eclectic mix of people – fathers carrying babies, bare footed women, children, elderly folk and tourists make this pilgrimage a remarkably friendly one.

Reaching the small, summit temple produces such feelings of euphoria that the fact the 'real' footprint is apparently beneath the cast you can see, detracts not at all. As dawn breaks pink and gold, you'll see the Hill Country rising to the east, while to the west you look all the way down to Colombo and the coast. Catching the awesome shadow on the clouds is the icing on the cake.

NGONG PING 360

Far East/China

WORTH A DETOUR:
The 'sharing experience' of
the Monkey's Tale Theatre –
a tale of 'greed, gluttony
and friendship'
in lurid Technicolor
computer graphics.

Ngong Ping theme park is a concept experience for tourists. The inspiration for it however, and still Ngong Ping's greatest attraction, is Ngong Ping 360, the amazing cable car ride that gets you there. From Tung Chung, on Lantau's waterfront, Ngong Ping 360's bi-cable gondola lift system crosses the bay to Hong Kong's new Airport Island, turns a 60-degree angle without stopping and heads on for 5.7 km (3.6 mi) to the plateau village. The 25 minute ride is certainly spectacular – and beautiful when fingers of sea mist thread the rolling grasslands below. The 360-degree panoramas from the gondolas make the most of the islands scattering the South China Sea to Macau; of the techno-sprawl of Chek Lap Kok's airport complex; of Lantau's own mountain crags (rising to 934 m/3,064 ft); and finally of Po Lin Monastery.

MACLEHOSE TRAIL

Far East/China

DON'T MISS
Pak Sha O –
a preserved village on
the Sai Kung peninsula.

The Maclehose Trail is a 100 km (62 mi) hike across Hong Kong's New Territories behind Kowloon. Most visitors to Hong Kong – and even a number of habitués – have no idea that huge tracts of beautiful hills and rugged wilderness exist so close to the compressed bustle of one of China's most dynamic cities.
The Maclehose, named after Hong Kong's longest-serving Governor during the colonial era, begins in Pak

Tam Chung, among the coves and rocky inlets of the Sai Kung peninsula where, despite the millions living nearby, the green hills drop to totally empty, curving white sand beaches like Tai Long Wan ('Big Wave Bay'). Most of Sai Kung's natural beauty is protected by Country Parks, but their rural isolation is real. No towns ever existed here. By the fifth of its ten stages, the Trail runs through woodland to the vast rock bulwark of Lion Rock, an abrupt cliff with Kowloon spread in miniature below. From there to Tuen Mun, the Trail is a series of glorious upland hikes round the slopes of Tai Mo Shan, Hong Kong's highest peak. There are streams and waterfalls in deep ravines full of subtropical birds and dense foliage, grassy moorlands, forests, and ancient hamlets and farms.

WALKING THE GREAT WALL
Far East/China

WORTH A DETOUR: The fortified stairways, cannon platforms and other Ming Dynasty (circa 1350) military detailing close to Jinshanling (northeast of Beijing).

The Great Wall of China is over 7,200 km (4,500 mi) long, and so familiar that it can seem to be universal property. In fact it was built over 2,000 years and consists of a network of structures reflecting China's expansion west and north.

Nothing could connect you to the past more than the Han Dynasty (206 BC – AD 220) Wall of concrete-hard reeds and mud, austere and magnificent in the wind-whipped wilderness of the Gobi Desert. Shorn of any outer brick casing, the two gateways of Yumenguan and Yangguan, near Dunhuang still bear majestic witness to imperial power as the two western gateways into 1st-century China.

Far fewer people walk the Wall east of Beijing. From Simatai you can follow one of the steepest and most dramatic sections through Huangyaguan, across razor-sharp mountain ridges with a watchtower on every one, to Jinshanling. But to appreciate the culture underwriting the Wall, you need to walk the long western stretches around Datong, beyond the Beijing crowds, but crammed with rich evidence of the Ming, Han, Qin and Wei Dynasties. In fact, for anything less than fourteen days, use a car or bus to cherry-pick the Wall's greatest features from Hongcibao, Motianling, Qidun, Kouzishang and Huashijian, staying in local farmers' houses alongside the Wall itself. Here, the Wall is no theme park. It feels more disused than ruined, and its threatening majesty retains all its power to shock. Sublime hiking.

- -

DON'T MISS
The beautiful calligraphy inscribed on rocks at beauty spots.

HUANGSHAN TREK
Far East/China

Huangshan means 'Yellow Mountain'. It's in Anhui province, south of the Yangtse flood plains and vast rice paddies, and it is China's most famous mountain.

The region includes dozens of peaks over 1,000 m (3,280 ft) and three ('Lotus', 'Brightness Apex' and 'Celestial Capital') over 1,800m (6,000 ft). The steep stone steps and chainlink rail to the summit of 'Celestial Capital' are typical of the often hair-raising paths and approaches to Huangshan's finest panoramas – but there are hundreds of beauty spots (with a directory of exotic names like 'Two Immortals Playing Chess', 'Grasping Beautiful Scenes Bridge', 'Beginning to Believe Peak', or 'Monkey Gazing at the Sea') which identify every rock, pine tree, cloud or hot spring. Huangshan is said to combine the four essences of aesthetic pleasure in perfect balance and harmony.

Right: The Great Wall of China

JIUHUASHAN TREK

Far East/China

Of China's four Buddhist sacred mountains, Jiuhuashan represents the South. Its temples are dedicated to Bodhisatva Ksitigarbha, lord of the earth and underworld. It rises on the northern edge of the Yangtze flood plains in Anhui Province, west of Shanghai. Above the glassy terraces of rice paddy, the road climbs into ragged pine forests, twisting deep into a landscape of forest-capped cliffs, cascades and massive, bizarre rock formations. In the mist creeping up from the valleys, shapes form in the washed-out colours of ancient Chinese paintings, and you feel a déja-vu familiarity. Though there are tea and vegetable plantations among the blossoming azaleas, these are cultivated by the monks and nuns of some 80 temples and sacred institutions, and they don't impinge on the otherwise authentic wilderness. But more than 1,500 years of sanctity means that Jiuhuashan's nine principal peaks, and every cave, stream, path, promontory, pool, waterfall, cliff, temple, pagoda and even the 'Ten Perfect Views', have names of meditational significance (like 'Celestial Presence at the Heavenly Pillar') – which transforms hiking on the mountain

into an involuntary pilgrimage whenever genuine pilgrims pause on the often narrow path.

It's no hardship. The goodwill you encounter trekking on Jiuhuashan enhances what is already an exceptionally lovely region. There is no development other than the stunning temple complexes, all of them integrated into the dramatic landscape according to the principles of the Tang, Ming and Qing dynasties in which they were built. You choose temple guesthouses over campsites, and seek out some of their 1,500 Buddha statues and thousands of important cultural relics – because rapidly you realize how their existence gives meaning to every rock and tree that you might hike past. With wafting incense, temple bells and a shrine on every corner, this is not normal hiking – but Jiuhuashan's natural magnificence and spiritual integrity make it abnormally rewarding.

WHEN SHOULD I VISIT?:
Year-round. Each season has its adherents – for example the Taoyan Waterfall, seen through the trees and tall bamboo of the Ganlusi ('Sweet Dew') Temple on Jiuhuashan's north side, is at its best after seasonal rain, when the river's force creates an all-pervading misty haze.

SHANGHAI'S MAGLEV TRAIN
Far East/China

HIGHLIGHTS: Seeing the driver of a Ferrari on the expressway shaking his fist at the Maglev speeding past. Floating on a magnetic cushion – a thought worthy of both Confucius and China's most imaginative poets.

A ride on Shanghai's Maglev (magnetic levitation) Train is a journey into the future of transport. The Maglev rail system might be only 30.5 km (19 mi) long, but that's enough to demonstrate its potential to transform national and international economies by bringing the most remote areas within reach of trade and tourism.

Although Maglev was created and developed in Germany, Shanghai is the first place in the world to use it successfully in a scheduled service, or indeed in any commercial venture at all, and the statistics are amazing. The train can reach 350 kph (220 mph) in two minutes, and is designed for normal operation with a maximum speed of 431 kph (268 mph). But during tests, the train reached a top speed of 501 kph (311 mph), an indication of what it holds in reserve. With no conventional engine, and on a (necessarily) dedicated track of electromagnetic power and guidance coils, the impetus of acceleration is spread throughout the train. The ride is as smooth as an airborne aircraft, without even the spine-pinning surge of 'take-off'. Looking ahead from the Maglev, you see how the swooping concrete curves of the track are banked; inside, you barely feel it. Once on board, a flickering display charts even the slightest variation in speed, and you can't help sharing the thrill of streaking past the fastest cars on the adjacent expressway.

SUZHOU TO HANGZHOU ON THE GRAND CANAL
Far East/China

WORTH A DETOUR: Qing He Fang Street in Hangzhou, much of which survives from the Southern Song Dynasty (1127–1279), and where the shops still sell silks, brocades, parasols, and Hangzhou's speciality fans.

China's Grand Canal is 2,000 years old, 1,764 km (1,103 mi) long, and connects all China's major, east-west running rivers, and thus most of its major cities, in a single, gigantic system. It is a unique guardian of Chinese history and culture – and nowhere on its length is that more evident than its southernmost stretch from Suzhou to its terminal at Hangzhou. The beauty of both cities is legendary, and the Grand Canal between them passes ancient water towns and villages, lakes and hanging gardens draped in antiquity. It is a privileged view of history, and China's greatest poets and artists have recognized and celebrated it since the Sui Dynasty 1,500 years ago.

From Suzhou's gardens, waterways and pagodas, you cruise past a traditional China from the 13th or 14th centuries to Wuxi, the 'Radiant Pear' of Taihu, a lake dotted with islands and gorgeous temples. There you can take a painted dragon-boat across the lake to Tongli, a medieval town split into seven parts by the fifteen river courses flowing through it. Living history just keeps coming for 147 km (92 mi), through Zhenjiang (girlhood home of American writer Pearl S. Buck), to the incomparable natural beauties of Hangzhou itself.

PEARL RIVER TWILIGHT CRUISE

Far East/China

WORTH A DETOUR: The '13 Hongs' – the line of warehouses along the Shamian waterfront where 19th-century foreign traders were allowed to do business.

The Pearl River Delta has been China's southern gateway for nearly 2,000 years, and the city of Guangzhou has been its significant port since the Tang dynasty (618–917). Formerly known as Canton, it accommodated first the Portuguese, then the British as predominant trade partners. Today, it is still one of China's fastest-growing cities, and just as devoted to international trade; but its success has been achieved at the cost of pretty well anything that speaks of its history or ancient culture.

Instead, Guangzhou is a testament to China's perception of modernity. Concrete confections stretch for blank miles along the Pearl River's broad stream, and river mists turn brown along the banks where they mix with traffic fumes. This is 'Metropolis', and even its residents criticize its lack of redeeming features. Guangzhou's (self-assessed) greatest attraction is to flee the fumes by boat – if only to cruise a short distance up and down the endless concrete shore. Then night falls, and the gorgeous butterfly of the Pearl River takes wing.

Where the Pearl River runs through the city, at night Guanghzou celebrates its industrial heritage and future in a blaze of lurid yellow, red and orange illuminations. Tombstone slabs of daytime grey become canvases for flashing, spinning, flickering sequences of neon. Hotels, shopping malls and high-rise office blocks on both banks create what look like rainbows arcing across the shimmering water. Some co-ordinate lighting sequences, creating themed patterns with names like 'Night Moon Over Goose Pool' and 'Red Heart of the Pearl River'. Multicoloured stroboscopic displays bounce reflections off every ripple, suggesting the hidden pulse of this endlessly energetic city. At any other time of day, a cruise on the Pearl River is merely dull. In the gloaming, the conspiracy of colour in frantic motion reminds you of Guangzhou's ancient, subtle, colourful Chinese soul.

WORTH A DETOUR: Lijiang, built in the late Song and early Yuan Dynasties, a UNESCO World Heritage Site where the traditional daily cultures of the Naxi and Dongba peoples are almost untouched.

TIGER LEAPING GORGE
Far East/China

Where the Yangtze, Mekong and Salween Rivers rush side-by-side out of Tibet and south along China's border with Burma, the towering ridge of Yulong Xueshan (Jade Dragon Snow Mountain) forces the Yangtze into an abrupt change of direction known as The Great Bend. It turns north, the mountains close in, and the river enters Hutiao (Tiger Leaping) Gorge, one of the world's deepest.

It is narrowest at its start, where a large rock in the middle defies the ferocity of the torrent in a chasm only 30 m (100 ft) wide. This is where a tiger once leaped across it – but its legendary name derives not from tigers' agility, but from their unpredictable savagery.

Entering its middle section, the water drops another 100 m (328 ft) without warning. Now at racing speed, whole blocks of water thunder and crash onto sharp outcrops of rock, and you can hear the greedy sucking of deep whirlpools pulling at the air. The third section of Hutiao's 15 km (9 mi) is even more dangerous and spectacular. The steeply-angled (70–90 degree) cliffs rise a sheer 18–2,400 m (6–8,000 ft) from the water, twisting and turning in a surge of high waves and filling the canyon in a haze of frothing spew. Beyond the gorge itself, the Great Bend continues for about 190 km (120 mi), turning south and east. The proximity of the Gorge to Lijiang, cradle of China's traditional Naxi and Dongba cultures justifies including this journey in any top-three wish list.

RAFTING NINE BENDS RIVER
Far East/China

WORTH A DETOUR: The 'fairy boats' – the boat-coffins dating back 4,000 years, stuffed into caves and fissures all along the soaring rock walls of the gorge, representing the philosophical and mystical unities of dozens of contrasting dynasties and regimes.

Wuyi Shan, in northern Fujian province, is southeast China's most remote mountain region. Its incomparable scenic beauty was recognized 4,000 years ago by the Yue people, and it became a site of pilgrimage for Taoism, Buddhism and Confucianism. Wuyi is the ultimate Chinese expression of the potential for harmony between nature and man. Its heart-stirring landscapes are littered with the temples, palaces and pavilions created in tribute to the aesthetics of Confucian philosophy, whose greatest spear-carrier, the 10th-century neo-Confucian Zhu Xi, lived and taught here for fifty years.

Jiuqu (Nine Bends) Gorge, a 10 km (6 mi) section of the 63 km (39 mi) Jiuqu River, is the geographical heart of this summation of Chinese history and culture – and the water element in the formula for harmony. So when you raft the Jiuqu Gorge, you embrace a welter of Chinese philosophy which dictates significance in every rock, every mist of spray, the towering cliffs and solitary, jungle-topped stacks wreathed in cloud; and in the deep placid green pools, the wind-dashed waterfalls and squabbling, rock-strewn rapids of the watercourse.

THREE GORGES: CRUISING THE YANGTZE

Far East/China

HIGHLIGHTS: The cliffs of Yellow Ox, Light Shadow and Yellow Cat gorges, filled with mist and mystery. The 12 Peaks of the Wushan Mountains, spread along both shores of the Wu Gorge.

From east to west, Xiling, Wu and Qutang Gorges stretch for 192 km (120 mi), compressing China's mighty Yangtze River into an angry torrent between Hubei and Sichuan Provinces. The Three Gorges may be the highlight of any journey along the Yangtze. Either you can take a short, local cruise from the dam site to Baidicheng ('White Emperor Town'),

at the western end of Qutang's north shore and a breathtaking sight of 2,000 year-old vermilion walls and flying eaves; or you must cruise from Shanghai all the way to Chongqing on one of the new 'tourist boats' which are now the only ones to be allowed to use the dam's five locks above Yichang, the eastern gateway to the gorges. You can no longer cruise just from Wuhan to Chongqing. Hopefully, visitors in the future may be allowed to travel on the Chinese commercial boats that lack any comfort, but stop everywhere.

WHEN SHOULD I VISIT?: June–October. Come in April only for the blossoming of 3,000 cherry trees (planted by the Japanese in the 1920s) at nearby Long Wangtang.

DALIAN COASTAL DRIVE

Far East/China

At the southern tip of northeast China's Liaodong Peninsula, Dalian is northern China's biggest port and a former colony of both Russia and Japan. Set between the hills of its own sub-peninsula, the city is unusual in China, because it is full of parks, woods, and green spaces that make the most of the beaches along its twisting shoreline. Dalian's deep-water industrial port is miles away – and the same meteorological quirk that keeps it ice-free makes Dalian a major domestic tourist resort. Since 1955, when the city became exclusively Chinese, its authorities have sought to retain some of the European ideas brought by the Russians – of wide boulevards, and, especially, the wonderful corniche called the Binhai Road. The Binhai Road runs for 42.5 km (26.6 mi) to Heishijiao, following every cove and promontory around the west and south of the city. It perches between the golden beaches (including two of China's designated top ten judged by colour, curve, breadth and fineness of sand) and the coastal hills of the nature park that fills most of the sub-peninsula. Visually, you could be near Sorrento or Cannes above the Mediterranean; but the thicker weight of the air and the sea mists are unmistakably oceanic. Dalian's city fathers proudly refer to their 'dancing silk ribbon', which begins at Asia's biggest plaza, Xinghai Square, and curls out and away among the woods and flower-filled cliff-sides. It's extremely pretty, but the Binhai Road is the centrepiece of a resort region, and nature has been tamed to comply.

THE SILK ROAD

Far East/China

WHEN SHOULD I VISIT?:
Year-round, according to which section you want to travel. A French team recently demonstrated that with meticulous planning, and travelling on horseback, you can travel the entire distance at the optimum season for each region.

The wayposts of the Silk Road are a litany of adventure and romance crossing half the world. Already ancient when Marco Polo set out from 13th-century Venice, the 13,900 km (8,700 mi) route to Kublai Khan's capital of Beijing is still fraught with the same historic dangers. War, pestilence, religious confrontation and plain banditry continue to influence travellers' choices – and are the reason why the Silk Road is not one, but a series of fragmented routes which tell a collective history.

Created by trade, the Silk Road has always been even more important as a conduit for ideas. The exchange of science and technology, of philosophy, religion and artistic culture has scored a trail of monumental magnificence across two continents. Venice, Istanbul, Bukhara, Samarkand, Tashkent, Kashgar, Urumqi, Dunhuang, Lanzhou and Xi'an stand out, but the mountain ranges, deserts, steppes, rivers and other natural obstacles between them hide a thousand treasures ranging from whole medieval cities to the most exquisite Islamic and oriental objets d'art. There are only two rules for travellers who want to make the most of the Silk Road: always expect the unexpected, and embrace cultural differences to the best of your diplomatic ability.

XINJIANG TO TIBET HIGHWAY

Far East/China

HIGHLIGHTS: Travelling the north slopes of the Himalayas – it feels like being on the dark side of the moon.
The monastery at Sagya – an oasis of human generosity, full of welcoming monks in a place of palpable antiquity.

Of the five overland routes into Tibet, the highest and most remote is the Xinjiang to Tibet Highway. It begins at Yecheng (Kargilik) in Chinese Turkestan, and climbs straight up the eastern edge of the Karakoram to Dahongliutan, at 4,900 m (16,000 ft) only just higher than the average altitude of the entire Highway. You need to be prepared, either with time to acclimatize, or ancillary oxygen. The rewards of entering Tibet this way are enormous. Over the Kunlun Mountains you skirt the western Tibetan plateau. Instead of people there are birds thronging the small lakes, and wildlife in extraordinary numbers. Mountain peaks form blue on vast horizons of grassland and rocky scrub. There will be a moment when you feel chastened by the biblical immensity of sky and earth and loneliness; and grateful for a human voice. Along the north slopes of the Himalayas into the desert terrain between Gerze and Nyima, only herds of antelope and wild yak disturb the ghosts at the ancient rock paintings at Rutog, among the ruins of the Guge Kingdom. It's a relief to joke with living monks at Tuolin, Sagya, and Tashilunpo monasteries.

WHEN SHOULD I VISIT?: From May–October, but for sheer romance, time your visit for the August historical festival in rural Numata, nestled at the foot of the Tamahara Highlands.

THE ROMANTIC ROAD

Far East/Japan

One of the loveliest but least known of Japan's scenic routes is the Romantic Road through the mountain heartland of central Honshu. It begins in the historic city of Ueda, once the feudal castle citadel of the Sanada family, and picks its way along the quietest backroads through the mountains of Gunma Prefecture to Utsunomiya. It leads to the double waterfalls of Fukiware, the rugged splendour of Lake Chuzenji and the natural glory of Nikko National Park; and to countless shrines, pagodas, castles, hot springs of all shapes, size and location, and ancient towns and villages that reveal some of old Japan's most enduring characteristics. For some 50 km (31 mi) of its 350 km (219 mi) length, the Romantic Road follows the base of Mount Asama, an active volcano. Old and new Japan accommodates itself to nature's dangerous beauty first, with a 1,000 year-old, three-storied pagoda of inspired grace, built at Miyota as protection against eruption; and second, with a miniature version of Tokyo's Ginza shopping district at the upmarket mountain resort of Karuizawa, further along the road. Both are charming. In the same way, the route passes by traditional and modern hot springs. The old style is for traditional architecture, and a beautifully composed natural setting; some of the newer springs like Kusatsu are factories of hydrotherapy.
You need a car to follow Japan's Romantic Road. It would be worth it even if you stopped only at the ultimate jewel – Nikko, home to Japan's most lavishly decorated shrine complex.

Right: Xinjiang to Tibet Highway

WALKING THE NAKASENDO

Far East/Japan

WHEN SHOULD I VISIT?:
April–October. Each season creates a new version of the Nakasendo's magic.

TIME IT TAKES:
1–12 days. The most popular stretch, Tsumago-Magome, is a 3–4 hour slow ramble, usually as part of a 1-day excursion. Ena-Narai is an easy to moderate 12-day hike of up to 20 km (12 mi) a day, with 2 rest days.

HIGHLIGHTS:
The hilarity of composing haiku, partly in sign language, for the Japanese families who run the minshuku, where all activities like eating and bathing are communal.
The historical integrity of the road – the restoration along the Ena-Narai section far transcends the usual 'theme-park' approach. This is all genuine and surprisingly moving.
The early morning mists, reinforcing the most powerful aesthetic in the predominant image of old Japan.

Developed from the 7th century onwards, the Nakasendo was formalized at the beginning of the Tokugawa Shogunate (1600–1868) as one of the five official roads for the use of the shogun and government dignitaries in ruling their territory. The Nakasendo was one of two highways connecting Edo (Tokyo) and Kyoto, and it runs through the forested heart of Japan across the mountains of Honshu and along its misty, green river valleys. There were 69 post towns and smaller stations established along its 534 km (332 mi) length – and long stretches, especially in the mountainous areas, remain now almost exactly as they were in the 17th century. Despite inevitable modernizing, it's still possible to hike the entire Nakasendo – but most visitors choose to spend 1–12 days on its pristine central section from Ena to Narai. Between these beautifully preserved Edo towns lies the fabulous Kiso Valley, a living vision of ancient, rural Japan. Huge stretches of the road are paved with their original ishidatami cobbles, curling through pedestrianized villages of traditional wooden houses, and stepped to follow the steep gradients of the forest hillsides. With volcanic Mount Ontake as a backdrop, the road reaches its zenith as custodian of Japanese rural cultural tradition between the villages of Tsumago and Magome. Achingly picturesque combinations of rocky hillsides, rivers, waterfalls and forests confound touristic cynicism with their enduring natural beauty. So much so that you appreciate the fact that even the postmen here wear full Edo-period costume. From Magome, some of the Nakasendo's loveliest landscapes unfurl on the steep climb to the Torii Pass, and culminate in the 17th–19th-century treasures of Narai. One terrific feature of the Nakasendo is the chance to stay in traditional minshuku – family-run inns where everyone eats and talks together. It's a rare opportunity for visitors to meet local people – it illuminates the journey.

Among the minshuku along the Nakasendo's central section are some of Japan's oldest and most famous inns – astonishingly, unwilling to capitalize on their fame and therefore still accessible to all travellers. That really is a cultural shock!

DON'T MISS
The 16th- century
Ujo ('Raven') Castle,
of Okayama.

SHINKANSEN – THE BULLET TRAIN FROM OSAKA TO HIROSHIMA

Far East/Japan

The high-speed Shinkansen is the pride of Japan Rail, and the core of its entire railway system. Even so, it has its own hierarchy. Though it serves all Japan's major cities, its newest, sleekest, fastest version is reserved for the Tokaido/Sanyo Shinkansen. Powered by the 300 km (188 mph) Nozomi Super-Express, it's the Tokyo-Kyoto-Osaka-Hiroshima-Hakata service, connecting the capital with the beautiful coastal region of Sanyo, the southern half of Honshu Island's panhandle, facing the Inland Sea.

The Shinkansen runs on a route parallel to the much older Sanyo Railway, celebrated for over 100 years as one of Japan's most scenic routes. Much like a dragon on old porcelain, the silver starship of the Shinkansen snakes through the traditional Japanese landscape of ancient, historic towns and villages, and of woods, water and arched bridges. It's a mighty metaphor for Japan's ability to synthesize the future with the past.

THE 88 TEMPLES OF THE SHIKOKU PILGRIM ROUTE

Far East/Japan

HIGHLIGHTS: Early 17th-century Matsuyama Castle, repository of Japanese history.
Bathing at Japan's oldest hot spring, Dogo Onsen.

The smallest of Japan's four main islands, Shikoku remains isolated by the Inland Sea, the loveliest and most bucolic region in the country. The south, especially, fits a traditional image of Japan – of fabulous mountain scenery, samurai castles, craft workshops, farming villages where oxen pull creaky wagons, and of small terraces of vegetable or orange trees cut into the hillsides of dense woodland.

This warming, humane landscape is the backdrop to Japan's oldest pilgrim circuit – the 1,450 km (906 mi) journey to 88 shrines established by the 9th-century Buddhist priest Kobo Daishi. Every year, more than 100,000 of his followers – called henro – complete the rite. Most, devout and determined but subject to modern pressures, do so by bus or car. A small proportion travel on foot, fulfilling the 'walk of life' that Kobo Daishi proposed as an opportunity for self-examination by confrontation with the unknown.

And you do confront it: even those who set out merely to enjoy the hiking discover that as a henro, they are drawn into a quite novel experience. Pilgrims wear white to show their status. Throughout Shikoku, they find they are the recipient of 1,000 small charities or gifts of food or money. These they must accept in humility as o-settai, gifts to help them on their way from people who cannot make the journey themselves. The constant exchange of moral responsibilities and actual goods adds a revelatory dimension to the usual introspections of a long, long hike.

THE PEARL ROAD

Far East/Japan

WHEN SHOULD I VISIT?:
Year-round, it's a lovely region
in which to unwind – and
easily accessible.

TIME IT TAKES:
One hour.

HIGHLIGHTS:
The Isa Grand Shrines –
Naiku houses the sacred
mirror of the Emperor – one
of the three essential pieces
of regalia of the Imperial
family.
The isolated, but perfect
white sand of Goza
Shirahama beach.
A boat trip among the
coves and islets of Ago Bay,
a marine landscape that
changes dramatically with
the weather, but always
enhanced by the sight of the
ama (female divers) diving
for pearls.

The Pearl Road is a skyline drive across the coastal edge of the Ise-Shima National Park on the Kii Peninsula in Mie Prefecture east of Nagoya and Nara. It overlooks the saw-tooth ria formations of deep indented bays and complicated fjords facing the Pacific, notably Ago-wan (Ago Bay), south of Toba city, where in 1893 Mikimoto Kokichi produced the first cultured pearl; and which is still the main centre of Japanese pearl production. In fact the Pearl Road begins at Mikimoto Pearl Island, where in addition to memorial statues and pearl museums, you can see the pearl ama – the highly trained, women pearl free-divers – at work. But Toba city is principally a resort centre, full of theme parks and huge groups looking for cheap excursion fun, and the Pearl Road provides an escape route to the tranquility of the lovely hills behind the otherwise gorgeous coastline.

It's fair to point out that the unbridled coastal development at Toba and elsewhere in the vicinity (all made misty by distance when you look down from the Pearl Road Observatory) owes its tacky existence to its proximity to one of Japan's most sacred Shinto shrines at Ise City. With so many visitors to the double shrines of Geku and Naiku, it's no wonder developers moved in to cater for them. From the Pearl Road, one side looks down on the shrine precincts. The stylized, traditional wooden buildings are set in ancient forests of sugi (giant cryptomaeria trees), with lakes, ponds and large stone formations of unfathomable symbolism all around. Established in the 3rd and 5th centuries, it's the image of the shrines and not the touristy horrors that you take away with you. They will outlast any modern development – and so will the Pearl Road's naturally beautiful marine landscapes.

YOU SHOULD KNOW
In the historic city of Matsukaka,
below the walls of the magnificent
castle there is a row of 19 houses
dating back to 1603. Six of them are
still occupied by descendants of
their original samurai owners.

WORTH A DETOUR: The 1.5 km (1 mi) of Edo-era merchant and domestic buildings at Seki in Mie Prefecture – completely undisturbed since that time.

THE TOKAIDO HIGHWAY
Far East/Japan

The Tokaido was designated Japan's most important thoroughfare at its creation in 1603. Now people travel on Japan National Route 1 or the Shinkansen, both of which parallel the old road. But the modern highway and express train both cut through hills and shave awkward angles in the name of passenger comfort; and their ribbons of steel and asphalt are anyway hemmed in by buildings. Almost forgotten, alongside but very much intact, the Tokaido remains, some of it accessible by car, and in some areas like Mie Prefecture, it is 95 per cent intact. Even where the new road is literally on top of the old, the Tokaido is signalled by the shrines, temples and official buildings of its former official status; and one section, in the lovely mountain region between Hakone and Machi has been officially 'preserved' – each November a Daimyo Gyoretsu ('feudal procession') of about 200 people acting as servants, porters, palanquin-carriers and spear-carrying guards re-enacts typical history.

TOKYO WATER CRUISE
Far East/Japan

HIGHLIGHTS: Plum Grove, at the eastern tip of the 62-acre Hama-Rikyu Gardens – an oasis of sylvan tranquility. Venus Fort, one of the giant shopping malls in Odaiba.

A ride in a suijo basu (river bus) provides a completely novel perspective on one of the world's most densely packed, urban maelstroms. From Hinode Pier green-glassed, sleek double-decker boats like rocket-ships make a futuristic statement for the Sumida River ferry, a service that started in 1885. Now, the ferry carries far more Japanese tourists and visitors than commuters on the 40 minute ride from the mouth of the Sumida River on Tokyo Bay upstream to Asakusa.

You pass Tsukiji's colossal Wholesale Market for fish and produce; the tidal duck ponds of the moated Hama-Rikyu Tei-En ('Detached Palace Garden'); old lumberyards and warehouses; the landmark green roof of the Kokugikan, housing the arena, museum and HQ of Japanese Sumo Wrestling; and, at Asakusa itself, the giant red lantern of Sensoji Temple, much loved by elderly Japanese.

Four other suijo lines start from Hinode, in various guises. The Harbor Cruise Line is a stern paddle-wheeler with a stovepipe stack – take it at dusk as the lights start to twinkle along the shore and across the Rainbow Bridge. Two more serve Odaiba, the massive artificial island in Tokyo Bay. The Odaiba Line goes to Seaside Park, where city folk come to frolic on the shipped-in beach and to practise romance on the boardwalk; others thread the network of man-made islands to the aquarium or the Kasai Sealife Park in Chiba. Travelling by river bus, you get a chance to reflect on what makes Tokyo's energy so exciting.

ENOSHIMA ELECTRIC RAILWAY

Far East/Japan

WORTH A DETOUR: Taking an escalator through the woods to the highest point of Enoshima Island – see the lovely Enoshima Benzaiten Shrine, a Shinto Shrine to the three sister goddesses.

It looks like a train, but the Enoshima Electric Railway has the soul of the much-appreciated local tram it used to be. It runs from Fujisawa, 51 km (32 mi) southwest of Tokyo, to the popular seaside resort of Enoshima and on to Kamakura, once capital of Japan and still the religious and historic hub of the Shonan region. The Railway has 15 stations on its 10 km (6 mi) length, with eclectic attractions in the vicinity of each, and there are special tourist tickets available to ensure you miss none of them.

Not even new rolling stock can disguise the Railway's alter ego of Tram. It follows the original tramlines laid out before 1910, at slow speeds determined by the sharp curves between the older buildings. Its narrow-gauge track squeezes between the backs of residential blocks and houses, bursting free of the inelegant tangle of wires and backyard detritus that makes all train journeys fascinating to reveal a procession of sights of extraordinary variety and interest. Most are partly visible from the train itself – like the unusual lighthouse at Enoshima Island, and some of the many shrines and temples for which Hase and Kamakura are famous. The Enoshima Electric Railway is a humble vehicle, but it takes you to some magical places. Get off at Hase for the 700 year-old brass Great Buddha at Kotoku-in Temple; or Kamakura, with 65 Buddhist temples, 19 Shinto shrines, and historic buildings going back to the city's foundation in 1192. Enoshima Island, a short walk away, offers amazing views of Mount Fuji in the distance, and a restful panorama of the beaches below.

WHEN SHOULD I VISIT?:
You can ski in winter, and Sorak's waterways and valleys respond to every shift of season and daily weather – but the reds and golds of autumn are glorious.

THE WINDING PATHS OF SORAKSAN

Far East/South Korea

Soraksan (san means 'mountain') Nature Reserve sits on the east coast of the central Korean peninsula, behind the South Korean resort city of Sokch'o. The region is a tumbling mass of cracked granite and gneiss peaks, many over 1,200 m (3,936 ft).

Threaded with plunging ravines of thick forest, streams and waterfalls, Sorak is full of hidden valleys and unexpected panoramas that take your breath away. A lattice of pathways and hiking trails leads into its remotest depths, but near the Reserve's entrance (just a 15 minute drive from Sokch'o's lovely beaches and resort razzmatazz) you understand what it means to be one of South Korea's most popular recreation sites. Even so, Soraksan has the grandeur to awe the biggest crowds, especially in autumn when its deciduous forests blaze with colour.

Its popularity as a natural wonder is combined with its cultural significance: several of South Korea's most famous temples can be found here. One, Allak-am, is placed above the Yukfam and Piryong waterfalls.

A TRIP TO ANAK KRAKATAO

South-East Asia/Indonesia

Anak is the offsping of the vanished volcanic island of Krakatao (sometimes misspelled as Krakatoa). Located in the Sunda Strait between Java and Sumatra, the parent island famously blew apart in the great eruption of 1883, with ensuing tsunamis killing tens of thousands after a 'big bang' that was heard 5,000 km (3,000 mi) away. Starting in 1929, the new island of Anak Krakatao emerged from the sea as the centre point of three encircling islands – the remains of Krakatao. It lies within the remote Ujung Kulon National Park in West Java, created by the Dutch in the late 19th century, and it is an active volcano that's growing steadily.

Depending on current volcanic activity, it is possible to land on Anak Krakatao and camp on the vegetated eastern shore of this young volcano before scrambling to the cone's summit – a demanding hike up a steep slope covered in lightweight ejecta (pumice-like rocks) that will take around two hours. But this is not a simple enterprise – the jump-off point is the port of Carita, a 120 km (75 mi) drive from Jakarta that alone takes the best part of half a day. From there, it is possible to hire a dilapidated fishing boat out to the Krakatao Islands, for the unique pleasure of exploring the world's most violent volcano.

HIGHLIGHTS:
The islands of Rakata (another name for Krakatao), Panjang and Sertung – for a chilling perspective on the size of the explosion that reduced the original large island to three fragments.
A side trip to Welcome Bay in the mainland portion of the Ujung Kulon National Park – don't miss the white rhino skeleton at the ranger station.

GUNUNG AGUNG
VOLCANO SCENIC ROUTE
South-East Asia/Indonesia

WORTH A DETOUR: Sideman, off the road between Selat and Duda, for stunning views down a valley of traditional rice terraces, over South Bali to the sea.

The island of Bali has a warm heart – the active volcano of Gunung Agung in East Bali's traditional Karangasem region, where local culture survives largely intact. This impressive peak rises above the mountains that form Bali's spine, towering to a height of 3,142 m (10,308 ft), and it is the site of Pura Besakih, Bali's sacred mother temple. The peak appears conical, but this fact actually conceals a massive summit crater. Strangely, Gunung Agung is covered in lush vegetation on the western side, while the eastern flank is barren. The best way to appreciate the brooding presence of this mighty volcano is to drive (or cycle) the scenic route along Gunung Agung's southern side from Rendang to the village of Bebandem near Amlapura. Reached via an attractive minor road from Bangli, Rendang is a pretty little town. From there, the winding road passes through the village of Muncan, set amidst some of the most attractive rice country on the island. The next ports of call are Selat and Pura Pasa Agung – starting point for the easier southern hiking route up Gunung Agung (the northern route is tougher, and the two are entirely separate). The road continues through Duda, and Sibetan to Bebandem. From there, it's a short step to the bustling centre of Amlapura – this old royal town is still the capital of East Bali, though somewhat reduced in importance after being isolated for three years following Gunung Agung's last major eruption, in 1963.

WORTH A DETOUR: The Cibodas Botanical Garden at Cianjur – this fabulous garden at the foot of Mount Gede near Jakarta displays the tropical and highland flora of western Indonesia.

JAKARTA TO BANDUNG
South-East Asia/Indonesia

One striking landmark in the centre of Jakarta in West Java is Gambir Station, with its lime green ceramic façade. This is the main starting point for long-distance trains to other major cities in the south and east – including one of Indonesia's most scenic railway journeys, the 180 km (110 mi) trip from Jakarta to Bandung. The most impressive landscapes will appear during the latter part of the trip, after the line starts climbing into the tranquil highlands. Along the way it passes through tunnels, also crossing spectacular viaducts, huge bridges and steel trestles constructed more than a century ago by Dutch engineers. The lush scenery outside the windows has – to a degree – been shaped by man, with terraced rice paddies against a mountain backdrop.

WORTH A DETOUR: Sunrise at the summit – the final climb is always done before dawn, so trekkers can enjoy the truly awe-inspiring sunrise.

GUNUNG RINJANI TREK

South-East Asia/Indonesia

One of the most spectacular volcanoes in Indonesia is Gunung Rinjani on the island of Lombok. The forested sides of the country's third-tallest mountain rise to a height of 3,726 m (12,224 ft) and the spectacular summit crater contains the vast, sacred lake of Segara Anak. One of the best short expeditions in South-East Asia is the Rinjani Trek from Senaru in the north, over the summit and down to Sembalun Lawang. Gunung Rinjani is a National Park, and this rewarding guided trek is a model for eco-tourism. It involves overnight camping on the mountain. It begins with a steep ascent through tropical forest and alpine meadows to the Senaru crater rim. The route traverses the spectacular rim ridge and descends to the emerald crater lake, before climbing back up the steep crater to the Sembalun rim. From there it's a hard climb to the summit, before the final descent to Sembalun Lawang to complete a memorable adventure.

PUERTO PRINCESA SUBTERRANEAN RIVER TRIP

South-East Asia/Philippines

DON'T MISS
Getting close to the lizards that frequent the forest and shoreline.

Located in the Saint Paul Mountains 50 km (30 mi) north of the city of Puerto Princesa on the island of Palawan, the Puerto Princesa Subterranean River National Park consists of a dramatic limestone karst landscape with a mountain-to-sea ecosystem that includes important forests.

The star feature is undoubtedly the navigable underground river that winds through a cave before discharging directly into an aquamarine lagoon on the South China Sea, a fact that makes the lower reaches of the river tidal. A 30 minute boat ride with great landscape views takes you to the river entrance.

From there, the journey continues in an outrigger canoe, a single lamp illuminating the extraordinary geological formations of the lofty cavern within. The knowledgeable guide will be a mine of information on life within this wondrous place – including fish, bats and the swiftlets whose nests are coveted for soup – as he quietly paddles around showing you the best stalactites and stalagmites. Although 8 km (5 mi) of this hauntingly beautiful underground river has been mapped, only 4 km (2.5 mi) is deemed navigable. A special permit is required to explore the full navigable stretch; the regular tour covers 1.5 km (1 mi).

BANAUE TO SAGADA BY ROAD

South-East Asia/Philippines

HIGHLIGHTS:
Sunrise Viewpoint near Banaue – the famous outlook over terraced hills that features on the local 1,000-peso banknote and is reached by a trail through the rice paddies.

The eerie cavern of Sumaging, near Sagada – like all the local caves it is unlit, so it's necessary for the explorer to go well equipped.

Asia's cities are mostly dirty, crowded places full of frenetic activity, but the very opposite is true of vast swathes of the continent's unspoiled countryside, where life often seems to go on pretty much as it has for centuries. Nowhere is this contrast more obvious than on the island of Luzon. To the south is the sprawling metropolis of Manila complete with 14 million people, while to the north is the sparsely populated Cordillera mountain range that forms the island's spine. Enjoying the unspoiled delights of the latter is no mean feat – by definition there is little tourist infrastructure and – far from the heavy hand of central government – the local Igorot people seem to be inclined to make sure that it stays that way. The two villages that must be seen are Banaue and Sagada. Reaching Banaue is a fairly major undertaking, with the usual method being jeep rental (with or without driver) in Manila, followed by an all-day drive. Be sure to make an early start, as Banaue shuts down for the night in the early evening.

The drive from Banaue to Sagada is awesome. The mountain scenery alone is breathtaking, with countless rushing streams and hilltops rolling away to the distant Mount Pulog, Luzon's highest point. But the bonus is the display of extraordinary rice terraces, created on the hillsides by Igorots over millennia. The road winds down into Bontoc Valley, and then makes the steep climb back up to Sagada, dramatically presented against a backdrop of limestone cliffs and pine forests.

It's more than tempting to make a full day of it, stopping to explore rice paddies, caves, forests and waterfalls, with a leisurely pause for a lunch of smoked meat, red rice and corn washed down with a glass (or two) of the local wine.

WHEN SHOULD I VISIT?:
April or May when the
swaying expanses of rice
are at their pre-harvest best.

RICE TERRACE HIKE

South-East Asia/Philippines

Once you've braved the difficulties of reaching the Cordilleras of northern Luzon, it's imperative to make the most of a very special place. The most striking feature of these mountains is provided by serried ranks of narrow rice terraces that climb the hillsides – now collectively listed as a UNESCO World Heritage Site.

The way to appreciate fully the endeavour that went into creating and maintaining these extraordinary 2,000-year-old man-made ledges is to get up close and personal by taking a hike. The paddies, with their high earthen walls, green pools and constantly trickling water, are often divided by bright red chongla plants. They are criss-crossed with paths and steps and there are numerous farms and dwellings that often look identical. It's easy to get disorientated, but local children are happy to act as guides for a few pesos and this is a worthwhile investment.

DEATH RAILWAY AND THE BRIDGE OVER THE RIVER KWAI

South-East Asia/Thailand

The journey along the infamous Death Railway and across the Kwai River Bridge is one of Thailand's best-known trips, taken by thousands of people each year. Many come to visit the spot where family members lost their lives.

In 1942, the Japanese needed an alternative supply route for their forces in Burma other than the dangerous sea voyage where they were under attack. They decided on a railway that had to be cut through difficult terrain of remote, jungle-clad hills. Tragically, there was an unlimited workforce to hand – 61,000 Allied prisoners of war, of whom 16,000 died here, and an enslaved population of some 200,000 Burmese, Thais, Malaysians and Indonesians, of whom 80,000 lost their lives.

Trains leave from Bangkok's Thonburi station, along the Death Railway line itself, reaching Kanchanaburi, before crossing the bridge. You can descend at the station just south of the Bridge and walk across the wooden planks, or just stay on board and rattle over at 10 km (6 mi) per hour. If you continue to the terminus at Nam Tok you will pass over the Wampo Viaduct, also POW-built. Looking at the lush vegetation and the tranquil river views, what happened here within living memory seems unimaginable.

HIGHLIGHTS:
Kanchanaburi POW Cemetery.
Chung Kai POW Cemetery.

CHEOW LAN LAKE AND NAM TALU CAVE

South-East Asia/Thailand

YOU SHOULD KNOW

In 2007 six tourists and two guides were drowned in a flash flood in Nam Talu. Take advice before going there.

Located in Thailand's southern province of Surat Thani, roughly halfway between the country's two coastlines, is the wonderful Khao Sak National Park. Covering an area of 739 sq km (285 sq mi), the park comprises the largest area of ancient rainforest in southern Thailand, complete with stunning karst topography – the highest formation is 960 m (3,200 ft). There are several different trails within the park, but one of the most exciting is to explore Cheow Lan Lake and Nam Talu Cave.

Cheow Lan was formed when the Ratchaprapha Dam was built in 1982. Some 169 sq km (65 sq mi), it is surrounded by rainforest and limestone crags, and contains over 100 islands. Basing yourself at one of the simple, bamboo floating bungalow operations, you can enjoy a few days of swimming and exploring the lake. Sitting quietly in a small cove, you'll see gibbons and macaques in the trees nearby, apparently totally unconcerned by the presence of humans. Your local guide will take you through the rainforest to Nam Talu cave. After beaching the kayak, you walk for a couple of kilometres looking out for tree snakes, orchids and otters, which inhabit the stream that winds its way through the jungle, to the 30 m (99 ft) entrance, inside which you will see stalactites, stalagmites and eroded stone formations. Thousands of bats inhabit this cave, which takes 90 minutes to walk through, but be warned: a stream runs through it, waist deep in parts, which has to be waded through.

WORTH A DETOUR: Nipping up to Mo Chit station on the Sukhumvit line to visit Chatuchak Weekend Market.

BANGKOK SKYTRAIN

South-East Asia/Thailand

The Skytrain has changed the face of travel in Bangkok. It used to be a nightmare of a city where one could easily spend two hours travelling a distance of about 5 km (3 mi) because the weight of traffic was bringing the whole place to a grinding halt. All this changed on 5 December 1999, King Bhumibol's birthday, when the luxurious Skytrain, with its ultra-modern elevated stations, opened.

Passengers get a fascinating, bird's-eye view of the city. Not only is one amazed by the vast quantity of skyscrapers, a symphony of chrome, steel, glass and concrete but, in among the hyper-modernity are glimpses of ancient temples, their sweeping roofs glittering red and gold in the sunlight, housing stock that varies from villas with flower-decked gardens to slums whose grimy windows are cheek by jowl with the track, advertising hoardings, monuments, traffic circulating and Thais going about their business. Several of the stations are linked to 'skywalks', elevated walkways leading to nearby shopping malls and other amenities such as the National Stadium, the Chao Praya River and the wonderful Chatuchak Weekend Market.

DON'T MISS
Ban Maeo Thai Boran –
where Siamese cats are
bred and conserved.

MAEKLONG RAILWAY – BANGKOK TO SAMUT SONGKHRAM

South-East Asia/Thailand

Built privately around the turn of the last century, the Maeklong Railway brought seafood from the fishing ports of Samut Sakhon and Samut Songkram to Bangkok – a distance of about 75 km (47 mi). The line was neaver connected to the main rail system, and is one of the capital's better-kept secrets. Leaving from Bangkok's west bank Wong Wian Yai station, take the train to Mahachai. Trundling along a single narrow track, you soon leave the city behind and find yourself in a fertile landscape of coconut palms, banana plants, lychee, guava and white pomelo orchards, interspersed with canals. There are numerous tiny stations along the way – blink and you'll miss them. The conclusion of the journey is almost the best bit, as the line goes through the middle of a large, colourful market. Stallholders clear awnings and goods from the track as the train approaches, putting them all back together again the moment it has passed.

SCENIC ROUTE TO CHIANG DAO CAVES

South-East Asia/Thailand

HIGHLIGHTS: Rafting on the Kok River from Fang to Pai. Doi Suthep, Chiang Mai's 1676 m (5,500 ft) peak, with its sacred temple, winter palace and delightful National Park.

The lovely northern city of Chiang Mai makes an excellent base for many different explorations. For this journey you'll need your own transport, to enable you to enjoy a roundabout journey to the Chiang Dao Caves, taking in some unusual, and un-touristy places en route.

The Dara Pirom Palace, former home of Princess Dara Rasamee and an absolute gem of a place, is full of fascinating personal effects and objects that give an insight into the royal lifestyle as it was lived about 100 years ago. Further north, Route 3010 winds through the forest to the much-revered Four Buddhas' Temple. Redeveloped over the years, it stands in a tranquil forest setting, little visited by foreigners.

Finally, you return to the main road, and head to Chiang Dao. You'll pass an elephant training camp on the way – well worth a visit if you have time. The cave complex is well signed and much visited: there are 100 named caves here, stretching over 10 km (6 mi) into the mountain. Currently only five can be explored, and you'll need to take a guide with a lantern for three of them.

HUE TO HOI AN ON HIGHWAY 1

South-East Asia/Vietnam

WORTH A DETOUR: The Cham Museum, founded in 1915, with its wonderful selection of ethnic sculpture and carving dating from the 7th–15th centuries.

The Hue, Da Nang and Hoi An coastal strip is one of the most-visited areas in Vietnam, with a great deal to offer. It is close to the former DMZ (Demilitarized Zone) between the old North and South, which were divided by the Ben Hai River. Much of the fighting in the 1960s Vietnam War took place thereabouts, and many interesting relics of that traumatic time remain to this day.

The Vietnamese Imperial City of Hue suffered serious damage in the conflict, but this UNESCO World Heritage Site remains a fascinating place that merits exploration. Hue is also the starting point for the drive south along Highway 1 via Da Nang to Hoi An. This magnificent coastal route is in much better shape than many roads in Vietnam, twisting and turning above the sea and rising to a dramatic high point at the Hai Van Pass (though a tunnel is under construction) where the panoramic view is sensational.

After crossing the pass, it's worth stopping at Da Nang to relax for a while on the splendid China Beach – though in fact there are other, rather more cultural side trips to consider here. These include the World Heritage Site of My Son, centre of the ancient kingdom of Cham and the extraordinary Marble Mountains, which are sculpted limestone hills containing pagodas, temples and grottos dedicated to Buddhist, Taoist and Confucian divinities.

Upon completing the scenic journey to Hoi An, the first thing to do is to explore the quaint old town, yet another World Heritage Site – be sure not to miss the Hoi An Museum, Phuc Kien Communal House, the Japanese Covered Bridge and the ancient Vietnamese houses. Another worthwhile outing is up the Thu Bon River to see traditional boatbuilding, woodworking and pottery-making villages like Kim Bong and Thanh Ha.

HEAVEN'S GATE PASS

South-East Asia/Vietnam

WHEN SHOULD I VISIT?:
March–May or
September–November.

To undertake this marvellous cycle ride, first take the overnight train from Hanoi across the Red River and on to Lao Cai. From there, a minibus will convey you and your trusty steed up through an impressive landscape of rice terraces to the picturesque village of Sa Pa, below Heaven's Gate. The onward climb from Sa Pa is steep, but the effort is worthwhile – after a refreshing pause at the Silver Waterfall, 3 km (2 mi) from the summit, more physical effort gets you to the top of the world... and the considerable rewards for Herculean pedal-pushing. You've reached the summit of the highest pass in Indochina, and the views of mountains and the Hoang Lien Valley below are breathtaking (assuming you've got any breath left to take). Having made it to the top, it's possible to turn around and let gravity hurry you back down to Lao Cai.

HANOI UNIFICATION EXPRESS

South-East Asia/Vietnam

This is a train journey that time forgot. The term 'express' is used loosely, as in averaging around 50 kph (30 mph) as opposed to the 15 kph (10 mph) achieved by local trains on the single track connecting Ho Chi Minh City (formerly Saigon) to Hanoi in the north. This amazing 1,725 km (1,100 mi) railway was built by the French along Vietnam's coastal spine a century ago and passes through wonderful countryside, though in truth the real reason for riding the Unification Express is to experience a railway journey like no other.

Rolling stock is old-fashioned and the train will be hot and crowded. There is a choice of seat (hard or not-very-soft) and sleeper (yes, hard or not-very-soft). Possessions left unwatched for a second will vanish like smoke in the wind. There will be frequent stops on sidings to allow trains to pass in the opposite direction and hordes of hustlers selling everything from food and drink to fake designer goods will appear at every stop. But this is a fascinating and worthwhile journey that will not only convey you through beautiful scenery, but also provide the opportunity to meet the people and experience the reality of Vietnamese life.

WORTH A DETOUR:
Cu Chi, the impressive underground tunnel network used by the Viet Cong during the Vietnam War.

PERFUME RIVER DRAGON BOAT TRIP
South-East Asia/Vietnam

WORTH A DETOUR:
The Imperial Citadel of the Nguyen Dynasty, damaged by American bombing during the Tet Offensive of 1968 but still mightily impressive.

Though not yet described as 'The Venice of the East', the imperial city of Hue – former capital of Vietnam's Nguyen Dynasty – is divided by the Perfume River and has numerous canals. So taking to the water is a great way to see the city's sights, and the famed Hue Dragon Boats – the local motorized equivalent of Venetian gondolas – are the way to travel. These long-tailed, brightly painted boats ply the Perfume River, and most do indeed have some resemblance to those fearsome if mythical fire-breathers, though tending to be of rather haphazard construction.

It's possible to enjoy the Dragon Boat experience by taking one as though it were a water taxi. Any trip around town will have the added dimension of revealing the sights and sounds of Hue's busy river life, with houseboats everywhere, laden sampans heading for market or undertaking another important mission like sand dredging… and of course there are more of those in-your-face Dragon Boats at every turn. This in itself is a worthwhile outing.

But the Hue area has many fascinating monuments and historical sights, and a Dragon Boat journey up river is a splendid way of visiting some of the best. There are many options to choose from, but a typical tour will include the Linh Mu (Thien Mu) Pagoda, Hon Chen Temple, Tu Duc Tomb, Emperor Minh Mang's Tomb amidst tranquil gardens and lakes and Khai Dinh Tomb. Some require a moto-taxi from the bank and the stops (usually 30–45 minutes) are not long enough to allow proper exploration, as these tombs are often large complexes. However, the Dragon Boat trip is an experience in its own right.

SAIGON TO ANGKOR WAT

South-East Asia/Vietnam

Don't be afraid to refer to Ho Chi Minh City as Saigon – most of the local people still do. And it's from Saigon that one of Indochina's great cycling expeditions begins, taking the adventurous pedal-pusher from the former capital of South Vietnam through the Mekong Delta and on to the drier country and contrasting sights of Cambodia, ending at the ancient city of Angkor Wat. This fabulous testament to the Khmer civilization was built between the 9th and 12th centuries. There are endless choices of route to follow, but one well tried and proven journey is from Saigon via My Tho, Tra Vinh, Can Tho, Long Xuyen, Chau Doc, Nha Bang (on the Cambodian border), Takeo, Phnom Penh, Tang Krasang and Phumi Loveay to Siem Reap. This scenic route weaves through rubber plantations, crosses rivers and passes through the paddy fields and lush countryside of the Mekong Delta before crossing into Cambodia – a land of traditional villages, busy markets, ancient temples and colourful pagodas. The locals do not see many foreigners, and those who venture into remote country areas on uncrowded back roads are invariably the subjects of great curiosity, especially to children. But the passers-by from another world are invariably received with warmth and hospitality in these backwaters.

WHEN SHOULD I VISIT?:
November–February.

HO CHI MINH TRAIL

South-East Asia/Laos

WORTH A DETOUR: Visit the UXO office in Xepon – view the collection of disabled ordnance here and talk to the experts who are clearing this deadly inheritance.

The Ho Chi Minh Trail began in North Vietnam, cut through the mountains and wound its way hundreds of kilometres south through both Laos and Cambodia to South Vietnam. This remarkable route enabled troops, arms and supplies to be moved south towards Saigon during the Vietnam War. As much of it was invisible from the air, the USA began a massive, secret campaign of bombing and defoliation, particularly in Laos, a country with which they were not at war. Between 1964 and 1973, over 2 million tonnes of bombs were dropped on Laos. Absolutely no reparations were offered subsequently, leaving eastern parts of Laos littered with UXO (unexploded ordnance) that kills and maims people to this day.

It is possible to travel on parts of the Trail in Laos, by mountain bike, motorbike or 4x4, but you must take a guide, and follow the route faithfully – exploring here could be fatal. Along the way you will see the debris of war – burnt out tanks, heavy artillery, scattered UXO and bomb craters. You will also see flowers planted in bomb casings, fences made from war detritus, tank treads used as bridges, and you will meet some amazing people, most of whom, remarkably, seem to hold no grudge.

DON'T MISS
The temples of Wat Xiang Thong, possibly the most beautiful in Laos.

MEKONG RIVER VOYAGE – HUAY XAI TO LUANG PRABANG

South-East Asia/Laos

Since Laos re-opened its borders to westerners in the late 1980s, the Mekong River voyage from Houay Xai to Luang Prabang has become an absolute classic. Crossing the river from Thailand takes a matter of minutes, and you will soon find the 'slow boats' that will carry you downstream. These are either cargo boats with enclosed sides, or riverboats that have a roof but are open-sided. The uncomfortable benches on the boats notwithstanding, it is perfectly lovely to be on the Mekong. Most of the passengers are young backpackers, and the atmosphere is sociable. You pass few villages en route, but you'll see fishermen on the river and people on the sandy beaches – tiny glimpses of local life – as well as lovely, riverside scenery. Arriving at the village of Pak Ben, your overnight stop, there seem to be more foreigners in Pak Ben than there are locals – all the slow boats stop here – and it's crammed with guesthouses, small shops and eateries.

In the morning, off you go again on this peaceful voyage: the sound of the water slipping past is hypnotic, though occasionally broken by noisy speedboats that complete the trip in a few hours. As you reach your destination, more villages and fantastic vegetable plots at the river's edge can be seen. The Mekong is wide and beautiful at Luang Prabang, with temples visible on each bank, and you'll be glad to reach dry land once more.

SIEM REAP TO BATTAMBANG

South-East Asia/Cambodia

In the northwestern rice-growing region, Battambang is Cambodia's second largest town, an interesting place with an old-fashioned provincial atmosphere as yet unaffected by the invasion of mass tourism. The architecture is a mixture of traditional Cambodian and French colonial, with streets shared by motorcycles, cars and horse-drawn vehicles. And for those who wish to see unspoiled rural Cambodia there couldn't be a better starting point – within a short distance of the town is a timeless land of small villages, rice paddies and farmland. There also may be found Angkorian ruins, pagodas, waterfalls and caves.

WORTH A DETOUR: The fabled temples of Angkor Wat.

Interesting though Battambang may be, the real attraction is getting to the place by boat from Siem Reap. A ferry leaves at 7 o'clock every morning, following a picturesque route across the northern tip of Tonlé Sap and up the Sangker River.

The Tonlé Sap becomes Asia's largest lake when it quadruples in size during the rainy season. It is a huge expanse of water that makes a vital contribution to the Cambodian economy, and the banks are lined with fishing communities. From there, the ferry enters the winding Sangker River and follows it for 40 km (25 mi) upstream to Battambang, through fields and forest.

Apart from the splendid scenery, this fascinating journey is part of everyday Cambodian life. Water is the lifeblood of local communities, and at every turn there will be something new to see along the bank.

SELANGOR RIVER CRUISE

South-East Asia/Malaysia

Despite intensive exploitation of Malaysia's abundant natural resources, many of this fascinating country's estuaries, rivers and jungles remain unspoiled – for now, so perhaps it's a case of 'catch them while you can'. One of Malaysia's natural wonders that you can't catch – but can definitely see – is the display put on as night falls by the fireflies (kelip kelip) that feed on the nectar of mangrove trees (berembang) near the mouth of the Selangor River. Colonies gather in individual trees and flash rapidly in unison as the insects seek mates.

A new dam upriver has disturbed the habitat and numbers are dwindling. Even so, this is still an amazing light show. Proceed to Kuala Selangor, northwest of Kuala Lumpur. This once sleepy town has started to show signs of tourist exploitation, but there is tasteful accommodation to be found on the riverbank for those who wish to stay over and explore the area's other attractions. But the main event is undoubtedly staged by the fireflies, which are actually small Lampyridae beetles.

Starting points for river cruises are the villages of Kampung Kuantan and Bukit Belimbing, where it is possible to embark on a small rowboat (tongkang) after 7.30 pm (though in the way of these things some cruises are now propelled by silent electric outboard motors).

Most of the 'flashers' have found a mate and switched off by late evening but in the meantime the synchronized, rhythmic (three flashes a second) display of blinking green lights puts the average Christmas tree to shame. No flash photography, noise or torchlight is permitted during the cruise, to ensure that the habitat of the fireflies is not unduly disturbed.

HIGHLIGHTS:
Touring the twin forts of Kuala Selangor, originally built to guard the mouth of the Selangor River in the early 16th century and subsequently expanded. The village of Tanjung Keramat with its picturesque lake and the fast vanishing ruins of another major fort. A visit to the Kuala Selangor Nature Park, home to a huge variety of wildlife including numerous species of resident and migratory birds.

TAMAN NEGARA EXPEDITION

South-East Asia/Malaysia

HIGHLIGHTS:

A night of animal watching from a hide – to give visitors the best chance of seeing larger animals, there are a number of observation hides overlooking clearings.

Visiting a settlement occupied by the semi-nomadic Batek people, who still practise their traditional way of life as hunter-gatherers within the Park.

The ear-shaped Gua Telingga Cave near the little town of Kuala Tahan.

One of the finest jewels in Malaysia's somewhat tarnished ecological crown is the vast and ancient (it's 130 million years old) rainforest within the Taman Negara National Park, in the formidable Titiwangsa Mountains of Pahang State. The Park has been protected for 70 years and remains a treasure trove of Mother Nature's riches – with undisturbed habitats and wonderful flora and fauna that have evolved undisturbed over countless millennia. This magical place may be reached by bus from Kuala Lumpur, with the final leg by boat from Kuala Tembeling Jetty. Once in the Park, it is possible to stay in an eco-friendly lodge, of which there are several.

The high point (literally) of any visit to Taman Negara is a journey along the extraordinary Canopy Walkway. This apparently flimsy ropewalk looks as though it's been there for generations, but is of fairly recent construction and is entirely safe. At 510 m (1,675 ft) it's the world's longest, weaving through the very tops of the trees at a height of 45 m (150 ft) to give a unique view of a sunlit jungle world that can only be guessed at from ground level.

But that's not all Taman Negara has to offer. There is a great variety of animal life within the Park – including headline species like elephants, tigers, leopards, sun bears and Sumatran rhino – but these are shy and rarely seen. However, long-tailed macaque monkeys are a common sight and there is plenty of visible birdlife (over 300 species recorded), plus reptiles aplenty. The adventurous visitor can undertake guided jungle treks by day or night, stroll along marked nature trails or even shoot the rapids on the Tembeling River.

CAMERON HIGHLANDS ROAD
South-East Asia/Malaysia

fter driving north from Kuala Lumpur for 90 minutes on the modern Expressway, take the turn-off for the town of Tapah and discover another world. For this is the gateway to the Cameron Highlands, named after a certain William Cameron who appreciated in the 1880s that these fertile mountains would be ideal for growing tea. The slopes were soon covered in plantations, and the British, who supervised humid lowland rubber plantations and tin mines, soon discovered that the cooler Highlands provided an ideal summer retreat. Today, relaxing colonists have been replaced by holidaymaking city dwellers who also appreciate the cool, fresh climate. The journey up into the Highlands from Tapah is a drive to remember, as the old road (Route 59) is very narrow, twisting and turning sharply through beautiful scenery. The tea industry remains, but today all sorts of vegetables, fruit (especially strawberries) and flowers are grown on farms mixed in with tea plantations in the hilly green landscape. The route goes through Ringlet, Habu and Tanah Rata to Brinchang.

Until recently, this was the only way into the hills, though there is now access from the north and east, so it's possible to enter or leave the Highlands via Gunung Brinchang (to the west) or Tringkap (to the east). This improved access will be sure to increase tourist and commercial pressure. There is already some modern tourist development, but for now the Cameron Highlands preserve much of their original character, with many bungalows from the colonial era still standing in stunning hillside locations. But the Highlands are becoming so popular that (even with the new roads) traffic is often slow-moving or at a standstill.

WORTH A DETOUR:
The free-entry Highlands Apiary Farm near Ringlet Lake, followed by a visit to the Boh Tea Plantation, said to be the largest in South-East Asia.

WORTH A DETOUR: Fort Cornwallis – an old star-shaped fort on the north-eastern coast of Penang Island.

PENANG FERRY
South-East Asia/Malaysia

In the 1780s, the port of Penang was established on the tropical island of the same name by Captain Francis Light of the British East India Company. From small beginnings, this strategically located Malaysian port in the Malacca Straits has become a major Far Eastern commercial centre with Freeport status. The capital of Penang State – George Town – is on the island, along with extensive port facilities and numerous high-tech industries.

The famous Penang vehicle and passenger ferry service is the oldest in Malaysia, having been established in 1920, and has long enjoyed iconic status. It connects the Sultan Abdul Halim ferry terminal near the station in Butterworth to the Raja Tun Uda terminal in George Town. The fleet of eight double-decker ferries constantly plies the waters of Penang's port from early morning until well after midnight. Once known as 'The Big Yellow Ferry', the boats have recently been repainted in an assortment of bright colours – oranges, yellows, reds, blues and greens – making them an even more distinctive feature of the busy waterway. From the ferry's top deck there is an excellent view of the impressive 13.5 km (8 mi) Penang Bridge.

SKRANG RIVER SAFARI
South-East Asia/Malaysia

HIGHLIGHTS: An amazing display of deadly blowpipe skills by proficient Iban hunters.
A stop at Serian to visit the bustling produce market.

Sarawak is located in northwestern Borneo, and is one of two Malaysian states on the island (the other being Sabah). With large tracts of tropical rainforest, Sarawak is separated from the Indonesian part of Borneo by the central mountain range, where several rivers rise. These include the shallow, fast-flowing Skrang River, fiefdom of the fearsome Dayak Iban headhunters. They believed that freshly gathered heads led to an abundant rice harvest, and celebrated their headhunting in the form of elaborate tattoos. Women, too, often bore tattoos that celebrated their skills as weavers.

The Skrang Ibans still have a traditional way of life, but happily there are no fresh heads hanging in the rafters of their huge longhouses along the riverbanks – just a few ancient skulls. Instead, the Ibans now supplement their subsistence economy by welcoming a select number of guests. But first there's a five-hour drive from the state capital of Kuching to the river, from whence a motorized longboat takes over.

It is possible to make scenic river trip through longhouse country, enjoying the verdant rainforest. This a is a genuine jungle safari, sometimes beneath overhanging foliage, and there are plenty of white-water rapids to add to the excitement.

MOUNT KINABALU TREK

South-East Asia/Malaysia

WHEN SHOULD I VISIT?:
March–October

TIME IT TAKES:
Four–six hours for the ascent
to Timophon Gate, two– four
hours from Laba
n Rata Guesthouse to the
summit (spread over
two days).

HIGHLIGHTS:
Plants galore – Kinabalu
National Park is full of rare
(often unique) plants.
A trip to Poring, 40 km
(25 mi) to the southeast of
Park HQ – for a great view of
the mountain, hot springs, a
butterfly farm, orchid centre
and canopy walkway.
A side trip to nearby Tuaran
Village to visit the crocodile
farm – be there at feeding
time for an impressive show
of reptilian greed.

YOU SHOULD KNOW
The trek is popular, so it is necessary to book
accommodation at Park HQ and Laban Rata
Guesthouse well in advance – no accommodation,
no trek.

The two-day trek up Mount Kinabalu in the Malaysian state of Sabah on Borneo follows a well-trodden path, but this doesn't mean it's easy. The mountain is located in Kinabalu National Park, a World Heritage Site noted for extraordinary biodiversity. Kinabalu is South-east Asia's fourth-highest mountain at 4,095 m (13,345 ft). The freezing summit at Low's Peak may be reached by anyone who is physically fit, without mountaineering equipment.

However, the climb may be attempted only with an experienced local guide. The journey begins with a stay at Park Headquarters, followed by a walk or minibus transfer to Timophon Gate at 1,800 m (5,900 ft). From there, the route continues up to the Laban Rata Guesthouse at 3,300 m (10,800 ft). Supplies to the hut are carried by porters, so that trekkers can enjoy a few basic home comforts like hot food, drinks and showers before attempting the final climb the next day. Some start to suffer altitude sickness at this height and should on no account continue the ascent.

The trek is quite often timed so climbers arrive at Laban Rata around dusk, to enjoy the fabulous sunsets and skyscapes, with an early start the following morning delivering a magnificent sunrise over the mountains, sometimes above the clouds. The final stretch to the summit is mainly over bare granite rock and – once there – panoramic views on a clear day are magnificent. The descent is steep and trekkers are more likely to suffer injury (happily usually minor) coming down than going up.

There is now an alternative route – the rugged Mesilau Trail – from the Mesilau resort some 15 km (9 mi) from Park HQ. This newer summit trail up the other side of Mount Kinabalu is much more challenging than the established route and thus appeals to those with a sense of adventure.

Right: Mount Kinabalu

EASTERN MED & MIDDLE EAST

BLUE VOYAGE

Eastern Mediterranean/Turkey

DON'T MISS

Cnidos; an important site in a wild and beautiful location.

Cevat Sakir Kabaagac, a Bodrum writer, recounted his travels by boat around the Carian and Lycian coasts and now the title of his book *Blue Voyage*, describes cruises in these Turkish waters. With rocky coastlines backed by dramatic forested mountains and waters of heavenly peacock hues, this is an idyllic region for a leisurely sea voyage.

Gulets are the graceful traditional Turkish motor-yachts, still constructed locally of the red pine that covers the hillsides. Most are now built for the tourist business and they're comfortable and well equipped. They may be chartered by groups, or a cruise can be an alternative 'package' holiday.

A typical Blue Voyage will sail from Bodrum to Marmaris by way of pretty Gökova, mooring here or at one of the neighbouring fishing villages or coves, and along the north of the narrow Datça Peninsula, doubling back to Datça, with its busy harbour and waterfront. Fjord-like Keci Buku Bay provides anchorage on the journey east to Marmaris, at the traditional fishing village of Selimye, or Bozburun, renowned for its boat building. Just short of huge, hectic Marmaris lie the more tranquil bays of Turunc and Kumlubük.

HIGHLIGHTS:

The Crusader castle of Saint Peter that dominates Bodrum Harbour.
The fascinating Museum of Underwater Archaeology.

The gulet will be at sea for several hours each day – possibly under sail – anchoring for swimming, visiting fishing villages or, for those with an interest in history, archaeological sites. The captain will establish his passengers' preferences. Scattered around the Gulf of Gökova are the remains of several ancient towns; at the tip of the Datça Peninsula the ancient city of Cnidos, and on a promontory south of Bozburun, are the ruins of Loryma, with its sheltered harbour.

THE LYCIAN WAY

Eastern Mediterranean/Turkey

WORTH A DETOUR:
The Lycians of Olympos worshipped a god of fire manifested in the Chimaera where inextinguishable flames still leap from crevices in the rocks.
Best seen at night.

The Lycians settled the wide peninsula between Telmessos (present-day Fethiye) and Antalya around 1400 BC. Archaeological remains, including the unique rock-tombs, dot the whole area.

The Way roughly follows the Turquoise Coast, sometimes cutting inland. The terrain is varied – rocky cliff-tops, steep scrambles down to isolated beaches, open stony hillsides, dense forest and shady valleys. Between Fethiye and Patara, along the western stretch, are the Lycian sites of Tlos, Pinara, Letoon and Xanthos and the Ottoman Greek ghost town, Kayakoy. South-coast Kas has a beautifully sited theatre, and Lycian tombs; inland you descend to Ucagiz and a cluster of historical sites along the shore and on Kekova Island.

GEORGIAN VALLEYS

Eastern Mediterranean/Turkey

The mountainous region north of Erzurum towards Artvin is an area of green valleys, waterfalls and orchards; the high forests are home to wild boar and ibex, the slopes are planted with fruit and vegetables, cotton and tea. The churches in the scattered villages are relics of Christian Georgia. Some have been converted to mosques, and are well preserved; others are in ruins. Most are built in the Armenian style, with drum and cone domes.

Erzurum, always a transport and military centre, is the largest city on the high plateau of Eastern Anatolia. The road northeast crosses a bleak, sparse landscape and drops into the valley of the Tortum, passing Tortum Lake. The river joins the Çoruh at the alpine town of Yusufeli; in places, the Çoruh Valley narrows to a gorge whose reddish cliffs tower above the rushing river. Local lads have always enjoyed spinning down the race on homemade rafts; now this is a popular location for white water rafting, which can be organized in Yusufeli. Yusufeli also makes a good base for exploring the countryside.

WHEN SHOULD I VISIT?:
May and June, after the snow has melted, for the best rafting; May–September for exploring.

KACKAR MOUNTAINS

Eastern Mediterranean/Turkey

DON'T MISS

The mountains to spot
birds of prey, including
the lammergeier.

The Kackar Mountains are part of the Pontic Alps, the formidable range running along the Black Sea coast, which for centuries provided defence against invasion and a refuge for minorities. The coast enjoys a damp climate and the lower slopes of the mountains are clothed in tea plantations, beech and chestnuts, with dense pine and 'rainforest' higher up; the southern slopes are alpine, with steep high summer pasture. The Kackars cover a relatively small area, but their close-packed snow-clad peaks, many of which are well over 3,000 m (9,750 ft), block paths from the valleys.

The mountains are increasingly popular with trekkers, and this is a lovely and rewarding area, rich in wildlife, dotted with small lakes and home, in the summer, to flocks and herdsmen. On the Black Sea sections, Ayder and Cat are good bases; both are reached via the beautiful Hemsin Valleys. On the southern side, above the Coruh and reachable from the Western Georgian valleys, Barhal, Hevek, Meretet and Tekkule are good starting points. The hikes are more gruelling from the south, but the weather is much better; the gentler northern slopes are covered in dense, damp cloud most afternoons. The villages have accommodation, and it is possible to hire guides or join an organized trek of anything from a day to a week. The highest mountain is Kackar Dagi – 3,932 m (12,779 ft) – and there are several others almost as high; climbing the peaks requires full kit and some experience, but there are some glorious one- and two-day walks below the highest parts.

WORTH A DETOUR: Kucuksu Kasri, near Anadolu Hisari. In the 19th century, the original wooden kiosk was replaced with an exquisite tiny Rococo palace.

BOSPHORUS FERRY TRIP

Eastern Mediterranean/Turkey

Istanbul, capital of mighty Christian and Islamic empires, was always a bridge between east and west; now Europe and Asia are linked by road, but ferries remain essential to life in this great city. The Bosphorus, the 30 km (19 mi) strait linking the Black Sea with the Mediterranean, remains an important trade route. Along both banks are royal residences (including the splendid Beylerbeyi Palace), villas, fashionable suburbs, boatyards, fortresses and working villages. Not many of the beautiful wooden yalis, the summerhouses of the wealthy, survive – many burned down, or were demolished. The waterfronts are punctuated by mosques, including the distinctive Ortaköy Mosque, just below the Atatürk Bridge. South of soaring Fatih Bridge, the twin castles – small Anadolu Hisar and the massive Rumeli Hisar, the Fortress of Europe – could effectively 'lock' the Bosphorus. Inland from the fashionable settlements on the European shore is Belgrade Forest, once a hunting preserve for the Sultans. The last ferry stop is at Anadolu Kavagi, on the Asian shore. Here there is time to explore and have a meal, or plan a return journey by bus, dolmus, and short ferry hops, visiting some of the places glimpsed on the journey.

YOU SHOULD KNOW
Tea-making is the only catering for the sleeping car. Take ample provisions and liquids. Also take toilet paper.

ISTANBUL TO ALEPPO ON THE TOROS EXPRESS
Eastern Mediterranean/Turkey

The original Istanbul to Baghdad railway was largely planned and financed by Germany, but the Toros Express (named for the mountain range it crosses) was inaugurated in 1930 by the Compagnie Internationale des Wagons-Lits, to extend its Orient Express service. Though trains no longer continue to Iraq, and the opulence has vanished (along with Belgian detectives), the Toros Express now runs from Istanbul to Aleppo once a week. Haydarpasa Station, on the waterfront south of Usküdur, is reached by ferry from Galata. This grandiose building, with its wood panelling and fine stained-glass, was presented to the Sultan by Kaiser Wilhelm in 1908.

The Syrian sleeping car, with its two-bed compartments and friendly, tea-making steward, is attached to a Turkish train. It heads out of Istanbul by the Sea of Marmara, and then eastwards along a broad valley. Then the line climbs southwards, and continues (past Afyon, where an ancient citadel crowns a dark crag) to the empty, arid plateau, where views expand – tawny plains, distant peaks, isolated villages and minarets. It is late by the time the train arrives in Konya (home to fine carpets and whirling Dervishes); overnight it runs, by way of innumerable tunnels and bridges, through the huge Toros range. In the early morning the train descends the southern slopes towards Adana. Then the line runs east through fertile plains to Febsipasa, where the sleeping car is uncoupled and joined to another train. At the border, after the normal delays, the train is coupled to a Syrian locomotive, and the journey continues through rocky hills and olive groves to the beautiful Syrian city of Aleppo.

HIGHLIGHTS:

The sheer romance of a journey like this – heading into the huge, changing landscape of Turkey and on into Asia Minor.
Descending the Toros at dawn: distant views from the craggy mountains of the green plain below, glimpses of the distant Mediterranean
Finally arriving in Aleppo: an exciting but easy-going city.

CAPPADOCIA CROSS-COUNTRY RIDE

Eastern Mediterranean/Turkey

WORTH A DETOUR: The underground settlements: complex warrens descending many levels, with deep ventilation shafts, wells, escape routes and sealable doors.

This part of Central Anatolia is famous for bizarre scenery, underground settlements and frescoed churches. The weird 'fairy chimneys' – toadstools, cones and pleated domes – were formed by erosion of the soft, volcanic tufa; unusually – most volcanic rock is black or grey – here the colours are soft golds and reds. These easily worked rocks have always provided refuge from raids and persecution; the underground

towns were probably dug in Hittite times – 1900–1200 BC – and used, extended and elaborated over the centuries. Caves are still used for stabling, storage and to keep pigeons; cultivation has also been continuous – the Hittites made wine, and grapes are still grown.

An excellent escape from the crowds into the extraordinary landscape is on horseback; several ranches offer anything from short sunset rides to cross-country trips of a week or more. These combine riding – through fertile valleys, narrow gorges, along winding tracks among the fairy chimneys and over the high volcanic mesas with visits to villages and sites of interest. Time is usually allowed in Göreme, where villagers are still troglodytic, to explore Göreme National Park, an open-air museum of many exceptional churches.

DON'T MISS
Adada has well-preserved buildings in a lovely hillside setting.

ST PAUL TRAIL

Eastern Mediterranean/Turkey

St Paul, a native of Tarsus in southeast Turkey, was, as an educated man and a citizen of the Roman Empire, able to travel and communicate freely. He spent about 20 years spreading Christianity and part of his first journey in AD 46 was from Perge near the Mediterranean coast to Antioch in Pisidia, a Roman colonial town north of Lake Egirdir.

Researched and established, like the Lycian Way, by Kate Clow, the St Paul Trail opened in 2004. The walk starts from Perge, skirting the Yazili Canyon, or from Aspendos, via the Koprolou Canyon. The routes into the wild hills of the Toros range meet at Adada, a little-visited site north of Sutculer, then pass Egirdir, crossing the lush agricultural western lakeshore to the attractive village of Barla. After a boat crossing comes a long climb to the Anatolian plateau and Antioch in Pisidia. Though little is left of the Church of St Paul, the extensive site is impressive.

HIGHLIGHTS:
Svetitskhoveli Cathedral at
Mtskheta. One of the world's
greatest cathedrals.
Tamara's Castle, at the
southern entrance to
the, vertiginous, gloomy
magnificence of the Darial
Gorge.
The tetraconch plan –
prototype for the whole of
the south Caucasus – of the
Great Church of the 6th-
century Djvari Monastery.

THE GEORGIAN MILITARY ROAD

Eastern Mediterranean/Georgia

Its name seems to encapsulate everything modern, so the first great surprise is that the Georgian Military Road is the historic name for the 2,000 year-old route linking Georgia with Russia, across the Caucasus Mountains. Apart from the 4 km (2.5 mi) Caspian coastal strip, completely blocked at Derbent in Russia, it's the only major route through the Caucasus. Just a rugged track until Russia annexed Georgia, the road was only surfaced between 1799–1863. For 208 km (130 mi) it follows the Kura River out of Tbilisi, climbing the Aragvi River Valley to the 2,379 m (7,815 ft) Krestovy Pass. The landscape is as wild and lawless as its history. Always magnificent, the looming crags and peaks now crowd into the awesome Baidarka Canyon, below Mount Kazbegi, Georgia's highest (5,033 m/ 16,508 ft) peak. Here, at the Russian border, the road runs for several kilometres on a shelf cut into the granite walls of the Darial Gorge – rising sheer for 1,500 m (4,900 ft) on both sides – before descending through the helter-skelter of the Terek River Valley tunnels to Vladikavkaz in Russia. Its treacherous hairpins and precipitous drops can still be genuinely frightening – but the road's natural drama is magnified by the accrued wealth of history.

At the city of Mtskheta, cathedrals, monasteries and palaces still guard Georgia's religious soul as they have since the 3rd century. Church and state again combine at the medieval fortress of Ananuri, with

two beautiful churches within its crenellated walls; and at the Church of the Trinity, the landmark on the skyline of Mount Kazbegi. The ruins of forts dating to the 3rd century BC are testament to an even older sequence of invasions, tribal migrations, and trade incursions. The Georgian Military Road is part of Georgia's national psyche, embodying the drama of its landscape and history. Its romantic imaginative appeal has inspired writers including Pushkin, Tolstoy, Dumas, Gorky, Lermontov and the hero/saint of Georgian nationalism, Ilya Chavchavadze.

MONASTERIES HIKE

Eastern Mediterranean/Armenia

Armenia became Christian in 301 AD and the countryside is scattered with old churches and monasteries and carved stone crosses, khatchkars. Beautiful, green Lori province has a concentration of medieval monasteries along the spectacular Debed Canyon.

From Tumanyan, the ruined 13th-century convent and the hamlet of Kobayr are visible. The roofless church still has some frescoes.

The large village of Odzun sits on a shelf over a steep drop to the Debed River; in the centre of the village, the sturdy church is 17th century, with an arcaded cloister once used as a school. On the edge of the cliff is another church and the remains of Horomayri Monastery cling to the slopes a little to the south.

Alaverdi is a quiet town lying in a bend of the canyon. There is a 12th century hump-backed stone bridge over the river, but this is mainly a modern copper mining town. The cable car provides an easy way up to the canyon edge.

WORTH A DETOUR:
Sanahin Monastery – the mossy complex of church, shadowy chapels, ancient graves, open archways and scattered khatchkars is bewitching.

WORTH A DETOUR: The Selim Caravanserai is the best preserved in Armenia. Built in 1332 of basalt blocks, it housed travellers and animals on the Silk Route.

LAKE SEVAN TO VAYOTS DZOR

Eastern Mediterranean/Armenia

This huge mountain lake, lying at just less than 2,000 m (6,500 ft) and covering nearly 1,000 sq km (400 sq mi), is famous for its glorious blueness, changing from duck-egg to turquoise to ultramarine with the weather. The Sevanank peninsula – an island until the water level dropped following irrigation/hydroelectric projects – is crowned by two early monastery churches; the climb to the hilltop gives views over the lake to a jagged skyline of surrounding volcanic peaks. South of Sevan town, well preserved Hayravank Monastery stands on a promontory, and the lovely old village of Noratus has a fine church, ruined basilica, enormous cemetery, and access to a quiet beach. At the medieval/modern cemetery the traveller may come across a Karasoonk marking the 40th day after a death – family, friends and musicians gather at the graveside before retiring for food, drink and storytelling.

From Martuni on the southern shore the newly repaired road runs through the Selim Pass to Yeghegnadzor, the main town of the remote region of Vayots Dzor. Small country roads lead off to hidden valleys and architectural delights.

WHEN SHOULD I VISIT?: November–March.
Camel racing takes place at Thumrait in
November and January.

RUB'AL KHALI –
THE EMPTY QUARTER
Middle East/Oman

Covering most of Saudi Arabia and slices of Yemen, Oman and the UAE, Rub'al Khali, the world's largest sand desert, occupies nearly a quarter of the Arabian Peninsula. Oman is a peaceable country, politically stable, with a calm, tolerant populace who are in no rush to sacrifice their national identity to tourism. The road from Salalah, a colourful south-coast port city with good beaches, crosses the fertile rolling plains and the Jebel Gara Mountains. This area enjoys monsoon rains, and is popular with Arabian visitors during the 'winds of plenty'. The landscape changes to dark gravel hills and narrow wadis – the home of the strange, gnarled frankincense tree. Thumrait, a stopping point for the ancient caravan routes, has a camel racetrack. Sisr, to the north, enjoys year round water; nearby Ubur is the site either of the 'Atlantis of the Sands', a lost Koranic city, or one of the caravanserai. Several towers, a waterhole and thousands of artefacts have been excavated.

THE INCENSE ROAD

Middle East/Yemen

WORTH A DETOUR:
The Wadi Hadramawt and
the many pretty villages,
mosques, tombs and
historical sites scattered over
its tributaries.

The wealth of the ancient kingdoms of Yemen depended on trade in frankincense and myrrh, highly valued throughout the civilized world. Part of the overland Incense Road, which stretched through Arabia to the Mediterranean, passes through several historically important places in Yemen.

Yemen's capital, Sana'a has one of the oldest intact medinas in the Arab world, a jumble of mosques, markets and unique tower houses. From Sana'a the road climbs through the mountains and descends to the eastern desert where, in the 8th century BC, a huge dam was built in what became known as Wadi as-Sudd (Wadi of the Dam) and the city of Ma'rib became capital of the Kingdom of Saba. But temples sank into the desert and the empty mud brick towers of Old Ma'rib are all that survive, though a new dam and oil finds offer new prosperity. The old city of Shabwa lies across the Ramlat as Sab'atayn desert. From the hill, where its remains are engulfed by sand and salt, a dramatic panorama covers the eastern end of the mighty Wadi Hadramawt, the largest wadi in the Middle East.

HARAZ MOUNTAIN TREK

Middle East/Yemen

WHEN SHOULD I VISIT?:
April, May, September
and October

HIGHLIGHTS:
The breathtaking, peaceful
countryside, and the
uncommercialized villages.
Some of the narrow terraces
are the width of just one row
of crops – from a distance
they look like giant ladders.
The ubiquitous Yemeni tower
houses in the villages are
stone; the decoration often
consists of ornate windows of
coloured glass.

The Haraz Mountains, west of Sana'a, is an area of step hillsides, high peaks and lovely stone villages. From the 12th century, the mountains served as refuge for descendents of the Ismaili Sulayhids, and many of the villages date from this period. During Ottoman occupation this was a strategic area where cannons guarded mountain passes. Farming is intensive – even the steepest slopes have been terraced, and monsoon rain is gathered for irrigation.

Trekking in Yemen is not organized, with no maps or marked trails, but the Manakha area is perfect for day-treks. Two of the villages, Manakha and Al Hajjara, have facilities for visitors and make good bases. Hostel accommodation offers packed lunches and evening entertainment of local music and dance, and can arrange guides and camping equipment for longer treks. Manakha is the market town for the surrounding region; Al Hajira, to the west, is a lovely fortified hilltop village.

There are many enjoyable circular day-walks using the network of paths between villages – south to Al-Khutayb, an Ismaili pilgrimage site, west to Jabal Masar and a scattering of historic hamlets, or Jabal Shibam, the highest peak in the region. Longer treks to the edge of the mountains, where peaceful villages look down over steep escarpments, or north and south out of the Manakha region can be arranged. Guides will arrange camping outside villages.

PETRA MONASTERY HIKE

Middle East/Jordan

Visitors to Petra may choose to escape the crowds and see Little Petra, a few miles north. This was an important suburb of Petra, a re-supply post for travellers and traders. Its Arab name is Siq Barid, 'The Cold' – it is entered by a slit in the rocks so narrow the sun scarcely filters through. The 400 m (1,300 ft) siq opens up into wider areas where the rock walls are crowded with houses, temples and triclinia, linked by rock-cut stairways in the cliff face. Floods have eroded lower facades but some of the higher ones are well preserved. As well as the dining rooms, there are a number of water channels and cisterns. A set of stairs at the bottom of the siq leads to a hidden canyon with views of the surrounding countryside.

A little south are the ruins of Al Beidah, a Neolithic village and one of the oldest sites in the Middle East. The remains are unremarkable, but some of the items found, dating to around 7000 BC, bear witness to early experiments in settled agriculture. The path drops to a wadi and from here a fairly easy hour's walk reaches the Monastery of Al Dier. Following small wadis through the rocks cuts out some of the hundreds of steps up to this inspiring monument. Near the top views open up over the mountains and valleys. The Monastery was actually a single chamber temple dedicated to a Nabatean king, probably used later as a church. The flat plaza to the front was levelled for ceremonials; the massive façade – nearly 50 m (162 ft) square – is carved into the mountainside; the doorway is bigger than a house.

DON'T MISS

The Painted House in Little Petra has the remains of AD 1st–century frescoed ceilings.

LAWRENCE OF ARABIA CAMEL TREK

Middle East/Yemen

HIGHLIGHTS: The spectacular landscape and the sheer scale of Wadi Rum.
The camel-mounted Desert Patrol Corps can be a stirring sight, robed and armed to the teeth.

In 1917, with Emir Faisal and the Arab warriors (and the support of General Allenby), T. E. Lawrence took Aqaba; he also attacked the Hejaz Railway on several occasions. Parts of Lawrence of Arabia were filmed here. The area around the main Bedouin settlement, Rum, is very busy, but even on foot it's possible to escape the crowds of day-trippers, exploring red sand corridors through ravines and valleys.

The ideal way to explore the desert is on a camel, with nights in Bedouin encampments. Basic camel riding can be quickly learned and most riders become fond of their silent mounts, despite their grumpy expressions. Long treks include the journey to Mudawarra on the Saudi border, where a railway carriage blown up by

Lawrence in 1917 (he made the trip in three days on a racing camel) still lies by the disused track.

After the daunting red cliffs of the Wadi Rum, the trek threads it way southeast through small wadis and hidden valleys to flatter terrain and darker rocks. Wadi Mhask is suddenly green (it lies above a huge underground water source); the jagged rocky cliffs near Mudawarra conceal canyons, home to wildlife including ibex and wolves.

WHEN SHOULD I VISIT?: March–May, September and October.
TIME IT TAKES: One hour plus.

JERUSALEM: THE VIA DOLOROSA

Middle East/Israel

Ancient Jerusalem has many sites of immense spiritual importance; for Judaism, the massive Western Wall is all that remains of the Great Temple; the majestic Dome of the Rock is, for Islam, more shrine than mosque. For Christianity, the Church of the Holy Sepulchre enshrines the last resting place of Christ, while the Via Dolorosa marks His final journey from trial to crucifixion.

The location of Calvary is undisputed, but Pilate probably lived in what is now the Citadel, not the Antonia Fortress (now a Muslim Madrasah) where the 'Way of Sorrows' begins. The 'Stations' of the Via Dolorosa, which runs east-west through the narrow streets of the Muslim Quarter, are marked with oratories and chapels (modest by comparison with the Gothic and Baroque splendours of Europe), plaques, crosses, and Roman columns. In the Christian Quarter, commerce and spirituality join in the 'pilgrim trade' shops lining the road to Calvary. A jumble of churches and hospices surrounds the huge Church of the Holy Sepulchre (originally built by Constantine at the request of his mother, St Helena), where the 10th–14th Stations are located.

Right: The Church of the Holy Sepulchre

ALONG THE EUPHRATES

Middle East/Syria

WORTH A DETOUR:
The Archaeological Museum in Deir ez-Zur is outstanding, with excellent well-labelled sections on Dura Europos and Mari.

The mighty green Euphrates rises in the mountains of eastern Anatolia and cuts a fertile swathe for 2,700 km (1,700 mi) through the deserts of Syria and Iraq; this was home to great civilizations and city-states. Control of the flow of water has always been contentious.

Along the Euphrates lie some fine archaeological sites. Travel is straightforward – roads with good bus links, and there's a railway line as far as Deir ez-Zur. East of Aleppo, Lake Assad is the huge reservoir formed by damming the Euphrates. From Ath Thawra (purpose built for construction workers and displaced villagers) a road runs over the dam to Qalaat Jaber castle, once high above a river crossing, now on the lakeshore.

Though little is left of busy Raqqa's former glory, a short detour south leads to Resafe, a remarkable ancient walled city in the desert. Downstream, twin Roman forts stand on either side of the river: Halebiye – built by Palmyra's rebel queen Zenobia – still has extensive walls; Zalebiye is fragmentary. Both have great views over the valley and desert.

Deir ez-Zur, a pleasant desert town, is a good base for visiting the southern sites (Abu Kamal is too close to the sensitive Iraqi border). Here, an elegant pedestrian suspension bridge crosses the wide, shallow river.

YOU SHOULD KNOW

The black, tent-like chador is issued for mosque visits, but even on the riverbank women must cover heads and general outline.

ISFAHAN RIVER BRIDGES WALK

Middle East/Iran

Isfahan is one of the most beautiful cities in the Islamic world. In the 16th and 17th centuries under the Safayids (particularly the inspirational Shah Abbas I), it was a city of exquisitely tiled mosques and palaces, paradise gardens, teahouses, fine carpets, and was a centre for the arts. Today, the old city remains a treasure house – squares, domes, minarets, courtyards, and an ancient covered bazaar. The Zayandeh River crosses the city just south of the centre – five of its eleven bridges are old and its banks make a fine walk. The teahouses built under or on the bridges make excellent refreshment stops.

HIGHLIGHTS:

Sunset and early evening at Si-o-Seh Pol when the light softens on the river and the distant mountains, and the bridges are illuminated.

From the bustle of Engelab-e Eslami Square, a path leads southeast to the river and a view of the Si-o-Seh Pol – The Bridge of 33 Arches – a very recognizable landmark, built in 1602. Walking east, the Chubi Bridge, designed to irrigate the gardens, was once joined to a canal system.

Khaju Bridge, built by Shah Abbas II, is two-layered; the bottom section, with locks incorporated into the arches, regulated the flow of the river. Stairs lead to the upper storey. A quiet walk east – 3.5 km (2.2 mi) – leads to the oldest bridge, Sharestan; a mostly stone and brick structure dating from the 12th century. The pleasantly shady south bank is popular with Isfahani picnickers.

Southwest of the Si-o-Seh Bridge is Jolfa, the Armenian quarter established by Shah Abbas.

CHALUS SCENIC ROAD

Middle East/Iran

WORTH A DETOUR:
Masuleh, with its fine
summer climate and tiers of
slate roofed cream houses
clinging to rocky, forested
slopes, is enchanting.

Tehran lies in the relatively temperate foothills of the Alborz Mountains that run the length of the Caspian Sea coast. The road from Tehran runs west, then north through the mountains. This marvellously unspoilt forested region of high peaks – several are over 4,000 m (13,000 ft) – is sadly threatened by plans for the Tehran-Somal Highway, which seem to be going ahead despite environmental objections. The road down allows panoramic views of the blue Caspian (rich in caviar and salmon) and the bright green coastal plains, where rice, cotton and citrus orchards thrive in the humid climate.

The development of the coast has been piecemeal – the previously charming twin villages of Chalus and Nosahar are now sprawling towns, though east of leafy Nosahar are some pleasant, undeveloped beaches. West of Chalus at Namak Abrud the popular cable car ascends the wooded slopes of Mt Medvin. Ramsar, where the coastal plain narrows and the mountains are a dramatic backdrop, is one of Iran's most pleasant seaside resorts. This is a relaxed, attractive place with good accommodation. In the little town of Lahijun, which still has some traditional Caspian architecture, is a museum of tea history – tea has been grown successfully in the Alborz foothills since about 1900.

YOU SHOULD KNOW

Driving can be hazardous – hire a driver, take a tour or use public transport.

BAKU TO SHEKISCENIC ROAD

Middle East/Azerbaijan

Until independence in 1991, Azerbaijan was ruled by great powers including Persia, Mongolia and Russia. Now this beautiful, hospitable little country is a Muslim state with a relaxed attitude to women's dress, alcohol and other faiths. Nineteenth century Baku was a major oil exporter, and international investment has once again made the big, cosmopolitan capital an oil-boom town. The old city seems unaffected by the turbulent 20th century: within its walls, amid cobbled lanes, colourful markets and medieval mosques, stands the massive Maiden's Tower (assumed to be defensive, but possibly an ancient Zoroastrian temple) and the medieval seat of Azerbaijan's ruling dynasty. Among several interesting museums is an excellent Carpet Museum. Along the bustling waterfront, the Caspian is turquoise, but thick with oil. Outside Baku are bleak reminders of the Soviet petrochemical industry, with views over the desolate coastal town of Sumquayit. Westward, the road hugs the foothills of the Caucasus. Shemaka lies in rolling countryside luxuriant with fruit, vegetables and vineyards; little remains of the ancient city but the hilltop ruins of Gulistan Castle. From Ismayilli, a scenic cliff top road leads to Lahic, a beautiful mountain village whose skilled carpet makers claim descent from the Persians. Near the pleasant market town of Qabala is the site of one of the oldest towns in Azerbaijan, dating from around the 3rd century BC. Sheki, in its glorious mountain setting, was a major staging post on the Silk Road – in its heyday there were five caravanserai – and its silk weaving industry continues, though now restricted to small workshops. This lovely town has museums, a royal palace and an attractive old town by the stream beneath a fortress.

HIGHLIGHTS:

The recently restored Palace of the Shirvan Shahs in Baku is a complex, fascinating site – a fine example of Shirvan architecture.

In the mountain village of Pirquli near Shamaka, the Observatory, an important Soviet space research centre, is open to visitors.

The Khan's Palace, Sheki, is beautifully decorated with tiles and carvings; the interior has murals of flowers and birds, battles and hunts.

INDEX

A Coruña to Madrid, Spain 191
Abel Tasman Coast Track, New Zealand 286
Adam's Peak, Sri Lanka 326
Adelaide, road trip from Perth to Adelaide, Australia 277
Aiguille du Midi cable car, France 176
Albanian coast from Corfu, Albania 251
Albertine Escarpment, Uganda 108
Aleppo, from Istanbul to Aleppo on the Toros Express, Turkey 367
Alexander the Great's footsteps across the Oxus, Tajikistan 302
Alice Springs to Coober Pedy, Australia 272
Alpine Pass hike, Switzerland 217
Alpine Road, Germany 227
Altai, Russian Federation 299
Amalfi Coast road, Italy 204
Amazon headwaters, Peru 81
Amazon journey, Brazil 75
Amber Trail, Hungary 243
Amsterdam tram, The Netherlands 169
Amur Highway, Russian Federation 299
Anak Krakatao, Indonesia 343
Andermatt to Grindelwald, Switzerland 220
Andes to the Atacama cycle, Argentina 90
Angel Falls, Venezuela 72
Angkor Wat, from Saigon to Angkor Wat, Vietnam 353
Annapurna Circuit Trek, Nepal 310
Antarctica cruise 294
Antrim Coast Road, Northern Ireland 163
Appalachian Trail, USA 29
Aranui cargo boat, French Polynesia 294
Arizona Trail, USA 45
Arkansas Highway 7, USA 36
Arnoweg, Austria 235
Asmara to Nefasit steam train, Eritrea 112
Atacama, cycle across the Andes to the Atacama, Argentina 90
Atlantic crossing by cargo boat, United Kingdom 162
Attic Coast Road, Greece 254
Australia, from London to 161

Badulla, Hill Country scenic train from Colombo Fort to Badulla, Sri Lanka 325
Baku to Sheki scenic road, Azerbaijan 379
Baltic to Crimea, Russia 142
Banaue to Sagada by road, Philippines 346
Bandung, from Jakarta to Bandung, Indonesia 344
Bangkok, Thailand
   Bangkok Skytrain 348
   Maeklong Railway Bangkok to Samut Songkhram 349
Barcelona, from Madrid to Barcelona, Spain 193
Barsey (Vershay) Rhododendron Sanctuary Trek, Sikkim 308
Battambang, from Siem Reap to Battambang, Cambodia 355
Bazaruto Archipelago, Mozambique 106
Beagle Channel, Argentina 89
Beartooth Highway, USA 39

Benedict Trail, Germany 224
Benone, from Bushmills to Benone, Northern Ireland 164
Bergen to Kirkenes, Norway 129
Berlin Wall Bike Trail, Germany 222
Bernese Oberland Hike, Switzerland 216
Birmingham, from London to Birmingham by Grand Union Canal, United Kingdom 154
Blue Mountain Downhill, Jamaica 63
Blue Mountains, Australia 272
Blue Nile Gorge, Ethiopia 113
Blue Ridge Parkway, USA 31
Blue Train, South Africa 95
Blue Voyage, Turkey 364
Bodø, from Trondheim to Bodø, Norway 127
Bohinj Railway, Slovenia 241
Boiling Lake trek, Dominica 64
Bosphorus ferry trip, Turkey 366
Bridges Cycle Route, Germany 224
Brine Trail, Austria 238
Brittany's Emerald Coast, France 184
Bruce Highway, Australia 271
Bruce Trail, Canada 12
Budva Riviera, Montenegro 248
Bullet Train from Osaka to Hiroshima, Japan 339
Bushmills to Benone, Northern Ireland 164

Cabot Trail, Canada 16
California, USA
   California State Route 1 24
   California Zephyr 49
Cameron Highlands Road, Malaysia 358
Cameroon, Mount 116
Canal du Midi, France 186
Caparú Plateau, Bolivia 82
Cape Cod Scenic Route 6A, USA 34
Cape Wine Route, South Africa 95
Cape York Peninsula, Australia 276
Cappadocia cross-country ride, Turkey 368
Cardamon Hills cycle, India 323
Carnic Peace Trail – via Alpina, Austria 240
Carretera Austral, Chile 86
Carrick-a-Rede rope bridge, Northern Ireland 164
Castle Road, Germany 231
Catania, from Rome to Catania, Italy 208
Cathar Castle Walk, France 186
Catskill Mountains, USA 34
Cerro Chirripo, Costa Rica 60
Chalus Scenic Road, Iran 378
Chamonix-Zermatt Haute Route, France 178
Channel Tunnel by Eurostar, United Kingdom 157
Chapman's Peak drive, South Africa 99
Charente River, France 182
Che Guevara's Revolutionary Road, Chile 91
Cheow Lan Lake, Thailand 348
Chesapeake Bay Bridge-Tunnel, USA 32
Chiang Dao Caves, Thailand 349
Chott el-Djerid, Tunisia 120
Cinque Terre, Italy 207

Circum-Baikal Railway, Russian Federation 300
Classic New Zealand Wine Trail, New Zealand 284
Coast Starlight Train, USA 26
Colombo Fort to Badulla by Hill Country scenic train, Sri Lanka 325
Connemara Coast Trail, Eire 167
Coober Pedy, from Alice Springs to Coober Pedy, Australia 272
Copenhagen waterbus, Denmark 136
Copper Canyon, Mexico 55
Copper Coast Drive, Eire 165
Coquihalla Highway, Canada 16
Corcovado Rack Railway, Brazil 78
Cordillera Blanca, Peru 79
Corfu, along the Albanian coast from 251
Corsican mule trails, France 189
Côte d'Alabâtre, France 172
Crete Senesi, Italy 211
Crimea, from the Baltic to Crimea, Russia 142
Curonian Spit Trail, Lithuania 141
Cuzco to Machu Picchu, Peru 78

Dajti Express Cable Car, Albania 250
Dalian coastal drive, China 334
Dalmatian Coast island hop, Croatia 248
Damaraland, Namibia 104
Danube Gorge, Romania 252
Darjeeling Himalayan Railway, India 316
Death Railway, Thailand 347
Death Valley, USA 44
Dempster Highway, Canada 15
Devil's Nose Railway, Ecuador 74
Dnieper River to the Black Sea, Ukraine 145
Douz, across the Chott el-Djerid from Tozeur, Tunisia 120
Dracula's Transylvania Tour, Romania 252
Drakensberg Traverse, South Africa 100
Drava River rafting, Slovenia 242
Dunajec Gorge, Poland 246

Eagle's Nest, Germany 229
East Coast Route, Denmark 135
East Coast Trail, Canada 13
echoes of Rimbaud & Verlaine, France 181
Edinburgh, from London to Edinburgh on the Flying Scotsman, United Kingdom 150
the 88 temples of the Shikoku Pilgrim, Japan 339
El Camino Real Historic Trail, USA 53
El Choro, Bolivia 82
El Greco Walk, Toledo, Spain 193
Elgon (Mount), Uganda 108
Emerald Coast, France 184
Empty Quarter Rub'al Khali, Oman 371
End of the World Train, Argentina 87
Enoshima Electric Railway, Japan 342
Ephrates, Syria 376
Espíritu Sanctu, Mexico 57

Fergana Valley, Tajikistan 302
Fiordland Long Distance Walk, New Zealand 287
Fish River Canyon Trail, Namibia 105

Flanders Fields, France 173
Florida Keys scenic drive, USA 26
Flüelen, from Lucerne to, Switzerland 216
Flying Scotsman, from London to Edinburgh, United Kingdom 150
Franz Josef Glacier, New Zealand 280
Fraser Discovery Route on the Rocky Mountaineer, Canada 11
Fraser Island Trek, Australia 274
French Riviera corniches 180

Galician Carpathians, Poland 245
Gambia River cruise, The Gambia 117
Ganges, India 322
Garden Route, South Africa 96
Georgian Military Road, Georgia 369
Georgian Valleys, Turkey 365
Gerlos Alpenstrasse, Austria 237
German Avenues: North to South, Germany 233
The Ghan, Australia 266
Gibb River Road, Australia 265
Glacier Bay National Park and Preserve, USA 25
Glacier Express, Switzerland 218
Glasgow to Mallaig, United Kingdom 149
Goa beaches, India 325
Gobi Desert Trek, Mongolia 304
Going-to-the-Sun Road, USA 52
Golden Mountains of Altai, Russian Federation 299
Golden Pass Panoramic Express, Switzerland 218
Golden Ring Towns, Russia 143
Gorée, Ile de, Senegal 117
Gorges du Verdon, France 176
Gota Canal, Sweden 132
Grand Canal, from Suzhou to Hangzhou, China 331
Grand Canal, Italy 213
Grand Circle Road Trip, USA 35
Grand Teton National Park, USA 36
Grand Trunk Road, Pakistan 313
Grand Union Canal, London to Birmingham, United Kingdom 154
Great Divide Trail, Canada-USA 21
Great Dolomites Road, Italy 206
Great Ocean Road, Australia 264
Great Sand Sea oases, Egypt 123
Great Wall of China 328
Green Spain 192
Grindelwald, from Andermatt to, Switzerland 220
Grossglockner Hochalpenstrasse, Austria 236
Gunung Agung Volcano Scenic Route, Indonesia 344
Gunung Rinjani Trek, Indonesia 345
Gustav Mahler Cycle Trail, Czech Republic 247
Gutan (Lake), Panama 61

Haervejen Oxen Trail, Denmark 135
Haleakala Highway, Hawaii 288
Hangzhou, from Suzhou to Hangzhou on the Grand Canal, China 331
Hanoi Unification Express, Vietnam 351
Haraz Mountain Trek, Yemen 372

Havel River, Germany 221
Heaven's Gate Pass, Vietnam 351
Hell Valley Railway, Germany 227
Helsinki to Tampere, Finland 138
Hetta-Pallas Winter Ski Trail, Finland 138
Heysen Trail, Australia 275
High Atlas mule trek, Morocco 120
High Coast Trail, Norway 131
Highway 1, USA 24
Highway 1, Vietnam 350
Highway 901, Puerto Rico 69
Hill Country scenic train – Colombo Fort to Badulla, Sri Lanka 325
Himalayas flight, Nepal 311
Hiroshima, from Osaka to Hiroshima on Shinkansen the Bullet Train, Japan 339
Historic Triangle, The Netherlands 171
Ho Chi Minh Trail, Laos 354
Hoi An, from Hue on Highway 1, Vietnam 350
home of the Sun God, Bolivia 83
Hortobagy Great Plains, Poland 243
Huancayo, from Lima to Huancayo, Peru 78
Huanchaca, Bolivia 82
Huangshan Trek, China 328
Huay Xai, Mekong river voyage to Luang Prabang, Laos 354
Huayhuash Circuit, Peru 81
Huckleberry Mountain Horse Trail, USA 47
Hudson River trip, USA 33
Hue to Hoi An on Highway 1, Vietnam 350

Icefields Parkway, Canada 17
Ile de Gorée, Senegal 117
Inca Trail, Peru 80
Incense Road, Yemen 371
Indian Pacific Railway, Australia 266
Ingapirca Inca Trail, Ecuador 74
Inlandsbanan, Sweden 133
Inside Passage Ferry, Canada 18
International Selkirk Loop, Canada 20
Ioannina to Méteora Road, Greece 258
Isfahan River Bridges walk, Iran 377
Isla del Sol, Bolivia 83
Isla Partida, Mexico 57
Isle of Man Steam Railway, United Kingdom 158
Issyk-Kul (Lake), Kyrgyzstan 301
Istanbul to Aleppo on the Toros Express, Turkey 367
Italian Riviera Day Train, Italy 214
Itria Valley Trulli, Italy 212

Jakarta to Bandung, Indonesia 344
Jebel Nafusa Mountain Drive, Libya 122
Jerusalem: the Via Dolorosa, Israel 374
Jiuhuashan Trek, China 330
Jobo Mountain adventure drive, Lesotho 103
John Muir Trail, USA 46
John O'Groats, from Land's End to John O'Groats, United Kingdom 150
Jonte River Gorge, France 185
Jungfraujoch Cog Railway, Switzerland 220

Kackar Mountains, Turkey 366
Kailash Kora (Mount), Tibet 306
Kalka to Shimla on the 'Toy Train' 320
Kamchatka Ring of Fire Trek, Russian Federation 300
Kanchenjunga Trek, Nepal 310
Karakoram Highway, Pakistan 315
Kastoria, Greece 258
Kauri Coast, New Zealand 281
Kerala Backwaters, houseboat cruise through, India 324
Keukenhof Gardens, The Netherlands 169
Khentii Mountains, Mongolia 305
Kilimanjaro (Mount), Tanzania 109
Kinabalu (Mount), Malaysia 360
King's Road Trail, Finland 137
Kirkenes, from Bergen to Kirkenes, Norway 129
Kokoda Track, Papua New Guinea 293
Kolkata heritage, India 323
Kom Emine Trail, Bulgaria 253
Krom River Trail, South Africa 94
Kullu Valley Trek, India 317
Kuranda Scenic Railway, Australia 273
Kvarken, Post Boat route across, Finland 140
Kwai Bridge, Thailand 347

La Alpujarra, Spain 200
La Méridienne Scenic Route, France 178
La Pedriza, Spain 194
La Rioja, Spain 196
La Ruta del Sol, Ecuador 73
La Ruta Maya, Guatemala 58
La Soufrière summit hike, Guadeloupe 64
Lake Gutan, Panama 61
Lake Issyk-Kul Trek, Kyrgyzstan 301
Lake Komani, Albania 250
Lake Manyara National Park, Tanzania 110
Lake Sevan to Vayots Dzor, Armenia 370
Lake Waikaremoana, New Zealand 283
Lake Windermere, United Kingdom 148
Land's End to John O'Groats, United Kingdom 150
Lauterbrunnen to Schilthorn, Switzerland 215
Lawrence of Arabia camel trek, Yemen 374
Leh, from Manali to Leh, India 318
Lena River, Russian Federation 298
Levada do Caldeirao Verde in Madeira, Portugal 200
Lewis & Clark's National Scenic Trail, USA 28
Lhasa-Gyantse-Xigatse scenic drive, Tibet 305
Liffey cruise, Eire 168
Lima to Huancayo, Peru 78
'Limes' Route, Germany 233
Lisbon Tram Line 28, Portugal 203
Llangollen Canal, United Kingdom 155
Lleida, from Tarragona to Lleida, Spain 198
Lofoten Islands, Norway 126
Loire Valley, France 183
London, United Kingdom
London market walk 153
London river journey 153
London to Australia 161
London to Birmingham by Grand Union Canal 154
London to Edinburgh on the Flying Scotsman 150
lost world of Huanchaca, Bolivia 82
Lötschberg, Switzerland 219
Lower Manhattan, USA 32
Luang Prabang, Mekong river voyage from Huay Xai, Laos 354
Lucerne to Flüelen, Switzerland 216
Luxembourg city walk 172
Lycian Way, Turkey 365
Lyse Road, Norway 130

Machu Picchu, from Cuzco to Machu Picchu, Peru 79
Maclehose Trail, China 327
Madrid, Spain
A Coruña to Madrid 191
Madrid to Barcelona 193
Maeklong Railway Bangkok to Samut Songkhram, Thailand 349
Maglev Train, China 331
Magellan Strait, Argentina 89
Majorca mountains, Spain 199
Mallaig, from Glasgow to Mallaig, United Kingdom 149
Manali to Leh, India 318
Manhattan, USA 32
Mani Peninsula, Greece 260
Mantario Trail, Canada 13
Manyara (Lake) National Park, Tanzania 110
Mariel to Valle de Vinales, Cuba 69
Marrakech Express, Ghana 118
Mason-Dixon Trail, USA 48
Matherah Hill Railway, India 319
Matilda Highway, Australia 269
Mekong river voyage – Huay Xai to Luang Prabang, Laos 354
Melbourne, from Sydney to Melbourne along the coast road, Australia 270
Mersey ferry crossing, United Kingdom 154
Messolonghi, from Patras to Messolonghi, Greece 256
Méteora, from Ioaninna to Méteora, Greece 258
Middle Rhine Valley, Germany 226
Mississippi riverboat cruise, USA 42
Mole National Park Safari, Ghana 118
Mombasa to Zanzibar cruise, Kenya 111
Monasteries Hike, Armenia 370
Monteverde Cloud Forest, Costa Rica 60
Montserrat Rack Railway, Spain 194
Moses's footsteps up Mount Sinai, Egypt 122
Mount Cameroon Trek, Cameroon 116
Mount Elgon & Sasa River Trail, Uganda 108
Mount Kailash Kora, Tibet 306
Mount Kilimanjaro, Tanzania 109
Mount Kinabalu trek, Malaysia 360
Mount Koghi Rainforest trek, New Caledonia 291
Mount Sinai, Egypt 122
Mount Washington Cog Railway, USA 50
Mountain Pine Ridge Forest Reserve, Belize 59

Mozart Cycle Path, Austria 239
Murray River paddle steamer, Australia 267

Nahanni River on a raft, Canada 20
Nakasendo, Japan 338
Nam Talu Cave, Thailand 348
Namib Desert, South Africa 101
Ned Kelly Trail, Australia 268
Nefasit, steam train from Asmara to Nefasit, Eritrea 112
Nestos Valley, Greece 257
The Netherlands waterway cruise 170
Ngong Ping 360, China 327
Ngorongoro Crater Highlands trek, Tanzania 111
Nile, Egypt 123
Nilgiri Mountain Railway, India 324
Nine Bends River rafting, China 333
Noguera Pallaresa River rapids 197
Norfolk Coast Path, United Kingdom 152
Normandy Beaches, France 184
Norsjö Cable-way, Sweden 134
North Cascades Scenic Highway, USA 37
North Mayo Drive, Eire 165
North Yorkshire Moors Railway, United Kingdom 146
Northern Loop, Argentina 89
Norway, spirit of 128
Nxai Pan Old Cattle Trek, Botswana 103

Oaxaca City to Puerto Angel, Mexico 57
Offa's Dyke Path, United Kingdom 151
Okavanga Delta, Botswana 102
Old Spanish Trail, USA 41
Omo River rafting, Ethiopia 114
Orange River, South Africa 97
Oregon Coast Trail, USA 30
Öresund Bridge, Denmark 137
Orient-Express to Venice, United Kingdom 160
Orkhon Valley, Mongolia 304
Orkney ferry, United Kingdom 146
Osaka, Shinkansen – the Bullet Train from Osaka to Hiroshima, Japan 339
Oxus, Tajikistan 302

Pacaya (Volcano), Guatemala 59
Pacific Crest Trail, USA 25
Padjelanta Trail, Sweden 132
Palace on Wheels, India 315
Pamir Highway, Tajikistan 303
Pan-American Highway, USA 54
Panama Canal 61
Pantanal Fazendas, Brazil 76
Paris, France 174
Patagonia, Chile/Argentina
Patagonian Channels 85
Patagonian Cordillera crossing 83
Patagonian Ice Cap Trek 90
Patras Dagi, from Venice to Patras Dagi, Italy 213
Patras to Messolonghi, Greece 256
Pearl River Twilight Cruise, China 332
Pearl Road, Japan 340
Peddars Way, United Kingdom 152
Pembrokeshire Coast Path, United Kingdom 152

INDEX

Penang ferry, Malaysia 359
Peneda-Gerês National Park, Portugal 201
Peninsula Valdes, Argentina 91
Perfume River Dragon, Vietnam 352
Perth to Adelaide road trip, Australia 277
Peter Norbeck Scenic Byway, USA 40
Le Petit Train Jaune, France 188
Petra Monastery hike, Jordan 373
Pico Duarte, Dominican Republic 66
Pinnacles Desert Walk, Australia 278
Piraeus to Santorini ferry, Greece 255
Port Philip Bay, Australia 273
Post Boat route across the Kvarken, Finland 140
Poznan to Warsaw scenic road, Poland 244
Prespa Lakes, Greece 258
P'Tit Train du Nord, Canada 14
Puerto Angel, from Oaxaca City to Puerto Angel, Mexico 57
Puerto Princesa Subterranean River Trip, Philippines 345
Punakaiki Horseback Ride, New Zealand 286
Purnululu National Park, Australia 279
Pyrenean Haute Route, France 189

Railway Trail, Bermuda 63
Rapa Nui Tour, Easter Island 292
Rasende Roland, Germany 229
Raumabanen Railway, Norway 130
Reisach Waterfall, Austria 239
Rennsteig Trail, Germany 228
Revolutionary Trail in the Sierra Maestra, Cuba 68
Rhine Valley, Germany 226
Rhône cruise, France 179
rice terrace hike, Philippines 347
Ridgeway National Trail, United Kingdom 160
Rif Road Trip, Morocco 119
Rim of the World Drive, USA 37
Rimbaud & Verlaine, France 181
Ring of Kerry, Eire 167
Rio Grande, USA 51
Rio Sonora, Mexico 55
Rio Usumacinta, Mexico 58
River Charente cruise, France 182
River Dnieper to the Black Sea, Ukraine 145
River Kwai Bridge, Thailand 347
River Lena cruise, Russian Federation 298
Riviera corniches, France 180
Riviera Day Train, Italy 214
The Road, Saba 65
Robben Island ferry, South Africa 98
Rocky Mountaineer, Canada 11
Romantic Road, Germany 225
Romantic Road, Japan 336
Rome to Catania, Italy 208
Roof of the World Express, Tibet 307
Roosevelt Island tramway, USA 33
Roraima Tepui, Venezuela 71
Rota Romantica, Brazil 77
The Route of Emperors and Kings, Germany 232
Route Napoléon, France 177
Route River Trail, USA 28

Route 66, USA 22
Rub'al Khali the Empty Quarter, Oman 371
Ruta de Califato, Spain 196
Ruta de las Nieves, Venezuela 70
Ruta de las Siete Lagos, Argentina 88

Sacred Valleys Trek, Bhutan 308
Sacred Way, Greece 259
Sagada, from Banaue by road, Philippines 346
Saigon to Angkor Wat, Vietnam 353
St Lawrence Seaway, Canada 19
St Paul Trail, Turkey 368
Salt Road from Timbuktu to Taoudenni, Mali 116
Samarian Gorge Hike, Greece 255
Samut Songkhram, Maeklong Railway from Bangkok to Samut Songkhram, Thailand 349
San Diego Scenic Drive, USA 39
San Francisco streetcar, USA 49
Sante Fe Trail, USA 41
Santiago de Compostela Pilgrim Route, Spain 190
Santorini, ferry from Piraeus to Santorini, Greece 255
Saputara Scenic Road, India 321
Sardinia, Italy 212
Sasa River & Mount Elgon Trail, Uganda 108
Schilthorn, from Lauterbrunnen to Schilthorn, Switzerland 215
Sea Islands, USA 45
Selangor River Cruise, Malaysia 356
Selvaggio Blu Trek in Sardinia, Italy 212
Semmering Railway, Austria 236
Sentiero del Viandante, Italy 208
Serra Verde Express, Brazil 75
Settle-Carlisle Railway, United Kingdom 145
Sevan (Lake) to Vayots Dzor, Armenia 370
Seward Highway, USA 52
Shanghai's Maglev Train, China 331
Sheki, scenic road from Baku to Sheki, Azerbaijan 379
Shenandoah Valley, USA 31
Shikoku Pilgrim, 88 temples of the, Japan 339
Shimla, 'Toy Train' from Kalka to Shimla, India 320
Shinkansen – the Bullet Train from Osaka to Hiroshima, Japan 339
Siem Reap to Battambang, Cambodia 355
Sierra Maestra, Cuba 68
Sierra Nevada, Spain 200
Silk Road, China 335
Simien Mountains, Ethiopia 115
Six Foot Track to the Blue Mountains, Australia 272
Skeena Train, Canada 11
Skeleton Coast, Namibia 104
Skrang River Safari, Malaysia 359
Skyrail Rainforest Cableway, Australia 274
Sligo Yeats Trail, Eire 166
Snaefellsnes National Park, Iceland 126
Snow Lake Trek, Pakistan 314
Soraksan, South Korea 342

Source of the Ganges, India 322
South Patagonia Ice Cap Trek, Argentina 90
South West Coast Path, United Kingdom 159
Southern Scenic Route, New Zealand 284
Southern Wine Road, Germany 230
Spree River, Germany 221
SR-20, USA 37
Sri Pada Pilgrim's route, Sri Lanka 326
Strait of Gibraltar, Spain 197
Suzhou to Hangzhou on the Grand Canal, China 331
Swat Valley, Pakistan 312
Sydney to Melbourne coast road, Australia 270

Table Mountain Aerial Cableway, South Africa 97
Tahoe Rim Trail, USA 47
Taman Negara Expedition, Malaysia 357
Tampere, from Helsinki to Tampere, Finland 138
Taoudenni, Salt Road from Timbuktu to Taoudenni, Mali 116
Tararua Mountains Southern Crossing, New Zealand 285
Tarragona to Lleida, Spain 198
Tasmania Coast Trek, Australia 279
Tazara Railway, Tanzania 110
Tea Road, Swaziland 106
Telefériço de Merida, Venezuela 70
Temple City Journey, India 320
Three Gorges: cruising the Yangtze, China 334
Three Rivers Ride, United Kingdom 156
Tibet, from Xinjiang to Tibet, China 336
Tiger Leaping Gorge, China 333
Timbuktu, Mali
  Salt Road from Timbuktu to Taoudenni 116
  Timbuktu by boat 114
Tokaido Highway, Japan 341
Tokyo Water Cruise, Japan 341
Toledo, Spain 193
Toros Express, Turkey 367
Torres del Paine 'W' Trail, Chile 84
Toy Train from Kalka to Shimla, India 320
Tozeur to Douz, across the Chott el-Djerid, Tunisia 120
Le Train des Pignes, France 179
Trans-Canada train journey, Canada 10
Trans-Oranje, Namibia 105
Trans-Siberian Railway, Russia 144
Tranzalpine Train, New Zealand 287
Tren Frances, Cuba 67
Tren a las Nubes, Argentina 87
Trondheim to Bodø, Norway 127
Tua Railway, Portugal 201
Twin Coast Discovery Highway, New Zealand 282

Umbria Hill Towns, Italy 210
Upano River rafting, Ecuador 72

Val Tremola, Switzerland 221
Valle de Vinales, from Mariel to Valle de Vinales, Cuba 69

Vancouver Island, Canada 14
Vayots Dzor, from Lake Sevan to Vayots Dzor, Armenia 370
Venice, Italy
  Grand Canal 213
  Venice to Patras Dagi 213
  Venice Simplon-Orient-Express 160
Verdon, Gorges du, France 176
Verlaine & Rimbaud, France 181
Vershay Rhododendron Sanctuary Trek, Sikkim 308
Via Alpina, Austria 240
Via de la Plata, Spain 190
Via Dolorosa, Jerusalem, Israel 374
Via Ferrata High Route, Italy 203
Via Francigena Pilgrim Trail, Italy 209
Vicentine Coast, Portugal 202
Victoria Falls, Zambezi River cruise to Victoria Falls, Zambia 107
Viti Levu, Fiji 290
Vltava River cruise, Czech Republic 247
Volcan Baru trail, Panama 62
Volcano Pacaya, Guatemala 59
Volga-Baltic Waterway, Russia 144
Vosges Wine Route, France 181
Vouraikos Gorge Railway, Greece 257
Vrsic Pass Road, Slovenia 242

Waikaremoana (Lake), New Zealand 283
Wainwright's Coast to Coast Walk, United Kingdom 151
Warsaw, scenic road from Poznan to Warsaw, Poland 244
Whanganui River Journey, New Zealand 282
white villages of La Alpujarra, Spain 200
Wicklow Way, Eire 166
Wild Waters Hike to the Reisach Waterfall, Austria 239
Windermere (Lake), United Kingdom 148
Winding Paths of Soraksan, South Korea 342
Wine Route, Chile 85
Wonder Trail, Canada 17
Wonderland Trail, USA 48

Xinjiang to Tibet Highway, China 336

Yangtze, China 334
Yucatán, Mexico 56
Yukon River canoeing, Canada 17

Zambezi River cruise to Victoria Falls, Zambia 107
Zanzibar, Mombasa cruise to Zanzibar, Kenya 111
Zermatt, Chamonix-Zermatt Haute Route, France 178
Zillertalbahn, Austria 2

archipelagos 18, 63, 85, 106, 126, 140, 213

battlefields 33, 173, 184
beaches 14, 30, 52, 69, 73, 184, 202, 270, 275, 286, 325, 350
birdlife 56, 60, 62, 63, 66, 73, 75, 76, 82, 94, 110, 114, 126, 185, 255, 274, 284, 286, 291
boat journeys 76, 324
  canals 132, 144, 154, 155, 170, 186, 213, 331
  cargo boats 81, 162, 294
  cruises 89, 111, 128, 213, 294
  ferries 18, 85, 98, 146, 154, 197, 250, 255, 355, 359, 366
  paddle steamers 216, 218, 267
  post boats 129, 140
  rivers 19, 33, 107, 114, 117, 123, 144, 145, 153, 168, 170, 179, 182, 226, 247, 282, 298, 332, 334, 352, 354, 356, 359
  sailing voyages 19, 88, 106, 282, 364
  steamers 148, 171
  waterbus 136, 250, 341
  see also canoeing; rafting
bridges 26, 32, 48, 64, 74, 131, 135, 137, 163, 164, 169, 241, 256, 302, 347, 357, 377
bus journeys 52, 161, 174, 220, 229, 318, 328

cableways and cable cars 33, 70, 97, 134, 176, 250, 274, 327, 378
camel rides 114, 116, 120, 122, 304, 374
canoeing 17, 51, 57, 72, 76, 97, 102, 197, 348
canyons 11, 35, 40, 42, 49, 51, 55, 58, 105
caves 40, 57, 59, 72, 119, 292, 314, 348, 349, 368
coastlines 30, 91, 99, 104, 152, 159, 167, 172, 180, 184, 202, 204, 207, 254, 260, 264, 270, 273, 277, 279, 281, 282, 286, 334, 350, 365, 378
cycling 14, 16, 20, 21, 36, 42, 43, 63, 70, 73, 79, 86, 88, 90, 126, 135, 137, 141, 150, 164, 169, 176, 181, 183, 184, 185, 196, 198, 202, 211, 212, 222, 224, 226, 232, 233, 237, 239, 247, 248, 252, 257, 273, 276, 323, 351, 353, 354

deltas 15, 102, 114, 145, 179, 257, 298, 324, 332, 353
deserts 90, 101, 105, 116, 122, 123, 272, 278, 304, 371, 374

fishing 16, 88, 94, 106, 132, 270, 283
fjords 85, 128, 129, 130, 287
floodplains 76, 102, 114, 328, 330
flora 29, 62, 63, 64, 65, 80, 81, 82, 96, 308, 310, 360
  meadows 14, 47, 48, 52, 83, 178, 189, 200, 220, 239, 310, 314, 345
forests 25, 40, 45, 57, 59, 60, 62, 66, 71, 73, 75, 78, 80, 81, 82, 86, 89, 200, 274, 276, 291, 357

gardens 14, 39, 96, 148, 169, 174, 183, 204, 233, 242, 247, 313, 323, 331, 341, 344, 348, 352, 377

glaciers 25, 52, 84, 87, 89, 216, 220, 280, 314
gorges 35, 72, 74, 113, 131, 176, 185, 226, 246, 252, 255, 257, 275, 314, 333, 334

helicopters 280
horse riding 20, 45, 60, 63, 66, 70, 73, 76, 83, 88, 103, 120, 156, 166, 243, 286, 304, 368

inland seas 144, 169, 339
islands 18, 19, 33, 43, 57, 63, 85, 98, 106, 111, 117, 126, 140, 146, 213, 248, 275, 290, 292, 294

jungles 56, 58, 59, 60, 61, 62, 66, 71, 72, 75, 81, 82, 89, 348, 356, 357, 359

lagoons 76, 141, 213, 291
lakes 17, 25, 40, 45, 52, 61, 64, 81, 83, 88, 106, 110, 148, 170, 208, 216, 219, 238, 250, 283, 300, 301, 314, 348, 355, 370

mangroves 57, 63, 69, 73, 76, 117, 275, 356
marine life 57, 89, 91, 96, 106, 255
motor-biking 54, 91, 237, 321, 354
mountain ranges 10, 11, 12, 15, 16, 21, 31, 34, 36, 40, 42, 43, 44, 45, 60, 63, 66, 70, 75, 78, 79, 81, 86, 90, 100, 109, 115, 119, 120, 122, 127, 178, 185, 189, 199, 206, 216, 217, 218, 220, 227, 228, 239, 240, 245, 246, 272, 285, 299, 303, 305, 310, 311, 314, 323, 324, 326, 360, 366, 372

National Parks 11, 16, 25, 31, 35, 36, 37, 42, 44, 48, 51, 52, 62, 64, 66, 68, 70, 71, 73, 78, 86, 88, 89, 90, 96, 110, 118, 126, 131, 151, 159, 185, 201, 202, 235, 244, 245, 246, 250, 264, 270, 276, 278, 279, 280, 282, 284, 286, 287, 288, 292, 305, 348, 360
nature reserves 94, 104, 106, 117, 140, 224, 233, 239, 298, 342

plane journeys 14, 311

rafting 20, 51, 58, 72, 88, 97, 114, 197, 242, 246, 333, 365
rainforest 62, 75, 86, 89, 274, 276, 291, 357
reserves 110, 111
rivers 11, 17, 20, 28, 40, 48, 51, 55, 61, 75, 81, 94, 102, 117, 145, 154, 170, 185, 197, 221, 226, 232, 257, 302, 322, 376, 377
  rafting 20, 72, 88, 97, 114, 197, 242, 246, 333, 365
  river cruises 19, 33, 72, 107, 117, 123, 144, 153, 168, 179, 182, 247, 267, 282, 298, 332, 334, 341, 352, 354, 356, 359
  subterranean rivers 345
road trips 32, 39, 55, 56, 57, 88, 108, 110, 120, 167, 225, 290
  coastal roads 73, 96, 99, 104, 163, 165, 180, 184, 202, 204, 251, 254, 256, 260, 264, 270, 277, 282, 334, 350, 378
  desert roads 123, 371
  gorge roads 113, 176

highways 15, 16, 24, 36, 37, 39, 52, 54, 69, 73, 269, 271, 299, 341
historic routes 22, 53, 54, 91, 177, 231, 232, 268, 272, 313, 334, 341, 369, 371, 379
long-distance 35, 41, 89, 231, 233, 265, 269, 271, 299, 313
mountain routes 31, 65, 70, 77, 103, 106, 119, 122, 130, 206, 221, 227, 236, 242, 258, 288, 303, 318, 336, 340, 346, 358, 369
off-road driving 47, 54, 71, 101, 103, 108, 265, 276, 284, 306, 354
scenic drives 20, 26, 34, 37, 40, 178, 244, 284, 305, 321, 336, 378
valleys 44, 312, 315
wine routes 94, 181, 196, 230, 284
rock formations 37, 42, 49, 79, 87, 88, 104, 105, 164, 264, 278, 368

sand dunes 101, 104, 106, 123, 141, 278, 304
ski resorts and skiing 20, 45, 88, 138, 176, 178, 206, 215
steppe 83, 91, 104, 142, 144, 299, 304, 335
streetcars 49
surfing 73, 202, 270

tea plantations 106, 110, 316, 325, 330, 358, 366, 378
tepui 71
train journeys 67, 110, 118, 127, 133, 149, 208, 214, 227, 257, 273, 347
  cog railways 50, 215, 218, 220
  electric railways 342
  high-speed 157, 331, 339
  intercity 105, 138, 142, 191, 193, 344, 349, 367
  long-distance 10, 11, 26, 49, 55, 144, 150, 192, 266, 351
  luxury 95, 160, 315
  mountain routes 74, 75, 79, 128, 130, 179, 188, 199, 201, 218, 219, 236, 287, 300, 307, 316, 319, 324, 325
  rack railways 78, 194
  skytrains 349
  steam trains 34, 87, 96, 112, 145, 146, 158, 171, 229, 234, 241, 316
  toy train routes 316, 320, 324
  wine trains 85
trams 169, 199, 203, 342
Transnational Parks 258
trekking and walking trails 16, 68, 84, 102, 118, 141, 166, 200, 291, 293, 327, 357
  canyons and gorges 105, 113, 176, 255
  city tours 153, 172, 323
  coastal paths 13, 30, 73, 131, 151, 152, 159, 167, 172, 207, 254, 273, 279, 281, 286, 365
  deserts 278, 304
  historic routes 135, 181, 328, 368
  icefields 90, 314
  lake-side hikes 208, 238, 283, 301
  long distance 12, 25, 29, 151, 160, 189, 235, 253, 275, 287, 327, 338
  monasteries, churches and castles 186, 370
  mountain routes 46, 48, 60, 64, 66, 71,

74, 80, 81, 82, 100, 108, 109, 111, 115, 116, 178, 189, 194, 199, 203, 212, 216, 217, 240, 253, 272, 285, 299, 305, 308, 310, 326, 328, 330, 342, 360, 366, 372
  national parks 190, 201, 209, 279
  pilgrim's trails 190, 209, 306, 326, 339
  railway trails 63
  rice terraces 347
  river-side 28, 94, 239, 322, 377
  valley walks 300, 308, 317
  volcanoes 59, 111, 344, 345
  wilderness treks 58, 132, 287
tunnels 32, 130, 157, 200

UNESCO Biosphere Reserves 12, 57, 69, 75, 84, 110, 159, 221, 230
UNESCO World Heritage Sites 25, 74, 75, 107, 131, 140, 159, 160, 183, 193, 204, 207, 212, 219, 231, 232, 233, 244, 251, 280, 284, 316, 347, 350, 360

valleys 257, 300, 302, 304, 308, 312, 317, 365
volcanoes 59, 62, 64, 108, 111, 116, 126, 288, 300, 343, 344, 345

waterfalls 10, 11, 12, 17, 20, 52, 58, 59, 63, 69, 72, 77, 79, 82, 94, 107, 108, 130, 215, 235, 239, 265, 274
wildlife 12, 14, 15, 16, 17, 18, 20, 26, 29, 34, 56, 57, 60, 75, 76, 91, 94, 102, 103, 104, 107, 111, 114, 115, 118, 201, 275, 300, 323, 356, 357
  see also birdlife; flora; marine life
wine routes 85, 94, 181, 196, 230, 284

123RF.com 3quarks 228; Aleksandrs Tihonovs 124; bennymarty 7 centre above, 261; Boris Stroujko 192, 224; Brian Waugh 148; danemo 293; Dawid Zagorski 245; deekleing 267; delcreations 187; Dmitry Rukhlenko 296, 353; Hywit Dimyadi 344; Iakov Kalinin 175; Israel Hervás 195; jakobradlgruber 213 below; jovannig 271; Kwan Wong 361; Liudmila Semenova 329; Lukasz Janyst 121; Malgorzata Kistryn 205; Maria Elena Pueyo Ruiz 223; monticello 6 centre below, 249; Narongsak Nagadhana 6 centre above, 80; Oleg Zhukov 140; Pere Sanz 128; Robyn Mackenzie 262; rognar 197; Rudmer Zwerver 282 above; Rudra Narayan Mitra 309; scanrail 139; Sean Pavone 136, 362-363, 375; Songquan Deng 38; stevanzz 166, 211; Thomas Fikar 8; Tom Baker 2, 328; tykhyi 242 below; Volha Kavalenkava 207; Wong Yu Liang 357; zechal 27. **4Corners Images** SIME/ Belenos PS 126; SIME/Spila Riccardo 176. **Alamy Stock Photo** Adam Deschamps 99; AEP 213 above; Alan Copson/Jon Arnold Images Ltd. 347 below; Allan Cummins 364; Amanda Ahn/dbimages 324 above; Andre Jenny 31; AndyLim.com 356; Arco Images GmbH 134; Arco Images/K Loos 167 above; Art Kowalsky 349 below; Auscape International Pty Ltd. 278; Banana Pancake 286; Bertrand Gardel/ Hemis.fr 19 365 above; Bertrand Rieger/hemis.fr 359; Best View Stock 332; Bill Bachman 270; Bjanka Kadic 73; Brad Mitchell 37; Brad Perks Lightscapes 6 above, 25; Brendan Hoffman 279; Bruce Percy 264; Casey Williams 48; Cephas Picture Library 196; Chad Ehlers 137 above; Christian Kober 355; Christian Ziegler/Danita Delimont 62; Ciaran MacKechnie/Aliki Image Library 68; Darrell Gulin/Danita Delimont 76; Dave Reede/All Canada Photos 13; David Cherepuschak 58 below; David Lyons 163; David Noble Photography 180; David Noton Photography 85; David Pearson 322; David R. Frazier Photolibrary, Inc. 16; David Robertson 230; David Wall 274, 275, 284 below, 287 above; Deborah Dennis 102; Dennis Cox 327 above; Deryck A Dillon 352; Don Smith/ Robert Harding Picture Library Ltd. 283; Duncan Soar 345 above; Eddie Linssen 234; Emil Enchev 253; eye35. com 202; Franck Guiziou/hemis.fr 318; Frank Blackburn 152; Friedrich von Horsten/Images of Africa Photobank 98; Galen Rowell/Mountain Light

84, 314; Gareth Leung 12; Gareth McCormack 90, 167 below; Gavin Hellier 248; Gavin Hellier/Robert Harding Picture Library Ltd. 301, 302; George and Monserrate Schwartz 47; Gordon Sinclair 57; Grant Rooney 316; Günter Gollnick/imagebroker 303; H. Abernathy/ClassicStock 36; Hans Winke 246; Hemis 137 below, 209; Henrik Lindvall 135; Hideo Kurihara 341; Horizon International Images Limited 287 below; Ian Paterson 281; Ian Shaw 242 above; imagebroker 226, 231, 233 below, 236; imagebroker/Kurt Mobus 233 above; Images&Stories 368 below; IML Image Group Ltd. 254, 256; INTERFOTO Pressebildagentur 54; International Photobank 215; Javier Etcheverry 87; Javier Pierini/Photodisc 88; Jeffery Drewitz/Cephas Picture Library 265; Jef Maion/Nomads'Land - www.maion.com 138; Jim Havey 21; Jon Arnold Images Ltd. 127, 247, 258 above, 339, 347 above; Jose Pedro Fernandes 201; Julia Bayne/Robert Harding Picture Library Ltd. 122; Jupiterimages/Agence Images 188; Karl Johaentges/LOOK Die Bildagentur der Fotografen GmbH 269, 330; Keren Su/China Span 334; Kevin Ebi 52; Lois Mason 51; LOOK Die Bildagentur der Fotografen GmbH 162, 193, 212; Lyndon Giffard 279 below; Marek Zuk 243 above; Martin Harris 319; Martin Harvey 100; Maximilian Weinzierl 311; mediacolor's 218 above, 219, 367; Michael DeFreitas North America 20; Michele Falzone 349 above; nagelestock.com 225, 238; Neil Grant 320 below; Neil McAllister 324 below; Neville Prosser 279 above; Nicolas Chan 272; Nicholas Pitt 273; Nico Stengert/imagebroker 86; Nik Wheeler 350; Patricia Berwick/Grapheast 313; Paul Carstairs 370; Pavel Filatov 299 below; PCL 260; Per-Andre Hoffman/ LOOK Die Bildagentur der Fotografen GmbH 74; Peter Adams Photography 216; Peter Erik Forsberg 244; Peter Fakler 277; Peter Titmuss 182; Philippe Renault/Hemis.fr 15; Photolibrary 268; Pies Specifics 81 above; Pixonnet. com 131; R A Rayworth 255; Richard Wareham/Sylvia Cordaiy Photo Library Ltd. 106; Robert Harding Picture Library Ltd. 153, 199, 206; Roberto Meazza/IML Image Group Ltd. 258 below; Robert Preston Photography 377; Rob Kavanagh 351; Romero Blanco 345 below; Ron Yue 327 below; Ross McArthur 323 below; Sherab 320 above; Sigrid Dauth Stock Photography 235; Stefan Auth/imagebroker 305;

Sue Cunningham Photographic 78 above; Suzy Bennett 78 below, 307; tbkmedia.de 243 below; Tibor Bognar 317, 368 above; Tom Mackie 151; Tom Till 169 below; Tony Waltham/Robert Harding Picture Library Ltd. 290, 306; Upperhall Ltd./Robert Harding Picture Library Ltd. 312; Walter Bibikow/Jon Arnold Images Ltd. 24, 358; Walter G. Allgöwer/imagebroker 378; Wolfgang Kaehler 55, 229, 300; Yadid Levy 326. **Alwyn Thomson** 250. **Corbis** Adam Woolfitt 252 below; Alan Copson/ JAI 191; Alison Wright 292; Amos Nachoum 65; Atlantide Phototravel 169 above, 373; Bertrand Rieger 129; Blaine Harrington III 259; Bob Krist 304 below; Bo Zaunders 32, 33; Catherine Karnow 252 above; Charles O'Rear 91, 343; Chico Sánchez/epa 71; Christophe Boisvieux 119, 304 above; Colin Garratt; Milepost 92 ½ 158; Creasource 161; Danny Lehman 61; Dave Bartruff 376; Dave G. Houser 50, 81 below; David Kadlubowski 35; Dean Conger 299 above; Derek Croucher 156; Diane Cook & Len Jenshel 66; Douglas Pearson 189, 210, 217; Emilio Suetone/Hemis 198; Epa 141; Franck Guiziou/Hemis 179; Franz Gingele/Handout/epa 295; Fred Derwal/ Hemis 325 above; Frédéric Soltan/ Sygma 323 above; Fridmar Damm/zefa 227; Galen Rowell 64; Gavin Hellier/Robert Harding World Imagery 194; George H. H. Huey 34; George Steinmetz 371 above; Gregor M. Schmid 143; Gunter Marx Photography 10; Hemis 183, 184; Hubert Stadler 79; Images&Stories 116 above; Jason Hawkes 159; John Miller/ Robert Harding World Imagery 177; Jon Sparks 374; José Fuste Raga 69, 284 above, 335; José Fuste Raga/zefa 208; Kazuyoshi Nomachi 75; Keren Su 170; Kubes Tomas/Isifa Image Service s.r.o. 116 below; Mark Karrass 7 above, 44; Martin Harvey 103; Martin Ruetschi/Keystone 218 below; Michael St. Maur Sheil 173; Michael T. Sedam 30; Michele Falzone/JAI 346, 372; Mike Nelson/epa 123; Natalie Fobes 11; Pablo Corral Vega 72; Paul A. Souders 17; Pat O'Hara 369; Pawel Wysocki/ Hemis 232; Peter Adams 371 below; Peter Adams/JAI 241; Peter Adams/zefa 150, 190; Rob Howard 113; Roland Gerth/zefa 221; Ron Watts 46; Sergio Pitamitz 107; Sergio Pitamitz/zefa 214; The Irish Image Collection 164, 165; Tim Tadder 203; Tim Thompson 168; Tom Bean 28; Walter Geiersperger

237, 240; Winfried Wisniewski/ zefa 101. **Crazy Horse Memorial Foundation** 40. **Eye Ubiquitous** Bryan Pickering/Hutchison 186. **Getty Images** Amanda Friedman 56; Ariadne Van Zandbergen 110; Dennie Cody 49; Franck Guiziou/Hemis 111; Gallo Images-Lanz von Horsten 94; Gavin Hellier 115; Hans-Georg Gaul 96; Jason Edwards 440; Jim Richardson 149; Michael & Patricia Fogden 104; Natphotos 153; Paul Joynson Hicks 109; Stuart D Franklin 97; Tim Fitzharris 45; Whit Richardson 41. **Halim Diker** Images&Stories 365 below. **Hedgehog House** Andy Reisinger 282 below; Colin Monteath 308. **James R. Page** 53. **Joshua Gitlitz** 60. **Lonely Planet Images** Sune Wendelboe 118. **National Geographic Society Image Collection** Otis Imboden 58 above. **Phil Lawson** 112. **Pictures of Britain** Gary Hutchings 155. **Pixabay** 6 below, 7 centre below, 7 below, 23, 29, 43, 77, 133, 142, 147, 157, 171, 251, 289, 337. **Unsplash** 92. **Renate Eichert** 298.

Every effort has been made to trace the copyright holders, and we apologise in advance for any unintentional omissions. We would be pleased to insert the appropriate acknowledgement in any subsequent edition of this publication.